PATERNOSTER THEOLOGICAL MONOGRAPHS

Jesus' Revelation of His Father

A Narrative-Conceptual Study of the Trinity with Special Reference to Karl Barth

PATERNOSTER THEOLOGICAL MONOGRAPHS

A complete listing of all titles in this series
and Paternoster Biblical Monographs
appears at the close of this book

PATERNOSTER THEOLOGICAL MONOGRAPHS

Jesus' Revelation of His Father

A Narrative-Conceptual Study of the Trinity with Special Reference to Karl Barth

Damon W. K. So

Foreword by Daniel W. Hardy

Paternoster:
thinking faith

MILTON KEYNES · COLORADO SPRINGS · HYDERABAD

First published 2006 by Paternoster

Paternoster is an imprint of Authentic Media
9 Holdom Avenue, Bletchley, Milton Keynes, Bucks, MK1 1QR
1820 Jet Stream Drive, Colorado Springs, CO 80921, USA
OM Authentic Media, Medchal Road, Jeedimetla Village,
Secunderabad 500 055, A.P., India
www.authenticmedia.co.uk
Authentic Media is a division of IBS-STL UK, a company limited by guarantee
(registered charity no. 270162)

12 11 10 09 08 07 06   7 6 5 4 3 2 1

Unless otherwise stated all Scripture quotations are taken from the
New International Version
Copyright © 1978 by New York International Bible Society

British Library Cataloguing in Publication Data
A catalogue record for this book is available from the British Library

ISBN 978-1-84227-323-4

Typeset by the author
Printed and bound in Great Britain
for Paternoster
by Nottingham AlphaGraphics

Series Preface

In the West the churches may be declining, but theology—serious, academic (mostly doctoral level) and mainstream orthodox in evaluative commitment—shows no sign of withering on the vine. This series of *Paternoster Theological Monographs* extends the expertise of the Press especially to first-time authors whose work stands broadly within the parameters created by fidelity to Scripture and has satisfied the critical scrutiny of respected assessors in the academy. Such theology may come in several distinct intellectual disciplines—historical, dogmatic, pastoral, apologetic, missional, aesthetic and no doubt others also. The series will be particularly hospitable to promising constructive theology within an evangelical frame, for it is of this that the church's need seems to be greatest. Quality writing will be published across the confessions—Anabaptist, Episcopalian, Reformed, Arminian and Orthodox—across the ages—patristic, medieval, reformation, modern and counter-modern—and across the continents. The aim of the series is theology written in the twofold conviction that the church needs theology and theology needs the church—which in reality means theology done for the glory of God.

Series Editors

David F. Wright, Emeritus Professor of Patristic and Reformed Christianity, University of Edinburgh, Scotland, UK

Trevor A. Hart, Head of School and Principal of St Mary's College School of Divinity, University of St Andrews, Scotland, UK

Anthony N.S. Lane, Professor of Historical Theology and Director of Research, London School of Theology, UK

Anthony C. Thiselton, Emeritus Professor of Christian Theology, University of Nottingham, Research Professor in Christian Theology, University College Chester, and Canon Theologian of Leicester Cathedral and Southwell Minster, UK

Kevin J. Vanhoozer, Research Professor of Systematic Theology, Trinity Evangelical Divinity School, Deerfield, Illinois, USA

To my wife, Yuen Ping;

and

in memory of our grandparents who perished in the Second World War and its aftermath,

and

in memory of the grandparents who survived and brought us up.

Contents

Foreword

Aspiring theologians, even those in established positions, so often limit themselves to cautious critical analysis of others that it is rare to find one with an important and comprehensive case to make. Damon So is such a person; and the proof lies in this book. The special value of his study lies in the ways he enlarges Karl Barth's view of revelation as the relation of Jesus and the Trinity. He does this by a variety of considerations, as to how we can discern the identity of Jesus in Scripture in relation to God, how we can find what is Jesus' relation (communion) with the Father and the Holy Spirit in salvation, and how this mirrors the Trinity of God. A further contribution of the book is its careful engagement with a variety of other people - Hans Frei, James Dunn and others - to assist in the development of his case. Altogether, this is an important study in the revelation of Jesus, his communion with the Father, the interpretation of Scripture, and the implications for the Trinity.

One of the major difficulties confronting theology today is the hiatus between biblical and doctrinal approaches, from which both are losers. So's attention to the narrative content of the Synoptic gospels alongside Barth's conceptual and interpretative categories shows how each benefits from the other. In such a way, Barth's discussions can be rooted more concretely in Scripture, and yet provide conceptual clarity for it: what emerges is a clear conception of Jesus' relation to the Father and the Holy Spirit. Both Jesus' words and actions are thus seen as revelation.

Another persistent issue in theology today is how the Holy Spirit is taken as seriously as it should be. So explores the Son's relation to the Father *through the Holy Spirit*, how the Holy Spirit is in Christ and his disciples, and whether the so-called Spirit- and Logos-Christologies do justice to the Holy Spirit in the Trinity. From careful Scriptural exegesis, and in contrast to Barth's view, So finds a 'non-linear concept of revelation' by which better to convey the communion of the Father with the Son in the Spirit, how the Son fully shares the presence and spirit of his Father. The unity of Jesus with the Father is found in Jesus' life and shows 'the plural sources of divinity in the Trinity' (how Jesus and the Spirit are united, and how Jesus and his Father are united in the life, experience and ministry of Jesus).

The combination of Scriptural and doctrinal study in this book is remarkable, and the case it presents is enriching for both. It is especially illuminating for its redevelopment of the notion of revelation, and for its understanding of the Spirit as the power in which Jesus moved, and at the same time the power of his Father present in him. As So vividly suggests, 'This is the mystery of the Trinity that Jesus himself experienced, the mystery of the community and unity of the Trinity expressed in the life-act and experience of Jesus Christ.' This is a profoundly helpful study.

Daniel W. Hardy
Cambridge,
December 2005

Acknowledgements

My loving gratitude goes first to my wife who has made considerable sacrifice to support me throughout my study at Oxford. The responsibilities that she has to shoulder in the past few years have been very great and the completion of this book is a mark of her earnestness and perseverance. Proverb 31:10-31 is an apt description of her and her work.

My gratitude also goes to The Chinese Church in London, especially Pastor and Mrs. Kah-Thuan Tan, whose prayers, support and encouragement have been instrumental particularly in the initiation of my study. I am also thankful to God for my experience of pastoring the Finsbury Park Congregation (of the CCIL) where some of my ideas on the Trinity began to be developed. Their humility and dependence on God still remain fresh in my memory.

Many individuals and families have encouraged and supported us in the course of my study and I am thankful to God for their partnership in this work. The following list of individuals and families is by no means exhaustive: Kit-Wan and Beh, Kit-Ling and Sammy Leung, Holly and James Chong, Robert and Lillian Tang, Anthony and Siu-Ping Hui, Chi-Keung Ng, Mr. and Mrs. Henry Mo, Iain and Estella Packwood, Mrs. Flora Wei, Dr. and Mrs. Daniel Mak, Mr. and Mrs. Danny Ho, the Wai family, Mrs. Ruth Lomas, William and Vivienne Chan, Auntie Oi (who is now with the Lord), May and Samuel Lee, and my parents-in-law.

My supervisors, Professor Haddon Willmer and Rev. Christopher Jones, had given me sharp and critical comments in the course of my research and these had been instrumental in shaping the direction of the research. I thank them for their patience and wisdom. My gratitude also goes to Heather Bliss who proof read the draft with great efficiency and diligence. Needless to say, the content and presentation of this book are entirely my responsibility.

The community at the Oxford Centre for Mission Studies have provided a loving Christian environment for worship, fellowship and research. I am thankful that I have the opportunity to meet and know many Christian leaders from different traditions and sections of the worldwide church. I am especially indebted to Dr. David Wenham who introduced OCMS to me as a place for theological research. I also thank the Oxford Chinese Christian Church (and its Student Fellowship) for their friendship, fellowship and prayers in the last few years.

I am grateful to Professor Daniel Hardy for the encouragement and support he has given me since the day I met him as my external examiner. His kindness and encouragement have been instrumental in realising the publication of this book.

Finally, I am extremely fortunate to have my two children, James and Rachel, who have been so supportive and understanding in the last few years. Through them and with them in our work and play, my wife and I have learnt much about God's fatherly affection, the Son's filial love and the meaning of fellowship in the Spirit.

Abbreviations

CD

Church Dogmatics (4 volumes, 12 parts; Edinburgh: T. & T. Clark, 1936-1977), by Karl Barth

TDNT

Theological Dictionary of the New Testament (10 volumes; Grand Rapids: Eerdmans, 1964), G. Kittel (ed.), G.W. Bromiley (tr.)

NIDNTT

New International Dictionary of New Testament Theology (3 volumes; Carlisle: Paternoster, 1986), Colin Brown (ed.)

CHAPTER 1

Introduction

1.0 The Importance of the Doctrine of the Trinity in Christian Theology

One of Karl Rahner's memorable comments in *The Trinity* was the neglect of this doctrine in Christian living and Christian literature.

> Despite their orthodox confession of the Trinity, Christians are, in their practical life, almost mere 'monotheists.' We must be willing to admit that, would the doctrine of the Trinity have to be dropped as false, the major part of religious literature could well remain virtually unchanged.[1]

He also commented that the Christian understanding of incarnation tended in a unitarian direction.

> Nor does it help to remark that the doctrine of the *incarnation* is theologically *and* religiously so central for the Christian that, *through it*, the Trinity is always and everywhere inseparably 'present' in his religious life. Nowadays when we speak of God's incarnation, the theological and religious emphasis lies only on the fact that 'God' became man, that 'one' of the divine persons (of the Trinity) took on flesh, and not on the fact that this person is precisely the person of the Logos. One has the feeling that, for the catechism of head and heart (as contrasted with the printed catechism), the Christian's idea of the incarnation would not have to

---

1 K. Rahner, *The Trinity* (London: Burns and Oates, 1970), J. Donceel (tr.), pp. 10-11.

change at all if there were no Trinity.[2]

Rahner was concerned to give the doctrine of the Trinity a central role in Christian doctrines and to revitalise this doctrine in the life of the church.[3] The contributors to *The Forgotten Trinity*, which include eminent theologians such as James Torrance, Alasdair Heron, John Zizioulas, Colin Gunton, Paul Fiddes and Tom Smail, share these concerns with Rahner.[4] They point out how the doctrine of the Trinity, far from being irrelevant to the church, can have an important impact on the church in a number of areas. Firstly, the fundamental question which this doctrine addresses is: who is the God whom Christians worship and serve? From this central question others are also raised. What is the nature of Christian worship? What is the church's understanding of the relationship between Jesus and the Holy Spirit? What is the nature of person and what is the nature of the church? What is the role of the Spirit in the church and in our communion with God? How does God relate to the world which he has created?[5] In particular, they attribute much imbalance of the church's faith and practice to her imbalance in relating to the three persons of the Trinity.

> If God's life is trinitarian, that should be reflected by the life of the Church, in which people are being renewed into the image of God. ... Much onesidedness and lack of balance in the faith and practice of churches can helpfully be understood in trinitarian terms as an over-emphasis on one or other of the Persons of the Trinity with a consequent failure to relate fully and freely to the remaining Persons.[6]

> ... But we do in general agree that conceptions of the Church derived from attention to one person of the Trinity only do tend to give rise to a variety of spiritual ills.[7]

---

2   *Ibid.*, p. 11. Italics his.
3   'We must point out in *every* dogmatic treatise that what it says about salvation does not make sense without referring to this primordial mystery of Christianity [Trinity].' *Ibid.* p. 21.
4   The British Council of Churches, *The Forgotten Trinity* (London: The British Council of Churches, 1989-91) in three parts.
5   *Ibid.*, 1, pp. 1-2. There are further questions relating to cultures and politics.
6   *Ibid.*, 2, p. 21, in 'The Trinity and Our Relationship with God'. See pp. 21-24 for details.
7   See the following longer quote. '[W]e need trinitarian controls on the ecclesiology imagery we use, if it is not to produce one-sided distortions. But it must be *trinitarian* theology as a whole that we use, not unconsidered appeals to persons of the Trinity. Suggestions we considered were that 'Father-only' images are associated with power-lust and domination; 'Jesus-only' images with moralistic activism or

One of the emphases in *The Forgotten Trinity*, on the role of the Spirit in trinitarian theology, is an attempt to redress this balance. Such an emphasis helps us to think of the natures of personhood and the church; i.e., the relational aspect of persons and the relatedness or communion amongst members of the church.[8] In the important area of mission, the need for a more balanced trinitarian theology of God was also called for. Lesslie Newbigin, in *Trinitarian Doctrine for Today's Mission*, wrote,

> The point has several times been made that a true doctrine of missions must make a large place for the work of the Holy Spirit; but it is equally true that a true doctrine of missions will have much to say of God the Father. The opinion may be ventured that recent ecumenical thinking about the mission and unity of the Church has been defective at both these points. The church-centric view of missions has perhaps been too exclusively founded upon the person and work of Christ and has perhaps done less than justice to the whole trinitarian doctrine of God.[9]

Concerning the place of the doctrine in preaching the gospel, Newbigin commented,

> [W]hen one goes outside the 'Christendom' situation to bring the Gospel to non-Christians, one soon discovers that the doctrine of the Trinity is not something that can be kept out of sight; on the contrary, it is the necessary starting point of preaching.[10]

And he gave reasons for this rather surprising comment.[11]

In the area of spirituality, James Houston, in 'Spirituality and the Doctrine of the Trinity', recognises the importance and benefits of recovering the doctrine of the Trinity, especially in the West.[12] Karl

---

individualistic pietism; 'Spirit-only' images with introspective escapism or charismatic excess. We would not necessarily agree with the precise form in which such points are made, particularly in view of the fact that matters of causality in these matters are notoriously difficult to discern. But we do in general agree that conceptions of the Church derived from attention to one person of the Trinity only do tend to give rise to a variety of spiritual ills.' *Ibid.*, 1, pp. 28-29.

8 See John Zizioulas, *Being as Communion: Studies in Personhood and the Church* (London: Darton, Longman and Todd, 1985), and his 'The Doctrine of the Holy Trinity: the Significance of the Cappadocian Contribution', in *Trinitarian Theology Today* (Edinburgh: T&T Clark, 1995), Christoph Schwöbel (ed.).

9 Lesslie Newbigin, *Trinitarian Doctrine for Today's Mission* (Carlisle: Paternoster, 1998. First published: Edinburgh House Press, 1963), p. 33.

10 *Ibid.*, p. 35.

11 *Ibid.*, pp. 35f.

12 James Houston, 'Spirituality and the Doctrine of the Trinity' in *Christ in our Place:*

Barth identifies a wider significance for the doctrine of the Trinity than its limited role in certain aspects of Christian theology or practice. For him, the doctrine is the most decisive of all Christian doctrines and it distinguishes the Christian doctrine of God from other conceptions of God.

> In giving this doctrine a place of prominence our concern cannot be merely that it have this place externally but rather that its content be decisive and controlling for the *whole* of dogmatics.[13]

> The doctrine of the Trinity is what basically distinguishes the Christian doctrine of God as Christian, and therefore what already distinguishes the Christian concept of revelation as Christian.[14]

And he quotes Herman Bavinck,

> With the confession of God's triunity stands or falls the whole of Christianity, the whole of special revelation. This is the kernel of the Christian faith, the root of all dogmas, the substance of the new covenant.[15]

Finally, the New Testament testifies that eternal life is to know the Father and the Son (John 17:3). Entering the rest in God's presence is to know the Father through the Son (Mt. 11:25-30).[16] And it is implicit that this knowledge of the Father and/through the Son is granted through the Holy Spirit (John 6:63, 14:26), who in giving this knowledge conveys the personal presence of God to us as we obey (John 14:15-23). Christian knowledge of God involves the three persons of the Trinity. Neglecting any one person of the Trinity will inevitably impoverish our knowledge of and relationship with God.[17] Despite the importance of the doctrine of the Trinity as presented above, the doctrine has not

---

The Humanity of God in Christ for the Reconciliation of the World: Essays Presented to Professor James Torrance (Exeter: Paternoster, 1989), T. Hart, D. Thimell (eds.), pp. 48-69.

13 *CD* I.1, p. 303. Italics mine.

14 *Ibid.*, p. 301.

15 Quoted on *CD* I.1, p. 302 from H. Bavinck's *Gereformeerde Dogmatiek*, vol. II, 4th edition, p. 346.

16 See exegesis in 4.0 of chapter 2.

17 In the author's pastoral experience, helping a congregation to know the Fatherhood of God, in addition to the Lordship of Christ, has been beneficial to their prayer life and relationship with God. The author has also sought to bring their attention to the role played by the Spirit who aids us to call out to God as 'Abba' and Jesus as 'Lord'.

always been in the forefront of Christian theology, beliefs and practice in the church, as Rahner observed. However, there are signs of progress in recent years as the following section on the context of the present study shows.

2.0 The Context of the Present Narrative-Conceptual Study of the Trinity

Every study of a particular subject has its own context. This study has very much been influenced by the renewed interest in the doctrine of the Trinity in recent decades. Its methodology, which takes up the use of gospel narratives in thinking about theology, also reflects the interest in narrative theology and narrative criticism in recent decades. Furthermore, the consideration of Jesus' relationship with the Spirit in this book echoes the recent interest in the Holy Spirit particularly raised by the charismatic movement. These four areas of interest which form the background of this study happen to have begun roughly at around the same time in the last century, that is, at the turn of the last quarter (or slightly earlier for the charismatic movement). The other essential background to this study is of course the work of Barth, which came to an end with his death in 1968.

2.1 Renewed Interest in the Doctrine of the Trinity

Rahner's observation regarding the actual significance of the Trinity was most probably true of the scene in British theology in the 1960s/70s. Maurice Wiles, who was Professor of Divinity at Oxford, wrote, 'The Trinity of revelation is an arbitrary analysis of the activity of God, which though of value in Christian thought and devotion is not of essential significance.'[18] Rahner's observation is also echoed by *The Forgotten Trinity* (mentioned above) which is a collection of preparatory papers published by The British Council of Churches in 1989-91 to raise the church's awareness of her neglect of this doctrine. The marginalisation of the Trinity could be attributed to at least three factors. Firstly, doctrinal criticism is inclined to understand doctrines as the products of historical circumstances rather than 'the inner logic of faith'.[19] Secondly, the influence of natural religion in modern theology had meant that God was conceived of in generic terms.[20] Natural

---

18 Maurice Wiles, *Working Papers in Doctrine* (London: SCM, 1976), p. 15.
19 From lecture notes on 'The Trinity in Twentieth Century Theology' by Professor John Webster, Oxford, 1999. See also the next two points and the recent renewal of trinitarian theology.
20 See Louis Dupré, *Passage to Modernity: An Essay in the Hermeneutics of Nature*

religion cannot in itself conceive specifically of the triune God who is made known only in revelation. Thirdly, from the early modern period, the discussion of the proof of the existence of God in theology, which cannot generate a conception of the Triune God, preceded the specific doctrine of the Trinity. Thus, God is not conceived of as the Trinity from the beginning but only in the later discussion of a systematic theology.[21]

The renewed interest in the Trinity in the last two or three decades of the 20th century was the result of at least three factors. Firstly, recent interest in and contact with the Eastern Christian tradition has influenced the development of social Trinitarianism with its emphasis on the role of the Spirit.[22] Secondly, the doctrine of the Trinity is increasingly deployed to tackle various doctrinal issues, e.g., theodicy by J. Moltmann in *The Crucified God* and creation by C. Gunton in *The One, the Three and the Many*.[23]

Thirdly, some approaches to theology maintain the importance of the doctrine of the Trinity despite its marginalisation. Barth is a prime example and Rahner's prophetic call to the church to return to the doctrine echoes Barth's emphasis and concern. Barth's treatment of the Trinity, in order and in significance, reverses that of Liberal Protestantism. Schleiermacher relegated the doctrine of the Trinity to the appendix of *The Christian Faith*. The lack of importance of the doctrine of the Trinity in his theology can be attributed to his whole approach to theology which is based on human subjective experience. He wrote in the appendix:

> But the assumption of an eternal distinction in the Supreme Being is not an utterance concerning the religious consciousness, for there it never could emerge. Who would venture to say that the impression made by the Divine in Christ obliges us to conceive such an eternal distinction as its basis?[24]

---

and Culture (New Haven ; London: Yale University Press, 1993), p. 184.

21 According to Rahner, this feature of the treatise of the one God preceding the treatise of the Trinity is found much earlier in the West. 'This separation of the two treatises and the sequence in which they are explained probably derives from the Augustinian-Western conception of the Trinity, as contrasted with the Greek conception, ... It begins with the one God, the one divine essence as a whole, and only *afterwards* does it see God as three in persons.' *The Trinity*, p. 17.

22 See, e.g., the work of John Zizioulas, *Being as Communion*.

23 Jürgen Moltmann, *The Crucified God: The Cross of Christ as the Foundation and Criticism of Christian Theology* (London: SCM, 1974), R.A. Wilson and J. Bowden (tr.). Colin Gunton, *The One, the Three and the Many: God, Creation and the Culture of Modernity* (Cambridge: Cambridge University Press, 1993).

24 F. Schleiermacher, *The Christian Faith* (Edinburgh: T. & T. Clark, 1956), p. 739.

For Schleiermacher, the subjective experience of God in our human history cannot and does not point to the eternal distinction of the Father, Son and Holy Spirit in God. It is interesting that Wilhelm Herrmann, Barth's teacher at Marburg, also reserved only a brief treatment of the Trinity for the very end of his *Systematic Theology*, which concludes with these sentences:

> By the doctrine of the Trinity we are reminded that we can find eternal life in communion with God only if he remains for us unsearchable and therefore an eternal mystery. The way to the Christian religion is the unconditioned will to truth or to submission to facts which we ourselves experience. But *its beginning and its end* is none the less man's humbling of himself before the unsearchable. 'God dwells in unapproachable light, whom no man has seen nor can see' (I Tim. 6:16).[25]

Herrmann, like Schleiermacher, based Christian religion on human experience but, unlike Schleiermacher, he did say that such human experience or religion has its beginning (and end) in man's self-humbling before the unsearchable - in this context, the Trinity. Barth commented that this remarkable statement at the end of *Systematic Theology*, which acknowledges the mystery of the Trinity as the beginning of the Christian religion, was unique in Herrmann's work.[26] Thus he implied that Herrmann in his life and work had not actually made use of this doctrine in any significant way. Could this statement have been a mere 'reflection of faith' by Herrmann which could have had little theological significance to him? Barth granted that Herrmann might well have thought so but he continued,

> Whether what is said here, once it has been thought and said, can be rendered harmless in such a way. ... If one has once thought that God is eternally Subject and never object, that he determines himself and is knowable exclusively through himself in 'pure act' of his Triune Personality - then one has thought it and must continue to think it. The thought cannot afterwards be put in brackets as just a "reflection of faith". ... It becomes obligatory to ask whether dogmatics does not have to begin

---

25 Wilhelm Herrmann, *Systematic Theology* (London: G. Allen & Unwin, 1927), N. Micklem and K.A. Saunders (tr.), p. 152. Italic mine.

26 K. Barth, 'The Principles of Dogmatics According to Wilhelm Herrmann' in *Theology and Church: Shorter Writings, 1920-28* (London: SCM, 1962), ed. T. Torrance, p. 255. In 1925, Barth's delivery of this lecture was occasioned by the publication of Herrmann's *Dogmatik* (i.e., *Systematic Theology*) after Herrmann's death in 1922.

where Herrmann ends. Herrmann on paper naturally rebuts me. But there is also a Herrmann in heaven, who perhaps does not offer a rebuttal.[27]

Whether Herrmann rebutted him or not, in 1932 Barth put the doctrine of the Trinity at the beginning of his *Church Dogmatics* (I.1) and truly began where Herrmann ended.[28] The doctrine of the Trinity is not only prominent in order but also in significance in Barth's theology. 'In one very important sense, the whole of the *Church Dogmatics* is a doctrine of the Trinity, both in its architectural conception and its specific content.'[29] Barth's insistence on the central importance of the Trinity in theology has its influence on theologians such as Colin Gunton, John Webster, Thomas Torrance, James Torrance, Alan Torrance and John Thompson on the British scene, J. Moltmann and E. Jüngel on the German scene.[30] These writers, not to mention those in America, have contributed significantly to the recent renewal of trinitarian theology.

2.2 The Rise of Narrative Theology

Narrative theology is not a uniform or well-developed discipline in theology, possibly because of its short history. There are at least three different types of narrative theology. The first uses the narratives of the lives of contemporary Christians, e.g., Martin Luther King, as the primary material to investigate the meaning of doctrines such as

---

27 *Ibid.*, pp. 255-6.
28 Barth's opposite treatment of the Trinity to those by Schleiermacher and Herrmann, i.e., putting it at the beginning of his *Church Dogmatics* rather than at the end, is a clear and significant sign of his break with and turning away from 19th century Liberal Protestantism after 1914.
29 John Webster, *Barth* (London: Continuum, 2000), p. 72.
30 See, e.g., C. Gunton, *The Promise of Trinitarian Theology* (Edinburgh: T. & T. Clark, 1991), *The One, The Three and the Many* (Cambridge: Cambridge University Press, 1993), *The Triune Creator* (Edinburgh: Edinburgh University Press, 1998); J. Webster, *Barth* (London: Continuum, 2000); A. Torrance, *Persons in Communion* (Edinburgh: T&T Clark, 1996); J. Torrance, *Worship, Community and the Triune Life of God* (Carlisle: Paternoster, 1996); T. Torrance, *The Trinitarian Faith* (Edinburgh: T. & T. Clark, 1988), *The Christian Doctrine of God* (Edinburgh: T&T Clark, 1996), *Trinitarian Perspectives* (Edinburgh: T&T Clark, 1994); J. Thompson, *Modern Trinitarian Perspectives* (New York; Oxford: Oxford University Press, 1994); Tom Smail, *The Forgotten Father* (London: Hodder and Stoughton, 1980), *The Giving Gift* (London: Hodder and Stoughton, 1988). See also E. Jüngel, *The Doctrine of the Trinity* (Edinburgh: Scottish Academic Press, 1976); J. Moltmann, *The Crucified God* (London: SCM, 1974), *The Trinity and the Kingdom of God* (London: SCM, 1981).

'atonement' which may be different from some traditional interpretations.[31] Secondly, 'others interested in narrative and theology wanted to begin with some theory about the narrative quality of human experience from which one could derive conclusions about the appropriateness of a narrative religious text.'[32] The third type uses biblical narratives as the source or basis for theology. Here, the interest will be in the last type of narrative theology. Although Hans Frei did not consider himself to be a narrative theologian because of his desire to distance himself from the first two types, his influence on the third type of narrative theology is significant and some of his ideas will be discussed in the following.[33]

Four important figures had crucial influence on Frei's 'narrative theology': Barth, H. Richard Niebuhr, Erich Auerbach, and Gilbert Ryle. In 1957 Frei wrote his doctoral dissertation on 'The Doctrine of Revelation in the Thought of Karl Barth, 1909-1922: The Nature of Barth's Break with Liberalism' under Niebuhr's direction.[34] Niebuhr's own writings in *The Meaning of Revelation* and *Christ and Culture* (especially the brief section entitled 'Toward a Definition of Christ') had a lasting impact on Frei.[35] Niebuhr brought his attention to the importance of story or narrative in theology. G. Stroup summarises his points succinctly when writing on Niebuhr's understanding of revelation and Christian identity:

> The first of these was Niebuhr's claim that revelation cannot be separated from history and that revelation has its true locus in the internal or personal histories of individuals and communities. Secondly, Niebuhr made the intriguing suggestion that when Christians articulate or give expression to their appropriation of Christian faith they do so by means of a story or narrative, 'the story of our life'. Finally, Niebuhr argued that the context in which this narrative recital of faith is learned and appropriated

---

31 For example, see James McClendon, *Biography as Theology* (Nashville: Abingdon Press, 1974).

32 Quotation from Hans Frei, *Theology and Narrative* (New York; Oxford: Oxford University Press, 1993), Hunsinger and Placher (ed.), p. 16. The classic source of this approach is Stephen Crites, 'The Narrative Quality of Experience,' *Journal of the American Academy of Religion*, 39 (Sept., 1971), pp. 291-311.

33 See Gerard Loughlin, *Telling God's Story* (Cambridge: Cambridge University Press, 1996) for an introduction to narrative theology. For an evaluation of narrative theology, see, e.g., Mark Wallace, 'The New Yale Theology' in *The Best in Theology*, vol. 3, (Carol Stream, Illinois: Christianity Today Inc., 1989), J. I. Packer (ed.), pp. 169-186.

34 See Frei, *Theology and Narrative*, p. 5.

35 H. Richard Niebuhr, *The Meaning of Revelation* (New York: Macmillan, 1941); *Christ and Culture* (New York: Harper, 1951).

is the shared life of the Christian community.[36]

Erich Auerbach, in his *Mimesis: The Representation of Reality in Western Literature,* commented that biblical narratives are realistic in the sense that they are life-like or history-like. But the biblical narratives have a crucial difference from other realistic literature.

> Far from seeking, like Homer, merely to make us forget our own reality for a few hours [the Bible] seeks to overcome our reality: we are to fit our own life into its world, feel ourselves to be elements in its structure of universal history.[37]

The Bible does not make neutral claims. It claims that its world is true and seeks to draw the readers into its own world, history and meanings. Frei found that Barth's analysis of the meaning of the text paralleled that of Auerbach: these narratives claim to define, in a way that any non-narrative translation loses, 'the one common world in which we all live and move and have our being.'[38] However, the question of truth concerning the narratives and the world of the Bible has yet to be answered. But according to Frei this was where the historians and apologists faltered and gave rise to the eclipse of biblical narratives in the eighteenth and nineteenth centuries.[39] They both failed to receive the literal meaning of the narratives, which Frei emphasised is the meaning for the reader. One should read the story within the bounds and the realistic world of the story. Regarding the question of truth, history or referential integrity, 'Frei thought that many of the episodes in the Gospels function as illustrative anecdotes: They show us the sort of person Jesus was, whether or not this particular incident took place.'[40] The story of the crucifixion and the resurrection, however, were thought by Frei to be genuine.[41] (For Barth's position on historicity, see 3.0 below.)

In 1975, Frei published his *The Identity of Jesus Christ: The Hermeneutical Bases of Dogmatic Theology* (Philadelphia: Fortress

---

36 *The Promise of Narrative Theology,* by George Stroup, p. 70.
37 Erich Auerbach, *Mimesis: The Representation of Reality in Western Literature* (Princeton: Princeton University Press, 1953), Willard R. Trask (tr.), 1953, p. 554.
38 See Frei, *Theology and Narrative,* p. 7. Quote taken from, Hans Frei, 'Eberhard Busch's Biography of Karl Barth,' in *Types of Christian Theology* (New Haven; London: Yale University Press, 1992), G. Hunsinger and W. Placher (ed.), p. 161.
39 See Hans Frei, *The Eclipse of Biblical Narrative* (New Haven; London: Yale University Press, 1974), pp. 28-30, pp. 130-136.
40 Frei, *Theology and Narrative,* p. 13.
41 *Ibid.*

Press, 1975), which was influenced by Gilbert Ryle. In his book *The Concept of Mind* (London, Hutchinson, 1949), Ryle attacked what he called 'Descartes' myth' or 'the myth of the ghost in the machine', where a certain separation of mind and body is imposed. Frei contended that a person's identity lay not in some inner essence but in the shape of the person's life, but he acknowledged that human beings have intentions as well as actions. When an intention turns into an action, 'There is a real or hypothetical "inside" description of that transition, of which all of us are aware but of which it is not easy to give an account.'[42] Frei's crucial point was that *it is the development of intention into action that constitutes the self. One is the person one has come to be through one's enacted intention.*[43] The gospels which narrate Jesus' words and actions are therefore able to present Jesus' identity: 'Jesus was what he did and underwent, and not simply his understanding or self-understanding.'[44] As David Kelsey puts it,

> A skilful storyteller can make a character 'come alive' simply by his narration of events, 'come alive' in a way that no number of straight-forward propositional descriptions of the same personality could accomplish. He can bring one to know the peculiar identity of this one unique person. Moreover, what one knows about the story's central agent is not known by 'inference' from the story. On the contrary, he is known quite directly in and with the story, and recedes from cognitive grasp the more he is abstracted from the story. So, too, biblical narrative can be taken as rendering an agent whose identity and actions theology is then to discuss.[45]

---

42 Hans Frei, *The Identity of Jesus Christ* (Philadelphia: Fortress Press, 1975), p. 43. See also 'Remarks in Connection with a Theological Proposal', in Frei, *Theology and Narrative*, chapter 1, p. 37.

43 *Ibid.*, see also 'Theological Reflections', chapter 2 in Frei, *Theology and Narrative*, p. 73.

44 See 'Barth and Schleiermacher', chapter 7 in Frei, *Theology and Narrative*, p. 184. Frei recognised two types of identity description: one is intention-action and the other is self-manifestation which is based on the first type. 'Self-manifestation description, on the other hand, tries to point to the continuity of a person's identity throughout the transitions brought about by his acts and life's events. ... This form of identity description deals with nothing less than the whole scope or stretch of a person's life, in vigourous contrast to the other type of description, which deals only with a specific sequence of events. It is evident, then, that self-manifestation description of Jesus involves the full scope of the Gospel story.' *The Identity of Jesus Christ*, p. 127.

45 David H. Kelsey, *The Uses of Scripture in Recent Theology* (London: SCM, 1975), 1975, p. 39.

Narratives can portray a person and his identity in such a way that cannot be captured or summarised by propositional statements such as are often found in doctrinal formulations. G. Stroup extends this idea of identity description to the triune God.

> The Trinity is, ..., a necessary description of God's identity, but it presupposes those narratives which witness to God's relation to the world. The claim that personal identity is always an interpretation of personal history applies to all persons - human beings and the triune God.[46]

In this book, attention is focused on knowing the person of Jesus Christ through his words and actions as given by the gospel narratives in Matthew but with the view that these words and actions of Jesus also witness to Jesus' relationship with his Father through the Spirit as he *reveals* his Father in these words and actions. The crucial idea connecting the identity description of Jesus Christ and that of the Father (and the Trinity) is Jesus' revelation of his Father (through the communion in the Spirit). The author is indebted to Barth for this crucial idea of revelation linking Jesus and the Trinity which will be made use of in this book.

2.3 The Rise of Narrative/Literary Criticism in Biblical Studies

From the late 1970s, there began a paradigm shift in biblical studies away from the strict historical approach towards a literary approach to the Bible.[47] The historical approach (or the diachronic approach) tries to reconstruct the author's circumstances and the history of the formation of the text (e.g., form criticism and source criticism), which cannot be directly yielded by the text itself. The attention focused on these issues and the minimalist approach adopted by some historians or scholars (such as Bultmann) make the literal meaning of the text almost invisible (this is the complaint of Frei in *The Eclipse of Biblical Narrative*). The literary approach (or synchronic approach) arose out of this context of biblical studies and seeks to study the text as it is, without reference to hypotheses that cannot be found within the text. Its aim in some respects is thus similar to that of narrative theology. However, compared to narrative theology, the discussion in literary criticism is much more specific regarding its methodology and its conceptual elements.[48]

---

46 G. Stroup, *The Promise of Narrative Theology* (London: SCM, 1984), pp. 245-6.

47 See Craig Blomberg, *Jesus and the Gospels* (Leicester: Apollos, 1997), chapter 5: 'Literary Criticism of the Gospels', pp. 99f.

48 For an introduction to literary criticism applied to the Bible, see Tremper Longman, III, *Literary Approaches to Biblical Interpretation* (Leicester: Apollos, 1987), A. K.

Narrative criticism, which is relevant to the present study, is a branch of literary criticism dealing with the particular genre of narrative.[49]

The following conceptual elements are often used in narrative criticism: plots, evaluative point of view, narration (narrator, implied author, real author), irony, narrative pattern and characterisation. For example, the plot in Matthew adopted in this book consists of Jesus' radical confrontation with the religious leaders concerning their narrow legalistic religion in Galilee, and the escalation of this conflict after his entry into Jerusalem, which culminates in his suffering and crucifixion. Within this plot or overall direction of the narratives, one can discern certain narrative patterns (see later chapters). An *inclusio* (a pair of brackets) is formed by Jesus' baptism and his death. The baptism of Jesus and his temptations are a kind of introduction (in narrative terms, the *preparation*) of his life, ministry and death. The main body of the gospel is therefore an explication, unpacking or unfolding (in narrative terms, the *particularisation*) of this preparation in his baptism and temptations. Within the inclusio and the particularisation of the preparation, there are the *pivot* and *repetitions* of Jesus' foretelling of his passion so that his life, ministry and predictions culminate in the *climax* of the whole narrative - his death on the cross.

Concerning characterisation, the narratives can either *tell* the readers of the traits of a character directly and explicitly, or *show* the readers these character traits implicitly through narrating his thoughts, words and actions. The gospels seldom explicitly tell the readers that Jesus is sinless or that he is gracious to sinners (as Paul used explicitly the word grace in his epistles), but in their narrative manner they portray Jesus as such in his words and actions (and sometimes in his thoughts). The narratives' showing the character of Jesus is analogous to the 'intention-action' identity description suggested by Frei in *The Identity of Jesus Christ*. It will be shown in later chapters that some of the crucial character traits of Jesus portrayed in Matthew's gospel are his radicalism, his lordship in exercising his authority in teaching and mighty works, his freedom, his unconditional love, his integrity and his humility. In these excellences, Jesus reveals his Father. It might be possible to draw from Jesus' revelation of his Father in these excellences some insight concerning the nature or content of Jesus'

M. Adam, *What is Postmodern Biblical Criticism?* (Minneapolis: Fortress Press, 1995); Norman Petersen, *Literary Criticism for New Testament Critics* (Philadelphia: Fortress, 1978). For an assessment and a bibliography of literary criticism, see Mark Powell, *The Bible and Modern Literary Criticism: A Critical Assessment and Annotated Bibliography* (New York; London: Greenwood Press, 1992).

49 For an introduction, see Mark Powell, *What is Narrative Criticism? A New Approach to the Bible* (London: SPCK, 1993).

communion with his Father, as will be attempted in chapters 3 and 4. The other crucial character traits of Jesus are of course his resolute obedience to his Father to the very end, the commitment and courage he shows in his path to the cross.

In studying the content of Jesus' revelation of his Father, the author has chosen to work mainly from the gospel of Matthew, though the pneumatology in Luke will also be made use of. It might be suggested that the gospel of John could be a more obvious choice than Matthew for studying Jesus' revelation of his Father. However, the appropriateness of Matthew for this purpose can only be assessed after an actual exercise or study with Matthew is performed. This question of appropriateness cannot be answered in the positive sense at the beginning of the book but only at the end. The use of Matthew has the advantage of being spared of the suggestion that its Christology is late and developed which is often directed at the gospel of John. It will be interesting to see if the concept and content of Jesus' revelation of his Father found in this synoptic gospel bear close resemblance to those of the fourth gospel.

2.4 The Rise of the Charismatic Movement and the Interest in the Spirit

In 1966, the publication of the first issue of *Renewal,* the magazine of the charismatic movement in Britain, probably marked the gathering momentum of this movement.[50] The exercise of charismatic gifts in this movement, e.g., speaking in tongues, prophecies and healings, highlighted some of the important works of the Spirit in Christian living and experience which might have been neglected in the majority of the churches. Some scholars or theologians who were aware of the neglect of the Spirit not only in Christian experience but also in Christian theology sought to recover the important place in theology which was due to the Spirit. Tom Smail, who once was the editor of the *Renewal* magazine, wrote *The Giving Gift* (London: Hodder and Stoughton, 1988), which deals with the theological issues relating to the Spirit (and Trinity).[51] James Dunn, from the perspective of biblical studies, first contributed to the discussions about the role of the Spirit in *Baptism in the Holy Spirit* (London: SCM, 1970) and then specifically dealt with Jesus' relationship with the Spirit in *Jesus and the Spirit* (London: SCM, 1975). Colin Gunton from the perspective of dogmatic theology highlighted the important role of the Spirit in the Trinity in 'Two Dogmas Revisited: Edward Irving's Christology' (published in 1988)

---

50 See the Foreword in *Living in the Light of the Pentecost: A Selection from Renewal Magazine, 1966-1990* (Crowborough: Highland, 1990), Edward England (ed.).

51 See *Ibid.*, p. 10 concerning Smail's editorship of *Renewal.*

and in his other writings.[52] The heightening of the role of the Spirit in Christian theology and church life is welcome, but these biblical and theological studies raise a question regarding Jesus Christ. In what sense was Jesus divine if the power in which he lived and by which he exercised his ministry was the power of the Spirit? Could Jesus of the gospels be interpreted merely as a Spirit-inspired man, as Dunn was so keen to emphasise? Or did Jesus' relationship with the Spirit have both continuity with and unique distinction from his disciples' relationship with the Spirit? The answers to these questions have a decisive consequence for orthodox Christian doctrines and the experience of Christians. These questions and answers will be closely examined in this book. If Jesus' 'divinity' could only be attributed to the Spirit, i.e., he has no inherent divinity of his own, then the doctrine of the incarnation and the doctrine of the Trinity could not stand. Also, the doctrine of atonement has to be drastically reinterpreted, for then it would not be God, but only a creature, who saves sinners. Furthermore, concerning revelation, the notion of Jesus' revelation of God his Father is severely undermined. This weakened sense of Jesus' divinity and revelation has its consequences for Christian discipleship and experience. Firstly, the power of the person of Jesus and the power of the words of Jesus will lose their decisive edge in Christian living and experience if his Lordship/divinity is diluted or denied. One can no longer perceive the sense of the decisive finality in Jesus' words and revelation; the Word that the Spirit wields has lost its sharpness, efficacy and cutting edge. Prayer and worship to Jesus can become difficult and meaningless. The result could be a kind of mysticism where the content of the person of Jesus Christ is emptied (Barth severely criticises mysticism, as did Herrmann). Barth quotes from *2 Clement* to emphasise the importance of acknowledging Christ's divinity:

> Brethren, we must think of Jesus Christ as of God, as of the judge of the quick and the dead. For we ought not to think meanly of our redemption. If we think meanly of Him, that means that we expect only mean things ... that we do not know whence and by whom and to whom we are called.[53]

This book will study Jesus' words and actions as presented in Matthew's narratives and the narrative patterns emerging from the narratives (chapters 3 to 5). From this narrative study, the Lordship/divinity of Jesus will emerge and an interpretation of Jesus' relationship with the Spirit will be made. An answer to the important question of the mutual compatibility between Logos Christology and

52 The paper appeared in *Scottish Journal of Theology*, 41 (1988), pp. 359-76.
53 *CD* IV.1, p. 160.

Spirit Christology will be attempted. A theology concerning Jesus' relationship with the Spirit and the Father's relationship with the Spirit will be suggested and the issue of *filioque* in the economic Trinity will be discussed, with possible implications for our understanding of the immanent Trinity (chapter 6). While the Lordship of Jesus will be maintained in this book on one hand, on the other some considerable effort will be made to understand the nature of communion between Jesus and his Father (with some reference to Geoffrey Lampe) and the crucial role played by the Spirit in this spiritual communion in the economic Trinity, with some possible implications for the understanding of the immanent Trinity and the relationship between the humanity and divinity of Jesus Christ (chapter 6).

3.0 Comments on Methodology

The methodology of this book has already emerged in the above discussion of its background and context. On one hand, it seeks to pay attention to the content of Jesus' revelation of himself and of his Father as narrated in the gospel narratives of Matthew. On the other hand, it tries to develop some conceptual understanding of the economic and immanent Trinity from the narrative study, hence the 'Narrative-Conceptual Study of the Trinity' in the title. This approach therefore may be distinguished from the traditional study of the Trinity in dogmatic theology, which often centres on the immanent Trinity and where the mode of discussion is often propositional, rational and abstract, but not narrative.[54] This book attempts to make the connections between the economic Trinity, which is more tangible and imaginable, and the less tangible immanent Trinity; in other words it attempts to understand the immanent Trinity via the economic Trinity through a narrative study of Jesus' revelation of his Father in history.

Rahner emphasised that the route to knowing the Trinity is via the economic Trinity. If one thinks of the Trinity merely in terms of divine essence, procession, relation and relative subsistence within the immanent Trinity, 'honesty forces us to admit that this does not lead very far.'[55] Catherine Mowry LaCugna echoed Rahner and lamented the

---

54 See G. Lindbeck's criticism of the Cognitive-Propositional approach to doctrines in his *The Nature of Doctrine* (London: SPCK, 1984). This book would retain the value of such an approach but suggests that it could be complemented by a narrative approach.

55 The quote is taken from a much longer complaint. 'As a result the treatise [the Trinity] becomes quite *philosophical* and *abstract* and refers hardly at all to salvation history. It speaks of the necessary *metaphysical* properties of God, and not very explicitly of God as experienced in salvation history in his free relations to his

neglect of the economic Trinity in the study of the Trinity through the centuries.

Given the trajectory set by Nicaea, in combination with the long-lasting controversies over Arianism and neo-Arianism, Christian theologians focused their attention more and more on the nature of *theologia per se*, that is, the interrelationship among the divine persons. While the motive was no doubt consistently soteriological, in time the economy became less and less decisive in shaping conclusions about the intratrinitarian relations. By the medieval period in both Byzantine and Latin theology, the divine persons were thought of as existing 'in' God, in a realm cut off from the economy of salvation history by virtue of an unbreachable ontological difference. In scholastic theology, the doctrine of the Trinity was identified as the science of God's inner relatedness. The result of this was a one-sided theology of God that had little to do with the economy of Christ and the Spirit, with the themes of Incarnation and grace, and therefore little to do with the Christian life. Greek medieval theology took refuge in an exaggerated agnosticism that relegated the trinitarian persons to a region far beyond our capacity to experience or understand. Hence, the defeat of the doctrine of the Trinity.[56]

Gordon Fee echoes LaCugna's observation: '[O]ur trinitarianism is terribly defective if we spend our labours on the ontological questions in such a way as to lose the essential narrative about God and salvation

---

creatures. For should one make use of salvation history, it would soon become apparent that one speaks always of him whom Scripture and Jesus himself calls the Father, Jesus' Father, who sends the Son and who gives himself to us in the Spirit, in his Spirit. On the other hand, if one starts from the basic Augustinian-Western conception, an a-trinitarian treatise 'on the one God' comes as a matter of course before the treatise on the Trinity. In this event, however, the theology of the Trinity must produce the impression that it can make only purely *formal statements* about the three divine persons, with the help of concepts about the *two processions* and about the *relations*. Even these statements, however, refer only to a Trinity which is absolutely locked within itself - one which is not, in its reality, open to anything distinct from it; one, further, from which *we are excluded*, of which we happen to know something only through a strange paradox. It is true that, in an Augustinian, 'psychological' theology of the Trinity efforts are made to give real content to such formal concepts as procession, communication of divine essence, relation and relative subsistence. But *honesty forces us to admit that this does not lead very far.*' Rahner, *The Trinity*, pp. 17-9. Italics mine.

56 Catherine LaCugna, *God For Us: The Trinity and Christian Life* (San Francisco: Harper; 1991), pp. 209-210. In stressing the importance of studying the economic Trinity - God for us - she might have overreacted when in her book she was unwilling to give equal consideration to the immanent Trinity - God in himself.

that raised those questions in the first place.'[57] Pannenberg also points out the importance of paying attention to the active relations in the Trinity, in addition to the relations of origin.

> When Scripture bears witness to the *active* relations of the Son and Spirit to the Father, it is not good enough to treat these as not constitutive for their identity and in this respect to look only at the relations of begetting and proceeding (or breathing), viewing solely the relations of origin which lead from the Father to the Son and the Spirit, as applicable to the constitution of the person. ... The Father does not merely beget the Son. He also hands over his kingdom to him and receives it back from him.[58]

Most of the salvific activities of the economic Trinity in the NT is found in the gospel narratives. But concerning these narratives, the biblical scholar, Tom Wright, laments the scant attention paid to the theological significance of Jesus' life and ministry as given in the gospel story in the last few centuries.

> The Reformers had very thorough answers to the question 'why did Jesus die?'; they did not have nearly such good answers to the question 'why did Jesus live?'... It would not, then, be much of a caricature to say that orthodoxy, as represented by much popular preaching and writing, has had no clear idea of the purpose of Jesus' ministry. For many conservative theologians it would have been sufficient if Jesus had been born of a virgin, lived a sinless life, died a sacrificial death, and risen again three days later. ... His ministry and his death are thus loosely connected.[59]

> For the same reasons, ... the reformers and their successors have seemed to be much better exponents of the epistles than of the gospels. Although Luther and the others did their best to grasp the meaning of (say) Galatians as a whole, and to relate it to their contemporary setting, little attempt was made to treat (say) *Matthew* in the same way, or to ask what the evangelists thought they were doing in not merely collecting interesting and useful material about Jesus but actually stringing it together in what looks for all the world like a continuous *narrative*, a *story*. My later argument will, I hope, indicate that these two weaknesses - the failure to ask about the *theological significance of the ministry of Jesus*, and the failure to treat the gospels with full seriousness as they

57 Gordon Fee, 'Paul and the Trinity' in *The Trinity* (Oxford: Oxford University Press, 1999), Stephen Davis, Daniel Kendall and Gerald O'Collins (eds.), p. 72.
58 W. Pannenberg, *Systematic Theology* (Edinburgh: T. & T. Clark, 1991), vol. 1, p. 320. Italics mine.
59 N. T. Wright, *Jesus and the Victory of God* (London: SPCK, 1996), p. 14.

stand, that is, as stories - are among the chief causes of much present confusion, and that they can and must be remedied.[60]

The systematic theologian, David Ford, argues for the primacy of the gospel story in Christianity,

> Just as Iris Murdoch supports the relative priority of her novels over her philosophy in rendering what is most important in human life, so I have argued for *the primacy of the gospel story's content and perspective* in Christianity. Systematic thinking has many roles in relation to this, but *crucial issues will concern the way in which it allows itself to be informed by this story*, and how far its system, whether critical or constructive, is appropriate to the story's form and content.[61]

This book then attempts to draw out the theological significance of Jesus' birth, baptism, ministry, death and resurrection as given by Matthew's narratives in a study of Jesus' revelation of his Father, his Lordship and the Trinity. But how does one progress from narratives to theological/conceptual/doctrinal formulations? Alister McGrath has the following comment.

> There is ... a dynamic relationship between doctrine and the scriptural narrative. That narrative possesses an interpretative substructure, hinting at doctrinal affirmations. It is evident that there are conceptual frameworks, linked to narrative structures, within scripture: these functions as starting points for the process of generation of more sophisticated conceptual frameworks in the process of doctrinal formulation. On the basis of these scriptural hints, markers and signposts,

---

60 *Ibid.*, pp. 14-15. Italics mine. Similar complaint can be found in George Hendry, *The Gospel of the Incarnation* (London: SCM, 1959), p. 31. When writing about the Royal Man in *CD* IV.2, p. 156, Barth also commented on the lacuna in traditional Christology, 'The older dogmatics was preoccupied with the general and fundamental question of the Godhead and manhood of Jesus Christ. And in this question it was more interested in the former than the latter. It did not, therefore, give any independent consideration to this fact. It was undoubtedly the presupposition and goal of its Christology, but no more. This *lacuna in its presentation must be filled.* The Son of Man, who is also the true Son of God, obviously wills to be considered and understood for Himself. He, the royal man belongs to the very substance of Christology. Indeed, as seen from the angle now under discussion, He is the substance of the whole.' Italics mine.

61 David Ford, 'System, Story, Performance: A Proposal about the Role of Narrative in Christian Systematic Theology' in *Why Narrative? Readings in Narrative Theology* (Grand Rapids: Eerdmans, 1989), S. Hauerwas and G. Jones (eds.)., p. 205. Italics mine.

doctrinal affirmations may be made, which are then employed as a conceptual framework for the interpretation of the narrative. The narrative is then re-read and re-visioned in the light of this conceptual framework, in the course of which modifications to the framework are suggested. There is thus a process of dynamic interaction, of feedback, between doctrine and scripture, between the interpretative framework and the narrative itself, paralleling the related process of mathematical iteration. There is an instructive parallel here with Hegel's understanding of *Vorstellung* and *Begriff*: the philosophical mediation of truth is characterised by the constant dynamic oscillation between representation and concept, as one is compared with the other and refined and modified accordingly.[62]

The initial conceptual framework for interpreting the narrative is to be discerned within, rather than imposed upon, the narrative.[63] In this book, Mt. 11:25-30 provides an initial conceptual framework (see 4.0 of chapter 2 on the concept of Jesus' revelation of his Father) for interpreting the narratives of Jesus' words and actions (see chapters 3 and 4). The interpretations of these narratives in turn inform further conceptualisations of Jesus' relationships with his Father and the Spirit, which are brought together in a *refined* concept of revelation and a theology of the Trinity (see chapter 6). Other conceptual elements, such as Jesus' Lordship (Mt. 3:3) and his conception by the Spirit (Mt. 1:20), will also play significant roles in the process of interpretations and further conceptualisations.

At this point, a brief treatment of Barth's view of the historicity of the gospel narratives is in order. Barth regards the gospel story as true even though its presentation may not reflect complete accuracy for the events being narrated. Concerning the intrusion of the terminology of later Judaism and extra-Judaic Hellenism into the gospels, Barth insists that the 'the human Word of Jesus was so constituted that objectively it was quite acceptable as a supremely particular and distinctive Word - His own Word - even in its formal and material similarity with so much of Rabbinism, even in the different versions given by the Evangelists, and even in its translation into Hellenistic thought forms and language.'[64] The word of Jesus, in virtue of its content, has its inherent power to

---

62 Alister McGrath, *The Genesis of Doctrine* (Oxford: Basil Blackwell, 1990), pp. 60-61.

63 'It [the conceptual framework] is not an arbitrary framework, however, but one which is suggested by that narrative, and intimated (however provisionally) by scripture itself. It is to be discerned within, rather than imposed upon, that narrative.' *Ibid.*, p. 59.

64 *CD* IV.2, p. 195.

burst through all its limitations, overcome all obstacles involved and came down to the first century community despite those intrusions. What Barth is saying is that the content of Jesus' word is preserved despite its possible outward adornments and changes in form induced by outside factors. That is, Jesus' word is still spoken and heard through its present embodiment as found in the gospels even though such embodiment may not be his word *ipsissima verba*.

David Ford, in *Barth and God's Story*, assesses Barth's attitude concerning the accuracy of the gospels by using Peter Stern's concept of 'middle distance' in fiction writing and comes to a similar understanding.[65] Central to this concept of 'middle distance' is the purpose of the story as a whole, and the level of accuracy employed should reflect or be consistent with this purpose: too low a level of accuracy is not sufficient for the purpose and too high a level of accuracy is not necessary. For Barth, the purpose of the gospel story is to present or portray the person of Jesus Christ in his words and actions. The gospels have 'the unmistakable unity of the picture which they draw of the totality of the activity of Jesus. The basic features of this portrait proved to be the same in all these recognised gospels.'[66] For Barth, the level of accuracy employed in the gospels is sufficient for the purpose of rendering the person of Jesus Christ in his words and action.[67] Barth's position concerning the referential integrity of the gospel narratives is much more affirming than those of many narrative theologians and biblical scholars.

---

65 'There is no valid description of 'the middle distance' or indeed of that mixture of meaning and fact and language we call realism ... except one that is related to "the purpose of the whole" for which the description is intended; and any description that takes the notion of accuracy from some other purpose is bound to be misleading ... "The purpose of the whole", or again "the proper point of perspective" that determines the middle distance of realism, is the most familiar thing in all literature: it is the fictional creation of people, of individual characters and lives, informed by what in any one age is agreed to constitute a certain integrity and coherence.' Peter Stern, *On Realism* (London: Routledge & Kegan Paul, 1973), pp. 120f; quoted by Ford in *Barth and God's Story* on pp. 54-5.

66 *CD* IV.2, p. 193.

67 "Barth is quite happy with contradictions and alternative accounts of the same events in the Bible, and even makes theology out of them, but without a certain 'middle distance' reliability (especially on the sequence of crucifixion and resurrection) many of his dogmatic arguments would be baseless. The literary judgment implied by the way he treats the gospel rendering of Jesus as normative, without being bothered by inadequacies or contradictions, is a recognition that the meaning of the story is grasped by appreciating it as a literary whole and accepting a middle distance perspective common to the evangelists." Ford, *Barth and God's Story*, p. 55.

4.0 Summary

Jesus' revelation of the Father is a key concept connecting Jesus with the Father and the Spirit. However, to gain some understanding of Jesus' relationships with the Father and the Spirit, i.e., the economic Trinity, it is essential but not sufficient merely to study this concept of revelation. The narrative content of revelation as given by the gospel narratives also needs to be studied such that the conceptual understanding of revelation and the economic Trinity can be 'fleshed out' by concrete tangible narrated events in the life, ministry and death of Jesus Christ. The vividness and the power of the story of Jesus can then complement the more reflective conceptual understanding of revelation and the Trinity. When speaking about the relationship between narratives and doctrines, Alister McGrath writes,

> Yet the neatness and conceptual clarity of the doctrine is offset by the vividness of the parable [or story], and its firm location in the world of human life. Perhaps we need to recapture the ability and will to restate doctrines in terms of stories, if their power, relevance and vitality are to be fully appreciated.[68]

And it is possible that in restating doctrines in terms of stories, the gospel narratives of Jesus might inform the conceptual understanding of revelation and the Trinity (cf. Ford's comment above and see chapter 6).

The following questions concerning revelation and the Trinity are addressed in this book. Firstly, the *conceptual* question will be asked in chapter 2: how does Jesus reveal his Father? The answer inevitably involves Barth's doctrine of the Trinity and the divinity of Jesus Christ but an important exegesis of Matthew 11:25-30 (which contains the so-called Johannine thunderbolt in v. 27) is also illuminating. In chapters 3 and 4, the second question, about the *content* of revelation, is asked: what has Jesus revealed of his Father through himself? The answer involves some detailed exegeses of selected gospel passages which witness to Jesus' Lordship/divinity as he reveals his Father in words and actions. The third question, which is a general question to be broken down into more specific questions, is: what is the emerging picture of Jesus' relationship with his Father and the Holy Spirit, given the answers to the first two questions? In particular, given the divine Lordship of Jesus, how can the problem of plural sources of divinity in the Trinity be solved? That is, (i) how can Jesus and the Spirit be united and (ii) how can Jesus and his Father be united, in Jesus' life,

---

68 Alister McGrath, *Understanding Doctrine: Its Purpose and Relevance for Today* (London: Hodder & Stoughton, 1990), p. 37.

experience and ministry? The former question prompts one to seek the compatibility between Logos Christology and Spirit Christology (chapters 5 and 6). A related issue concerns *filioque* and *per filium* in the context of Jesus' life and ministry, as opposed to the usual context after Pentecost or in the immanent Trinity in which these issues are discussed (chapter 6). The other question (ii) concerning Jesus' unity with his Father is crucial to his revelation of his Father. This unity and revelation involves Jesus' obedience to his Father and his communion with his Father which in turn are critically related to his divinity. Barth's notion - Jesus Christ has to be divine in order to reveal God - will therefore be unpacked in terms of Jesus' obedience, communion and unity with his Father. By using three senses of the word 'spirit' and with some references to G. Lampe and P. Tillich, the meaning and nature of Jesus' communion with his Father is further explored with some possible implications for a more refined understanding of the concept of revelation and a trinitarian approach to Christology (chapters 6 and 7).

The attempted answers to the questions concerning the Trinity and revelation will be justified on the basis of the narrated events of Jesus Christ in the economy and some conceptual framework or conceptual elements already found in the narratives, though some further conceptual formulations or rationalisation will also be necessary, especially for the refined concept of revelation (hence the narrative-conceptual approach of this book). The attempted answers concerning the economic Trinity (before Pentecost, because only the gospel narratives are used) will be used to inform our understanding of the immanent Trinity. This concrete handling of the economic Trinity and its subsequent linking with the immanent Trinity is one of the distinctive contributions of this book.

The Lordship of Jesus plays a very important role in this book and this is due to the influence of Barth. It is natural then, when dealing with this essential aspect, to quote Barth's expositions of Jesus' Lordship, which are often used not only Christologically but also in relation to the Trinity. Since Barth expounds his Christology using both doctrinal concepts and gospel narratives in *CD* IV.1,2 (which is quite unique in contemporary theology in view of the comments of the last section), his work will be helpful and relevant to those chapters which deal with the conceptual or narrative aspect of the study.

CHAPTER 2

The Concept of Jesus' Revelation of His Father

Summary: This chapter is a study of the concept of Jesus' revelation of his Father. In Barth's thought, revelation and Trinity are closely related together. Two key elements of the concept will be considered here - the identity of Jesus Christ and Jesus' communion with the Father, corresponding to Mt. 3:3 (or Mt. 1 to 3) and Mt. 11:25-30.

The questions which will be considered in this chapter are:
(i)   What is the identity of Jesus in his revelation of his Father?
(ii) How does Jesus reveal his Father in heaven according to Mt. 11:25-30?

These two questions are treated in this chapter as conceptual questions in that their answers are provided by looking at the corresponding concepts presented in Matthew. Matthew also provides answers to these questions in a non-conceptual manner, i.e., through the concrete and more detailed words and actions of Jesus presented in the narratives; these will be dealt with in the next two chapters. This chapter, which deals with the concept of revelation in a schematic manner, provides the interpretative framework for studying Jesus' revelation of his Father through words and actions in the next two chapters. These two chapters will therefore complement the present one by giving some concrete details and examples embodying the concept of revelation.

A crucial question in the concept of Jesus' revelation of his Father pertains to the identity of Jesus Christ. Jesus is clearly presented as a human being in Matthew, especially in his identification with Israel. But does Matthew present Jesus as equal to God or Yahweh in his revelation of God? Does Matthew in any way identify Jesus with Yahweh in his gospel? What is the nature of that identification if there is one? These questions are important for a proper concept of revelation, because if Jesus Christ is less than God, the possibility or the capacity of Jesus to reveal God is put into serious question (cf. Barth, see later). The opinions of biblical scholars need to be considered and contended with for many of them are not favourable to the idea of finding the divinity of Jesus Christ in the synoptic gospels. For this purpose, a detailed exegesis of Mt. 3:3 is necessary, along with a careful examination of the narrative structure of Matthew relevant to this important aspect of the identity of Jesus Christ.

Mt. 11:25-30 provides the most explicit statement of the concept of revelation found in Matthew. It therefore deserves detailed examination. Matthew, by placing this passage after the presentation of Jesus' teaching and mighty works in chapters 5 to 9 (and the disciples' mission in chapter 10), has the strategic purpose of providing a conceptual framework for making sense of Jesus' words and works, especially how Jesus is related to his Father, given the extraordinary authority that Jesus displays in those chapters and elsewhere. The exegesis of this passage therefore provides an invaluable insight into Jesus' relationship with his Father in the context of his revelation of him. In the next two chapters, this insight will be made use of in interpreting Jesus' words and actions in Matthew's gospel according to the intention of the evangelist.

1.0 Kingdom of God and Messiah

The discussion in this section is based on N. T. Wright's *The New Testament and the People of God* and *Jesus and the Victory of God*.[1]

> Israel would at last 'return from exile'; evil would be defeated; Yahweh would at last return to 'visit' his people. Anyone wishing to evoke and affirm all this at once, in first century Palestine, could not have chosen a more appropriate and ready made slogan than 'Kingdom of God'.[2]

To the Jews of the first century, Israel whose land was occupied and ruled by the foreign Romans was still in a state of 'exile', despite the fact that they were living in that land. They longed for Yahweh to intervene decisively on Israel's behalf, to restore her fortune, to end her bitter period of exile, to bring about a new situation where Israel would

---

1 N. T. Wright, *Jesus and the Victory of God*, (London: SPCK, 1996), *New Testament and the People of God*, (London: SPCK, 1992).

2 Wright, *Jesus and the Victory of God*, p. 227.

have victory over the nations, the land would be cleansed, the temple rebuilt, and Yahweh would at last return to visit his people, dwell in the temple on Zion, overcome the evil in the world and established his reign.[3] God's deliverance of Israel would have both political/physical and spiritual elements.[4] There was also an expectation that God would inaugurate a new covenant with his people where there would be forgiveness of sins and God would pour out his Holy Spirit so that the people would keep the Torah from the heart (Jer. 31:31f, Ezek. 11:19f, 36:22-32, Joel 2:28, Is. 32:15, Zech. 12:10).[5] The various strands of Jewish expectation of the Kingdom of God in the first century were by no means uniform in detail but they had common elements. They were expecting God to come to visit his people, liberate them from the harsh foreign rule and restore Israel from her 'exile'. This expectation of the Kingdom of God, or God's rule, or God's coming to visit his people was influenced by Israel's history of exodus and liberation from the bondage in Egypt.

The expectation of a Messiah (or two Messiahs as in the Qumran Community) was only one aspect of the wider and far more frequent expectation of the Kingdom of God.[6] There were no strong connections between the Kingdom of God and the coming Messiah. The apparent tension of Yahweh as King and Messiah as King did not really arise because the two were not usually spoken of in the same text.[7] The expectation of a Messiah was comparatively infrequent (with respect to the Kingdom of God) and completely unsystematised. In some writings, the Kingdom of God involved a Messiah; God ruled Israel and the world through the appointed Messiah.[8] God's agent, the Messiah, was believed to be a this-worldly human ruler or judge who would arise within Israel and who would enact the divine judgement and vengeance on Israel's oppressors.[9]

The above is a brief summary of the expectation of the Kingdom of God and the associated Messiah which could be held in various shades and forms by the Jews of first century Palestine. The New Testament, which was not strictly bound by these forms of expectation, was free to bring out its own concretised versions of the Kingdom of God and the

---

3 See Wright, *The New Testament and the People of God,* pp. 306-7, and *Jesus and the Victory of God,* pp. 206-7.

4 Wright, *The New Testament and the People of God,* p. 334.

5 *Ibid.,* p. 301.

6 *Ibid.,* p. 300.

7 *Ibid.,* p. 307.

8 *Ibid.,* p. 302. But in some writings, God's rule could also involve a line of true priests in addition to the Davidic King (Messiah), see p. 307.

9 *Ibid.,* pp. 319-20.

Messiah. The New Testament versions have similarities and continuities with some of these forms of expectation but the writers also felt free to differ from them. In particular, the relationship between the coming of God (or his Kingdom) and the coming of the Messiah in the New Testament is an interesting and important one. Even though the relationship was not clearly and firmly established in the various forms of Jewish expectation, the New Testament presents the concrete form of fulfilment. In the fulfilment found in the New Testament, indeed God's agent the Messiah has come; he is Jewish and human as in the expectation, and he has established or inaugurated God's rule. But the Messiah presented in the New Testament is more than a human figure in that he is strongly identified with God himself. The Messiah's strong identification with God in the New Testament captures the main thrust of the hope of the Kingdom of God - that God himself will come to visit his people to bring about a decisive change and liberation - which was more prevalent than the idea of a human Messiah. The two strands of expectation - the coming of the human Messiah and the coming of God himself - seemed to have been fulfilled by Jesus, according to the witness of the New Testament. Jesus' fulfilment of these two strands of expectation raises the question of his identity.

2.0 Jesus as the Coming Lord

2.1 Matthew 3:3 and the Associated Narrative Structure

'The voice of one crying in the wilderness, "Prepare the way of the Lord. Make straight his paths."' (Matthew 3:3)[10]

This verse is almost a verbatim quote of Isaiah 40:3. An obvious reading of this verse in Matthew would understand that in its fulfilment 'the Lord' and 'his' correspond to Jesus because John the Baptist was clearly the forerunner who prepared the way for Jesus who came after him (3:11). Apparently, it was the Baptist himself who first understood the fulfilment of this prophecy in Isaiah and identified himself as the voice calling in the desert (see John 1:23 where it was the Baptist himself who uttered these words), but in his understanding he might not identify Jesus with 'the Lord'. In all probability, the Baptist did not expect the Lord - Yahweh himself in the context of Isaiah 40:3 - literally to come himself and establish his Kingdom and reign. For the Baptist, the coming of the Lord, for which he prepared, probably had a metaphorical rather than a literal meaning, such that the coming of the Lord meant the

---

10 Translation taken from Donald Hagner, *Word Biblical Commentary: Matthew 1-13* (Dallas: Word Books, 1993), p. 44.

establishment of God's reign on earth which would be fulfilled by an agent - the human Messiah - who would come after him and baptise with the Holy Spirit and fire (3:11-12).[11] In that case, in the Baptist's mind the human agent who came to establish the Kingdom was not to be identified with Yahweh himself; only the work of this human agent was to be identified with the reign of Yahweh. But there are at least two reasons why Matthew's usage of Isaiah 40:3 here may be different from the Baptist's understanding.

Firstly, in contrast with John 1:23, Matthew, as in Luke and Mark (or the tradition they received), *deliberately* takes the verse away from the lips of the Baptist so that Matthew (or the tradition) is not presenting the Baptist's understanding of the fulfilment of Isaiah 40:3 here (an important feature not noted by commentators, see the following footnotes). Rather, Matthew is presenting his own understanding of the fulfilment, which could be different from the Baptist's, so that it is possible that Matthew might have identified Jesus with Yahweh - the Lord.[12] Secondly, if Matthew is to follow the Baptist's understanding, he could have quoted Isaiah 40:3 entirely verbatim from the LXX translation. In that case, the straight paths made would be 'of our God/τοῦ θεοῦ ἡμῶν' rather than 'his/αὐτοῦ' so that Jesus could not be identified with 'our God'.[13] Nor would he be identified with 'the Lord' since 'the Lord' and 'our God' are parallels and therefore identical in Isaiah 40:3. However, Matthew is not satisfied with a verbatim quote of Isaiah 40:3 and he changes 'of our God' to 'his'. The reason is evident: this deliberate change would break down the barrier to identifying Jesus with 'our Lord' such that in the context of Matthew 3:1-12, where the Baptist prepares for the coming of Jesus, 'his' paths prepared by the Baptist in 3:3 is Jesus' path and 'the Lord' is identified with Jesus.[14] And it must be remembered that in the context of Isaiah

---

11 J. Hughes claims that the Baptist regards the coming one as Yahweh himself, see his 'John the Baptist: The Forerunner of God Himself', *Novum Testamentum*, 14 (1972), pp. 191-218. But D. Hagner disagrees, '... the forerunner precedes the one who will bring the kingdom. While the Baptist expects a triumphant Messiah, it is probably going too far to conclude that he regards the coming one as none other than Yahweh. The words that immediately follow are only appropriate to a human agent such as the Messiah.' Hagner, *Matthew 1-13*, p. 51, commenting on Mt 3:11.

12 In John's gospel (1:23), there is no need to take this sentence from the Baptist's lips in order to open up the possibility of identifying Jesus with Yahweh because there Jesus has already been identified with God (John 1:1-2).

13 'God' in Matthew is always reserved for the Father. It is not used for Jesus except perhaps in the brief elaboration of Immanuel - 'God with us' - which applies to Jesus. For details of the different translations, see Hagner, *Matthew 1-13*, p. 48.

14 'In Isaiah the "voice" preceded the coming of God; here the phrase *his paths*, instead of Isaiah's "a highway for our God", allows the reader to see *the Lord* as Jesus.' R.T.

40:3, 'the Lord' refers to Yahweh. Therefore, by his double action of *deliberately* taking this verse away from the lips of the Baptist (thus allowing a different interpretation) and *intentionally* changing the quotation of Isaiah 40:3, Matthew *purposefully* identifies Jesus with the Lord in the Old Testament - *Yahweh*. However, this identification cannot be an identical identification with Yahweh because in Matthew and the other gospels only the Father (or God) is identical to Yahweh of the Old Testament. What then is the nature of this identification? Matthew's identification of Jesus with the Lord is not unique in the New Testament, where Jesus is often referred to or identified as the Lord. It is probable that Matthew's use of 'the Lord' for Jesus in Mt. 3:3 has close connections with those in the New Testament. This possibility is considered here. The following is a brief summary of how Jesus is acknowledged as Lord in the NT epistles.

> The confessional cry used in worship, Jesus is Lord, ... is one of the oldest Christian creeds, if not the oldest. With this call the NT community submitted itself to its Lord, but at the same time it also confessed him as ruler of the world (Rom. 10:9a; 1 Cor. 12:3; Phil. 2:11; ...). God has raised Jesus from the dead and exalted him to the position of universal *kyrios*. Moreover, he has 'bestowed on him the name which is above every name' (Phil. 2:9f; cf. Isa. 45:23f.), i.e., his own name of Lord and with it the position corresponding to the name. The exalted *kyrios*, Christ, rules over mankind (Rom. 14:9). All powers and beings in the universe must bow the knee before him. When that happens, God the Father will be worshipped (cf. Eph. 1:20f; 1 Pet. 3:22). This is further implied in the fact that Christ is called the ruler over all the kings of the earth, Lord of lords and King of kings (Rev. 1:5; 17:14; 19:15f). In this way Jesus Christ received the same titles of honour as God himself (1 Tim. 6:15; cf. Dan. 2:47).[15]

France, *The Gospel According to Matthew: An Introduction and Commentary* (Leicester: Inter-Varsity, 1987), p. 91, where the RSV is used for quoting Scripture. See R.H. Gundry, *Matthew: A Commentary on His Literary and Theological Art* (Grand Rapids: Eerdmans, 1982), p. 45, for the same point. Interestingly, E. Schweizer, *The Good News According to Matthew* (London: SPCK, 1976) and U. Luz, *Matthew 1-7: A Commentary* (Edinburgh: T. & T. Clark, 1990) in their commentaries bypass Matthew's deliberate identification of Jesus with the Lord/Yahweh here. Also, even though F.W. Beare, in *The Gospel According to Matthew* (Oxford: Blackwell, 1981) notices and mentions the change from 'our God' to 'his', he severs the meaning of Mt. 3:3 from its original context in Isaiah 40:3, removes Jesus' identification with Yahweh, and declares that all the verse says is that the Baptist is the one who prepared the way for Jesus (p. 90).

15 *NIDNTT*, vol. 2, p. 514.

Barth connects the usage of Lord in the NT epistles with the usage in the gospels in the following way:

> [A]t that time it [Lord] was also used in a more precise sense, amongst Greek-speaking Jews as a translation of the Old Testament name for God, ... And if in the New Testament Epistles, which for the most part *precede the Gospels*, the title κύριος is consistently applied to Jesus Christ in the strictest sense, we can gather from this that even *when it is used of Him in the Gospels it has this precise and emphatic sense*, expressing in a comprehensive way the sovereignty which made an ineffaceable impression on the community as the distinctive mark of the being of Jesus.[16]

Barth's point is that since the epistles (or most of them) were written earlier than the gospels and these epistles acknowledged Jesus as Lord in the strictest sense (in the sense of God or equality with God), the gospels also used 'Lord' to refer to Jesus in this sense of sovereignty. According to Barth, this was how the community recollected the presence and being of Jesus in his earthly life - he was already Lord in the highest sense. But the following precautionary consideration needs to be taken.

When κύριος is directly applied to Jesus in Matthew, all the twenty-five cases are in the vocative, i.e., in the form of respective address, Κύριε.[17] Such addresses in the original contexts, i.e., on the lips of those who used this address to Jesus, did not bear the sense of divine majesty. This is R.T. France's and D. Carson's position.[18] However, G. Bornkamm observed the following.

> [I]t is very significant that though Matthew frequently uses the title διδάσκαλος or alternatively ῥαββί, he never uses it as a mode of address in the mouth of the disciples, with one exception - Judas Iscariot. The Pharisees and strangers call him διδάσκαλε. His disciples call him Κύριε. This observation is the more weighty since the received tradition, as Mark shows, very frequently and ingenuously places the term of address διδάσκαλε or ῥαββί in the mouth of the disciples (Mark 4:38; 9:5; 9:38; 10:35; 13:1; ...). Matthew, on the other hand, quite consistently changes to Κύριε (cf. 8:25 and Mark 4:38; Mt. 17:4 and Mark 9:5; Mt.

---

16 *CD* IV.2, p. 162. Italics mine.

17 The κύριος in Mt. 21:3 may refer to God, Jesus or the donkey's owner. That is the only possible use in Matthew which could refer to Jesus directly as κύριος.

18 R. T. France, *Matthew - Evangelist and Teacher* (Exeter: Paternoster, 1989), pp. 287-8; and D. Carson, 'Christological Ambiguities in Matthew', in *Christ the Lord* (Leicester: Inter-Varsity, 1982), H. Rowdon (ed.), pp. 108-9.

20:33 and Mark 10:51; ...). Those who do not belong to the disciples say
to the disciples 'your master' (9:2; 17:24); likewise, over against the Jews
he is designated by the disciples as 'the Master' (26:18), but among the
disciples themselves this title is not adequate for him, but only the Lord-
title will do.[19]

Bornkamm's point is that Matthew intentionally redacted his source to
have the disciples uniquely addressing Jesus with this title - Lord. After
adducing further evidences, Bornkamm concluded, 'From the evidence
presented, it follows: the title and address of Jesus as Κύριος in
Matthew have throughout the character of a *divine name of majesty*. The
legitimation of this from Scripture is found in Psalm 110:1 (Mt.
22:41ff).'[20] Most scholars have accepted Bornkamm's view.[21] In
particular, Jack Kingsbury analysed the relationships between 'Lord'
and other christological titles - Son of Man, Son of God, Christ - and
concluded that it is used in conjunction with these titles to denote Jesus'
divine authority and majesty.[22] To many scholars, 'The inevitable
implication, of course, is that the Evangelist was anachronistically
reading back a view of Jesus not actually found until the time of his own
Sitz in Leben.'[23] But this suggestion of anachronistic reading by
Matthew is denied by Carson and France who maintain that Κύριε was
only a form of respective address. However, France does acknowledge
that in Matthew Jesus is expected to be addressed as 'Lord' when he
comes as the eschatological judge and as the Son of Man in his glory
(7:21-22; 25:11, 37, 44) and it is likely that Matthew exploited the fact
that it was also used for the divine title in LXX.[24] Carson also points out
other equivalences between Jesus and God (e.g., Mt. 3:3; 11:9-11,
where Jesus equivalenced John the Baptist with Elijah who was God's
messenger to prepare for the coming of Yahweh, see Malachi 3:1, 4:5-
6). Instead of seeing the use of 'Lord' as anachronistic, Carson's subtle
approach is similar to France's.

> Certainly Matthew rather favours *kyrios* and *proskyneo*; doubtless some
> of the reasons cannot be retrieved with any degree of certainty. But it
> appears that one of the contributing factors, at least in some of his usages,

---

19 G. Bornkamm, G. Barth, and H. Held, *Tradition and Interpretation in Matthew*
(London: SCM Press, 1963), p. 41.

20 *Ibid.*, pp. 42-3. Italics mine.

21 Carson, 'Christological Ambiguities in Matthew', p. 108.

22 J. Kingsbury, 'The Title "Kyrios" in Matthew's Gospel', *Journal of Biblical
Literature*, 94 (1975), pp. 246-255.

23 Carson, 'Christological Ambiguities in Matthew', p. 108.

24 France, *Matthew: Evangelist and Teacher*, p. 288.

is that the words are ambiguous. Interpreted narrowly, the words do not permit an anachronistic reading of the church's mature theology back into Jesus' day; yet at the same time, no reader in Matthew's day could fail to read those same words without recognising that the full response of worship before Deity is required by his or her full understanding of the Gospel, an understanding achieved in part by being located a little later in the flow of redemptive history than those who knew Jesus in the days of his flesh.[25]

[E]nough has been said to conclude that Matthew successfully attempted to distinguish between his own Christological understanding at the time he wrote, and that of Jesus' contemporaries, including his disciples, during the days of his ministry. Yet at the same time, he set forth his Gospel in such a way that he revealed his own Christological commitments, and showed what conclusions he expected his readers to draw. All of the titles take on new light in the wake of the cross and the empty tomb; and yet the pre-passion usages anticipate and point to the fullness of revelation about to dawn.[26]

It is clear that the change of perspective to one acknowledging Jesus' Lordship occurred at the point of the resurrection and Jesus' receiving all authority in heaven and on earth (Mt. 28:18), which is also Barth's position.

[T]he knowledge of Jesus Christ, and the presentation in the whole of the New Testament and therefore from the very outset in the Synoptics, rests on the self-declaration in which He revealed Himself to His disciples in the resurrection and ascension. The New Testament attestation would be valueless, and His history and He Himself as the royal man obscured, if we tried artificially to divert this light of His self-declaration and consider the pre-Easter prelude in abstraction from its Easter sequel. From the very first, and wherever it has been alive, the Church has lived by and with the Jesus Christ of the New Testament, i.e., of the New Testament as written and read in the light of His resurrection and ascension.[27]

---

25 Carson, 'Christological Ambiguities in Matthew', pp. 110-111.

26 *Ibid.*, p. 114.

27 *CD* IV.2, p. 156. J.D. Kingsbury, in *Matthew as Story* (Philadelphia: Fortress, 1988), p. 38, also writes, '[L]ike the implied author, the implied reader, too, has a place or position of his or her own within the world of Matthew's story. This position lies, as the passages 24:15; 27:8; and 28:15 reveal, at some distance from the resurrection but short of the Parousia. It is, in fact, identical with the place of Matthew as implied author. From this vantage point in time, the implied reader likewise oversees the story of the life and ministry of Jesus of Nazareth as Matthew conveys this through

One can interpret the disciples' addresses to Jesus as Lord in Matthew as follows. Mark certainly refers to Jesus as 'Lord' *directly* and *indirectly*. Like Mt. 3:3, Mark 1:2-3 identifies Jesus with the Lord (Yahweh) in Isaiah 40:3 (and Malachi 3:1). The Lord to whom David referred in Mark 12:37 (Psalm 110:1) was understood to be Jesus. The Syro-Phoenician woman addressed Jesus as Lord (Mark 7:28). The Son of Man, Jesus, is Lord of the Sabbath (Mark 2:28). All these four (direct) references to Jesus as Lord are shared by Matthew (3:3; 22:44; 15:27; 12:8). Mark quite deliberately equivalences the Lord (God) with Jesus in the exorcism of the man in Gerasenes (5:19-20, indirect reference), which is left out by Matthew for the sake of brevity.[28] Therefore, it is quite certain that in the tradition that Matthew received, there were some tendency for *direct* references to Jesus as the Lord and there is some tendency for *indirect* references to Jesus as the Lord. And it is probable that Matthew strengthens the tendency for direct references by shaping the disciples' addresses to Jesus into a uniform pattern - Κύριε, and strengthens the tendency for indirect references by including further equivalences between Jesus and Lord (Yahweh; see France's *Matthew: Evangelist and Teacher*, pp. 308-317.[29] See also his *Jesus and the Old Testament*). Matthew is therefore *highlighting a theological point* which was there in the tradition (cf. Bornkamm and Kingsbury). The overall picture he presents is that *Jesus is equivalenced with 'Lord' (Yahweh)* and Jesus' disciples consistently addressed him as Lord. Even though his disciples did not appreciate this full and legitimate meaning and its implications at the time; they can be understood by Matthew's readers, who are positioned at a post-resurrection point in time, as speaking better than they realised. The references to Jesus as Lord in Matthew therefore can be understood at two levels - as an address of respect and at a deeper level of divine Lordship. The same can be applied to references to Jesus as Lord in other gospels.[30] In that sense, Barth's interpretation of the 'Lord' in the

---

his voice as narrator, and he or she can comprehend the whole of this story.'

28 Matthew often gives summary versions of Mark's pericopes. See France, *Matthew: Evangelist and Teacher*, pp. 133-5.

29 For example, the authority and glory of the Son of Man sitting on his throne pronouncing divine judgment (Mt. 25:31f).

30 All three synoptic gospels have Jesus' alluding himself to be the Lord in Psalm 110:1 (Mt. 22:41-45; Mark 12:35-37; Luke 20:41-44). Also, Luke 3:4 equivalences Jesus with 'Lord' (Yahweh) in Isaiah 40:3 and has even more references to Jesus as Lord than Mark and Matthew. H. Conzelmann wrote in *The Theology of St. Luke* (London: Faber, 1960), p. 176, 'For Luke Jesus is already on earth Christ, Son and Lord.' Interestingly, Mark's equivalence between Jesus and Yahweh at the beginning of his gospel is even more pronounced than Matthew and Luke, using both passages from Isaiah 40:3 and Malachi 3:1. Mark's ending, if 16:9-20 is included, has Jesus

highest sense in the gospels can be justified more fully.

Matthew's deliberate identification of Jesus with Yahweh in Mt. 3:3 near the beginning of the gospel and Jesus' exaltation to universal Lordship at the end in Mt. 28:18 prompt one to consider the possible presence of an inclusio as a literary device in the structure of Matthew's gospel highlighting Jesus' divine Lordship. Bearing in mind the other and wider inclusio formed by Jesus' title - Immanuel (Mt. 1:23) - and his universal presence in Mt. 28:20, the following literary pattern has emerged.

> X: Immanuel - God with us (Mt. 1:23)
>> Y: Jesus identified with the Lord (Mt. 3:3)
>>> Z: Jesus' baptism, his Lordship in his ministry, ... death, resurrection
>> Y': Jesus' universal Lordship (Mt. 28:18)
> X': Jesus' universal presence with his disciples (Mt. 28:20)

The formation of an *inclusio* by Mt. 3:3 and Mt. 28:18 (YY', on the theme of Lordship), in addition to Matthew's highlighting Jesus' Lordship in his disciples' address to him (see above) and his exercise of his Lordship in words and actions in his ministry (Z; see chapters 3 and 4), witness to the author's intention of consistently presenting Jesus' Lordship throughout the gospel. Put in other literary terms, Y is a *preparation* on the theme of Jesus' Lordship which is unpacked or elaborated through the ministry of Jesus (Z), reaching its *climactic* expression in Y'.[31] However, it must be remember that Jesus' Lordship

---

explicitly referred to as 'Lord' twice in succession (16:19-20). The double equivalences at the beginning of his gospel and the double explicit references to Jesus as Lord at the end therefore form an inclusio, the theme of which is Jesus' divine Lordship. This Lordship is expressed in narrative form in the body of the gospel bracketed by the inclusio. It would be unreasonable, then, to suggest that only Matthew, not Mark and Luke, intended to present Jesus' divine Lordship while it is true that he specifically heightened some aspects of it by his redactions.

31 However, J. Kingsbury insists that the Christological title most appropriate to Mt. 28:18-20 (Y'X') is 'Son of God' and refuses to entertain the thought that the Christological titles of Son of Man and Lord (to Kingsbury the two are related) are also proper ('The Composition and Christology of Mt. 28:16-20', *Journal of Biblical Literature*, vol. 93, 1974, p. 580). Kingsbury follows Tödt's argument that exaltation is not associated with the Son of Man (H. E. Tödt, *The Son of Man in the Synoptic Tradition* (London: SCM Press, 1965), pp. 287-91). But Tödt himself did not exclude the idea of Mt. 28:18 expressing Jesus' Lordship even if he gave the caution that this is the only place where such universal Lordship of Jesus is expressed in Matthew (*Ibid.*, pp. 290-1). Kingsbury, who intends to relate 28:18-20 solely to the Christological title 'the Son of God', seems to have been too exclusive by

must not be viewed on its own for Matthew (Mark and Luke) presents his Lordship via his identification or equivalence with Yahweh. His Lordship means he is equal with his Father and because of this equality he can be properly called Lord; Jesus is not Lord in his solitary self. His Lordship and equality with the Father is further highlighted in the second last verse of Matthew's gospel, where the disciples are to be baptised in the name (singular) of 'the Father and of the Son and of the Holy Spirit.' Matthew, apart from highlighting the Son's *equality* with the Father (or the Son at the same rank as the Father and the Spirit) in this verse, also brings the reader's attention to their *unity* through his deliberate use of the singular for name (ὄνομα).

It is reasonable to raise the question of whether Matthew intends his reader to appreciate Jesus' divine Lordship and his equality with his Father by reading Mt. 3:3 (Y) alone. Although from the literary structure of his gospel and the general use of 'Lord' in the transcendent sense for Jesus in the early church one may be quite sure that Matthew himself understands and uses it in that sense, he might not expect his readers to appreciate its ultimate significance in their first reading. However, his narratives will lead the readers to a deeper appreciation of Jesus' authority and Lordship in his words and actions which will culminate in the cross, resurrection and Jesus' universal Lordship at the end of the gospel (Y'X'). It may well be that it is only after completing the first reading of the gospel and in a subsequent re-reading of Mt. 3:3 that his readers may appreciate what he means by Jesus' identification with Yahweh of the OT - *Jesus is everything the name of Yahweh represents* or *his equality with his Father*. It is by such a hermeneutical spiral that the readers are expected come to a better appreciation of Jesus' identity as presented by Matthew.[32] His presentation of Jesus'

---

disallowing 'Lord', or Jesus' Lordship, to be a Christological theme here. In any case, arguing against Tödt, France shows that a proper understanding of Mt. 26:64 allows the Son of Man in Daniel 7 to be closely related to this passage (*Matthew: Evangelist and Teacher*, p. 315). There is no reason why, then, the Christological titles - Son of Man and Lord - should not be related to 28:18-20. Also, clearly Jesus' universal Lordship after his resurrection is presented there. Therefore, one cannot agree with Kingsbury that the Christological title or theme, 'Lord', is inappropriate to 28:18 (Y') while one can agree with him that the other title, Son of God, is also clearly in view (cf. 11:27). It has not been found amongst the literature a sustained effort to relate Mt. 3:3 (and Isaiah 40:3) together with Jesus' universal Lordship and presence at the end of the gospel (though there are general acknowledgement of the connection between Immanuel in 1:23 and Jesus' continuing presence with his disciples in 28:20, e.g., France, *Matthew Commentary*, p. 80, and Hagner, *Matthew 1-13*, p. 21). The identification of the literary structure concerning Jesus' Lordship as given above, though not a profound one, apparently is unique.

32 The reader, like the first disciples, needs to go through a phrase of transformation as

divine Lordship and equality with his Father is therefore less explicit than John's gospel. However, there are some similarities between Matthew and John in this respect. John, whose prologue can be interpreted as a kind of *preparation*, elaborates his prologue throughout his gospel by elucidating Jesus' relationship with his Father. It is only by reading the whole of John's gospel that one may appreciate Jesus' equality and relationship with his Father given in the prologue. This hermeneutical procedure is essentially the same as that of Matthew. But Matthew could not be as explicit as John in ascribing deity to Jesus probably because of the strict monotheistic belief of his more Jewish audience. Nevertheless, he subtlely leads his readers to the same conclusion as one might arrive at by reading John (see also 3.3.2 later on the role of the Holy Spirit).[33]

In 3.0 of chapter 1, McGrath's comment on the dynamic interacting relationship between narrative and theological/conceptual/doctrinal formulations was quoted. He suggests that 'narrative possesses an interpretative substructure, hinting at doctrinal affirmations.' The literary pattern identified above and the identification of Jesus with Yahweh in Mt. 3:3 are good examples of such interpretative substructure and doctrinal hint respectively. But the interpretative substructure and the doctrinal hint related to Jesus' identity found in Matthew cannot stand on their own. They need to be affirmed by the narratives of Jesus' life, ministry, death and resurrection. Effectively, these narratives help to clarify and locate the significance of the interpretative substructure and the meaning of Mt. 3:3. In this move, Mt. 3:3, the interpretative substructure and the narratives are taken up in a conceptualisation (or doctrinal formulation) of the identity of Jesus Christ - Jesus' equivalence with Yahweh and his divine Lordship. (For Barth, this move has to be the move by the Holy Spirit, see 3.3.2

---

he follows through the narratives of Jesus life, ministry, death, resurrection and universal reign before he comes to a better appreciation of the person of Jesus.

33 Concerning Matthew's Christology, U. Luz's judgment is that 'Matthew advocates a Christology "from above", but not in the sense later espoused by the Old Church. It is not his primary intent to define the figure of Jesus as one thing or another - for example, as God. What he does say, however, is that in the *story* of the man Jesus, God *acts*. In other words, his Christology is conceived from a narrative standpoint.' *The Theology of the Gospel of Matthew* (Cambridge: Cambridge University Press, 1995), p. 32. While it is true that Matthew's Christology is very much presented through the narratives, as this book concurs, it is not necessary to imply that Matthew is not interested in any other (e.g., more explicit) form of Christology. Mt. 3:3 and Mt. 28:18 (YY'), as has been argued, is a deliberate and explicit form of high Christology (though not as explicit as in John and the Old Church) employed by Matthew who uses it together with his narratives to present a Christology from above, while acknowledging Jesus' true humanity.

below.) With such clarification, affirmation and conceptual formulation of Jesus' identity, the narratives can be re-read and re-visioned in the light of Jesus' identity (see chapters 3 and 4). Such re-readings may prompt further and clearer understandings of Jesus' relationships with his Father and the Spirit (see, e.g., chapter 5), which in turn may call for further conceptualisations or doctrinal formulations towards a theology of the Trinity (see chapter 6). This may be an example of what McGrath calls 'a process of dynamic interaction, of feedback, between doctrine and scripture, between the interpretative framework and the narrative itself, paralleling the related process of mathematical iteration.'

2.2 The Origin of the Confession of Jesus as Lord

Bousset and Bultmann espoused the theory that cultic devotion to Jesus, and hence the high Lordship (or divinity) of Jesus, originated in gentile churches rather than Jewish Palestinian churches so that they were not genuinely connected with the historical Jesus.[34] According to this view, the strict monotheistic belief of Jewish Christians could not have tolerated and originated a devotion to Jesus as Lord. However, the gentile pluralistic environment was much more conducive to this kind of devotion to Jesus alongside God. The NT epistles, which were written mostly to gentile churches and confessed the high Lordship of Jesus, reflected the gentile origin and influence of this Lordship. Such gentile influence was carried into the writing of the gospels which took place later than the epistles, such that some devices were invented by the church or its evangelists to present the high Lordship of Jesus in the gospels, e.g., the miracle stories of Jesus.[35] In this view, the high Lordship of Jesus presented in the gospels cannot be trusted. Against this view, there are scholars such as C.F.D. Moule, L. Hurtado, R. France, R. Bauckham, M. Turner (and Barth) who argue that such high Lordship of Jesus can be traced back to the Jewish Palestinian church (rather than gentile churches) or to the historical Jesus himself.

Hurtado, in *One God, One Lord,* strongly advances the following thesis:

---

34 W. Bousset, *Kyrios Christos* (Nashville: Abingdon Press, 1970), pp. 119-52; R. Bultmann, *Theology of the New Testament* (London: SCM Press, 1952-1955), 1:42-53, especially pp. 51-2.

35 'Bultmann's view is that they were narrated as proofs of the Messianic power and divine might of Jesus.' Vincent Taylor, *The Formation of the Gospel Tradition* (London: Macmillan, 1960), p. 131. However, Bultmann did not think the evangelists, *except Luke*, used the title 'Lord' in a divine majestic sense. Bousset took a similar view, *Kyrios Christos*, pp. 79f. Luke does use 'The Lord' in the exalted sense, see Conzelmann, *The Theology of St. Luke*, pp. 176-9.

[T]he evidence suggests strongly that ... within the first two decades of Christianity, Jewish Christians gathered in Jesus' name for worship, prayed to him and sang hymns to him, regarded him as exalted to a position of heavenly rule above all angelic orders, appropriated to him titles and Old Testament passages originally referring to God [e.g., Lord], sought to bring fellow Jews as well as Gentiles to embrace him as the divinely appointed redeemer, and in general redefined their devotion to the God of their fathers so as to include the veneration of Jesus.[36]

Again, concerning the times of the hymns sung to Jesus:

There is a scholarly consensus that embedded within the New Testament are examples of 'Christ hymns' which certainly include some from the first half of the first century C.E.: John 1:1-18; Col. 1:15-20; and Phil. 2:5-11 are widely accepted as major passages where early Christian hymns concerning Christ have been incorporated.[37]

These Christian hymns acknowledged and celebrated the Lordship of Jesus, his supremacy over creation and his equality with God. In terms of time, these compositions seems to have originated from Christian groups from the very beginning.[38] In terms of the breadth of usage, some of them were used both in Jewish and gentile churches.[39] It is probable that such celebration of Jesus' Lordship goes back to Jewish Palestinian church. This is consistent with the fact that we have no record of Jewish Palestinian church criticising Paul and the gentile churches for worshipping Jesus as Lord though there were other criticisms (e.g., concerning circumcision of gentiles).

Also, there is the Aramaic prayer, *maranatha*, which originated from Jewish Aramaic speaking church and was used in gentile churches.[40] The ending of Paul's first letter to the Corinthians (16:22) contains such an example without translation to Greek. *Maranatha* means 'Our Lord (or Lord) come!'. The immediate context of 1 Cor. 16:22-23 shows that the prayer was addressed to 'Lord Jesus'; the wider context of 1 Cor.

36 Larry Hurtado, *One God, One Lord* (London: SCM Press, 1988), p. 11. Before Hurtado, R.T. France also drew attention to the important factor of the worship of Jesus in reflecting on the identity of Jesus. See 'The Worship of Jesus: A Neglected Factor in Christological Debate?' in *Christ the Lord*, H. Rowdon (ed.), pp. 17-36.

37 *Ibid.*, p. 101

38 *Ibid.*, p. 102, Hurtado quotes J.D.G. Dunn, *Jesus and the Spirit* (London: SCM Press, 1975), pp. 157-96 for support.

39 *Ibid.*, p. 102, point 3.

40 *Ibid.*, pp. 106-108.

11:26 - 'You proclaim the Lord's death until he comes'- indicates that this prayer was invoked in the eschatological expectation of the return of the Lord and was therefore addressed to Jesus. And most scholars think Rev. 22:20 - 'Come, Lord Jesus!' - is a Greek translation of this Aramaic prayer. '[T]here are good reasons for concluding that the use of *marêh* ['Lord'] for Christ did connote the conviction that he had been made to share in divine glory and transcendence and therefore was to be reverenced in terms of actions characteristically reserved for God.'[41] For further arguments by Hurtado concerning the worship of Jesus as Lord in early Jewish Palestinian churches, see his *One God, One Lord,* pp. 100-24.

France lists the references to Jesus as Lord at the beginning of the Christian church - Acts 2:36; 4:33; 7:59; 10:36; etc.[42] Acts 2:36 relates to Jesus' resurrection and exaltation to the right hand of God. Acts 7:59 is Stephen's prayer to 'Lord Jesus'. Peter in Acts 10:36 acknowledged Jesus as 'Lord of all'. For France, the NT account of the early church indicates that the 'phenomenon of the worship of Jesus developed remarkably quickly' after Jesus' resurrection.[43] He also surveys Paul's letters and the NT as a whole concerning the worship of Jesus and attributes such worship to 'what was already there *in the traditions and experiences of his ministry and teaching*, ... a new and essentially unparalleled experience of God in Jesus'.[44] It was this unparalleled experience of God in Jesus which drove the Jewish Christians to worship Jesus.[45]

---

41 *Ibid.*, p. 107.

42 France, 'The Worship of Jesus: A Neglected Factor in Christological Debate?', p. 29.

43 *Ibid.*

44 *Ibid.*, p. 23. Italics mine. This point is reiterated in his article 'Development in New Testament Christology', *Themelios*, 18 (1993), no. 1, p. 8. Apart from attributing the worship of Jesus to his ministry and teaching, France also includes the power of the risen Christ as a reason. 'I am suggesting that the incarnational Christology of the New Testament had its roots ... in Christian experience of Jesus, both in his earthly ministry and in his risen power, and that it was the natural translation of this experience into an attitude of worship which provided the seedbed for New Testament Christology.' *Ibid.*, p. 33.

45 'This worship was no easy option for pious Jews. If their own monotheistic upbringing rebelled against it, they could be sure it would provoke the violent hostility of their fellow-Jews. Even among Gentiles it was a preposterous idea, as is vividly illustrated by the famous Alexamenos *graffito* from third-century Rome: a young man worshipping a crucified human figure with a donkey's head, over the caption 'Alexamenos worship his god.' Men do not gratuitously court such opposition and ridicule merely out of a dispassionate search for a new religious ideology. *There must have been an irresistible compulsion, so that they could do no other.*' France, 'The Worship of Jesus: a Neglected Factor in Christological Debate',

Scholars such as Bornkamm and those who follow him in his interpretation of 'Lord' in Matthew point to Psalm 110:1 (Mt. 22:41f) as the legitimation of this use of 'Lord' for Jesus.[46] Vincent Taylor, when commenting on the parallel passage in Mark 12:35-36, wrote,

> The allusive character of the saying favours the view that it is an original utterance; it half conceals and half reveals the "Messianic secret". It suggests, but does not state the claim that Jesus is supernatural in dignity and origin and that His Sonship is no mere matter of human descent. It is difficult to think that the doctrinal beliefs of a community could be expressed in this allusive manner ... [D]emonstrably, it is not the tone or the method of primitive Christianity.[47]

Taylor's observation strengthens France's point that the disciples' worship of Jesus as Lord was rooted in Jesus' own teaching and ministry.

The article by R. Bauckham, 'The Worship of Jesus in Apocalyptic Christianity', also negates the theory of alien influence on the worship of Jesus in the Christian church.[48] Bauckham's point is that the apocalyptic tradition in early Christianity distinguished between angels and God sharply - angels must not be worshipped while God must be, and Jesus was regularly placed on the divine side of the divide. Bauckham argues that in terms of Christian religious practice the divinity of Jesus was already recognised from a very early date.

M. Turner, by studying Peter's preaching at the Pentecost (Acts 2:14-39), argues that the divine Lordship of Jesus could be acknowledged as early as the beginning of the church after Jesus' resurrection and ascension.[49] Peter proclaimed that God's promise through Joel, that he will pour out his Spirit on all people (Joel 2:28-32; Acts 2:17-21), had been fulfilled in Jesus, who, having received from the Father the promised Spirit, had poured out the Spirit on his disciples at Pentecost (Acts 2:33). Jesus' pouring out the Spirit has great significance.

---

p. 35. Italics mine.

46 Bornkamm, Barth, and Held, *Tradition and Interpretation in Matthew*, pp. 42-3. Psalm 110:1 reads, 'The Lord says to my Lord: Sit at my right hand until I make your enemies a footstool for your feet.'

47 Vincent Taylor, *The Gospel According to St. Mark* (London: Macmillan, 1952), pp. 492-3.

48 R. Bauckham, 'The Worship of Jesus in Apocalyptic Christianity', *New Testament Studies,* 27 (1980-1), pp. 322-41, especially pp. 333f.

49 Max Turner, 'The Spirit of Christ and Christology', in *Christ the Lord*, H. Rowdon (ed.), pp. 168-190. More briefly in *The Holy Spirit and Spiritual Gifts: Then and Now* (Carlisle: Paternoster, 1996), pp. 175-8.

[Jesus] now has the *power to administer the operation of the Spirit as the Spirit of prophecy.* ... [H]e is now able to distribute its individual and varied charismata (2:33). Through this means he will direct and empower the church's mission to outsiders (*e.g.,* Acts 2:4; 4:8, 31; 8:29; 10:11-21; 11:12; 13:2, 4, 9; 16:6f; *etc.*), and he will give charismatic wisdom and revelation where it is needed either for the defence and propagation of the gospel (*cf.* Acts 6:3, 5, 10 and Lk. 21:25) or for the direction, sanctification and upbuilding of the church (*cf.* Acts 5:1-11; 9:10ff., 31; 11:28; 13:52; 15:28; *etc.*).[50]

As the Spirit had mediated God's activity, and thus his presence, amongst his people, so, according to the perspective of Acts 2:33, the Spirit has now become the means of Jesus' presence and activity too. ... [O]nce Christians ever begin to speak of the Spirit mediating the activity and presence of Jesus, they would be drawn irresistibly towards a divine Christology. The Acts account of the Pentecost speech suggests that this move had already been taken by Peter. If, for him, Jesus' functions have become so aligned with Yahweh's that both can be said to pour out the Spirit (*cf.* 2:17, 33) then there is nothing to prevent the Christological application of the Joel citation being carried through at every point. Jesus can barely be other than the one denoted by Joel's expression *to onoma kyriou* ('the name of the Lord': *i.e.,* the Lord himself) upon whom all men are to call for salvation (compare 2:36, 38f. with 2:21, 33); so he is to be acknowledged as 'Lord', and that in its transcendent sense.[51]

Thus Jesus' ascension and the church's experience of his pouring out of the Spirit on her played a pivotal role in her recognition of his divine Lordship. Turner's argument brings the origin of the acknowledgement of the divine Lordship of Jesus back to the time of the Pentecost in Jerusalem on Palestinian soil. However, it is important to note that (i) Jesus' indelible impact on his disciples in his ministry and teaching (pre-Pentecost, stressed by France but not exclusively), (ii) his pouring out of the Spirit at Pentecost (stressed by Turner but not exclusively) and (iii) the experience of Jesus by early Christians especially in visions (post-Pentecost, stressed by Hurtado but not exclusively) *all* worked constructively together to guide the church to acknowledge and worship Jesus as the divine Lord.[52][53]

---

50 *Ibid.,* pp. 180-1.
51 *Ibid.,* pp. 183-4.
52 For Hurtado's emphasis on visions, see *One God, one Lord,* pp. 115-122.
53 Turner, 'The Spirit of Christ and Christology', p. 189, outlines several factors which
    could have contributed towards the church's understanding of Jesus as the one who

C.F.D. Moule, after studying the words for 'Lord' in Hebrew, Aramaic and Greek contexts, also rejected Bousset and Bultmann's theory of gentile influence in the use of the title 'Lord' for Jesus.

> I have selected only four words or phrases - 'the Son of Man', 'the Son of God', 'Christ', 'Lord' - by way of demonstrating how high a degree of continuity may be detected between, one the one hand, what, so far as any reading of the evidence can probe, seems to have been *implicit in the earliest impact made by Jesus himself*, and, on the other hand, the usage of those periods in which the New Testament documents were taking shape.[54]

> [T]here is a continuous identity between the Christ of the ministry and the Christ of the first believers after Easter; and that the characterisations of Christ in the New Testament are better accounted for as springing from contact with Jesus himself than as springing from contact with extraneous

---

sent the Spirit to the church. However, the following factor should also be considered. All three synoptic gospels witness to Jesus giving his disciples the power to heal and exorcise within his earthly ministry (Mt. 10:1; Mk. 3:14-15, 6:7; Lk. 10:19). There are very good reasons for believing that power was the power of the Holy Spirit. Therefore, before the Pentecost, Jesus had already given his disciples the power of the Holy Spirit for their short-term mission, in anticipation of Jesus pouring out the Holy Spirit on to the disciples for their long-term mission. It is probable that the disciples at the time did not appreciate what this implied, but their experience of the reality of the power of the Holy Spirit, given to them by Jesus and working through them in their mission of miraculous healings and exorcisms, would have been indelible. And this indelible memory and recollection would surely encouraged them to interpret the Pentecost event as *Jesus* (and the Father) pouring out the Holy Spirit upon them because they had already experienced another 'similar' event in which *Jesus* gave them the power of the Spirit. The similarity is heightened by the fact that the gift of the power of the Spirit was for the purpose of mission and witness on both occasions. It is possible that the Pentecost event in turn helped the disciples to understand why Jesus had been able to give the power of the Spirit to them within his earthly life for their short-term mission - he is and was the Lord of the Spirit. With this understanding, the evangelists could give the account of Jesus giving the power of the Spirit to his disciples for their short-term mission without inhibition, in a plain and unencumbered manner - 'He ... gave them authority to drive out evil spirits and to heal every disease and sickness' (Mt. 10:1). Thus, in the disciples' understanding, the event of the short-term mission and the event of the Pentecost could interact constructively with one another to give them a more comprehensive understanding of Jesus and his divinity. This illustrates why it is important to take all the evidences, pre-Pentecost and post-Pentecost, in seeking to understand how the church came to acknowledge and worship Jesus as the divine Lord.

54 C.F.D. Moule, *The Origin of Christology* (Cambridge: Cambridge University Press, 1977), p. 44. See pp. 35-44 for Moule's argument. Italics mine.

sources.[55]

Finally, Barth was well aware of the kind of proposition from the school of the history of religions concerning the divine Lordship of Jesus and wrote against this view.

> He [Jesus Christ] has put these titles of majesty on their lips. They do not try to crown Him in this way, but they recognise Him as the One who is already crowned, to whom these titles belong. ... It is not they who represented Him, but He who represented Himself to them, in this majesty. He is to them the Christ, the *Kyrios*, the Son of Man and the Son of God, the One who is absolutely different and exalted, even before they describe Him in this way. And when they do describe Him in this way, they appeal in some sense to Himself - that He Himself continually attests Himself as such.[56]

> [T]his [biblical] witness is to the simple effect that, prior to any attitudes of others to Him or statements of others about Him, the man Jesus did in fact occupy this place and function, that, prior to any knowledge of His being or temporally conditioned confession of it, He actually was and is and will be what He is represented in the reflection of this witness, the Son of the Heavenly Father, the King of His kingdom, and therefore 'by nature God'.[57]

The debates concerning gentile influence on the confession of the high Lordship (or divinity) of Jesus continue.[58] This book will align itself with the position of Barth, not only for the intellectual reasons given above but also for another reason associated with Barth which will be discussed later in 3.3.2.

There are good reasons, then, to believe that the early churches, Jewish and gentile, celebrated Jesus' divine Lordship and equality with the Father and therefore the origin of such celebration can be traced back to the Jewish Palestinian church (or the ministry, death and resurrection of Jesus himself). The writers or redactors of the gospels

---

55 *Ibid.*, p. 135.

56 *CD* IV.1, p. 162.

57 *Ibid.*, p. 163

58 For example, M. Casey supports Bousset in 'Chronology and the Development of Pauline Christology', in *Paul and Paulinism: Essays in Honour of C.K. Barrett* (London: SPCK, 1982), M. D. Hooker and S. G. Wilson (eds.), pp. 124-34. Hurtado argues against Bousset in his *One God, One Lord* and also 'New Testament Christology: A Critique of Bousset's Influence', *Theological Studies,* 40 (1979), pp. 306-17.

had clear knowledge of and familiarity with the confession of 'Jesus is Lord' in the highest sense. And it is reasonable to expect that when Matthew (and the other evangelists) identified Jesus with the Lord in Mt. 3:3 (Mark 1:2-3, Luke 3:4), he (they) had this highest sense in mind - Jesus in his Lordship is equivalent to (or equal with) God even though he is distinct from him, being his Son. The title given to Jesus early in Mt. 1:23, Immanuel - 'God with us' - confirms this usage, as do Matthew's narratives which contain the concrete expressions of Jesus' divine Lordship and equality with his Father in his words and actions, and this will be shown in chapters 3 and 4. Meanwhile, it is necessary to consider Jesus' relationship with his Father in terms of the concept of revelation and the doctrine of the Trinity because this book is not merely interested in Jesus' expression of his divine Lordship in his life, ministry and death but also his revelation of and relationship with his Father.

3.0 The Identity of Jesus Christ, Revelation and Trinity

The identity of Jesus Christ and the doctrine of the Trinity are inextricably linked with the concept of revelation in Barth's thought. And Jesus' identity involves his divinity and his humanity. In this section, these four crucial elements of Christian doctrines will be discussed in relation to Barth. Also, Jesus' humanity as presented by Matthew, in particular his identification with Israel, will be discussed while Jesus' divine Lordship in Matthew has been treated above. Barth's doctrine of the Trinity will be evaluated before the concept of revelation given by Mt. 11:25-30 will be considered.

3.1 The Divinity of Jesus Christ

For Barth, the Lordship or divinity of Jesus is paramount for knowing who Jesus is and for God's revelation.

In distinction from the assertion of the divinisation of a man[59] or the humanisation of a divine idea,[60] the statement about Christ's deity is to

---

59 'To the "eye of faith" a remarkable man who had once been known as such, and who strictly was always kept in view, was idealised upwards as God ... This is Ebionite Christology, or Christology historically reconstructed along the lines of Ebionitism.' *CD* I.1, p. 403.

60 By 'the humanisation of a divine idea', Barth means the attractive idea of the communion of deity and humanity (or God's condescension and self-manifestation) is expressed or personified in a human symbol - Jesus Christ. What is important in this approach to Christology is the attractive idea, not the concrete historical reality

be understood in the sense that *Christ reveals the Father*. But this Father of His is God. He who reveals Him, then, reveals God. *But who can reveal God except God Himself?* Neither a man that has been raised up nor an idea that has come down can do it. These are both creatures. Now the Christ who reveals the Father is also a creature and His work is a creaturely work. But if He were only a creature He could not reveal God, for the creature certainly cannot take God's place and work in His place. *If He reveals God, then irrespective of His creaturehood He Himself has to be God.* And since this is *a case of either/or*, He has to be full and true God without reduction or limitation, *without more or less*. Any such restriction would not merely weaken His deity; it would deny it. *To confess Him as the revelation of His Father is to confess Him as essentially equal in deity with this Father of His.*[61]

Barth will not settle for a diluted or reduced form of Christ's divinity. It is not a case of more or less; it is a case of either or. For Barth, a weakened or diluted divinity is no divinity at all. This important point will be taken up when considering a form of Spirit Christology proposed by Dunn in chapters 5 and 6.

Section 2 above attempts to show that Matthew's gospel, and the synoptic gospels in general, present Jesus' divine Lordship from a post-Easter perspective. In this respect of Jesus' divine Lordship, the synoptic gospels are therefore similar to John's gospel. Barth concurs with these observations; or rather the view presented in section 2 has been greatly influenced by Barth who writes:

Inwardly and essentially they [synoptic gospels] start from the fact that the man Jesus of Nazareth, "the carpenter's son" (Mark 6:3), shows Himself in his resurrection from the dead to be the Messiah and the Son of God. *In that light they look back and understand all His words and actions. The revelation of this man as God and Lord that takes place in His resurrection is the very thing they wish to say and attest.* ... According to John, the great mystery is that God assumed humanity in Jesus. That in this man divinity appeared among us, the divinity of Christ, is the *same* mystery according to the Synoptists.[62]

---

of the symbol Jesus Christ. This approach to Christology is related to an interpretation of the gospel of John and is criticised by Barth as docetic Christology for in this Christology God did not truly become man. See *CD* I.1, pp. 402-5.

61 *CD* I.1, p. 406. Italics mine.

62 *CD* I.2, p. 22. Italics mine. Again, 'The starting point of Synoptic thought, which finds *God* in Jesus, is the fact, manifest to certain men, of the divine envoy as such. ... And the starting point of Johannine thought, which finds God in *Jesus*, was the fact, manifest to certain men, of the divine mission, message and revelation which

For Barth, the starting point of New Testament thought - the true divinity of Jesus Christ - has crucial implications not only for the *revelation* of God but also for man's effective *reconciliation* with God. He exposes the inadequacy of subordination Christology and modalistic Christology for a proper doctrine of reconciliation.[63] Barth in his writings tirelessly and vigourously refutes any Christology which undermines or dilutes the divinity of Jesus Christ. He points out that the divinity of Jesus Christ is the axiomatic starting point of the New Testament (see below) and quotes *2 Clement* to emphasise the importance of acknowledging Christ's divinity,

> Brethren, we must think of Jesus Christ as of God, as of the judge of the quick and the dead. For we ought not to think meanly of our redemption. If we think meanly of Him, that means that we expect only mean things ... that we do not know whence and by whom and to whom we are called.[64]

In comparing orthodox Christology with Herrmann's Christology, Barth again comments on the supreme importance of the truth of Christ's divinity and that its power for accomplishment is incomparable to any diluted form.

> But this truth is the beginning, the basis and the presupposition apart from which Christian preaching and dogmatics cannot say one meaningful word concerning Christ. Without that truth, they both remain undeniably

---

they found in Jesus ... In the light of these real starting points of the New Testament thought, and already with these starting points, the common goal, the statement about Christ's deity, is easy to understand.' (*CD* I.1, p. 404).

63 Concerning subordination Christology, Barth writes,'[The subordinationists] interpreted the assertion [of Christ's deity] in such a way that its content was explained away and lost. They did not see that in doing this they destroyed the meaning and weight of the witness to the humiliation and the lowliness and the obedience of Christ... [I]t was and is impossible to see how many can be made righteous by the obedience of a being which is not properly God, of a supremely qualified creature.' *CD* IV.1, p. 196. Concerning modalistic Christology, Barth writes, '... if He can be the humiliated and lowly and obedient One only in a mode of appearance and not in His proper being, what is the value of the true deity of Christ, what is its value for us? It is as the humiliated and lowly and obedient One that He is the Reconciler. But can He reconcile if He has no proper being as the Reconciler, but only that of a form of appearance of the one true God, who has no part in the atonement?' *Ibid.*, p. 197. In Barth's understanding, in modalism Christ was only in an appearance of God, not God in his true self.

64 *CD* IV.1, p. 160.

stuck fast in history. Here no other 'way' whatever exists except the road
from above downward. Orthodox Christology is a glacial torrent rushing
straight down from a height of three thousand metres; it makes
accomplishment possible. Herrmann's Christology, as it stands, is the
hopeless attempt to raise a stagnant pool to that same height by means of
a hand pump; nothing can be accomplished with it.[65]

It is safe to say that without holding firmly to the full divinity of Jesus
Christ, Barth would not have written his *Church Dogmatics* as
energetically, patiently and powerfully as he did. The divinity of Jesus
Christ, or the divine Person of Jesus Christ, was the glacial torrent
which drove him to such a sustained effort and its accomplishment. In
the next two chapters, we shall explore in Matthew's narratives how
Jesus reveals himself to be the Lord in his words and actions, and we
shall verify if Jesus' Lordship thus revealed is indeed the divine one, as
Barth insisted. We shall also explore how Jesus' Lordship is related to
the Lordship of the Father, in particular how Jesus' Lordship reveals the
Lordship of the Father.

3.2 The Humanity of Jesus Christ

Matthew applies a double identification to the person of Jesus in his
gospel. On the one hand, Jesus the Son of God is identified with
Yahweh the Lord, as discussed above. On the other hand, Jesus is
identified as the true Israel, the truly obedient Son of God.

In the genealogy of the first chapter of Matthew, Jesus is presented as
the descendant of Abraham, David and the son of Mary. Jesus was a real
man. As a real man he could represent Israel the nation; he was the true
Israel. His identification with Israel can be seen quite clearly in the
following. If (i) the infant Jesus' exile to Egypt and return in chapter 2 is
read in conjunction with (ii) his baptism in the Jordan, followed by (iii)
the forty days of temptation in the desert, it only takes a small step of
imagination to see that Matthew is drawing a parallel between Jesus and
Israel which (i) was brought out of the exile in Egypt, (ii) crossed the
Red Sea and (iii) spent forty years in the wilderness before entering
Canaan. In particular, Matthew in 2:15 uses Hosea 11:1 - 'Out of Egypt
I called my son,' which refers to Israel as God's son - as an Israel-Jesus
typology and sees Jesus as the fulfilment of Israel.[66] Jesus' identification

---

65 K. Barth, 'The Principles of Dogmatics According to Herrmann' in *Theology and
   Church: Shorter Writings, 1920-28* (London: SCM Press, 1962), T. Torrance (ed.), p.
   265.

66 For a more thorough treatment of the Israel-Jesus typology, see France's *Matthew:
   Evangelist and Teacher,* pp. 207-210. See also C. H. Dodd, *The Founder of*

with Israel can be further confirmed by 8:17 - 'He took up our infirmities and carried our diseases.'[67] The old Israel had failed to obey God and fulfil his righteousness and mission to the nations. She was put into exile. Jesus, by representing Israel, or being the true Israel, fulfils God's righteousness, saves the people from their sins (1:21) and ends their exile (1:17). In Jesus Christ, Israel is truly liberated from their sins and exile in foreign territory.

Barth expounds on this aspect of Jesus' identification with Israel in *CD* IV.1 in the section 'The Way of the Son of God into the Far Country.' He affirms the importance of acknowledging the fact that Jesus was a Jew and warns of the danger of seeing Jesus 'in the empty sphere of abstract principles and relations or in the sphere of myth.'[68] The Jewishness of Jesus is important for appreciating his identification with Israel. Barth elaborates this identification by first establishing how the specific term - son of God - was used in the Old Testament to denote Israel, its kings and priests.[69] The Old Testament verses he uses includes Hosea 11:1 which was used by Matthew in 2:15. Then he makes the connection between Israel the son of God and the Israelite Jesus - the Son of God.

> But where in the Old Testament we find Israel, or the king of Israel, in the New Testament we find the one Israelite Jesus.[70]

For Barth, Jesus' humanity and Jewishness are crucial for the doctrine of reconciliation. In his genuine humanity and Jewishness, Jesus identifies himself with sinful Israel.

> The place taken by the one Israelite Jesus according to the New Testament is, according to the Old Testament, the place of this

---

Christianity (London: Collins, 1971), p 106, where he wrote, 'The Messiah is not only founder and leader of the Israel-to-be, the new people of God; he is its "inclusive representative". In a real sense he *is* the true Israel, carrying through in his own experience the process through which it comes into being.' C. F. D Moule, 'Fulfilment-Words in the New Testament', *New Testament Studies,* 14 (1967-68), pp. 300-1, found applied to Jesus in the New Testament as a whole 'a great convergence of Israel-titles and other collectives ... Servant of Yahweh, Son of Man, Zechariah martyr, rejected-but-vindicated stone, cornerstone, foundation stone, stumbling-stone, temple, ... This marks him as, in the estimate of Christians, the climax of the pattern of true covenant-relationship ... Thus, to a unique degree, Jesus is seen as the goal, the convergence-point, of God's plan for Israel, his covenant-promise.'

67 A prophesy from Isaiah 53:4, according to Matthew.

68 *CD* IV.1, p. 166.

69 *Ibid.*, pp. 169-70.

70 *Ibid.*, p. 170.

disobedient son, this faithless people and its faithless priests and kings.[71]

> The Son of God in his unity with the Israelite Jesus exists in direct and
> unlimited solidarity with the representatively and manifestly sinful
> humanity of Israel.[72]

And Jesus publicly expresses his solidarity or identification with Israel
in his baptism. For Barth, Jesus' baptism symbolises the eventual death
of Jesus in which his solidarity with sinners reaches its climax.

> His first public appearance is that of a penitent in *unreserved solidarity*
> *with other penitents* who confess themselves to be such in the baptism of
> John, and can look only for the remission of their sins in the coming
> judgment (Mt. 3:15) - *a clear anticipation of the story of the passion*,
> towards which the narrative in all the Evangelists hastens with a
> momentum recognisable from the very first, and at the climax of which
> Jesus is crucified between two thieves (Mt. 27:38).[73]

It is in this solidarity with sinful humanity that Jesus was able to bring
an end to sinners and sin in his death. His interpretation of the
atonement is somewhat different from Anselm and hinges on Jesus'
identification with humanity.

> If Jesus Christ has followed our way as sinners to the end to which it
> leads, in outer darkness, then we can say with that passage from the Old
> Testament (Isaiah 53) that He has suffered this punishment of ours. But
> we must not make this a main concept as in some of the older
> presentations of the doctrine of the atonement (especially those which
> follow Anselm of Canterbury), either in the sense that by His suffering
> our punishment we are spared from suffering it ourselves, or that in so
> doing He 'satisfied' or offered satisfaction to the wrath of God. The latter
> thought is quite foreign to the New Testament. And of the possible idea
> that we are spared punishment by what Jesus Christ has done for us we
> have to notice that the main drift of the New Testament statements
> concerning the passion and death of Jesus Christ is not at all or only
> indirectly in this direction. The decisive thing is not that He has suffered
> what we ought to have suffered so that we do not have to suffer it, the
> destruction to which we have fallen victim by our guilt, and therefore the
> punishment we deserve. This is true, of course. But it is true only as it
> derives from *the decisive thing that in the suffering and death of Jesus*

---

71 *Ibid.*, p. 171.
72 *Ibid.*, p. 172.
73 *Ibid.*, p. 165. Italics mine.

> *Christ it has come to pass that in His own person He has made an end of us as sinners and therefore of sin itself by going to death as the One who took our place as sinners. In His person He has delivered up us sinners and sin itself to destruction.*[74]

Because Jesus has identified himself closely with sinful humanity, what he has gone through in his suffering and death has the corresponding result in humanity. Because Jesus is the bearer of sins and the representative of sinners, he is able to put an end to sins and sinners by his suffering and death. With the death of the 'one great sinner', sinful humanity is spared and saved from death and thereby reconciled to God.[75] For Barth, a necessary and crucial factor for man's true reconciliation with God is Jesus' true humanity and his identification with humanity (or Israel). Without this factor, his death has no connection with and significance for humanity. That is why Barth is extremely vigilant in refuting Docetism. He insists that Jesus was a true man, a true Israelite.

The treatment of Jesus' humanity by Matthew and Barth can be compared in the following. In Matthew, Jesus' humanity is affirmed and his identification with Israel can be inferred as shown at the beginning of this section. Concerning Jesus' identification with Israel/humanity in his death, in Matthew Jesus is indeed the servant in whom God delights (Mt. 12:18 and Isaiah 42:1), who 'took up our infirmities and carried our diseases' (Mt. 8:17 and Isaiah 53:4), who gave 'his life as a ransom for many' (Mt. 20:28) and whose blood was 'poured out for many for the forgiveness of sins' (Mt. 26:28). The theme of Jesus taking the place of many on the basis of his identification with Israel/humanity (found in Matthew) is consistently applied by Barth in the doctrine of reconciliation, as shown above. In terms of covenant Barth wrote, 'In Him [Jesus] the covenant which God has faithfully kept and man has broken is renewed and restored. Representing all others in Himself, He is the human partner of God in this new covenant - He in the authenticity, validity and the force of His suffering and dying.'[76] In Matthew, the blood of Jesus is the 'blood of the new covenant' poured out for many (26:28). Barth's understanding of the humanity of Jesus, his identification with Israel and the significance of his death for humanity and Israel in the new covenant therefore have very close parallels with Matthew (even though Matthew does not have a doctrine of reconciliation as explicit as Barth's). This is not surprising since

---

74 *Ibid.*, p. 253; pp. 253-6 are particularly crucial for appreciating Barth's understanding of atonement. Italics mine.
75 *Ibid.*, p. 254. The 'one great sinner' or Representative refers to Jesus Christ.
76 *Ibid.*, p. 251.

Barth's method of doing dogmatics is the exegesis of Scripture.

The discussion on the identity of Jesus above shows that Matthew has indeed applied a double identification to the person of Jesus in his gospel. He is identified closely with Yahweh and equally closely with Israel. He is Immanuel, God with us (1:23), identified with Yahweh (3:3) and at the same time Jesus of Nazareth, the son of Mary (1:21). He is the exalted Lord and at the same time the humble servant who gave his life and died. Matthew does not explain how these two identifications of Jesus can co-exist with one another or how they can be reconciled. He merely presents a narrative which embraces these two aspects of Jesus simultaneously. Likewise, Barth holds firm these two aspects of Jesus simultaneously.

> For this one man ... is the Son of God who is one with God the Father and is Himself God. God is now not only *the electing Creator, but the elect creature*. He is not only the giver, but also the recipient of grace. He is not only the One who commands, but the One who is called and pledged to obedience.[77]

Like Matthew, Barth does not explain how these two aspects of Jesus can possibly be held together in his one person. He does not argue for such a possibility inductively from some prior principles. For Barth, the actual existence of Jesus in these two aspects witnesses to the possibility. (The possibility is inferred from the actuality.) In the final analysis, the fact that this possibility exists and was actualised in the person of Jesus was due to the freedom of God.[78] In exercising his freedom to condescend to become true man, the Son of God does not cease to possess his Lordship and divinity.

> He remains Himself. He does not cease to be God. ... He does not forfeit anything by doing this. In being neighbour to man, in order to deal with him and act towards him as such, He does not need to fear for His Godhead. On the contrary. We will mention at once the thought which will be decisive and basic in this section, that God shows Himself to be the great and true God in the fact that *He can and will let His grace bear this cost, that He is capable and willing and ready for this condescension*, this act of extravagance, this far journey. What marks out God above all false gods is that they are not ready for this. ... God is not proud. In His high majesty He is humble. It is in this high humility that He speaks and

---

77 *Ibid.*, p. 170.

78 George Hunsinger, 'Karl Barth's Christology', in *The Cambridge Companion to Karl Barth* (Cambridge: Cambridge University Press, 2000), John Webster (ed.), p. 133.

acts as the God who reconciles the world to Himself.[79]

In God's sovereign freedom, he is able to be divine and human at the same time.[80] But how is the divinity and humanity of Jesus related to God's revelation and how is God's revelation related to the doctrine of Trinity?

3.3 Revelation and Trinity

3.3.1 THE IDENTITY OF JESUS CHRIST AND REVELATION

The discussion in 3.1 and 3.2 brings out how in Barth's thought the divinity of Jesus and the humanity of Jesus are crucial for a proper reconciliation between God and man - only the true God can save sinful humanity but only a true human representative can suffer and die for sinful humanity. The discussion in 3.1 on the Lordship of Jesus also highlights the importance (for Barth) of Jesus' divinity for a proper revelation from God - only God can reveal God or only the divine Jesus (Lord) can reveal God. The next question which comes to mind is: how is the humanity of Jesus important for God's revelation? What is Barth's answer to this question and does Matthew have anything to say regarding this? Barth's straightforward answer is: 'A man we can see, physically or spiritually or both at once. Jesus Christ can reveal God because He is visible to us men as a man.'[81] 'His humanity is the covering which He puts on, and therefore the means of His revelation.'[82] Furthermore, God does not reveal himself to us in his divine majesty which is not veiled, but veiled in humanity and human suffering.

His actual entry into this visibility signifies, let us remember, the entry of the eternal Word of God into veiling, into *kenosis* and passion.[83] But this

---

79 *CD* IV.1, p. 159; Italics mine. Also, 'God's freedom for us men is a fact in Jesus Christ, according to the witness of Holy Scripture. The first and the last thing to be said about the bearer of this name is that He is very God and very man. In this unity He is the objective reality of divine revelation. His existence is God's freedom for man. Or vice versa God's freedom for man is the existence of Jesus Christ. And now we continue by saying that in this objective reality of the divine revelation there is presupposed and grounded and brought within our knowledge its objective possibility.' *CD* I.2, p. 25.

80 See also *CD* IV.1, p. 177 and pp. 187-8 for Barth's passionate affirmation of the divinity and humanity of Jesus Christ.

81 *CD* I.2, p. 36.

82 *Ibid.*, p. 35.

83 By *kenosis* , Barth does not appeal to the kenotic theory but means humiliation or in a 'servant form.' *Ibid.*, p. 37.

very veiling, *kenosis* and passion of the Logos, has to take place in order that it may lead to His unveiling and exaltation and so to the completion of revelation. God's revelation without this veiling or in the form of an unknown being from another world would not be revelation but our death.[84]

When the veil of human suffering in the man Jesus Christ is unveiled (i.e., its true meaning and significance are recognised), he is exalted and his revelation of God is completed. But this means that God's revelation is dependent in the first place on the Son of God going to the far country to accomplish the work of reconciliation in which the Lord is the servant who takes on human suffering and passion. Here we see the close relationships between Jesus' divine and human identities, reconciliation and revelation. As seen in 3.1 and 3.2, Jesus' divine and human identities are necessary for the work of reconciliation. And it is in this reconciliation wrought by the divine and human Jesus that God is revealed to us. For Barth, reconciliation and revelation are tied to the one and same event of Jesus Christ.[85]

Revelation (and reconciliation) as it is actualised in Jesus, then, depends on his true humanity and his true divinity. Or as John has put it succinctly, 'The Word became flesh' (1:14) and made the Father known (1:18). For Barth, the divinity and humanity of Jesus Christ is the starting point of his doctrine of revelation.

> Our crucial first statement, 'that the eternal Word of God chose, sanctified and assumed human nature and existence into oneness with Himself, in order thus, as very God and very man,' signifies the mystery of the revelation of God in Jesus Christ. That is to say, in this statement we describe absolutely the sole point in which the New Testament witness originates, and therefore, also the sole point from which a doctrine of revelation congruous with this witness can originate. We do not look for some higher vantage point from which our statement can derive its meaning, but we start from this point itself. This, of course, we cannot do by our own authority and discretion. We can only make it clear from the Evangelists and apostles what it will mean to *start from this point*, and then try to make clear what our own starting point is. But we cannot get 'behind' this point. Therefore we cannot derive or prove the statement, in

---

84 *Ibid.*, p. 36.

85 'God reveals himself in reconciling acts.' Trevor Hart, 'Revelation' in *The Cambridge Companion to Karl Barth*, p. 55. Or in Barth's own word, 'Revelation in fact does not differ from the person of Jesus Christ nor from the reconciliation accomplished in Him.' *CD* I.1, p. 119.

which this point is to be described, from a higher discernment.[86]

'Jesus Christ is very God and very Man,' is the assumption upon which all further reflection must proceed.[87]

The divinity and humanity of Jesus Christ is a given and its possibility cannot be proved from other sources but only inferred from its actuality. This is an important insight by Barth which reminds us of the futility of trying to find such a proof. However, given that it is an actuality, the question of how the divine and human nature of Jesus Christ are possibly related to one another may be raised. This difficult question he deals with in *CD* IV.2 and will be discussed in chapter 7 with reference to the possible meanings of 'spirit'.

3.3.2 THE HOLY SPIRIT AND REVELATION

The discussion in section 2 on 'Jesus as the Coming Lord' centres around the issues of Matthew's intention of presenting Jesus as the divine Lord and the probable origin of the confession of and devotion to Jesus' Lordship in Jewish Palestinian church. No matter how convinced one is of this intention of Matthew and the historicity of this origin, according to Barth *these in themselves do not actually make one believe that Jesus is the divine Lord.* All the discussions in New Testament scholarship on Christological titles, his pre-existence and his divinity, even if one takes the conservative position, are not in themselves sufficient to make one confess that Jesus is Lord. Nor would taking a narrative approach looking at his life, ministry, death and resurrection as adopted by this book, in recognition of the fact that Jesus cannot be captured by mere Christological titles (cf. E. Schweizer's 'The Man Who Fits No Formula'[88]), be sufficient to make one confess Jesus' Lordship. In Barth's understanding, they are merely human activities of no avail unless they are taken up by the Holy Spirit in revealing Jesus as Lord to us in the event of revelation.[89]

The arguments which we can raise for the divinity of Jesus Christ and his equality with his Father are intellectual and 'objective' ones. Even if we can accept them to be true, they are information in our heads and can remain so. But mere information is not a true knowledge of Jesus Christ. Barth's teacher, Wilhelm Herrmann, made this powerfully clear (and so

---

86 *CD* I.2, p. 124. Italics mine.

87 *Ibid.*, p. 131.

88 'The Man Who Fits No Formula' in E. Schweizer, *Jesus* (London: SCM Press, 1971).

89 For the meaning of the event of revelation or the event of God's Word, see *CD* I.1, pp. 111-20.

Barth had followed him on this right to the end).[90] It is only when these 'objective' and intellectual informations are taken up, with the narratives, by the Holy Spirit in a personal (and sometimes ineffable) encounter with Jesus Christ that one comes to acknowledge in heart and mind that Jesus is Lord. As one is moved by the Holy Spirit and sees Jesus moving in his freedom and majesty, in his radical speech and unconditional love, in his relentless authority and in his gentle humility, in his amazing wisdom and full integrity, in his compassion and empathy, in his courage and dependence on his Father, in his resolute obedience to and trust in his Father, in his intimate knowledge of and love for his Father, in his powerful acts and in his lowly sorrows, in his glorious liberation of others and in his own painful suffering, in his death and resurrection, in his humiliation and universal reign ..., that one comes to know the meaning of his divine majesty and Lordship. In that encounter, it is he who defines the meaning of divine Lordship to us and we totally concur with him as we also surrender to him, and as we surrender to him any pre-notions of Lordship.

Barth, as Herrmann, does not base his faith on the human activities of historical research, philosophy, anthropology, science, ... His basis of faith is the self-revealing and self-authenticating Word.[91] And no human control can be exercised upon God's Word; it cannot be captured by human scholarship and stored in one form or another, nor can one know how human words can become the divine Word of God.[92] The event of the Word of God, or the event of revelation, is God's own free and sovereign act which can be experienced but cannot be explained. Barth tirelessly rebutted and warned against taking human beings as having autonomy over the Word of God in *CD* I.1. It is only in God's divine action that one comes to a personal encounter with the living Word in which faith is created and established, the possibility of knowing the Word of God is created and actualised, obedience is called for and yielded, relationship is transformed and life renewed, God is

---

90 'Information concerning God, therefore, although it may claim to be of divine revelation, can only bring that troubled piety which lives by no delivering act of God, but by men's own exertions. ... For in such doctrines, however true they may be in themselves, we are not brought face to face with that reality which gives faith its certainty; they simply tell us something, and we are then expected by our own efforts to hold that information to be true.' W. Herrmann, *The Communion of the Christian with God* (London: SCM Press, 1972), p. 58.

91 See G. Dorrien, *The Barthian Revolt in Modern Theology: Theology Without Weapons* (Louisville: Westminster John Knox Press, 2000).

92 '[T]o receive the Word of God does not mean ... to be able to see and know and state between the two sides, to be able to say why and how far the veiled Word now means unveiling ... If we could know and state this, the Word of God would obviously cease to be a mystery.' *CD* I.1, p. 174.

experienced and known through Jesus Christ in this event of revelation from God. This divine act of revelation, this event of God's free act, is accomplished none other than by the Holy Spirit who is the sovereign Lord in revelation. The Holy Spirit is God in the action of revelation and it is only by the Holy Spirit that one comes to know the Lordship of Jesus and confess him as Lord (cf. 1 Cor. 12:3 - 'No one can say "Jesus is Lord" except by the Holy Spirit.').

The sovereign Spirit moves wherever he pleases; we cannot tell where he comes from or where he is going, i.e., we cannot trace his path or gain any control of his activities.[93] This is so in the Spirit's revealing the divinity of Jesus and his equality with his Father to us. With our human mind and with our objective/intellectual arguments, we cannot prove Jesus' divinity and his equality with his Father in the way the Spirit witnesses to and convicts us of Jesus' divinity and his equality with his Father, though our objective and intellectual understanding can be taken up by the Spirit. We cannot trace his path and thereby repeat his work by our own means and engineering. We can only *see* Jesus' divinity and his equality with his Father by the grace of the sovereign Spirit.[94] And even if Matthew is to be read apart from the intellectual arguments in 2.2, the Spirit can still open our eyes to see the divine Lord who is equal with his Father, or in Matthew's terms the risen Lord is present to reveal his Lordship to us in a personal manner (Mt. 28:20).[95] And our questions and doubts (if they arise) about not having a full and iron-cast human proof, within Matthew itself, of Jesus' divinity and his equality with his Father will evaporate in the personal face of Jesus Christ, who as far as the involved reader is concerned, is Lord and the Son of God who has equality with his Father.

In an attempt to gain some understanding of the mystery of Jesus' communion with his Father through the Spirit, again it is the Spirit who alone can reveal to us the mystery of this communion. Jesus' personal experience of his Father through the Spirit is ultimately unfathomable and beyond the mere description in human words. If the reader is to appreciate this crucial aspect of his life to some degree, he himself needs to have some pre-understanding of this experience of God. Without such pre-understanding or experience, what the gospels say about Jesus' communion with or experience of his Father can make very little sense to him. Nothing in the world can avail meaning to the reader regarding this spiritual aspect of Jesus' inner dimension. Only the Holy Spirit can give him his own personal experience of Jesus Christ or the Father to help him to appreciate to some degree Jesus' communion with

---

93 See John 3:6-8.
94 Cf. John 1:39 and the repeated seeing till 1:51 and beyond.
95 This may be why Matthew does not have the Pentecost.

his Father. And such spiritual experience in the Spirit can come through encountering Jesus in the gospel story as briefly described above, or through prayer, worship and other forms of receiving God's presence. The Spirit thus reveals to us Jesus' Lordship and *equality* with his Father as well as his relationship of communion and *unity* with his Father.

The Spirit is sovereign in the revelation of God through Jesus Christ. He takes the reader from the level of narratives and story to the level of encounter with God; he lifts the reader from the domain of human description to the domain of divine self-description; from the realm of human activities to the realm of divine action. The Holy Spirit is the epistemological link between Scripture and theology, theology understood as receiving God's revelation.

3.3.3 BARTH'S DOCTRINE OF THE TRINITY

In the discussion in 3.1, it has been noted that for Barth Jesus Christ has to be divine for a true revelation of God. In the discussion in 3.3.2, the Holy Spirit is Lord in revelation. These two important considerations are the basic elements in his enquiry into the nature of God who has thus revealed himself.

One of Barth's favourite sentence in *CD* I.1 when he is expounding his doctrine of the Trinity is 'God reveals himself as the Lord'.[96] He relates God's Lordship closely with freedom and speaks about God's Lordship and freedom in revelation. In *CD 1.1* he spends relatively little time on how God exercises his Lordship and freedom as given in the biblical witness (he does talk briefly about Jesus' Lordship and authority, and very briefly about the Spirit's Lordship in directing the church, e.g., the apostles' journey).[97] Rather, he concentrates on the *concept/schema* of revelation, rather than the narrative *content* of revelation as given by biblical witness, in speaking about the threefold Lordship of God in revelation. In this schema of revelation, firstly the subject of revelation is God the Father (the revealer) himself and therefore *God* reveals himself. *God* reveals himself to be the Lord in revelation because God can freely choose to reveal or veil himself (even after he has revealed himself through Jesus Christ).[98] Secondly, because Jesus Christ is equal with God, God reveals Himself *through Himself* (or God *reveals* Himself, or Jesus Christ is God's revelation). And God *reveals* Himself to be the Lord in his words and actions in his ministry, exercising his supreme authority.[99] His Lordship and freedom is also

---

96 *CD* I.1, p. 307.
97 *Ibid.*, p. 306.
98 *Ibid.*, p. 324.
99 *Ibid.*

revealed in his freedom to differentiate from God the Father when he takes temporal form in revelation.[100] Thirdly, the Holy Spirit is the One who effects the Revealness of God (or the revealness of the revelation) such that God reveals *Himself*. The Holy Spirit is the One who imparts the event of Jesus Christ as 'a fact over which there is no court by reference to which it may be regarded as a fact'[101], a fact of special historicity, not only of general historicity.[102] The Holy Spirit thus reveals himself to be the Lord in his sovereign divine act to make revelation effective in man.[103] To summarise, God reveals himself to be the Lord three times in the single action of revelation. Therefore, revelation is closely related to the doctrine of the Trinity.

What we are saying is that revelation is the basis of the doctrine of the Trinity; the doctrine of the Trinity has no other basis apart from this. We arrive at the doctrine of the Trinity by no other way than that of an analysis of *the concept of revelation.*[104]

And after a *side-glance at the passages in the biblical witness* which directly reflect the doctrine of the Trinity, we have enquired what revelation means in the Bible, asking, but asking concretely with reference to the biblical text, whether the statement that God reveals Himself as the Lord really has a *threefold meaning* and yet *a simple content* in these texts. ... [I]f our threefold conclusion that God reveals Himself as the Lord is not then, an illicit move but a genuine finding; if in this statement we have really said *the same thing* three times in three indissolubly different ways, then we may now conclude that revelation must indeed be understood as the root or ground of the doctrine of the Trinity.[105]

Barth also observes another interesting relationship between revelation and Trinity: the three forms of the Word of God - revelation, Scripture and proclamation - is the only appropriate analogy, *vestigium*,

---

100 *Ibid.*, p. 320.

101 *Ibid.*, p. 329.

102 General historicity is to do with the outward form of an event that is observable. But the event is open to all the possibilities of interpretation. A general historical understanding of Jesus of Nazareth is not revelation. It is only when the Holy Spirit imparts the correct interpretation and understanding in faith that the true significance of Jesus is recognised and his history becomes a special history to the receiver. See *Ibid.*, pp. 325-7.

103 *Ibid.*, p. 331.

104 *Ibid.*, p. 312. Italics mine.

105 *Ibid.*, p. 332. Italics mine.

for the Father, Son and Holy Spirit.[106]

Barth is heavy on divine unity or simplicity and at the same time he insists on the distinction in God. He prefers to use the term Triunity to denote the threeness and oneness of God in a simple word. In section 9 of *CD* I.1 on the Triunity of God, Barth expounds in details the doctrine of the Trinity after treating the relationship between the doctrine and revelation in section 8. One of the most significant treatment in this section is on the understanding of person.

> 'Person' as used in the Church doctrine of the Trinity bears no direct relation to personality. The meaning of the doctrine is not, then, that there are *three personalities* in God. This would be the worst and most extreme expression of tritheism, against which we must be on guard at this stage.[107]

> What is called 'personality' in the conceptual vocabulary of the 19th century is distinguished from the patristic and mediaeval *persona* by the addition of the attribute of *self-consciousness*. This really complicates the whole issue. One was and is obviously confronted by the choice of either trying to work out the doctrine of the Trinity on the presupposition of the concept of person as thus accentuated or of clinging to the older concept which since this accentuation in usage has become completely obsolete and is now unintelligible outside monastic and a few other studies.[108]

For Barth, the Trinity is not three personalities each with a centre of self-consciousness; the Trinity is a single subject who is referenced by the pronoun 'I', 'He' or 'Thou'. He quotes Diemkamp to say that there is only one self-consciousness in God, 'In God, as there is one nature, so there is one knowledge, one self-consciousness.'[109] But Barth does insists on the real distinctions in the Trinity and uses the term 'mode of being' instead of 'person' to denote such distinctions.

> The statement that God is One in three ways of being, Father, Son and Holy Ghost, means, therefore, that the one God, i.e., the one Lord, the one personal God, is what He is not just in one mode but - we appeal in support simply to the result of our analysis of the biblical concept of revelation - in the mode of the Father, in the mode of the Son, and in the

---

106 *Ibid.*, p. 347.
107 *Ibid.*, p. 351. Italics mine.
108 *Ibid.*, p. 357. Italics mine.
109 *Ibid.*, p. 358.

mode of the Holy Ghost.[110]

The modes of being are then the different ways of possessing the essentiality (*CD* I.1, p. 360) and the one unique essence of God corresponds to the one 'personality' of God (*CD* I.1, p. 350). The three modes of being, which are essential to the Trinity, are to be understood in terms of their 'distinctive genetic relations to each other', their 'dissimilar relations of origin to one another' or their distinctive modes in the concept of revelation.[111]

Because of Barth's emphasis on divine unity and his use of the term 'mode of being', he is sometimes criticised as a modalist. But he does see the Father, Son and Spirit as truly distinct and 'there is also fellowship - a definite participation of each mode of being in the other modes of being.'[112] And he quotes John of Damascus on the doctrine of perichoresis to which he certainly subscribes as the 'final sum of the two factors under discussion' - unity in Trinity and Trinity in unity.[113] Barth has therefore partly answered the criticism that he so stresses divine unity at the expense of communion within the Trinity.[114] But the real difficulties of his doctrine of the Trinity in *CD* I.1 lie in (i) his over-reliance on the linear concept of revelation and (ii) his use of the singular 'I' (or 'He') for God as the speaking subject of revelation. These two difficulties will be dealt with in the given order.

Firstly, he expounds the doctrine of revelation in a rather *linear* manner: the Father speaks the Word which is made effective by the Holy Spirit. In Rowan Williams' interpretation and critique of Barth (see the following quote), this linear concept of revelation is intimately related to Barth's conception of the Trinity as a divine speaking subject. It is linear in the sense that the direction of revelation goes in one way without recourse to the bi-directional communion between the Father and the Son through the Spirit. The over-reliance of Barth's doctrine of the Trinity in *CD* I.1 on this particular linear *concept* of revelation, rather than the narrative *content* of revelation and *other concepts* (e.g., a non-linear concept) of revelation which emphasise the notion of communion, means that this linear concept/schema of revelation makes

---

110 *Ibid.*, p. 359.
111 *Ibid.*, p. 363
112 *Ibid.*, p. 370.
113 *Ibid.*, pp. 370-1.
114 For such criticisms, see Alan Torrance's *Persons in Communion* (Edinburgh: T&T Clark, 1996), p. 241; J. Moltmann, *The Trinity and the Kingdom of God* (London: SCM Press, 1981); Rowan Williams, 'Barth on the Triune God', in *Karl Barth: Studies of His Theological Method* (Oxford: Clarendon Press, 1979). See also LaCugna, *God For Us*, pp. 254-5.

it very difficult to explore more on the intra-relationships amongst the Father, Son and Holy Spirit even though he claims to subscribe to the doctrine of perichoresis. Rowan Williams interprets Barth's doctrine of the Trinity in *CD* I.1 as follows.

> What I have called "linear" view (God - the Word - the hearing of the Word) is no help at all in thinking about God's "immanent" being, and the idea of the Spirit as *donum* (gift) or *nexus amoris* (bond of love) has to be developed. ... God's otherness to himself in his Word is the existence in him of response, mutuality, not simply a "self-expression" of some sort. He is not, in short, a self. The basic weakness of a self-interpretative model is its implied conviction that we are dealing with something comparable to an individual human subjectivity, rather than a unity consisting in a system of relations. Barth (as we have seen) insists that the Trinity of God is indeed a special kind of unity; yet his view of revelation in I/1 necessarily dictates that God be thought of as a single self analogous to human selves. If there is one speaker, there can be only one subject; hence the aporia of I/1.[115]

The second problem with Barth's doctrine of the Trinity concerns his insistence on God as a single subject with one centre of consciousness. Williams' interpretation of Barth - concerning the ideas of a linear view of revelation and a single speaking subject in *CD* I.1 - is helpful and faithful to Barth's understanding of revelation and Trinity, but his suggestion that - because Barth understands the Trinity as a single speaking subject he is not dealing with a system of relations (see last quote) - is not so accurate. Barth does conceive the Trinity as a system of relations for he does subscribe to the doctrine of perichoresis. Even in the linear concept of revelation, a linear system of relations is in view (Father speaks his Word which is made effective by the Spirit). The (second) problem with Barth is that on one hand he insists the Trinity is a single subject (with one self-consciousness) who speaks (*Deus dixit*) but on the other hand he maintains that the Trinity is a system of relations amongst three modes of being. It is difficult to see how a single subject can also be a system of relations at the same time - the problem of incompatibility. It is hard to conceive God as a single speaking subject with one centre of consciousness and at the same time participating in mutual fellowship. The incompatibility between the two can only be removed by compromising the former or the latter. As his later volumes of the *Church Dogmatics* show, the idiom of God as a single speaking subject gives way to a more pluralistic understanding of

---

115 Williams, 'Barth on the Triune God', p. 181. Williams' critique of Barth is a careful one, according to Webster (see his *Barth*, pp. 71, 74).

the Father, Son and Holy Spirit even though the theme and concept of revelation remains strong, e.g., *CD* IV.[116] In particular, his much more detailed study of the narrative *content* of revelation (rather than depending merely on the linear *concept* of revelation), e.g., in 'The Lord as Servant' and 'The Servant as Lord' in *CD* IV.1 and 2 , has enabled him to be much more explicit in speaking about the plurality in the Trinity, e.g., the following aspects of the Son's relationship with God the Father: obedience, reflection, conformity and correspondence. However, even there the notion of the Father's communion with the Son through the Spirit is not an evident one. The following are two possible reasons accounting for this feature.

Firstly, Barth still very much conceives the relationship between the Father and the Son in terms of the linear concept of revelation which in itself is true and proper (even though it is a limited concept). However, he has not considered adequately the narrative content of this revelation which might inform this linear concept: *what the Son has revealed embraces not only the Father but also the Son's relationship with the Father through the Spirit.* Even though the idiom of God as a single speaking subject has relatively subsided in *CD* IV, perhaps his linear concept of revelation still has not developed into a more bi-directional, or non-linear, concept embracing the crucial mutual communion between the Father and the Son through the Spirit in the very act of revelation (see next section for the latter concept). The second reason for Barth's relative reticence on Jesus' communion with his Father is that such kind of spiritual fellowship/communion invariably involves speaking about Jesus' experience of his Father in his consciousness and inner being. But the inner life of Jesus, the jewel in Herrmann's theology, is something Barth would wish to avoid because of its association with Schleiermacher and 19th century Protestant theology which Barth reacts against. Once this spiritual or inner aspect of Jesus is avoided for the sake of considering merely his sensible words and actions, it will be difficult for Barth to speak of the profound communion between the Father and the Son through the Spirit in the earthly human existence and experience of Jesus Christ - i.e., in the economic Trinity, even though Barth is prepared to speak of this communion in the immanent Trinity as the discussion above shows.

---

116 A defence for Barth's doctrine of the Trinity is given by J. Webster: *CD* I.1 is not the only volume where the doctrine is treated, even though it is explicitly treated there; other volumes should be included in the evaluation of his doctrine. Webster writes, 'In one very important sense, the whole of the *Church Dogmatics* is a doctrine of the Trinity, both in its architectural conception and its specific content, and criticisms of his explicit exposition of the divine triunity sometimes need to be set in the light of what happens elsewhere.' *Barth*, p. 72.

Barth then has made considerable improvement from *CD* I.1, where he majors on the linear *concept* of revelation, to *CD* IV where the *narrative content* of Jesus' life, ministry, death and resurrection are used much more in his expositions of dogmatics. However, his *linear concept* of revelation has yet to be informed and transformed by the narrative content which he has recovered but whose witness to the bi-directional/mutual nature of the crucial communion between the Father and the Son through the Spirit in a non-linear concept of revelation has still to be fully made use of. This book seeks to bring forth both this *non-linear concept* of revelation and the expression of this concept in the narrative *content* of revelation as witnessed by the *gospels*, Matthew in particular, hence the emphasis of 'narrative-conceptual' approach to the Trinity in the book title.

The divinity of Jesus Christ is fundamental to Barth's concept of revelation - Jesus Christ has to be equal with God in order to reveal God. However, it will be suggested in the next section and elaborated further in chapters 7 and 8 that Jesus' communion with and obedience to his Father are expressions of his divinity; they are some of the crucial elements of what it means for Christ to be divine. In chapters 7 and 8, it shall be shown that communion is not a concept separate and distinct from divinity but is subsumed under it. Barth, in emphasising Jesus' divinity in his revelation of his Father, should have equally emphasised his communion with his Father in that revelation.

4.0 A Non-linear Concept of Revelation: Exegesis of Mt. 11:25-30

[25]At that time Jesus said, 'I praise you, Father, Lord of heaven and earth, because you have hidden these things from the wise and learned, and revealed them to little children.[26] Yes, Father, for this was your good pleasure.[27]All things have been committed to me by my Father. No-one knows the Son except the Father, and no-one knows the Father except the Son and those to whom the Son chooses to reveal him.[28] Come to me, all you who are weary and burdened, and I will give you rest.[29] Take my yoke upon you and learn from me, for I am gentle and humble in heart, and you will find rest for your souls.[30] For my yoke is easy and my burden is light. (Mt. 11:25-30)

The context of this passage needs to be noted before its exegesis. This passage is preceded by the summary of Jesus' ministry in 4:23-25; the Sermon on the Mount which witnesses to his authority in teaching; Jesus' ministry (chapters 8, 9) which witnesses to his authority in healing, exorcism and over nature; another summary of Jesus' ministry in 9:35-38; the second discourse on the disciples' mission (chapter 10) and the response of John the Baptist to this mission (11:1f) which raised the question of Jesus' identity (11:2). From 11:20, it is about Jesus' response to the result of the disciples' mission.[117] He denounced the cities - Korazin, Bethsaida and Capernaum - for their lack of repentance despite the miracles performed there. The passage of 11:25-30 is not only a continuation of that response but it is also an insight given to his disciples about the basis of his extraordinary teaching and ministry that have happened so far (bracketed by the summaries in 4:23-25 and 9:35-38) and those that will follow. W.D. Davies and D.C. Allison commented that this passage is 'a capsule summary of the message of the entire gospel.'[118] And according to E.P. Blair, Matthew's gospel is 'simply a commentary on the crucially important passage 11:27-30.'[119] The central theme of this passage relates to the concept of Jesus' revelation of the Father which is also the theme of this chapter. Matthew has placed this passage after his ministry of words and works in Galilee (chapters 5-9) so that this conceptual understanding can shed light on the nature of Jesus' ministry. For the purpose of focussing our attention on the theme of Jesus' revelation of his Father in this book, the order of presentation in Matthew is adjusted. This conceptual passage is treated here in this chapter before attending to the narratives in the next two chapters of this book where Jesus' concrete revelation of his Father in his ministry of words and works will be considered in the light of this concept of revelation. The adjustment of the order of presentation does not violate Matthew's intention of juxtaposing the concept of revelation and Jesus' ministry of revelation of his Father, and will serve the purpose of this book. The use of Mt. 11:25-30 (and Mt. 3:3) as a conceptual framework, already found in Matthew's narratives, for interpreting the narratives echoes McGrath's comment on the dynamic interacting relationship between conceptual framework and narratives quoted in 3.0 of chapter 1. The interpretations of the narratives with this conceptual framework concerning revelation will give a clearer understanding of Jesus' relationship with his Father through the Spirit (see chapters 3 and 4), which in turn will prompt a search for a more refined concept of revelation (see chapter 6).

The disciples' mission and his own ministry in Galilee were not entirely without success. The wise and the learned had indeed rejected him, his message and his miracles, but those who were like little children had received the revelation of the Father. In Jesus' spontaneous

---

117 Luke 10:21-22, the parallel passage to Mt. 11:25, appears after the mission of the seventy-two, not twelve, but without the Baptist's response.

118 W.D. Davies and D.C. Allison, *A Critical and Exegetical Commentary on the Gospel According to Saint Matthew* (Edinburgh: T. & T. Clark, 1988-1997), 2:29b.

119 E.P. Blair, *Jesus in the Gospel of Matthew* (New York: Abingdon Press, 1960), p. 108.

praise to the Father (in Luke 10:21 he was inspired by the Holy Spirit), he gave thanks to the Father for his pleasurable will in withholding 'these things' from the wise and learned but revealing them to little children (vv. 25-26). The crucial factor for properly receiving the Father's revelation lies in an appropriate attitude - childlikeness.

Continuing the theme of the Father's revelation, v. 27 expands on the nature of such revelation. It turns out that it is the Son, referring to Jesus the Son of God in Matthew, who reveals the Father. Because of the strongly Johannine theme of this verse, it has been called the Johannine thunderbolt. But its authenticity has also been called into question for this very reason.[120] However, two reasons can be given for its defence. Firstly, the concept of Jesus as the Son of the Father is a familiar one in Matthew as in John (see 3.2). Secondly, in Matthew Jesus reveals God's righteousness in his teaching and Jesus the perfect Son reveals the Father's presence (1:23) through his embodiment of God's righteousness (5:48). Therefore, Jesus' Sonship to the Father and his revelation of the Father found in v. 27 are concepts local to Matthew. (See footnote for further defence of the authenticity of this verse.)[121] What is especially important about v. 27 in Matthew is that it spells out more clearly how it was possible for the Son to reveal the Father - the crucial reason for this possibility is the mutual exclusive knowledge between the Father and the Son.

It should be noted that Matthew here is perhaps portraying a Wisdom Christology (note Jesus' earlier reference to wisdom in 11:19). God knows the personified Wisdom (Sirach 1:6-9), Wisdom knows God (Wisdom 8:4) and conveys the knowledge of God to others (Wisdom 9:17-18). The two verses after v. 27 also have a strong wisdom motif (see later). If Matthew does employ Wisdom Christology here, he is drawing the reader's attention to wisdom's existence with God before

---

120 'This "meteorite from the Johannine heaven" (von Hase) is undoubtedly a theological (Christological) composition from the hand of an unknown mystic of the early church. It teaches that the knowledge of God is a mystery which cannot be attained except by revelation, and the revelation is mediated only through the Son (Jesus). Not only that, but the knowledge of Jesus himself is a mystery which is reserved for the Father alone.' Beare, *The Gospel According to Matthew*, p. 266. See also U. Luz, *Matthew 8-20* (Minneapolis: Fortress 2001), p. 158; Schweizer, *The Good News According to Matthew*, p. 271.

121 'Is it a legitimate canon of criticism that any synoptic saying which has a parallel in John must *ipso facto* be spurious? ... Without such points of departure in the synoptic tradition it would be an eternal puzzle how Johannine theology could have originated at all!' D. Hill, *The Gospel of Matthew (New Century Bible)* (London: Marshall, Morgan and Scott, 1972), p. 205. See also A.M. Hunter, 'Crux Criticorum - Matt. XI. 25-30 – A Re-appraisal', *New Testament Studies,* 8 (1961-62), pp. 244-5; Dunn, *Jesus and the Spirit,* pp. 27-34.

the beginning of the world (Prov. 8:1-23, 32-36; 9:4-6). However, Matthew does not make Wisdom Christology explicit here. The most one can say is that he alludes to it. But what is clear is that Jesus' revelation of the Father depended on his unique relationship of mutual knowledge with the Father. This mutual knowledge is not confined to an intellectual knowledge. In the OT, to know someone is to be in an intimate relationship with the person.[122] ἐπιγινώσκει in v. 27 with the preposition prefix ἐπι intensifies this knowing to mean 'know completely, through and through'.[123] For Jesus in Matthew, this ἐπιγινώσκει involves the Son knowing intimately the Father's will as much as the Father knows his. But it is not a case where the Father's will known to Jesus is different from Jesus' own will. Jesus knows his Father's will which, in his obedience, corresponds to his own will and is expressed in his obedient thoughts and actions. This is the basis of Jesus' revelation of the Father. The Son's will, attitude and purpose correspond to, reflect and reveal that of his Father. In this correspondence, the Father's will and Jesus' will are one and the same, which is expressed in Jesus' words and actions. His words and actions (as given, e.g., in the Sermon on the Mount in chapters 5-7 and his healing ministry in chapters 8-9) are therefore channels for knowing the will of Jesus the Son and thus the will of the Father. Matthew does not explain why Jesus, as a man, can know his Father's divine will and share his Father's divine will so completely, through and through, beyond the limit of the knowledge of his Father by any being in heaven or on earth. One might explain this by appealing to the Lordship of Jesus as given via 3:3. As Jesus is the Lord who is everything the name of Yahweh represents, he is in a position to, and has the capacity to, resonate with his Father, share his Father's will and unite himself with his Father through perfect obedience. But this will of Jesus the Lord is the will of Jesus the man in Matthew. It is the will of the one person of Jesus but it can be looked at from the two perspectives of his humanity and divinity. (Matthew does not seem to think in terms of two wills in

---

122 'The organ of knowledge is the heart (Jer. 24:7; Ps. 49:3), which suggests that knowledge is experiential and not merely speculative. One knows war (Judges 3:2) or God's displeasure (Num 14:34) by experiencing it. Yahweh's special relationship with Moses is described as knowing Moses face to face (Deut. 34:10; cf. Ex. 33). While Samuel certainly knows who Yahweh is, he does not know God until he experiences a theophany (1 Sam 3:7).' *The Oxford Companion to the Bible* (New York; Oxford: Oxford University Press, 1993), M. Coogan, B. Metzger (eds.), pp. 416-7. 'The OT regards knowledge as something which continually arises from personal encounter.' *NIDNTT*, vol. 2, p. 396.

123 *A Greek-English Lexicon of the New Testament* (New York: United Bible Societies, 1988), p. 291. Luke 10:22 does not have the prefix ἐπι and so Matthew deliberately emphasises this knowing.

Jesus - one human, one divine - but only one, see chapter 7 for discussion.) This then reflects the double identifications of Jesus in Matthew, with man and God. And it is through the agent of the divine and human Jesus that the divine Father reveals himself to humanity. This divine and human agent takes hold of what are his Father's and reveals them (or 'these things' in v. 25 and 'all things' in v. 27) through his own personal existence on earth. On one hand, the divine Lordship of Jesus is necessary for this revelation, for who, without divine Lordship, can know the Father to the extent that the Son does - exclusively, completely, through and through, i.e., in the same manner as the Father himself knows the Son? And without this thorough knowledge of God and resonance with him, how can one truly reveal him? (In this sense, 11:27 echoes the Lordship of Jesus presented in Mt. 3:3.) On the other hand, the humanity of Jesus is necessary for this revelation for it is in his earthly existence that we as humans can understand and know him, and through him know his Father. Put together, the divine Lordship of Jesus and the humanity of Jesus are both necessary for his revelation of his Father on earth. Barth expresses the same idea when he interprets this passage in 'The Way of the Son of God into the Far Country'.

'All things are delivered unto me of my Father.' Again in accordance with the sense Schlatter underlines the fact 'that Πάντα [all] does not carry any limitation ... there are no limits for the giver and therefore *no limits* for the recipient.' Therefore, this saying implies the *deity* of Jesus. But it is in complete hiddenness that He is who and what He is. 'No man knoweth the Son, but the Father; neither knoweth any man the Father, save the Son, and he to whomsoever the Son will reveal him.' But that means that who and what He is as *the human bearer of that unlimited omnipotence*, and who and what is the One who has given it to him, what there is of divine majesty in giving and receiving of it - this and the revelation of it is not something which can be laid down and judged and evaluated from without. ... The door to the majesty of Jesus can open only from within. And when it does open it is this door - the poor *humanity of the divine being* and activity, the strange form of the divine majesty, the humility in which God is God and the Son is Son, and to that extent the Father the Father, ...[124]

Barth concurs with the above idea that only a divine Lord can know (or receive all things from) the Father completely, through and through. Only the divine Lord can be the bearer of that unlimited omnipotence. It is inconceivable that a lesser being can know the Father to the same

---

124 *CD* IV.1, p. 178. Italics mine.

extent as the Father knows the Son, i.e., completely, so that in resonance and consonance with his Father he can truthfully reveals the Father as he is. But at the same time, it is through the concrete existence of the man Jesus that the door of divine revelation is open.[125]

Within the wider context of Matthew's gospel, the mutual and intimate knowledge between the Father and the Son is more than the sharing of will and purpose but also includes the fellowship of love. According to 3:17, the Father's words at Jesus' baptism, this mutual knowledge involves the Father's love for the Son and the Son knowing his Father's love for him. And from Jesus' obedience and his teaching on the greatest commandment to love God (22:37, for Matthew Jesus has fulfilled this commandment), this relationship also involves the Son's love for the Father. In other words, the mutual relationship in 11:27 seen in the context of Matthew involves the mutual love between the Father and the Son. It is this mutual relationship of knowledge, fellowship and love that underlies Jesus' referencing or calling out to God intimately as 'Abba' (forty-four times in Matthew, all on Jesus' lips).[126] In view of Jesus' intimate relationship with and knowledge of his Father, one is led to consider the possibility of conceiving of his experience of his Father in terms of his experience of his Father's presence. This possibility is strengthened by the episode of Jesus' baptism where the Spirit of God descended on the Son like a dove (and the further reference to the Spirit on Jesus in 12:18 following 11:25-30). The Spirit is an expression of God's presence and activities in the OT and that presence can be a personal presence (Psalm 51:11). In view of Jesus' intimate relationship with his Father given by 11:27, it is perhaps legitimate to suppose that Jesus lived in the presence of his Father through the presence of the Holy Spirit. Also, Davies and Allison have interpreted 11:25-30 in terms of what might be called a Moses typology based on Exo. 33:12-14 which involves the notion of God's gift of his presence and rest to Moses.[127] It is difficult to know whether Matthew, apart from Wisdom Christology, also had in mind the notion of God's

---

125 The question of how Jesus as a human being knows the will of the Father will be dealt with at the end of the next chapter.

126 'Abba' is the Aramaic original of Father, according to J. Jeremias, *The Prayers of Jesus* (London: SCM Press, 1967).

127 'Moses said to the Lord, "You have been telling me, 'Lead these people,' but you have not let me know whom you will send with me. You have said, 'I know you by name and you have found favour with me.' If I have found favour in your eyes, teach me your ways so I may know you and continue to find favour with you. Remember that this nation is your people." The Lord replied, "My Presence will go with you, and I will give you rest"' (Exo 33:12-14). For Davies and Allison's interpretation, see their *A Critical and Exegetical Commentary on the Gospel according to Saint Matthew*, Vol II, pp. 278-93.

gift of presence of rest specifically from Exo 33:12-14, but his understanding of the intimate Father-Son relationship of love and the Father's Spirit on Jesus might probably have included these notions of presence and rest, as will be shown in the following.

Very often, the interpretation of vv. 25-27 and that of vv. 28-30 are relatively loosely related in commentaries. Here an attempt to connect vv. 25-27 and vv. 28-30 is to be made. If vv. 25-26 is about the object or recipients of the Father's revelation - little children (or those like them, see 18:3-4), then v. 27 is about how the Father reveals himself - through the Son who knows him and is known by him. Jesus' invitation to come to him in vv. 28-30 to find rest may be related to receiving the revelation of the Father through him (the theme in vv. 25-27). This proposition is consistent with the parallelism between Jesus and the personified Wisdom probably alluded to here. The personified Wisdom reveals knowledge of God to those who come to her and gives them rest, and Jesus is playing a similar mediating role here in vv. 25-27 and vv. 28-30 respectively.[128] The reason that those who come to Jesus can find rest is because Jesus knows the Father and reveals the Father to them; thus vv. 25-27 and vv. 28-30 could be closely related through the person of Jesus. However, it is customary in commentaries to treat the theme in vv. 28-30 rather separately from vv. 25-27: vv. 28-30 are Christological in nature with no mention of the Father while the theme in vv. 25-27 is the Father's revelation through the Son.[129] But this rather compartmentalised treatment of vv. 25-27 and vv. 28-30 does not do justice to the unity of the whole passage of vv. 25-30. It will be shown that vv. 25-27 and vv. 28-30 are linked together by the Son who features in both, and by the notion of humility which can be found in either. This unitary approach will bring out more clearly the relationships between God's Fatherhood and sonship, humility and rest.

The 'weary and burdened' in v. 28 could refer to those who are suffering and labouring under the tyranny of legalism. The Pharisees and teachers of the law 'tie up heavy loads and put them on men's shoulder'(23:4).[130] The 'weary and burdened' could also include Jesus'

---

128 Sirach 51:23-27 provides a promising background to 11:28-30. There the personified Wisdom invites people to come 'to me'. The reference to needy 'persons', the call to take the 'yoke' of instruction, the reference to a light 'labour' and the promise of rest that is to be 'found' are in that passage. But there one has to labour a 'little' before one can find 'much rest'. See Hagner, *Matthew 1-13*, pp. 321, 323.

129 See, e.g., commentaries by Beare, *Matthew*, p. 267; Luz, *Matthew 8-20*, pp. 172-4; Hagner, *Matthew 1-13*, pp. 316-325; France, *Matthew Commentary*, pp. 198-201; and Gundry, *Matthew: a commentary*, pp. 218-20.

130 The Pharisees spoke of 613 commandments and their rulings involved a

disciples.[131] The invitation to come to Jesus is open to all/ πάντες who are weary and burdened. Jesus will give them rest.[132] Jesus giving rest to people who come to him in v. 28 and his revelation of the Father to them in v. 27 are clearly linked by his person. This will become even clearer later.

'Take my yoke upon you and learn from me' in v. 29 invites the people to follow Jesus' new teaching and follow his example. The yoke symbolised obedience to the law in Judaism.[133] 'My yoke' refers to the obedience to Jesus' new teaching. But was Jesus' yoke only for others to carry so that he was spared from carrying it himself? In Matthew, Jesus the perfect Son fulfils his own teaching so that 'my yoke' is not only to be taken by others, it could also be taken by himself, on himself.[134] (The commentaries consulted, except Luz's, only see this yoke to be carried by others, not Jesus himself.)[135] This interpretation of Jesus carrying his own yoke is confirmed by the immediately succeeding and parallel clause 'learn from me for I am gentle and humble in heart.' This clause, parallel to 'take my yoke', is not 'learn from me for I teach you to be gentle and humble in heart.' In that case, the yoke is for others, not Jesus. But in v. 29, Jesus set himself as the example: 'I am gentle and humble in heart.' Learning from his concrete example is part and parcel of taking up his yoke - the second clause elaborates the first clause. But this means that Jesus in his exemplary attitude and life-style has originally taken the yoke upon himself. 'My yoke' therefore refers to the yoke that Jesus himself carries, which is

---

complicated casuistry, see Hagner, *Matthew 1-13*, p. 323.

131 G. Stanton, 'Matthew 11:28-30: Comfortable Words?', *Expository Times,* 94 (1982), pp. 3-9.

132 Note it was Yahweh who gave Moses rest in Exo 33:12-14.

133 Mishnah *Aboth 3:5, Berakoth 2:2;* see also *NIDNTT* vol. 3, pp. 1161-64.

134 G. Strecker makes the link between Jesus' teaching and his life. '... Matthew wants to say thereby that Jesus realises in himself the directives that he gives. From this the Christian community can learn how it is supposed to deal with the demands of the Preacher on the mount.' *The Sermon on the Mount* (Edinburgh: T. & T. Clark, 1988), p. 95. J. Kingsbury also wrote,'The human being in Matthew's Gospel who is whole in his relationship to the Father, in whom God's kingdom is a present reality, and who does God's will perfectly is of course Jesus the Son of God. He it is who stands before disciples as the one who realises in his life the ethic of the greater righteousness. Accordingly, bound to him in trust and assured of his forgiveness, disciples "follow after him" as they hear his call and lead the life of the greater righteousness.' 'The Place, Structure, and Meaning of the Sermon on the Mount Within Matthew', in *Interpretation,* 41 (1987), p. 143.

135 '... Jesus, on the other hand, lives what he teaches, and it is precisely the example that he gives - according to Matthew in distinction from the Pharisees (23:4!) - that makes his yoke "kind and light".' Luz, *Matthew 8-20* , p. 174.

now also to be taken up by those who come to him.

Those who learn from Jesus and follow his gentleness and humility will find rest for their souls (v. 29). But Matthew does not explain explicitly why this is so. What is special about gentleness and humility that these will lead them to rest? And why was Jesus able to give rest to those who come to him? Hagner contrasts Jesus' humility with the pride of the Pharisees and thereby deems Jesus as more trustworthy with his new teaching than the Pharisees with their laws, i.e., Jesus can give rest because he is a better teacher.[136] France comments generally that Jesus' yoke is easy (and so the disciples find rest) because they enter into a disciple-relationship with the one who is gentle and lowly in heart,[137] i.e., Jesus can give rest because he is gentle with his disciples. But these explanations of the humble and gentle Jesus giving rest neglect the reference to the little children in v. 25 who are examples of obedience and humility (18:3-4, humble/ $\tau\alpha\pi\epsilon\iota\nu\grave{o}\varsigma$ and meek/gentle/ $\pi\rho\alpha\ddot{\upsilon}\varsigma$ are essentially synonymous and include the meaning of submission and obedience as opposed to unrepentance as in 11:20). If the connection between those who are humble and gentle in v. 29 and the little children in v. 25 is made, then the Father who reveals himself to the little children in v. 25 also reveals himself to those who are gentle and humble in v. 29. It is this revelation of the Father to the gentle and humble that gives them rest. But this revelation of the Father is given through Jesus the Son (vv. 27-28) so that the burdened and weary have to come to Jesus to receive this revelation and rest from the Father. And what is the content of revelation that they receive through Jesus of the Father which can give them rest? In Matthew, this content of revelation through Jesus can be summarised as the righteousness of God, the Fatherhood of God and the Lordship of God (e.g., the Sermon on the Mount includes all three). Coming to Jesus, receiving the Father's revelation through him, means relating to God as he has revealed himself through his Son. That is, they are to humbly seek God's kingdom and submit to God's righteousness (taught and exemplified by Jesus) like little children in the context of the Father's loving care, forgiveness, unconditional love, attentiveness to their prayers (6:33, 12; 5:45,48; 7:11), and his sovereign Lordship. As the disciples do these according to Jesus' revelation and yoke, they shall find true rest. But since Jesus' yoke originally belongs to him in that he himself takes up his own yoke, he is the first one, the archetypal example to his disciples, who seeks God's righteousness, fulfils it, enjoys God's Fatherhood and finds this rest in his Father. 'My yoke is easy and my burden is light' in v. 30 refers to Jesus' own burden and yoke, not a yoke merely for others

---

136 Hagner, *Matthew 1-13*, p. 324.
137 France, *Matthew Commentary*, p. 201.

to carry. As the obedient Son of God with a gentle and humble heart knows the Father and finds rest in him, so the obedient sons of God who come to Jesus and share in his meekness and humility may also know their Father through him and find rest. Hagner understands this rest as 'a realisation of a deep existential peace, a shalom, or sense of ultimate well-being with regard to one's relationship to God and his commandments.'[138] The above interpretation of 11:25-30, which treats Jesus as the archetypal example to his disciples, would understand that Jesus the perfect Son lives in such a shalom, peace with his Father. Put in other terms, Jesus lives in the very personal presence of his Father (through the Spirit) and enjoys rest in that presence, or as v. 27 puts it, the Father knows the Son and the Son knows the Father. Barth in his exegesis of 11:25-30, unlike other commentators, perceptibly and remarkably does connect Jesus' rest with this mutual communion or unity with his Father and acknowledges Jesus' yoke as the yoke he himself carries.[139]

> It is to these [the weary and burdened] that He promises rest, a fulfilment which the others can never enjoy, because they do not know of it, because it cannot mean anything to them, *His own rest, the rest of His own being in the unity of the obedient Son with the will of the Father and with the Father himself.* It is these that He summons to come to Himself, to be with Him in this rest, to take His yoke upon them. *His rest consists in the fact that He carries the yoke and burden of the obedience of the Son to the Father* - an easy yoke, a light burden, as whose bearer He is really at rest, and can promise rest to those whom He calls ...[140]

Is it possible to detect some signs of Jesus' rest in the Father in his teaching and his life-style? If what Jesus reveals about the Father flows from his personal knowledge of the Father (v. 27), then what he teaches about the Father may well reflect his personal relationship with him and his rest in him; it will be difficult to imagine that what Jesus teaches about his Father is alien to his own relationship with his Father.[141] A clear example in the Sermon on the Mount is that he teaches his disciples to pray to God intimately as 'Our Father' (6:9). But this

---

138 Hagner, *Matthew 1-13*, p. 324.
139 Schweizer's comment is less direct but does allude to Jesus having this peace in his relationship with his Father. 'Because Jesus is himself among those who are tired and burdened, he can inspire the disciple to follow his life of total openness to God and thus attain true peace ...' *The Good News According to Matthew*, p. 273.
140 *CD* IV.1, p. 179. Italics mine.
141 See footnote 134 about the comments by Strecker and Kingsbury that Jesus fulfils his own teaching. This should also apply to relationship with God as Father.

teaching reflects his own personal intimate prayer to God in which he also prays to God as Father (11:25) though using his unique address 'My Father'(26:39). His Father is the source of his rest as the Father is the source of his disciples' rest. Likewise, in teaching his disciples to trust in their Father in heaven for provisions (6:25-34), this teaching may well reflect his trust and rest in his Father for his provisions. Accordingly, even though Jesus the Son of Man has no place to lay his head (8:20), one cannot detect any anxiety on Jesus' part concerning the physical needs of himself and his disciples; he entrusts all these needs to his loving Father and so finds rest in him. As he teaches his disciples that they are highly precious in their Father's eyes (6:26, 10:31), this may reflect his knowledge of how his Father treasures and loves him (3:17). As he teaches his disciples that when they are tried before local councils the Spirit of the Father will speak through them (10:20), this may reflect his own experience of inspiration by the Spirit of his Father. Teaching his disciples to pray to their Father for strength in the face of temptation (26:41) may well reflect his prayer to his Father in his hour of need, seeking strength to overcome his own temptation in the Garden of Gethsemane. Teaching his disciples that not even one sparrow falls to the ground apart from their Father's will (10:29) may reflect his absolute trust in his Father's sovereign rule, knowing that his Father is ruling in and working out all things to fulfil his purpose - his own fall to the ground (cf. 10:28 about killing the body) will be within his Father's will and purpose. With this trust in his Father, he repeatedly predicts his death to his disciples. Accordingly, he unswervingly walks the path of the cross, courageously confronting the religious leaders, facing persecutions, temptations, trials and insults, not doubting if his Father's purpose is being fulfilled through evil men but trusting his sovereign Father to work out his saving purpose for Israel and the nations even through his insults, sufferings and death. These are some of the hints in Matthew of Jesus finding rest in his Father despite the great challenges that he faces.[142]

Jesus the perfect Son not only trusts his Father's loving and sovereign care and so finds rest in him, but he - the one gentle and humble in heart - also always chooses to obey his Father, uniting himself with his Father in his will, sharing the same purpose, mind and spirit with his Father, keeping himself in communion with his Father in the Spirit. Without

---

142 To follow Jesus and fulfil the righteousness as taught in the Sermon on the Mount is extremely difficult. However, the level of difficulty is somewhat offset by Jesus' teaching on the loving and caring Fatherhood of God in the sermon. Without the rest and assurance in the Father, the Sermon on the Mount becomes impossible to fulfil indeed. That is probably why Matthew skilfully balances the teaching on God's righteousness and God's Fatherhood in the Sermon on the Mount.

Jesus' obedience to his Father, his will and actions will differ from his Father's and he cannot be properly in a perfect communion and correspondence with his Father to reveal him. Jesus' obedience is part and parcel of his unity and communion with his Father and thus his revelation of his Father. Hence the close connections between Jesus' obedience (gentleness and humility in v. 29), the knowledge of and communion with his Father (v. 27), his rest in the communing presence of his Father (vv. 28-30) and his revelation of his Father (v. 27) in Mt. 11:25-30. These connections will be further elaborated in chapter 6. Here, it is explained why the concept of revelation given by Mt. 11:25-30 should be called a non-linear concept. In the linear concept of revelation (see section 3.3), the Father speaks his Word which is made effective by the Spirit to the hearers. The direction of revelation or communication is unidirectional - from the speaker via his Word to the hearer. However, within this process the Word spoken and the speaker are in mutual knowledge and fellowship through the Spirit which is reciprocal or bi-directional. The Father wills, the Son responses to his will with obedience; the Father loves the Son and grants him rest in his communing presence, the Son returns this love with his own love through the Spirit. It is in this mutual/reciprocal/bi-directional relationship of fellowship, trust and love in the Spirit that Jesus resonates with and maintains consonance with his Father and so reveals him on earth. This is why this concept of revelation is called a non-linear concept. Barth, when expounding Mt. 11:25-30 also sees this connection between reciprocal communion and revelation.

> [T]he revelation imparted to the νηπίοι (Mt. 11:25 and Luke 10:21) is grounded in a preceding movement in God Himself between the Father and the Son; ... He was the Father who loves the Son and the Son who loves the Father, and as such, *in communion and reciprocity of this love*, as God the Father, Son and Holy Ghost, the God who is self-moved, the living God, *the One who loves eternally and as such moves to love.*[143]

Despite Barth's perceptive observation of the connection between reciprocal communion and revelation here, he does not make much use of this connection in his presentation of Jesus as 'The Royal Man' earlier in *CD* IV.2 where the concepts of reflection and correspondence in revelation dominate, as will be shown in chapter 4.[144] This book emphasises that reciprocal communion is fundamental to Jesus' correspondence to, reflection and revelation of his Father.

---

143 *CD* IV.2, p. 759, in the subsection 'The Basis of Love.' Italics mine.
144 That is, Barth's rather linear concept of revelation still exerts its considerable force on his presentation of Jesus' relationship with his Father.

5.0 Concluding Summary

The Jewish historical background of the coming of God and the coming of a human Messiah has been briefly presented. That background paves the way for considering the identity of Jesus Christ who has fulfilled both the coming of God and the coming of the Messiah in his own unique manner. Jesus' double identifications in Matthew, with Israel and with Yahweh, has been considered in some detail. Contrary to many New Testament commentators, Barth maintains that Jesus is understood and presented as the divine Lord in the synoptic gospels, basing this firm conviction on the fact that the evangelists recollected the event of Jesus Christ and wrote their gospels from a post-resurrection perspective. By studying how Matthew (or the tradition he received) intentionally took Mt. 3:3 away from the lips of the Baptist and deliberately but subtlely changed the LXX translation of Isaiah 40:3, Matthew's (also Mark's and Luke's) purposeful identification of Jesus with the Lord (Yahweh) has been recognised. This strategic move by Matthew at the beginning of his gospel couples with Jesus' universal Lordship at the end of his gospel to form an inclusio. Within the inclusio, Matthew elaborates what this Lordship of Jesus consists of in his narratives about Jesus' life, ministry and death (see next two chapters).

The importance of the dual identifications of Jesus, his humanity and divinity, has been briefly discussed for Barth's doctrine of reconciliation. Jesus' divinity and humanity are also necessary and crucial for a proper revelation of his Father. In the above discussion, Jesus' divinity and humanity are not considered under the question and theme of how the two natures of Jesus Christ can co-exist together in him, though there will be discussion on human-divine compatibility in chapter 7 in the context of trinitarian theology.

A detailed exegesis of Mt. 11:25-30 yields some insights concerning Jesus' knowledge of his Father as the basis of his revelation of his Father: it is in the rest afforded by the communing presence of his Father, and his obedience to his Father, that Jesus reveals his Father in words and actions. Contrary to many, if not most, New Testament commentators, Barth's perceptive understanding of the connections between Jesus' unity/communion with his Father, his rest in his Father and his revelation of his Father in a few passages in *CD* IV.1,2 agrees with the results of the exegesis here. Barth does have some very good understanding of Jesus' experience of and communion/unity with his Father in his earthly life even though Barth does not emphasise these aspects. His doctrine of the Trinity, which has often been criticised for its lack of emphasis on the aspect of communion, could have been much more developed along the lines which he has already obtained and indicated in *CD* IV.1,2. This is precisely the direction in which this book seeks to move.

By establishing Jesus' identification with Yahweh and Israel/humanity, by emphasising the importance of communion in Jesus' revelation of his Father, this chapter thereby has prepared the conceptual framework for considering Jesus' revelation of his Father in his concrete words and actions in the next two chapters.

CHAPTER 3

Jesus' Revelation of His Father through His Words

Summary of chapters 2 and 3: These two chapters will answer the question 'What has Jesus revealed of his Father through his concrete words and actions as witnessed by Matthew's narratives?' Within the scope of this book, the answer to this question has to be selective but representative of some major elements of Jesus' teachings and acts. In his words and actions Jesus reveals his Father but the unique manner of his revelation of the Father raises the questions of his identity and his relationship with his Father. These questions can only be adequately answered in the light of the non-linear concept of revelation (and Jesus' identification with Yahweh) discussed in chapter 2. With the help of the answer from the concept of revelation, his revelation of his Father and his revelation of his relationship with his Father in words and actions can be interpreted as the embodiment or realisation of the concept or principle of revelation.

1.0 Introduction

In 'The Royal Man' in *CD* IV.2, Barth rightly observes that there cannot be any separation between the person of Jesus Christ and his life-act which consists of both his words and his actions.[1] The person of Jesus Christ is known through his life-act; or the life-act of Jesus witnesses to who Jesus is. There cannot be an abstract imagination or knowledge of Jesus which bypasses his words and actions. Both mysticism and other

---

1 *CD* IV.2, p. 194.

so-called spiritual experiences are targets of Barth's attack.[2] Barth expresses the coincidence between the person of Jesus and his life-act thus,

> We must now attempt ... to understand Jesus in the act accomplished by Him. *It is in the act of His life that the distinctiveness of His existence and His likeness to God are actual and can therefore be seen and comprehended.* His life was His act, and it has therefore the character of history. The community in which the New Testament originated looked back to this history, which was also its present and future. *No distinction was then made, as later, between His person and work.* It looked to His completed work, which was regarded as of absolute significance as the work of this person. And it looked to His person, which was regarded as of absolute significance as the Subject of this work. In His history, and therefore in His life as this act, Jesus was there for His community, not only as past, but also as present and future. The totality of His *being* in its scope for them and the whole world was identical with *the totality of His activity.*[3]

This quote, especially the last sentence, is reminiscent of Barth's concept of being and act in 'The Being of God in Act' in *CD* II.1. There he applies the relationship between being and act to God.[4] God reveals himself in his action in event and history. The way to seek, find and know God is therefore through his action in history. Barth understands that the God who reveals himself in his action in history is Father, Son and Holy Spirit, who is the revealer, the act of revelation, the revealed according to his concept or scheme of revelation. This is a valid way of knowing the Father, Son and Holy Spirit - by analysing the act of

---

2 E.g., *CD* IV.2, pp. 361f; *CD* I.2, pp. 318-20, pp. 750-1. Herrmann also attacked mysticism severely in the early chapters of his *The Communion of the Christian with God.* It is possible that Barth was influenced by Herrmann on this criticism of mysticism which neglects the content of revelation - the concrete life and acts of Jesus.

3 *CD* IV.2, p. 193. Italics mine.

4 'God is He who in this event is subject, predicate, and object; the revealer, the act of revelation, the revealed; Father, Son and Holy Spirit. God is the Lord active in this event. ... Seeking and finding God in his revelation, we cannot escape the action of God for a God who is not active. This is not only because we ourselves cannot, but because there is no surpassing or bypassing at all of the divine action, because a transcendence of his action is nonsense. We are dealing with the being of God: but with regard to *the being of God*, the word 'event' or 'act' is final, and cannot be surpassed or compromised. To its very deepest depths God's Godhead consists in the fact that it is an event - not any event, not events in general, but *the event of his action*, in which we have a share in God's revelation.' *CD* II.1, p. 262-3. Italics mine.

revelation and its conceptual formulation. However, there is more one can learn about the Father, Son and Holy Spirit in the act of revelation - by looking at the narrative content of revelation in addition to the concept of revelation.[5] The narrative content of Jesus' words and actions witnesses to and therefore reveals Jesus himself, and through Jesus his Father is revealed. This is what Barth consistently and correctly upholds and emphasises. However, Jesus' words and actions - the contents of his revelation - also reveal or bear witness to his *relationships* with his Father and the Spirit. Therefore, the three emphases of (i) Jesus' revelation of his own identity, (ii) his revelation of his Father and (iii) his revelation of his relationship with the Father through the Spirit will be borne in mind in this chapter and the next when considering Jesus' revelation through his words and actions.

Both Jesus' words and his actions witness to Jesus himself. Barth is careful to avoid the liberal tendency to neglect the actions of Jesus and insists that his actions, including his mighty works, also witness to him. Barth does not see Jesus' words and actions as two separate unrelated avenues for knowing Jesus Christ; for him the two are closely connected. His action is the fulfilment or confirmation of his own speech so that his speech and action complement one another in witnessing to the person of Jesus Christ.

> His activity was as it were the kindling light of His speech - the light of the truth of His speech kindling into actuality. More pertinently, it is the demonstration of the coincidence, or identity, of his proclamation of the kingdom of God, the lordship of God, the divine *coup d'état*, with the event itself. It is not for nothing that in the first instance the activity itself usually consists in a Word which He speaks, but then in the Gospel record this Word tears aside the illusion that it might perhaps be 'only' a Word, an event in the spiritual sphere, by immediately accomplishing the corresponding change in the material and physical sphere, in the visible and palpable circumstances of the world around.[6]

Barth observes that in the gospel narratives the accounts of Jesus' speech are always accompanied and confirmed by his concrete actions. Again, regarding the nature of the relationship between Jesus' words and actions, he understands the activity of the Son of Man as 'an actualisation of His Word and commentary on it.'[7] But at the same time Barth acknowledges that there is a distinction and order between Jesus'

---

5 Barth does look at the concept as well as the content of revelation.

6 *CD* IV.2, p. 209.

7 *Ibid.*, p. 225. Cf. Strecker's and Kingsbury's comments that Jesus' action fulfils his own word, see chapter 2, footnote 134.

word and action - the word of Jesus is the 'primary and controlling aspect of His life-act'.[8] Barth's observation is correct: without the words of Jesus, his actions could be misinterpreted and misunderstood. But when his action in the kingdom of God confirms his word of the kingdom and his word interprets his action, we have a most satisfactory understanding of Jesus, as will be seen in the following interpretations of some gospel narratives. In these interpretations, there are three significant themes which run through both Jesus' words and actions - his Lordship, the radical nature of his life-act and his unconditional or undiscriminating love. These of course correspond to God's Lordship, God's radical nature compared to the world and God's unconditional love. Jesus' faithful correspondence to God in these bears witness to his relationship of communion and unity with his Father.

In studying Jesus' words and actions, selections will be made from Jesus' teaching from the Sermon on the Mount in chapters 5 to 7 in Matthew (in this chapter), followed by some of his words and actions in chapters 8 and 9 immediately after the Sermon (next chapter). Both his teachings in the sermon and the succeeding actions pertain to the Kingdom of God, the former as Kingdom Manifesto or Kingdom Ethics,[9] the latter as the manifestation of the power of the inbreaking kingdom of God. The study of Jesus' revelation of his Father through his concrete words and actions in the present and the next chapter will be important for considering Jesus' identity in relation to the Father and the Spirit in chapter 5, where different opinions will be verified with respect to Jesus' concrete words and actions. Chapter 6, where a theology of the Trinity will emerge, will also make use of the understandings gained in these two chapters with references to tangible concrete narratives.

---

8   *Ibid.*, p. 194. In the discussion of the unity of the body and soul in Jesus (in *CD* III.2), Barth ascribes precedence to the soul relative to the body and observes an analogous order in Jesus' word and action. 'All this [the precedence of the soul in the unity of the person of Jesus] must naturally be applied also to the oneness and wholeness of the work of Jesus and therefore to the relationship between His words and acts. Here, too, as we have seen, there is no dualism. The unity of the person of Jesus is reflected intact in the unity of his work [words and actions] also. But here too there is order - superiority and inferiority. The Word leads; the sign follows. The Word affirms; the sign confirms. The Word is the light; the sign its shining. The two cannot be separated; but they are to be seen in this relationship to one another. ... The Word is the proper revealing movement of His work, the act the confirmatory. The act never occurs alone and for itself or for its own sake. It can only be misunderstood, if considered, desired or admired for itself. It is produced by the power of the Word. Indirectly, it is itself Word, *verbum visibile*; and it wills to be accepted as such.' *CD* III.2, pp. 339-40.

9   France, *Matthew: Evangelist and Teacher*, p. 164.

1.1 The Teaching of Jesus

Jesus is presented in the gospels as an itinerant preacher, travelling from village to village. It is highly probable that there was a basic core in his message and he delivered substantially the same or a similar message during his itinerant journeys.[10] The parables he gave could be retold many times with minor variations, and the list of beatitudes he gave could be modified according to different contexts of delivery.[11] The basic core of Jesus' message was the arrival of the Kingdom of God which the Jews had been waiting for, or longing for (Mt. 4:17). Luke expresses it in terms of liberation and God's Jubilee favour in 4:18-19. Unlike the teachers of the Law, Jesus spoke with authority and power. With decisiveness, his vivid words demanded a response or decision from his hearers regarding the message of the kingdom . The following may give a glimpse of Jesus' ministry of preaching and teaching.

> [W]e may catch something of the required flavour if we say that Jesus was more like a politician on the campaign trail than a schoolmaster, more like a composer/conductor than a violin teacher; more like a subversive playwright than an actor. He was a herald, the bringer of an urgent message that could not wait, could not become the stuff of academic debate. He was issuing a public announcement, like someone driving through a town with a loudhailer. He was issuing a public warning, like a man with a red flag heading off an imminent railway disaster. He was issuing a public invitation, like someone setting up a new political party and summoning all and sundry to sign up and help create a new world. He was, in short, in some respects though not all, quite similar to the other 'leadership' prophets of the first century. The fact that he was not arrested sooner was due to his itinerant style, and to his concentration on villages rather than major cities, not to anything bland or unprovocative about the content of his message.[12]

In this chapter, the questions relating to Jesus' revelation of his Father are partly answered by looking at Jesus' teaching, much of which is radical and provocative. Because of the constraint of space, only the

---

10 Wright, *New Testament and the People of God*, pp. 422-44.

11 'He has regular phrases with which he urged repentance, commanded faith, encouraged the desperate, rebuked those he considered hard-hearted, spoke words of healing. The chances of his finding totally new things to say all the time, so that everything he said once and once only, must be reckoned at nil. Theissen's picture, of those who had heard him comparing memories and coming up with similar, though not identical, ways of retelling his stories rings thoroughly true (Theissen, 1987, *The Shadow of the Galilean*).' Wright, *Jesus and the Victory of God*, p. 170.

12 *Ibid.*, p. 172.

most relevant aspects of his teaching to this study will be treated. The Fatherhood of God is a highly important theme in Jesus' teaching and will be considered. If Jesus teaches about his Father according to his own knowledge of his Father (11:27), then his teaching may well reflect his relationship and experience of his Father, particularly in his humanity for he teaches how man should relate to the Father. The other teaching to be considered is the righteousness of God as given in the Sermon on the Mount. In particular, the antitheses are especially informative regarding the radical nature of Jesus' teaching on the Kingdom of God, and his remarkable authority and Lordship in giving these commands. The questions raised are: how is Jesus related to God when he exercises his *Lordly authority* and issues these radical teachings? And how is the *humanity* of Jesus involved in these seemingly sovereign utterances?

2.0 The Fatherhood of God

In Matthew, the term 'Father' appears forty-four times and every time on the lips of Jesus. In the Sermon on the Mount alone, Jesus uses it seventeen times. He teaches his disciples to follow his example and call upon God as Father and pray to him as such. However, while his disciples pray to God as 'our Father'(6:9), Jesus addresses or prays to God as 'my Father'.[13] According to Jeremias' *The Prayers of Jesus*, the Aramaic form for Father, *abba*, is an unusual and rather intimate form of address to God.[14] The form that Jesus uses, 'my Father', makes his prayers even more personal and unique. 'Jesus' use of this unusual and intimate form for addressing God in prayer suggests strongly that Jesus' religious life was characterised by relating to God in a very intense and

---

13 Mt. 7:21; 10:32, 33; 11:27; 12:50; 15:13; 16:17; 18:10, 19, 35; 20:23; 25:34; 26:39, 42, 53.

14 '... *abba* as a form of address to one's father was no longer restricted to children, but also used by adult sons and daughters. The childish character of the word ('daddy') thus receded, and *abba* acquired the warm, familiar ring which we may feel in such an expression as 'dear father'. Nowhere in the entire wealth of devotional literature produced by ancient Judaism do we find *abba* being used as a way of addressing God. The pious Jew knew too much of the great gap between God and man (Eccl. 5:1) to be free to address God with the familiar word used in everyday family life.' *NIDNTT*, vol. 1, p. 614. It was Jeremias' conclusion that Jesus' addressing God as *abba* in prayer was unprecedented and unique, *The Prayers of Jesus*, pp. 57-62. But there was one example of a Jew saying 'my Father' to God in Eccl. (Ben Sira) 51:10. However, the word used is πατήρ in Greek, not *abba* in Aramaic. In any case, Jesus' far more frequent and regular use of *abba* was certainly unique for his time, see Dunn, *Jesus and the Spirit*, p. 23.

personalised way that is not fully paralleled even in other examples of very devout spirituality in the ancient Jewish setting.'[15] 'Jesus seems to have thought of himself as God's son in a distinctive sense.'[16] But this distinctive sense of Sonship does not exclude the possibility of others addressing God in a similar fashion. Rather, this distinctive and intimate sense of Sonship which he enjoys (with the attendant rest in his presence) may serve as a driving force for him to call others to come alongside him, draw near to God, call upon him as *abba* and also enjoy rest in his presence.[17] By encouraging his disciples to pray to God as *abba*, Jesus is teaching them that God is not a transcendent God who is remote from his people, but a God who desires to draw his people close to himself in a highly personal and intimate manner. The exegesis of Mt. 11:25-30 in the last chapter confirms that Jesus is in just such an intimate relationship of mutual fellowship with his Father, where he finds rest in his Father's communing presence of love. The disciples are to be like the teacher (10:25); they, likewise, are to seek this rest and fellowship with their Father. Barth concentrated his attention on the understanding of God as Father and the Christians' relationship with him as sons near the end of his life (see *The Christian Life: Church Dogmatics IV.4 Lecture Fragments*).[18] And Barth spoke not merely of Jesus' obedience to his Father, but also his childlike trust in his Father (p. 74). However, the latter aspect, Jesus' trust or rest in his Father, is apparently rare in Barth's writings but is brought out more prominently here in this book (but see Barth's reference to Jesus' rest in *CD* IV.1, p. 179, quoted in 4.0 of chapter 2).

---

15 *Dictionary of Jesus and the Gospels* (Downers Grove; Leicester: InterVarsity Press, 1992), J. Green, S. McKnight, I.H. Marshall (eds.), p. 275.

16 Dunn, *Jesus and the Spirit*, p. 38.

17 Dunn convincingly demonstrated that the prominent notion of Father-son relationship between God and Jesus' followers in the New Testament can be traced back to Jesus' own awareness of his unique Sonship to God. See Dunn, *Jesus and the Spirit* , pp. 11-40, 62-7. Also, Jesus is also unique in this encouragement to others to relate to God as Father. L. Hurtado writes, 'Whatever the partial analogies offered (e.g., by Vermes) for Jesus' own intimacy with God among ancient Jewish holy men, there is no parallel for Jesus' sense that God called him to become the pioneer and catalyst for a special filial relationship to God to be enjoyed by his disciples.' *Dictionary of Jesus and the Gospels*, p. 276.

18 See K. Barth, *The Christian Life: Church Dogmatics IV.4 Lecture Fragments* (Edinburgh: T. & T. Clark, 1981). See for example his comment on p. 102, 'As we have described it thus far, the invocation of God by his children [i.e., Father] in which the spiritual life and also the witnessing ministry of Christians in the world have their *basis*, *root*, and norm, and which is the nerve of their whole Christian existence, is an integral part of the history of the covenant between God and men.' Italics mine.

The Father's promise of *rest* and his Fatherly *love* go hand in hand with his demand for *obedience*, and vice versa. These two aspects are clearly found in Jesus' teaching. The exegesis of his words in 11:25-30 shows that the way to enjoy the Father's rest is to be his obedient and humble child, as Jesus is the obedient and humble Son. On the one hand they are encouraged, or commanded, to seek the Father's kingdom and righteousness so that they can be light of the world and salt of the earth, and their good deeds may honour their Father in heaven (5:6; 6:33; 5:13-16). Their goal is to be perfect as their heavenly Father is perfect (5:48). On the other hand, as they set their hearts on this course rather than other courses, such as amassing wealth for themselves (6:24), they shall experience the Father's detailed loving care. They are not to worry about their financial needs because they are assured of their Father's provision. Jesus uses his powerful rhetoric in 6:25-33 to makes this point emphatically - the sons of the Father are incomparably more precious than other creatures and God will surely and lovingly take care of them in his providence. Jesus again reassures his disciples of their Father's detailed providential care in 10:29-30 as he sends them out to mission.[19] Concerning prayer, Jesus uses his potent rhetoric in 7:9-11 to emphasise the Father's loving attentiveness to the prayers of his children.[20] Concerning rewards, their Father knows their good deeds done in secret and will surely reward them (6:1-18). All these teachings by Jesus concerning the Father witness to the central theme of the Father's love for his children and his desire for his children to obey him, draw near to him, receive his forgiveness and acceptance, and enjoy his provisions, presence and rest in the sure knowledge of his unconditional love (5:45-48).[21]

The relationship between Jesus' teaching of the Fatherhood of God and his own experience of his Father will be considered in the following. Since Jesus teaches about his Father according to his own knowledge of his Father (Mt. 11:27), his teaching of God's Fatherhood (briefly given above) may well reflect his relationship with and

---

19 'Are not two sparrows sold for a penny? Yet not one of them falls to the ground apart from the will of your Father. And even the very hairs of your head are all numbered. So don't be afraid; you are worth more than many sparrows.'

20 'Which of you, if his son asks for bread, will give him a stone? Or if he asks for a fish, will give him a snake? If you, then, though you are evil, know how to give good gifts to your children, how much more will you Father in heaven give good gifts to those who ask him!'

21 Concerning the Father's love for his children, Israel and all nations, even though Matthew does not make it explicit as John does (in 3:16), it is implicit that the Father reveals his love to his children, Israel and the nations climactically in the death of his Son who identifies himself with Israel/humanity and saves them from their sins.

experience of God his Father, or, *it is probable that out of his own experience of his Father he teaches his disciples about the Fatherhood of God.* His teaching on the Father's love and the children's obedience indeed echoes his own experience of his Father's love and his obedience to his Father. For instance, his baptismal experience is an important example of (i) his own personal experience of his Father's love and presence through the Spirit and (ii) his Father's call for obedience, which has definitive significance for him and his mission.[22] Also, at the end of the exegesis of 11:25-30 in the last chapter, it has been shown with examples how Jesus trusts in his Father's love and sovereign care and finds rest in him despite a lifestyle of poverty, and despite the persecutions and fatal danger that encroach upon him. As for his obedience, he obeys his Father from the wilderness of temptations to the cross, faithfully fulfilling his own teaching on God's righteousness and his Father's mission for him. Therefore, Jesus is the fulfilment of his teaching on knowing the Father's love and obedience to the Father, and his teaching is probably borne out of his own relationship with God as his Father. Indeed, according to the non-linear concept of revelation, as discussed in the exegesis of Mt. 11:25-30, the knowledge of God as his Father and his corresponding identity as the Son of God is the foundation on which Jesus lives, breathes, acts and finally dies as he reveals his Father in all these.[23] And it is on the same foundation - his relationship and fellowship with God as Father - that he teaches his disciples about the Fatherhood of God. This is saying no more than the

---

22 His Father's words to him - 'This is my Son, whom I love, with him I am well pleased.' - are usually associated by commentators with Psalm 2:7 where the Messianic Davidic king is in view, and, Isaiah 42:1 where the servant is eventually identified as the suffering servant in Isaiah 53. The combination of these two OT verses means that Jesus the Son of God is also the suffering servant. However, Jeremias, *New Testament Theology* (London: SCM Press, 1971), 1:53-55, argues that the background to this voice from heaven was solely Isaiah 42:1, not including Psalm 2. He conjectures that the υἱός/son here was originally παῖς which can mean 'servant' or 'son'. The servant and God's delight in him in Is 42:1 will therefore closely parallel the utterance of this voice from heaven. However, the ensuing temptations presupposes Jesus as the Son/υἱός of God and therefore υἱός is probably correct here. See Hagner, *Matthew 1-13*, p. 59. Hence, Jesus' experience of God's Fatherhood in his baptism is maintained.

23 J. Kingsbury shows that the presentation of Jesus as the Son of God is central to Matthew's christology, see his *Matthew: Structure, Christology, Kingdom* (Philadelphia: Fortress, 1975), pp. 40-127; 'The Figure of Jesus in Matthew's Story: A Literary-Critical Probe', *Journal for the Study of the New Testament*, 21 (1984), pp. 3-36. France, *Matthew: Evangelist and Teacher*, p. 295, '[T]he freedom with which he speaks of God as his Father shows that Matthew has no doubt that Jesus not only was but was conscious of being the Son of God.'

fact that Jesus' revelation of the Fatherhood of God is a particular example or concretisation of the non-linear concept of revelation.

There is an important corollary to be drawn in the following concerning revelation. It has been established that Jesus does not only teach others to trust in God's love and obey him; he himself trusts in his Father's love and obeys his Father from the beginning to the end. The activity of the Son of Man is indeed 'an actualisation of His Word and commentary on it' (Barth). Jesus therefore reveals God's Fatherhood not only through his teaching but also through commenting on his teaching by his perfect example of Sonship, his own relationship with his Father. Conversely, his teaching on God's Fatherhood is a commentary on his relationship with his Father. This is how Jesus reveals God's Fatherhood: by his words, and by giving us a glimpse of his own relationship with his Father through his life of obedience and trust, both of which complement with and act as commentary on the other. But this means that *Jesus in his words and actions does not only reveal God's Fatherhood to us, but he also reveals and comments on his own relationship with and experience of God as his Father.*[24] One of Barth's emphases concerning revelation is that Jesus Christ reveals God to us. This notion of Jesus' revelation of his Father is of fundamental importance to Christian faith and theology. One of the aims of this book is to complement Barth's emphasis by showing that in Jesus' revelation of God, he also reveals his relationship with God to us. The above discussion concerning Jesus' revelation of the Fatherhood of God is a valid example of this. Another example is Jesus' teaching on the righteousness of God.

3.0 The Righteousness of God in the Sermon on the Mount

Jesus teaches his disciples not only to enjoy the Fatherhood of God but also to seek first his kingdom and righteousness. The Sermon on the Mount covers both aspects of Jesus' teaching. In the last section, it was seen that studying Jesus' teaching on the Fatherhood of God can give some insight into his relationship with his Father. It is possible that studying his teaching on righteousness could give further understanding of his relationship with his Father.

The sermon in Matthew is most probably a compilation of Jesus' sayings which were used in his itinerant journey, rather than one contiguous sermon. Many of the sayings are scattered in Luke; see, e.g., Robert Guelich, *The Sermon on the Mount* (Waco: Word Books, 1982),

---

24 His teaching of the *abba* prayer and his own call to his Father as *abba* is a clear example of this.

p. 34, for the correspondence. The sermon, in Matthew's arrangement, begins with the beatitudes where Jesus promised that God's favour is granted to those who are poor in spirit, mourning, meek ... and who are persecuted because of Jesus himself (5:1-12). Contrary to some opinion, there is grace for those who are weak and acknowledge their need.[25] There are blessings also for those who hunger and thirst for righteousness, who are merciful and pure in heart. The beatitudes are followed by Jesus' exhortation for his disciples to live as salt and light to the world (5:13-16). (In this respect, Jesus himself is the great light; 4:16). Their good deeds will bring praise to their Father in heaven. Then Matthew presents Jesus' direct continuity with the Torah - that he came to fulfil the Law and the Prophets (5:17-20). The six antitheses, where Jesus openly alters the Torah and even abrogates some of the provisions, illustrate this meaning of fulfilment which bears the notion of going beyond what has been given.[26] It is interesting that in the last antithesis the indiscriminate grace of God to sinners is used as a pattern for the disciples' grace to others. There is grace in the sermon to be discerned. (See also the petition for God's forgiveness in 6:12.) The three basic aspects of Jewish piety - almsgiving, prayer and fasting - are then presented (6:1-18). The emphasis is not on the outward action only, but on the motivation and attitude that goes with the act. This emphasis very much echoes the demand for inner purity in the second and fourth antitheses. Then a decision to serve God or mammon is called for (6:19-24), with the promise of God's loving providential care if one chooses the former - seeking first God's kingdom and righteousness (6:25-34). After treating the disciples' attitude towards God and mammon, Matthew presents Jesus' teaching on the disciples' attitude towards others who have wronged them (7:1-6), which echoes the teaching against anger in the first antithesis, the teaching on forgiveness in the Lord's prayer and the teaching on unconditional love in the last antithesis. Again, God's loving care to the disciples is emphasised in 7:7-11, where it is taught that it is impossible or inconceivable for the heavenly Father not to give good gifts to his children in answer to their

---

25 The Lutheran view is that the idealism of the sermon demonstrates our need of grace and hence drives us to the gospel. However, there is God's grace already to be found in the sermon itself and it is of fundamental importance, as the beatitudes show. Cf. Hagner, *Matthew 1-13*, p. 83. The theme of the liberation of the poor and needy is also found in Luke 4:18-19, which, together with the first two beatitudes in Matthew, are linked to the liberation theme in Isaiah 61:1-2.

26 See Hagner, *Matthew 1-13*, p. 105 for the various interpretations of fulfilment. The author would add that Jesus' fulfilment of the Law and Prophets also involves his own life and actions which embody his teaching of righteousness, thus concretely fulfilling it.

prayers. The verse in 7:12, the golden rule - to do to others what one would have others do to one - is a summary of the righteousness toward others demanded by Jesus. Following the golden rule are challenges and exhortations to obey Jesus' teaching on righteousness, as given in the sermon. Two metaphors, gate and road, and two parables, fruit of a tree and the two builders, are used in calling for a decision for obedience by the readers/hearers. The presentation of the sermon finishes with the crowd being amazed or overwhelmed (ἐξεπλήσσοντο) at the teaching of Jesus who taught as one who had authority (εξουσίαν).

Some have viewed the Sermon on the Mount as kingdom ethics for Jesus' disciples to follow, but in view of God's promises of blessings, grace, forgiveness, his Fatherly providential care and attentive listening to his children's prayer, it is perhaps appropriate to call it the *Kingdom Manifesto*[27] - God as Father is reaching out to the people with his promises of blessings, grace and care, inviting them to take part in this programme of revolutionary living, which is the hallmark of his Kingdom and reign amongst his people.[28]

3.1 The Authority of Jesus in the Sermon on the Mount

Even though the sermon is understood as God's prophetic word through Jesus to the people concerning right relationships with God and others, the teacher himself - Jesus - features prominently in the sermon. 'Blessed are you when people insult you, persecute you ... because of *me'* (5:11). 'Do you think *I* have come to abolish the Law or the

---

27 Hagner, *Matthew 1-13*, p. 83, calls the sermon 'The Ethics of the Kingdom', while France calls it a 'manifesto setting out the nature of life in the kingdom of heaven', *Matthew: Evangelist and Teacher*, p. 164. Here, it is called explicitly the Kingdom Manifesto.

28 For the debate concerning whether the Sermon on the Mount is an integral part of Matthew, see H. D. Betz, *Essays on the Sermon on the Mount* (Philadelphia: Fortress Press, 1985), pp. 17-21, 89-93 and the responses in G. Stanton, *Gospel for a New People* (Edinburgh: T. & T. Clark, 1992), pp. 307-325, and France, *Matthew: Evangelist and Teacher*, pp. 163-5. Betz proposed that the Sermon on the Mount was a pre-Matthean single unit of discourse which was incorporated wholesale into Matthew's gospel with no or little modification. The theology of the Sermon on the Mount is quite different from the rest of Matthew and contains a minimal Christology. Against Betz's suggestions, the author contends that the sermon is integral to Matthew and is inextricably linked to the rest of Matthew because the teaching here is a commentary on Jesus' life and ministry presented in the rest of Matthew, or, Jesus himself is the fulfilment of his teaching in the sermon. In the light of this, instead of having a minimal Christology, the sermon is Christologically centred and should be interpreted as such, while remembering that this sermon is also Jesus' teaching for his disciples who follow him.

Prophets; *I* have not come to abolish them but to fulfil them. *I* tell you the truth (αμὴν γὰρ λέγω ὑμῖν) ... For *I* tell you that unless your righteousness surpasses that of the Pharisees and the teachers of the law, you will certainly not enter the kingdom of heaven'(5:17-20). There are six examples of 'But *I* tell you ...' in the six antitheses, with the first antithesis reinforced with '*I* tell you the truth (ἀμὴν λέγω σοι)'(5:26). And each of the teachings on the three aspects of Jewish piety is reinforced with '*I* tell you the truth (ἀμὴν λέγω ὑμῖν) ...' (6:2, 6:5, 6:16). The teaching on trusting God's Fatherly provision begins with 'Therefore, *I* tell you ...' (6:25) and was rammed with another '*I* tell you' in 6:29. In the scene of the eschatological judgment, Jesus speaking as the Judge responds to those who claim their merit but disobey his word (or his Father's will) with 'Then *I* will tell them plainly, "*I* never knew you. Away from *me*, you evildoers"'(7:23)! There are twenty direct references to the speaker himself in the sermon (compared with twenty-three references to God or Father). And each of the references to the speaker pertains to his authority or loyalty to him. It is also interesting that in none of the sayings where the self-references occur does the speaker invoke the authority of God, any other authority or inspiration by the Spirit.[29] It has emerged that the speaker invokes and exercises his own authority in the whole of the Sermon on the Mount. We might call this self-referencing authority 'egocentric authority' (ἐγώ taken from ἐγὼ δὲ λέγω ὑμῖν/but I tell you, which is used six times in the six antitheses and many other Jesus' self-references), which is not to be interpreted in a pejorative sense but in a positive self-referencing sense. The speaker does not say he is merely an agent who has heard the prophetic word of God concerning the Kingdom and passed it on, as the Old Testament prophets invariably did in their own contexts. Their typical style of speech was 'This is what the sovereign Lord says ...' (Amos 3:11, cf. Amos 1:3, 9, 2:1; Haggai 1:2; Jer. 8:4; Is. 29:22); or 'Hear the word of the Lord ...' (Hosea 4:1); or 'The word of the Lord has come to me ...' (Joel 1:1; cf. Obadiah 1:1; Micah 1:1; Ezekiel 6:1; Jer. 2:1,2; Is. 1:1). The Old Testament prophets never invoked any authority of their own, never used the sentence 'I say unto you ...' to pass on the message from God. They were careful to make clear that the authority of what they said came from God, not from themselves.[30] And they never expected their hearers to obey them either, only Yahweh. The prophetic utterances of Jesus, by the sheer exertion of his own authority, mark him out from all Old Testament prophets,

---

29 Regarding the inspiration by the Spirit, it might be more correct to say that the writer does not invoke Jesus' inspiration by the Spirit as an editorial comment.

30 T. W. Manson, *The Teaching of Jesus* (London: Cambridge University Press, 1931), p. 106.

and for that matter, from all New Testament apostles who confessed their authority as deriving from God or Jesus Christ (Acts 2:17-18; Rom. 1:1-5; 1 Cor. 1:1; 2 Cor. 1:1; Gal. 1:1; Eph. 1:1 ... Rev. 1:1-2).

The nature of Jesus' authority came into sharp focus when he abrogated or extended some of the Old Testament laws and provisions in the six antitheses in Matthew. E. Lohse demonstrated that the antithetical form of sayings was not original to Jesus, being used in rabbinical arguments concerning their interpretation of the Torah.[31] In the rabbinical use of this form, a premise or thesis concerning a doctrinal view or position is put first, followed by the antithesis - 'but I say to you ...'. The thesis could not be the Torah itself for the rabbis would not wish to contradict God's written sacred Law. The thesis could be some oral tradition or an interpretation of Torah but not the Torah itself. Was Jesus' use of the thesis-antithesis structure the same as those of the rabbis or radically different?

The theses in Matthew begin with 'You have heard that it was said' (Ἠκούσατε ὅτι ἐρρέθη) or the abbreviated form 'It was said' (Ἐρρέθη). Do the six theses using these phrases in Matthew refer to some oral traditions (which are to be distinguished from the written Torah, cf. Mt. 15:3, Mark 7:5), an interpretation of the Torah or the Torah itself? This question is significant because the answer to it will determine whether Jesus' new positions are in fact standing with respect to the Torah or something much less authoritative.[32] Guelich, by incorporating the works of Lohse, Lohmeyer and Manson, shows convincingly that the proper meaning of 'You have heard it was said' is not the hearing of some oral tradition or interpretation of the Torah but the hearing of the Torah itself, most probably in the context of the readings in the synagogue or temple worship.[33] Thus, the rabbis might debate amongst themselves using the antithetical form, concerning matters of interpretation of the Torah or oral tradition, and in those contexts contribute their 'but I say to you'. However, Jesus used the antithetical form to put forward the theses as given in the Torah and then declared his 'but I say to you' to pronounce his new teaching with respect to the Torah. Such a bold move to alter the teaching of the Torah would not be attempted by the rabbis in their debates, but Jesus revealed and claimed his own unmistakable authority by making such a unique move, without even invoking God's own authority or divine inspiration

---

31 See Strecker, *The Sermon on the Mount*, p. 62, for Lohse's reference.

32 For the scholars' view for the latter (Dalman, Kümmel, G. Barth, Klostermann), see Guelich, *The Sermon on the Mount*, pp. 179-81.

33 Guelich, *Sermon on the Mount*, pp. 179-82. For a similar judgment, see also R. Banks, *Jesus and the Law in the Synoptic Tradition*, (Cambridge: Cambridge University Press, 1975), pp. 186-203.

by the Holy Spirit.[34] To appreciate the force of Jesus' unique authority, it is necessary to examine the content of the theses and antitheses. Only the last three antitheses will be presented but they are sufficient to illustrate the radical nature of Jesus' teaching and his relentless authority. Because of the constraint of space, detailed exegeses will be performed only on these three antitheses in considering Jesus' teaching on righteousness in the Sermon on the Mount. However, these, especially the last two, are the core of Jesus' teaching on righteousness and will link up well with Jesus' practice of unconditional love in his ministry, which will be studied in the next chapter.

3.2 The Antitheses

3.2.1 OATH (MATTHEW 5:33-37)

Again, you have heard that it was said to the people long ago, 'Do not break your oath, but keep the oaths you have made to the Lord.' But I tell you, do not swear at all: either by heaven, for it is God's throne, or by earth, for it is his footstool, or by Jerusalem, for it is the city of the Great King. And do not swear by your head, for you cannot make even one hair white or black. Simply let your 'Yes' be 'Yes', and your 'No', 'No'; anything beyond this comes from the evil one. (Mt. 5:33-37)

The provision of oaths and vows were not only permitted and assumed in the OT but in some cases they were actually commanded (Num. 5:19f). Often the name of God was invoked in making an oath: 'May God deal with me, be it ever so severely, if ...'[35] Yahweh is the defender of oath; he who does not keep his oath will be dealt with by Yahweh.[36] However, in Jewish-rabbinical teaching the name of God could be avoided in oath through some circumlocutions; such as heaven, earth and Jerusalem in 5:34-35, and temple or its gold, altar or the gift on it in

---

34 This critical feature of Jesus cannot be erased from the gospel records because if it is attributed to the church or any other sources it amounts to holding the church or the sources responsible for altering the Torah. But if the rabbi dared not tamper with the sacred Torah, it is safe to conclude that any Jew who was loyal to the religion of their fathers would not do so either. It is difficult to imagine the source of the alteration to be someone other than Jesus himself. Bultmann was indecisive concerning whether the antitheses (he was referring to the first three) go back to the historical Jesus, while E. Käsemann found these to be the heart of Jesus' proclamation (Strecker, *Sermon,* p. 65 and footnote 4). See also Guelich, *Sermon on the Mount,* pp. 198-9 for the positive evaluation of the authenticity of the antitheses.

35 1 Sam. 14:44, 20:13, 25:22.

36 See also Lev. 6:1f; Zech. 8:17; Ezek. 16:59.

23:16-19. But the proliferation of these different forms of oath had raised the question of their relative validity (see Jesus' comments in 23:16f). These questions occupied the rabbis to the extent of writing several tractates of the Mishnah on this subject.[37]

The thesis here, strictly speaking, is not a verbatim quotation of an OT passage but it is an undisputed summary of the clear permission of oaths and the requirement to keep them in the OT.[38] But Jesus starkly abrogates these provisions for oaths by declaring 'But I tell you, do not swear at all ...' He, by prohibiting all forms of oath in his new teaching, stands directly opposed to the provisions in the Torah. He further points out that swearing by the circumlocutions - heaven, earth and Jerusalem - are to be avoided because they do implicate God in the oath and in that sense are valid oaths (Mt. 23:22). The need to use an oath arises from a lack of credibility on the part of the one who makes it. And to use God's name to buttress one's word is to exploit God's name. The true remedy to the situation is to be completely honest in whatever one says (let your 'yes' be 'yes' and your 'no' 'no', v. 37) so that others may find one trustworthy even without the use of oaths. The question of the authority exercised by Jesus is heightened here because the OT teaching is not preserved and extended as in the first two antitheses but abrogated altogether! The immediate question that arises is: who has the authority to cancel a law in the Torah? And the second question is: how can this new teaching be a fulfilment of the Law and the Prophets? It can be a fulfilment of the Torah if one understands that the God of the OT is the God of truth, it is always in God's original will for men to be honest, and the new teaching of Jesus here fulfils that original will by demanding men to be completely transparent and honest in every word that is uttered, even without the use of oaths.

It needs to be noted that Jesus was not the only one who spoke against the use of oaths. Josephus (*Jewish War* 2.8.6, 135) wrote of the Essenes (or the Qumran Community), 'Any word of theirs has more force than an oath; swearing they avoid, regarding it worse that perjury, for they say that one who is not believed without an appeal to God stands condemned already.' Philo (*Decal.* 84) also criticised the use of oaths.[39] But two distinctions must be made between these and Jesus' prohibition of oaths. Firstly, Jesus' absolute rejection of oaths exceeded the teaching of the Essenes, whose prohibition was not absolute, i.e., some oaths were allowed. Jesus stood alone in contemporary Judaism with his absolute prohibition of oaths. Secondly, the opinions of the Essenes and Philo were expressed, or even practised, at a distance from

---

37 France, *Matthew Commentary*, p. 124.
38 See, e.g., Lev. 19:12; Num. 30:2; Deut. 23:21.
39 Josephus and Philo are quoted by Hagner, *Matthew 1-13*, p. 128.

the Torah. They never dared to take their opinions to the Torah and set them in opposition to it. But Jesus set out the provision in the Torah plainly in the thesis and then contradicted it starkly in the antithesis of his new teaching! It is this blunt abrogation of some OT teachings that marks Jesus out from other Jewish teachings, along with his stricter and absolute prohibition of oaths. But Jesus gives no apology or shows no hesitancy in his abrogating this clear provision in the Torah. He who brings in the Kingdom of God exercises his own authority, makes known the ultimate and radical will of his Father and thus *reveals* him. But the manner of his revelation of his Father's will, i.e., the exercise of supreme authority in relation to the Torah, raises the question of his own identity and his relationship with God. Who is he and what kind of relationship with God does he have that allows him to speak with such authority? These questions, which will be taken up further in 4.0 and chapter 6, can only be adequately answered with reference to Jesus' identification with the 'Lord' (Yahweh, Mt. 3:3) and the non-linear concept of revelation in Mt. 11:25-30.

Jesus' teaching on honesty and truth as an aspect of God's righteous will does not only apply to his disciples but also to himself. As he is the one who fulfils his own teaching, his teaching on honesty acts as a commentary on his own life of truth and faithfulness which he exercises in obedience to his Father. His supreme fulfilment of this teaching can be seen in the way he truthfully and faithfully realised his words concerning his journey to Jerusalem with the impending suffering and death (Mt. 16:21; see next chapter). He did not fail to keep his words; he did not retreat from that journey; he was truthful before man and before God. As with Jesus' teaching on the Fatherhood of God, his revelation of this aspect of God's righteousness (honesty and truth) in words and in actions also serves to reveal and comment on Jesus' relationship with his Father - his life of righteousness and truth before God.

3.2.2 NON-RETALIATION BUT COMPLIANCE (MATTHEW 5:38-42)

> You have heard that it was said, 'Eye for eye, and tooth for tooth.' But I tell you, do not resist an evil person. If someone strikes you on the right cheek, turn to him the other also. And if someone wants to sue you and take your tunic, let him have your cloak as well. If someone forces you to go one mile, go with him two miles. Give to the one who asks you, and do not turn away from the one who wants to borrow from you. (Mt. 5:38-42)

The thesis is quoted from Exo. 21:24, Lev. 24:20, Deut. 19:21. A similar principle of retribution was also found in Hammurabi (18 century B.C.).[40] Here in the Torah, these are the legal/judicial prescriptions for a proportionate retribution to the wrongdoer. Its purpose in the judicial system is to limit the extent of revenge to be inflicted, rather than to encourage violence. By the time of Jesus, such physical penalties had been replaced by financial ones. A victim is therefore legally entitled to exact a proportionate compensation or penalty from the wrongdoer.[41]

However, Jesus in the antithesis boldly counteracts this OT prescription by saying 'But I tell you ...' and teaches his disciples to forgo this legal right. 'Do not resist' (μὴ ἀντιστῆναι) could mean 'do not take legal action against'.[42] This legal interpretation follows the thought of legal retribution in the thesis and thus affords a proper antithesis. Evil (τῷ πονηρῷ) does not mean 'the evil one' nor an evil principle but rather 'evil deed' (Hagner, *Matthew 1-13,* p. 131) or an evil person (France, *Matthew Commentary,* p. 126). Jesus is not here condoning evil social principles/ethics or evil politics, nor is he reforming the judicial system by abolishing the rule for retribution. He is teaching his disciples to renounce the legal rights that they are entitled to in terms of recompense.

There follow after the antithesis four illustrations of this non-retributive approach to life. To strike someone on the right cheek was 'a blow with the back of the hand, which even today in the East expresses the greatest possible contempt and extreme abuse'.[43] The penalty for such an offence was a very heavy fine.[44] But Jesus teaches his disciples not only to refrain from demanding a lawful recompense, but to offer the other cheek! This kind of compliance to one's adversary (implied) was unheard of and contrary to common sense. Non-retaliation or giving up the right of recompense may be practicable. One wonders whether turning the other cheek to invite or allow further contempt and damage is literally to be obeyed. It might be a very vivid and surprising rhetoric to imprint this teaching on the minds of the hearers. Perhaps it is a radical spirit of total forgiveness which is in view here.

In response to litigation claiming one's tunic (undergarment), one should put up no defence and surrender not only the tunic but also one's cloak, which is more essential![45] 'Force you to go one mile'

---

40 France, *Matthew Commentary,* p. 125.

41 *Ibid.,* pp. 125-6.

42 *Ibid.,* p. 126.

43 Jeremias, *New Testament Theology,* p. 239. Quoted by France's *Matthew Commentary,* p. 126.

44 See Mishnah, B.K. 8:6, referenced by France, *Matthew Commentary,* p. 126.

45 Even though a cloak is not to be taken away from its owner overnight on humanitarian ground (Exo 22:25-27).

(ἀγγαρεύσει) was a term for a Roman soldier's practice of enforcing someone to be a porter, which was greatly resented by the Jews. But rather than refusing to yield to such foreign imposition, Jesus' disciples were to volunteer to go twice the distance. Lastly, there is to be a total compliance to anyone who seeks to borrow from the disciples! To practise the above literally in an evil and greedy world would quickly make one bankrupt, exhausted and injured. These rhetorical remarks were probably meant to illustrate, with shocking and lasting effect on the audience, how one might lead one's life in a radical spirit of forgiveness, generosity and selfless grace which is utterly different from, in fact the opposite of, the spirit of the world where retributive vengeance, greed, self-preservation and the exploitation of others almost have their universal reign.

It should be noted that non-retaliation was taught in Prov. 20:22, 24:29 and at Qumran (1 QS. 10:18-19).[46] For example Prov. 24:29 reads, 'Do not say, "I'll do to him as he has done to me; I'll pay that man back for what he did."' But these are not truly comparable to Jesus' new teaching here in terms of thoroughness, powerful illustrations, and the spirit of positive/active grace as opposed to passive non-retaliation. Moreover, again Jesus sets his new teaching against the OT provision of retribution, which is not paralleled by any Jewish teaching.[47] Therefore, here again Jesus, who brings in the Kingdom of God, exercises his authority as the Lord and *reveals* the ultimate and radical will of his Father. He stands fearfully alone not only in contemporary Judaism but also in the history of religions in terms of the content, rhetoric and *authority* of his *radical new* teaching. This already powerful and shattering antithesis paves the way for the final climax of the antitheses.

3.2.3 LOVE YOUR ENEMIES (MATTHEW 5:43-48)

You have heard that it was said, 'Love your neighbour and hate your enemy.' But I tell you: Love your enemies and pray for those who persecute you, that you may be sons of your Father in heaven. He causes his sun to rise on the evil and the good, and sends rain on the righteous and the unrighteous. If you love those who love you, what reward will you get? Are not even the tax collectors doing that? And if you greet only your brothers what are you doing more than others? Do not even pagans

---

46 Hagner, *Matthew 1-13*, p. 131.

47 'Compliance and humility are also commended in the rabbinic literature as model attitudes. Matthew goes beyond the rabbinic norm of behaviour by setting the directive of compliance against the Old Testament-Jewish legal system.' Strecker, *The Sermon on the Mount*, p. 83.

do that? Be perfect, therefore, as your heavenly Father is perfect. (Mt. 5:43-48)

The first half of the thesis, 'Love your neighbour', is found in Lev. 19:18, in which context the neighbour was a fellow Israelite. 'Hate your enemies' is not explicitly found in the OT but is rather an interpretation based on passages such as Deut. 7:12; 23:3-6, 30:7; Ps. 139:21-22. This may be seen as a collective attitude towards a hostile foreign community.[48] The Qumran sect concretised this attitude of hatred in their Qumran Manual - 'that they may love all the sons of the light ... and hate all the sons of darkness (1 QS 1:3-3, 9-10; 19:21-22).[49]

Jesus' antithesis - 'But I tell you: Love your enemies and pray for those who persecute you' - could well be a shocking bolt of lightning to the first hearers (as opposed to Christians in the twenty-first century) who were unaccustomed to Jesus' teaching because it went against human common sense and practice. In the context of the gospels, 'love' and 'prayer' are the two most positive actions that one could do for others. Here, the beneficiary of these actions are to be your enemies, who are actively persecuting you![50] It is this unusual behaviour and attitude of the disciples which mark them out as sons of the Father in heaven who showers his grace of sun and rain on people in an undiscriminating manner. The disciples of Jesus must rise above the ordinary norm of behaviour, i.e., the reciprocating love which could be found even amongst the tax-collectors and gentiles. Their love of others is not to be conditioned by the expectation of reciprocating reward. It is a self-giving, unconditional, undiscriminating love for all people. It is in this exercising of this love that the disciples attain τέλειός - which incorporates the meaning of perfection, wholeness and completeness[51] - in the sight of God who himself possesses these qualities and this love.[52]

Some comparisons with other teachings can be made to illustrate the uniqueness of Jesus' teaching here. Stoics and Cynics spoke about loving all people including the ungrateful (Strecker, *The Sermon on the Mount*, pp. 89-90) and Prov. 25:21-22 teaches about feeding your enemies. But the former does not bring out the force of Jesus' singling out one's enemies as objects of one's love; it does not have the *intensity*

---

48 It should be remembered that an individual alien in the land of Israel was to be welcome, Deut. 10:19; Lev. 19:34.

49 France, *Matthew Commentary*, p. 128.

50 The enemies could refer to those who persecuted the Matthean community but that should not be the exclusive meaning.

51 Bultmann, *Jesus*, pp. 102-3.

52 'Be perfect, therefore, as your heavenly Father is perfect.' echoes closely 'Be holy because I, the Lord your God, am holy' (Lev. 19:2). See also Lev. 11:44-45, 20:26.

of Jesus' antithetical teaching here.[53] The latter has expectation of reward in mind. In Jewish literature, there was the mention of prayer for one's foes but this too was conditioned by the hope of their conversion to Judaism.[54] However, Jesus' teaching is total and intense: *loving* your *enemies* and *praying* for them purely for their sake without the motivation for reciprocating reward or gratitude. His teaching, taking the logically extreme position, has reached perfection without remainder. Moreover, his teaching is not merely an advice, a mention of a philosophical ideal, or an inspired opinion without obligation to obey it. His teaching is his concrete demand on his disciples invested with his own divine authority. It exceeds the demand to love one's neighbour in the Torah and in that sense extends and fulfils the Torah. His disciples are expected by the teacher to imitate the Father in heaven by an actual practice of this new teaching, this unconditional love. It is the mark of his disciples in the Kingdom of God and by it they are to be salt and light of the world (5:13-15). In this unique and revolutionary teaching, Jesus has no parallel and no genuine comparison can be made with him; he stands in unadorned singularity at an unapproachable height not only in contemporary Judaism but also in the history of religions in the world.[55] This is the teacher being portrayed in the Sermon on the Mount. This is the Son who *reveals* not only the radical will of his Father but also his relentless egocentric authority, through which the relentless authority of his Father is also revealed.

This idea of unconditional love - already indicated in the first antithesis, underlying the thoughts in the second and the third antitheses,

---

53 'Seneca gives the advice: "When you imitate the gods ... then give good also to the ungrateful, for the sun also rises over the criminals, and the ocean is open to the pirate" (*de benef. IV* 26). At this point the Stoic philosopher, of course, is thinking of the regular operation of nature, to which he is supposed to accommodate himself in his thinking and acting, in order to reach the ideal of a dispassionate, wise person. But the Q tradition of our saying is different - not an ideal of humankind but the unconditional demand of Jesus, not the regularity of nature but the self-identical action of the Creator independent of human effort.' Strecker, *The Sermon on the Mount*, p 90.

54 *Ber.* 10a; *Sanhedrin* 37a, *Midr Ps.* 41 *(Str-B* 1:370-371), quoted by Strecker, *The Sermon on the Mount*, p. 89, footnote 63.

55 'The commandment to love one's enemy is an example of the independence of Jesus' ethical radicalism both vis-à-vis his Jewish surroundings and in comparison with the Christian church. In this absolute orientation, the commandment is not attested in its religious-historical environment.' Strecker, *The Sermon on the Mount*, p. 88. Also, 'R. Bultmann is therefore correct when he claims of this and the related sayings that they "contain something characteristic, new, reaching out beyond popular wisdom and piety and yet are in no sense scribal or rabbinic nor Jewish apocalyptic."' Banks, *Jesus and the Law in the Synoptic Tradition*, p. 201.

and ringing out loudly in the fifth antithesis - is here brought to the clearest, most direct and climactic expression and fulfilment. It shatters our normal human ethical expectation and practice. It exposes ruthlessly our human inadequacy and bankruptcy. It shines the light of truth into the darkened human heart. It awakens and humbles every complacent soul and calls for a true moment of decision. It *reveals* the heart of the Father and the heart of Jesus in this revolutionary, awe-inspiring teaching of the unconditional love of God, which in due course finds its concrete and climactic expression/fulfilment in the passion narrative of the Son, who is like his Father in every way, even in this perfect divine love (cf. Mt. 5:48).

3.3 Conclusions from the Antitheses

It should be evident by now that the antithetical form of Jesus' teaching in Matthew is extremely important for portraying the unique teaching and authority of Jesus. Granted, there might be teachings in Judaism and Hellenistic philosophy which bore some resemblance to his teaching. However, there are some crucial differences.[56] The Jewish teachings never set themselves against the teaching of the Torah. They either espoused their opinions as interpretations of the Torah, or, expressed their opinions at some distance from the Torah when these opinions differed from or contradicted the Torah itself (e.g., the Essenes, or the Qumran Community, on not using oaths). In both cases, potential conflict with the Torah was avoided. However, in Matthew Jesus boldly set up a teaching from the Torah in the thesis, and then in the antithesis altered it by intensifying/extending/surpassing its meaning or abrogating it altogether.[57] In short, Jesus made alterations to the Torah in his new teaching.[58] But he gave no apology for his action. He did not soften the

---

56 'Despite the many attempts among Jewish, and some christian, scholars to fit the authority of Jesus within the general framework of Pharisaic Judaism, at almost every point we have noted a formidable gap between them. Where rabbinic methods or argument appeared to be present, only formal similarities could be detected ... [I]n both aspects [the teaching of Jesus and his person] he broke through and transcended the categories of contemporary Judaism. Other endeavours to find similarities between the form of Jesus' teaching and that of rabbis indicated that, while verbal parallels sometimes do exist, ... substantial differences occur in the instruction that is given and the authority with which it is conveyed. Most significant is the culmination of Jesus' instruction in the command to follow him, a call to a life of discipleship for which no real parallel can be found in the rabbinic writings. His was a unique ministry expressing itself in a unique teaching and stemming from a unique authority.' Banks, *Jesus and the Law in the Synoptic Tradition*, p. 262.

57 This is also true of the first three antitheses. Hence, this is true for all six antitheses.

58 'As for the relationship between Jesus' authoritative utterances and the Old

potential conflict with the Torah by diluting/relativising his teaching. Rather, he purposefully intensified and absolutised his teaching to the limit in order to fulfil the Law and the Prophets, even at the cost of being misunderstood as speaking against the Torah (Mt. 5:17). His teaching was not given in the form of advice, a personal opinion or even some ethical ideal as in Hellenistic philosophy, such that the hearers had no obligation to obey it. His approach to his hearers was far from casual. He confronted his hearers with his personal authority - 'But I say to you' - and demanded them to make a decision concerning him and his teaching for he would be their eschatological judge (Mt. 7:21-23).[59] As Barth comments, his presence demands a response and decision from them.

> The exciting of that astonishment [at Jesus' presence] was not an end, let alone an end in itself. His existence was not in any sense neutral. There could be no neutrality, therefore, in face of it. It was a question which demanded either a Yes or No. And if the answer was Yes, it meant a resolute redirection and conversion of the whole man ... His existence, which derived from a prior decision, involved decision in those whom He encountered. It brought to light what was in them, who and what they were. It divided them both within themselves and among themselves. It brought about separations between and among themselves. It brought about separations between man and man which had nothing whatever to do with other differences or antitheses, but ran right across them, and even across the closest of ties. He was present and decided as the Judge, bringing about and bringing to light the final divisions in and among men.[60]

Jesus was well aware of the momentous significance of his teaching - it is the new teaching of the Kingdom of God, it is the radical will of his Father. He was aware of the very high and even sovereign authority that was necessary in order to wield this new teaching with power and decisiveness. Yet he did not cringe from exercising this high authority

---

Testament words with which they are introduced, we have noted once again that it is a surpassing or transcending of the Law that is the keynote throughout. His teaching cannot be regarded merely in terms of the "exposition" or "completion" of the Law, its "radicalisation" or "sharpening", or the "abrogation" of some or all its commandments.' Banks, *Jesus and the Law in the Synoptic Tradition*, p. 203. Also, 'The Kyrios stands over the Torah; his authority makes it possible to be critical of the Torah, which leads even to dissolving individual commandments and setting up new instructions.' Strecker, *Sermon on the Mount*, p. 62.

59 Strecker has pointed this out very well, *Sermon on the Mount*, pp. 88-90.

60 *CD* IV.2, p. 157.

in a public manner. He was not found wanting in the delivery of his speech. (The fact that the Sermon on the Mount is a collection of his sayings does not detract from this point. Rather, it shows the ubiquitous nature of Jesus' authority in his preaching ministry.) Characteristically he spoke with supreme conviction, certainty, boldness and confidence. This manner of speech is not found only in the six antitheses, nor only in the Sermon on the Mount, nor only in Matthew. It is a ubiquitous feature of all the four gospels. In this connection, Jeremias' study of the 'amen' sayings of Jesus in the four gospels is instructive.[61] According to Jeremias' finding, what has been observed in the three (or six) antitheses of the Sermon on the Mount is also true of the four gospels: Jesus always spoke with his characteristic authority, without compromise and without the fear of men. He sometimes punctuated his sayings with the *amen* clause, at other times his egocentric authority came through the manner and content of his speech. But he was not one who blindly exercised this authority without the quality of his teaching for its match. No, his authority was always matched by the wisdom, depth, liveliness, power and intensity of his speech so that his words came as an amazement to his hearers (Mt. 7:28,29; Mark 1:27; Luke 4:32). He struck at the heart of the matter when he taught about human relationships and their relationships with God. He saw through the

---

61 'It has been pointed out almost *ad nauseam* that a new use of the word *amen* emerges in the four gospels *which is without analogy in the whole of Jewish literature and in the rest of the New Testament.* Whereas according to idiomatic Jewish usage the word *amen* is used to affirm, endorse or appropriate the words of another person, in the tradition of the sayings of Jesus it is used *without exception* to introduce and endorse Jesus' own words. The formula is always ἀμὴν λέγω ὑμῖν (σοι) in the synoptics, and ἀμὴν, ἀμὴν λέγω ὑμῖν (σοι) in John. There are 13 instances in Mark, 30 in Matthew, 6 in Luke and 25 in John. *So we have a completely new manner of speaking, strictly limited to the gospels and here again limited to the sayings of Jesus.* Here the *amen* serves to replace oath-like formulae of asserveration which Jesus forbids in Mt. 5:33-37 because they are a misuse of the divine name; it is even more likely that the formula *amen* should be seen as an alternative to the authoritative prophetic formula "Thus says the Lord", which avoids using the divine name. The only question is whether it is probable that on occasion the tradition has introduced this *amen* into the sayings of Jesus.' Jeremias, *The Prayers of Jesus,* p. 112. By comparing the parallel sayings in the synoptic gospels, Jeremias found that the tendency was for these *amen* introductory clauses to be dropped, rather than introduced. It is therefore possible that there were more such sayings imbued with Jesus' personal authority in the traditions than what we can find in the synoptic gospels. Jeremias concluded, 'So, in the *amen* sayings, too, we have the emergence of a new and completely unique manner of speaking. And once again, the new form is matched by a new content. *Here is a consciousness of rank which lays claim to divine authority.* Once again, we have here without question an incontestable linguistic characteristic of the *ipsissima vox Jesu.*' *Ibid.,* p. 115. Italics mine.

bankruptcy of the human heart - its hypocrisy and its pride (see his teaching on almsgiving, prayer and fasting in 6:1-18), its disrespect for fellow human beings male or female (see first three antitheses), its deceitfulness (fourth antithesis), its vengefulness, its lack of generosity, its limited and conditional love (fifth and sixth theses). He taught his disciples the true righteousness of God which exceeded the legalism and externalism of the Pharisees and teachers of the law, which called for no half measures but their full and total commitment. He used vivid and powerful imageries and parables (and ironies too) to bring out the *intensity* of his teaching (e.g., turning the other cheek, cutting off the right arm, gouging out the right eye, go a second mile, do not let your left hand know what your right hand is doing, why do you look at the speck of sawdust in your brother's eye and pay no attention to the plank in your own eyes? ...). He often delivered his line with a punch: love your enemies; let your 'yes' be 'yes', and your 'no' 'no'; do not give dogs what is sacred; do not throw your pearls to pigs (7:6) ... When he spoke about his disciples' relationship with God, in a revolutionary manner he taught them to call upon God intimately as *abba* - Father. By comparing the value of the disciples, the birds of the air and the grass of the field in their Father's eyes, his rhetoric most powerfully forced them to conclude that there was no way the Father's loving providential care would leave them (6:25-34; cf. 10:29-31). Likewise, if earthly fathers know how to give good things to their children, the disciples have to conclude that it is impossible that their Father in heaven will disregard their prayers (7:7-11). The four gospels are full of the wisdom of Jesus which is delivered with great liveliness, intensity, power and his personal authority. The temple guard sent by the chief priests to arrest Jesus witnessed to this ubiquitous feature of Jesus as they returned to the chief priests empty-handed and declared, 'No-one ever spoke the way this man does'(John 7:46). Barth likewise described Jesus' presence amongst the people as an 'amazing presence' and an 'unforgettable presence' in 'The Royal Man' of *CD* IV.2 .

> [I]t is obvious that those who report it [Jesus' impact on the people] wish to point through and beyond these to the One who spoke and acted. He Himself was a source of amazement and even alarm to the people. He was an absolutely alien and exciting *novum*. This was how He was seen by His community. This was How He was present to them.[62]

As one ponders upon the nature of the characteristic authority that he exercised, one can only describe this authority as constant, relentless and insuperable. As E. Käsemann commented, 'Jesus felt himself in a

---

62 *CD* IV.2, p.157.

position to override with an unparalleled and sovereign freedom, the words of the Torah and the authority of Moses.'[63] But as only God himself has the proper authority to change or abrogate parts of the Torah, the authority with which he spoke, for example in the six antitheses, can only be God's sovereign authority. The immediate question is: God was in heaven and Jesus was on earth, why was it that Jesus was able to exercise this sovereign authority in his teaching on earth? The question of his authority was the one raised by the chief priests and the elders in Jerusalem (21:33). The related question is about his wisdom: how did he receive such wisdom in his teaching? This was the question raised by the people of his home town - Nazareth - when they heard him there (13:53-56). The former question regarding Jesus' authority will be dealt with initially in section 4 and in greater detail in chapter 6. Concerning the latter question of Jesus' wisdom, or his knowledge of his Father's righteous will, one can infer that he knows his Father's will intimately and without a shadow of doubt; otherwise he would not have been able to teach his Father's righteous will with such conviction, certainty, force and intensity. His certain and intimate knowledge of his Father's righteous will can only be explained by the non-linear concept of revelation given by Mt. 11:25-30 and will be considered further in section 5.

It has been mentioned that Jesus fulfilled his teaching in the fourth antithesis on honesty and truth by faithfully completing his journey to the cross. Likewise, his teachings on non-retaliation and unconditional love in the fifth and sixth antitheses respectively were also fulfilled in his suffering and death.[64] It has now become evident that, indeed as Barth observes, Jesus' teaching and action were inextricably linked together. As he *fulfilled* his own teaching on righteousness *in his own life and action* (cf. Mt. 5:17), his teaching comments on his life and action, and vice versa, so that we are presented with a more comprehensive picture of Jesus Christ.[65] Considering this in terms of

---

63 E. Käsemann, 'The Problem of the Historical Jesus' in *Essays on New Testament Themes* (London: SCM Press, 1964), p. 40.

64 Jesus' teaching and action often come to their climactic end in his suffering and cross, as already indicated.

65 Matthew has alluded to Jesus' self-fulfilment of his teaching in 10:24,25 - 'A student is not above his teacher, nor a servant above his master. It is enough for the student to be like his teacher, and the servant like his master.' On one hand, the disciples are to seek the righteousness as taught by the teacher in the Sermon on the Mount. On the other they are to be like the teacher. These mean that if they succeed to realise the righteousness in the Sermon on the Mount they will be like their teacher. But this requires the precondition that the teacher himself has fulfilled, or will continue to fulfil, the righteousness he teaches. Mt. 16:24 - 'If anyone would come after me, he must deny himself and take up his cross and follow me.' - also alludes to the same

revelation, Jesus *reveals* his Father's righteousness in words and in actions as the picture of Jesus we see *reflects* God. But as he reveals his Father's righteousness in these, his relationship with his Father is also revealed in the following manners. Firstly, it is revealed that he is the Son *like* his Father who is perfect and complete (cf. Mt. 5:48). Secondly, he *loves* his Father and *obey* his Father's righteous and perfect will from beginning to end (cf. Mt. 22:37). Thirdly, as mentioned above, he *knows* his Father's will surely and intimately as witnessed by the certainty of his teaching concerning that will (cf. Mt. 11:27). Thus it can be concluded that as Jesus reveals his Father on earth, he also reveals his relationship with his Father who is in heaven. This dual revelation is not surprising in view of the fact that the basis of his revelation of his Father is his intimate relationship with his Father. In Jesus' revelation of his Father, in one way or another this basis of revelation - characterised by knowledge, love, obedience and likeness - is also revealed. Accordingly, this book emphasises Jesus' intimate relationship with his Father both in the basis of revelation and in the content of revelation, which characterises the non-linear concept of revelation.

4.0 Jesus' Lordship and His Revelation of His Father's Lordship

Jesus' teaching of the kingdom of God was radical, different and unique in that it transcended normal human understanding and expectation. But it is also radical in that it extended and fulfilled the OT teaching. Barth writes concerning the radical and uncompromising nature of Jesus' teaching and his person,

> For Jesus, and as seen in the light of Jesus, there can be no doubt that all human orders are this old garment or old bottles, which are in the last resort quite incompatible with the new cloth and the new wine of the kingdom of God. The new cloth can only destroy the old garment, and the old bottles can only burst when the new wine of the kingdom of God is poured into them. All true and serious conservatism, and all true and serious belief in progress, presupposes that there is a certain compatibility between the new and the old, and that they can stand in a certain neutrality the one to the other. But the new thing of Jesus is the invading kingdom of God revealed in its alienating antithesis to the world and all its orders. And in this respect, too, the dictum is true: *neutralitas non valet in regno Dei*. There is thus concealed and revealed, ..., the radical and indissoluble antithesis of the kingdom of God to all human kingdoms, the

---

point. See the similar comments by Strecker and Kingsbury in chapter 2, footnote 134.

unanswerable question, the irremediable unsettlement introduced by the kingdom of God into all human kingdoms.[66]

[W]e do not really know Jesus (the Jesus of the New Testament) if we do not know Him as ... this revolutionary.[67]

To be able to teach in the radical way as Jesus did, one must have supreme confidence in one's authority. The authority that his teaching called for, and the authority that he wielded, was nothing less than the authority of God. Jesus thus revealed himself to be the Lord through his radical and authoritative teaching. Barth eloquently writes,

There can be no doubt about the full and genuine and individual humanity of the man Jesus of Nazareth, but in that man there has entered in and there must be recognised and respected One who is *qualitatively* different from all other men. He is not simply a better man, a more gifted, a more wise or noble or pious, in short a greater man. But as against all other men and their differences we have in the person of this man One who is their Lord and Lawgiver and Judge. He has full power to condemn them or to pardon. He has full power to call them and bind them to Himself. ... In attestation of this understanding of the man Jesus the New Testament tradition calls Him the Messiah of Israel, the *Kyrios*, the second Adam come down from heaven, and, in a final approximation to what is meant by all this, the Son or the Word of God. It lifts Him right out of the list of other men, and as against this list (including Moses and the prophets, not to mention all the rest) it places Him at the side of God.[68]

In the last chapter when considering the identity of Jesus Christ in Matthew, it was noted that Matthew deliberately takes Mt. 3:3 from the lips of the Baptist and changes the LXX translation of Isaiah 40:3 in order to identify Jesus with Yahweh, meaning Jesus is everything the name of Yahweh represents. This is done with the clear understanding of Jesus' post-resurrection universal Lordship. Jesus' identification with Yahweh at the beginning of the gospel together with his universal Lordship at the end form an inclusio which brackets Jesus' life, ministry and death. Within this bracket, Matthew expounds by his narratives what Jesus' Lordship, or his identification with Yahweh, comprises.[69]

---

66 *CD* IV.2, p. 177

67 *CD* IV.2, p. 180

68 *CD* IV.1, p. 160. Italics mine.

69 Hence, Luz's judgment that Matthew advocates a Christology "from above" from a narrative standpoint without identifying Jesus as God is not entirely true. See his *The Theology of the Gospel of Matthew*, p. 32. Matthew does present his Christology

With such an understanding of the literary structure in Matthew, Jesus' Lordship and sovereign authority expressed in his teaching, the Sermon on the Mount in particular, can be readily appreciated. The expression of this Lordship in sovereign authority in his life and ministry is of a piece with his identification with Yahweh at the beginning and end of Matthew's gospel. This is how Matthew presents his Christology comprehensively and skilfully, both by titles and by narratives. However, J.D.G. Dunn understands Jesus' authority in a very different manner, attributing it to the inspiration of the Spirit, but not to his inherent Lordship. His view raises serious questions about the identity of Jesus and his relationship with the Spirit, which will be dealt with in chapters 5 and 6.

Jesus' Lordship also raises the question of his relationship with the Father, apart from his relationship with the Spirit. To the readers of Matthew's gospel, the question might be: do not Jesus' Lordship and his Father's Lordship constitute a double or dual Lordship? This question concerning unity will be tackled in chapter 6. But the Jesus in Matthew does not seem to have any difficulty in exercising his own Lordship/authority and at the same time acknowledging his Father's Lordship/authority. From the manner of his speech, one can only conclude that he felt it was his Father's will for him to proclaim this new teaching with a sovereign/insuperable authority which is equal with his Father's, without even invoking the name and authority of his Father or the inspiration of the Spirit, such that people's attention was drawn to him who had such authority.[70] He seemed to understand that his exercise of Lordship and authority did not threaten his Father's Lordship and authority but in fact was fulfilling his Father's pleasurable will.[71] And he might well understand that *it is only in his undiminished Lordship and authority that he can truly reveal his Father's Lordship and authority in person*. Otherwise, his speech would have been a prophet's speech (thus says the Lord ...), not God's direct and powerful speech (but I tell you ...), and he would have been unable to reveal his Father's sovereign Lordship on earth *in person*. For God's revelation *in person* to take place, there has to be a *personal correspondence and likeness* between the person revealing God and God himself. Jesus possesses this *personal correspondence and likeness*, here in terms of the sovereign authority in speech. And being in correspondence to God and likeness of God in person, being in full consonance with God in the spirit of

---

using narratives but he also identifies Jesus with Yahweh even though he does not use explicitly the term 'God'.

70 Regarding the inspiration of the Spirit, it might be more correct to say that the writer does not invoke Jesus' inspiration by the Spirit as an editorial comment.

71 Cf. Phil. 2:11.

authority and majesty through the Holy Spirit, Jesus was able to speak with sovereign authority as God personally would speak and thus faithfully revealed his Father *in person* on earth. Barth's emphatic point, Jesus Christ has to be God in order to reveal God, is true. Any dilution of the divine Lordship and sovereign majesty of Jesus Christ disqualifies him from a true and undiminished revelation of his Father's divine Lordship and sovereign majesty on earth.

5.0 Jesus' Humanity in Knowing His Father's Will

The Lordship of Jesus plays a crucial role in his teaching and revelation of his Father's righteous will. But do his true humanity and the Holy Spirit also have important roles to play in this revelation? This question will be answered by considering how Jesus in his genuine humanity knew his Father's righteous will for him and for the disciples in the kingdom. After the people of his home town, Nazareth, heard his teaching, they questioned the source of his wisdom and teaching (Mt. 13:53-56). If one takes the humanity of Jesus seriously as people in his home town did, this question inevitably arises. The answer to this question may lie in Mt. 11:25-30, where we are given the insight of the basis of Jesus' revelation of his Father - his close communion with and intimate knowledge of his Father. It is possible that Jesus in his genuine humanity received the content of the new teaching of the Kingdom of God from his Father as he drew close to his Father through prayer and meditation of the OT Scripture in the Spirit. The time Jesus spent in the wilderness might be a time such as this, when after his baptism he was led by the Spirit to draw close to his Father in prayer and fasting before launching into his ministry. However, this time also turned out to be a time of temptations.

Commentaries on Matthew (e.g., France, Hagner and Schweizer) have correctly observed that Jesus' responses to the temptations were all drawn from Deut. 6-8. While the words of the second temptation explicitly came from Psalm 91, it will be shown that in the first and third temptations Scriptural passages from Deut. 6-8 might also have been used to tempt Jesus, as Jesus' responses, also from Deut. 6-8, indicated. In these temptations, the idea of Jesus' identification with Israel is crucial. The passage probably relevant to the first temptation is Deut. 8:2-3 where Moses reminded the Israelites how during the forty years of testing in the wilderness Yahweh provided them (his children or *son*, 8:5) with manna for food.[72] Now, Jesus the *Son* of God was in the forty days of temptation and became hungry. It is probable that while meditating over these verses, Jesus was confronted with the

---

72 France, *Matthew Commentary*, p. 98.

interpretation suggested by the devil that, since he was the Son of God, miraculous provision to fill the Son's hunger would not be out of order given his parallel with Israel as suggested by Deut. 8:2-3. It was an attractive interpretation both physically and spiritually (spiritually because of his identification with Israel and his recapitulation of Israel's experience from Egypt to Jordan and the wilderness). But this interpretation or application was a dangerous one, being contrary to the will of his Father which was for him to identify with Israel/humanity in such a way that he truly shared their real struggles and experiences. It is possible that the Spirit who led Jesus into the wilderness also led Jesus to this passage in Scripture in his meditation but, while the devil suggested an attractive but dangerous interpretation, the Spirit conveyed the true significance of these verses to him - obedience, living by the word of God (Deut. 8:3), not filling his hunger (or using his power for his own convenience or gain). Max Turner also arrives at a similar interpretation regarding the role of the Spirit in affording Jesus 'charismatic wisdom and insight, which is the basis of the hoped-for Messiah's redoubtable righteousness'.[73]

The words of the second temptation explicitly comes from Psalm 91 and do not need to be treated here for the present purpose of considering the means by which temptations came to Jesus. The context of the third temptation is probably Deut. 6:10-12, where Israel was promised that it would inherit the land of Canaan with 'large and flourishing cities ..., houses filled with all kinds of good things ..., wells ..., vineyards and olive groves ...', from which the Israelites would eat and be satisfied.[74] And Israel was reminded: after receiving this inheritance from Yahweh, 'be careful that you do not forget the Lord who brought you out of Egypt, out of the land of slavery'(v. 12). It is possible that Jesus while meditating on this promise to Israel in Deut. 6:10-12 was confronted with the suggestion by the devil that likewise he, the fulfilment of Israel, should also inherit the land and build a kingdom of splendour of his own in the world.[75] After all, he was God's beloved Son brought out of

---

73 Turner, *The Holy Spirit and Spiritual Gifts: Then and Now*, pp. 29-30.

74 See France, *Matthew Commentary*, p. 99-100 for this possible context. And Moses' view of the promised land from Mount Nebo in Deut. 34:1-4 could also be relevant.

75 The trip to a high mountain to see *all* the kingdoms of the world is probably a subjective visionary experience as there could not be such a mountain nearby. See France, *Matthew Commentary*, p. 99 and Hagner, *Matthew 1-13*, pp. 63, 68. Likewise, the trip to the temple may also be non-literal, and it does not need to be literal in a mental temptation. As Matthew clearly states that the temptations happened in the wilderness, two physical trips to a high mountain (to see all kingdoms of the world) and the temple are probably not meant. This observation strengthens the hypothesis that the temptations happened mentally as the Spirit led Jesus to meditate over passages of Scripture, especially those in Deuteronomy.

Egypt (Mt. 2:15, cf. Deut. 6:12). Should he not inherit the land as Israel did? Should not the Davidic king and Messiah build a kingdom of power and splendour as his forefather did? But to tread that path of worldly kingdom and splendour amounted to worshipping and serving a different god who was no god at all but Satan. It is true that path would win him great popularity, support, wealth, power, luxury and pleasure in that kingdom of the world, and spare him from the humble and in the end lonely and painful path to the cross. It had all these attractions but in the end it would be a denial of the true God and a spurning of his calling and mission. Jesus in his wisdom through the Spirit distinguished the world of difference between these two choices of serving God and serving Satan and vehemently rebuked Satan with the words of Deut. 6:13, 'Worship the Lord your God, and serve him only.'

The Moses-Jesus typology and the Israel-Jesus typology will be considered for a further interpretation of Jesus' temptations. Moses received the ten commandments (Law) from God, in his intimate presence, on Mount Sinai (wilderness) in *forty* days and *forty* nights before delivering them to Israel (Exo 34:28-29, Matthew uniquely amongst the evangelists includes forty nights to reflect Jesus' parallel with Moses as the Law-giver). Israel spent *forty* years in the wilderness and was tempted.[76] Jesus' temptations in the wilderness for *forty* days and *forty* nights could allude to these two events together in the following way. In drawing close to his Father in prayer and fasting in the forty days, Jesus was seeking his Father's will for his forthcoming ministry, e.g., the content of the new teaching (the new Law which will soon be delivered to Israel in the Sermon on the Mount), by meditating over Scripture and being guided by the Spirit throughout the whole time of fasting, prayer and meditation (Moses-Jesus typology). But it was in this time of Spirit-led meditation that dangerous interpretations of passages of Scripture were suggested to him by the devil (Israel-Jesus typology). It could be that Jesus through the Spirit knew his Father's will by discerning the correct interpretation for him concerning his identification with Israel (Son and son) and thereby obediently and resolutely aligned his will to his Father's.[77] It is true that the interpretation of Jesus' temptations and the role of the Spirit presented above is a theoretical one because Matthew does not explicitly *tell* his readers those connections. But in view of the Moses-Jesus typology in Matthew (e.g., both as law-giver who spent forty days and forty nights before God),[78] in view of Jesus' close identification with Israel as the

---

76 For the allusions to Moses and Israel regarding the figure 'forty', see Hagner, *Matthew 1-13*, p. 64.

77 Again, see Turner's *The Holy Spirit and Spiritual Gifts*, pp. 29-30.

78 See France's *Matthew: Evangelist and Teacher*, pp. 186-9.

Son of God and his recapitulating Israel's path from Egypt through the water and the wilderness to the promised land, and in view of the close association of the temptations with specific passages of Scripture (especially from Deuteronomy), Matthew might be *showing* his readers (possibly Jewish) that such an interpretation of Jesus coming to seek and know his Father's will in the wilderness in a subjective spiritual experience involving the Spirit and Scripture is a genuine possibility.[79]

If this possibility is not discarded, then one might understand that Jesus did not bypass his humanity in his communion with God and approach to God. In particular, he receives his Father's righteous will in intimate fellowship with his Father through the Spirit before revealing it to the people in his life and speech. This is what Mt. 11:27 strongly indicates, as shown in chapter 2 on the non-linear concept of revelation. It is true that Jesus possessed and exercised his divine Lordship and *authority* in his teaching, which cannot be attributed to his humanity. But in the process of receiving the *content* of his teaching from his Father through the Spirit, his humanity may still be very much involved though perhaps not at the exclusion of his divinity (cf. Barth's comment on the Son receiving 'all things' from the Father without limit, quoted in 4.0 of chapter 2 from *CD* IV.1, p. 178). Jesus Christ, in receiving his Father's will and proclaiming his will, is both Lord and servant, who identifies with humanity in drawing near to God and makes his Father known through his Lordship.

---

79 There is a further reason for seeing the events in the wilderness as Jesus' spiritual experience of his Father through the Spirit, not only as facing temptations from Satan. This reason is based on a certain uniformity regarding Jesus' experience of his Father presented in Matthew. Jesus' spiritual experiences of his Father explicitly presented in Matthew are his baptism, his transfiguration and his forsakeness on the cross. These spiritual experiences of Jesus all have to do with the Father's will (particularly on the servant's suffering) and Jesus' obedience: the first two concern Jesus' receiving his Father's will and mission for him, which is completed in the third. The events in the wilderness were also about Jesus' obedience to his Father's will, and are tightly tied to the themes of the baptism episode - his identification with needy humanity and his eventual death (see Barth's interpretation of Jesus' baptism and his temptations in 3.1 of chapter 4). If these events in the wilderness are treated as Jesus' spiritual experience of his Father as suggested, then they fall in line with Jesus' other spiritual experiences of his Father presented in Matthew, i.e., all these spiritual experiences of Jesus in Matthew concern his Father's will for him (including his death) and his resolute obedience.

CHAPTER 4

Jesus' Revelation of His Father through His Actions

At the end of Jesus' speech in the Sermon on the Mount in Mt. 5-7, the crowd were amazed at his authority which set him apart from other teachers of the law (7:29). In Jesus' works in Mt. 8-9, Matthew continues to present Jesus' relentless authority. The dominant impression the reader receives throughout chapters 5 to 9 is therefore the unparalleled authority (and Lordship) of Jesus.[1] The other element which runs through these chapters on Jesus' words and actions is closely associated with Jesus' authority and Lordship - his radicalism. Jesus not only gives radical teachings in relation to the Old Testament and Jewish practices (as in the Sermon on the Mount), he also acts radically in his works amongst the people, crossing boundaries and barriers set up in Jewish traditional beliefs and customs. It takes authority and courage to challenge and overcome these barriers which were steeped in these Jewish traditions and beliefs. But Jesus in his Lordship has no hesitancy in exercising his authority to bring in the radical new acts of the kingdom of God, so that the people in need can be touched, healed and liberated by the undiscriminating love of God (5:45). As the story in Matthew develops, Jesus' radicalism is increasingly opposed by the Jewish religious leadership, to the extent that the leaders decide the author of this 'dangerous' radicalism has to be removed. However, this 'dangerous' radicalism which they decide to stamp out along with its author is precisely the radicalism of God, a radicalism which cannot be commensurate with the thinking of the world and cannot be overcome by the world.

Strictly speaking, Jesus' actions in Matthew chapters 8 and 9 also involve his words but these activities of Jesus are grouped under the

---

1 W.D. Davies, *The Setting of the Sermon on the Mount* (Atlanta: Scholars Press, 1989), pp. 90-1.

heading of actions in order to differentiate them from Jesus' discourses where only his words are involved. Because this chapter and the last deal with the common theme of Jesus' revelation of his Father through his life-act, Barth's comments on Jesus' life-act and his correspondence to God, and the concluding summary, presented in this chapter inevitably relate also to the last chapter.

1.0 The Radical Liberating Acts of Jesus

1.1 Healing of the Leper (Mt. 8:1-4)

When he had come down from the mountain, large crowds followed him. And look, a leper came to him and knelt down before him, saying, 'Lord, if you want to, you are able to cure me.' And Jesus extended his hand and touched him, saying, 'I do want to. Be whole.' And he was immediately cleansed of his leprosy. And Jesus said to him, 'Be careful not to tell anyone of this. But go and show yourself to the priest and bring as an offering the gift commanded by Moses, as a witness to the people.'[2]

This is the first miracle of Jesus presented by Matthew in his gospel. The desperate state of the leper could be understood not only in terms of his physical suffering but also in terms of the devastating psychological effect of this disease.[3] A leper is ceremonially unclean and lives away from his family and the community.[4] He is to announce his proximity to other people by calling out 'Unclean! Unclean!'[5] No one is to make any physical contact with him; a person who touches him becomes unclean.[6] The lepers are therefore the untouchables of the society/community who live in hopeless misery. It is in this desperate state of need that this leper approaches Jesus and seeks his healing and cleansing, saying, 'Lord, if you want to, you are able to cure me.'

Jesus responds to this leper positively and heals him by his action and by his word. He extends his hand to touch him and verbally confirms his willingness to heal by saying, 'I do want to. Be whole.' He could have healed the leper by merely uttering the word of healing (see 8:8 of the immediately succeeding miracle), but Jesus in a radical expression of his love is not hindered by the taboo of touching an unclean man, deliberately extends his hand to touch and heal him. And he does this

---

2   Translation by Hagner, *Matthew 1-13*, p. 196.

3   The disease could be what is now known as Hansen's disease or some other less serious skin disease. These are all covered by the term 'leprosy' in the Old and New Testament. See Hagner, *Matthew 1-13*, p. 198.

4   Leviticus 13:45-46.

5   *Ibid.*

6   Leviticus 5:3.

apparently in front of a large crowd. What is the significance of his action?

One can entertain the thought that Jesus thoroughly understands the leper's need and his physical touch on this untouchable may bring him psychological healing and loving acceptance. This could be an important aspect of his healing. Here the significance which is to be focused on is that Jesus wills not to heal him from afar, he wills not to let any barrier bar him from drawing close to this leper, that he confronts this ritual barrier, breaks it and transcends it by purposefully extending his hand to touch and heal the leper. There can be no holding back of his love to this needy person; there can be no prevailing obstacle obstructing his love. In this he, as the perfect Son who is like the Father, reveals his Father's undiscriminating, compassionate and radical love on earth (5:45-48). This radical and undiscriminating love of God overcomes and transcends all boundaries and barriers to reach humanity in need, as shall be seen also in other acts of Jesus. Jesus in revealing his Father's love reveals his radicalism in this move. Just as he was ready to transcend the Torah with his radical new teaching in the Sermon on the Mount, here he is prepared to transcend the Torah's prohibition on touching the unclean with his radical new action. In his radicalism, Jesus is bringing what is new and liberating in the kingdom of God (cf. 9:17 about new wine). But bringing and wielding what is new and radical in God's rule or kingdom requires authority and boldness for it to be decisive and effective. One without authority and courage simply cannot bring oneself to such ground-breaking work. Here, Jesus' authority is already seen, not only in the direct, unencumbered and bold manner in which he extends his hand to the leper and breaks the ritual barrier, but also in the manner of his speech and the result that it brings. The words - 'I do want to. Be whole. (Θέλω, καθαρίσθητι)' - betray the underlying fact that it is within Jesus' own will, freedom and authority to decide the fate of this man, whether he will be cleansed and liberated or remain bound as he was. He does not need to ask a higher authority for miraculous power, or solicit help by some kind of incantation in order to heal.[7] Who is he that he is able to do all these? According to Matthew, he is the Lord (Mt. 3:3) and therefore has his own proper authority and freedom not only to transcend ritual barriers, but also to bring healing to the needy and the sick. Lastly, his Lordship, freedom and authority, manifested in his radical act and comforting speech, is vindicated, confirmed and revealed in the miraculous recovery of the leper. His recovery shows that Jesus' Lordship, freedom,

---

7 For Barth's comments on the distinctive aspects of Jesus' miracles compared to other so-called miracles of the time which involved elaborate procedures, see *CD* IV.2, pp. 214-9.

radicalism and undiscriminating love are not in vain, that his act and speech are not those of a self-deluded fanatic with an inflated ego. His radical act and speech are indeed those of the true and compassionate Lord who has the authority to bring in the liberating rule and kingdom of God.

In Matthew's presentation, Jesus is the Lord (3:3) who in every way - in his will, word and action - shows himself to be the true author of this healing. He does not invoke another authority or another name in healing as some do, e.g., in 7:22 those who drive out demons and perform miracles in Jesus' name (cf. Acts 3:6 where Peter heals a crippled beggar in Jesus' name). Rather, he exercises his own will and his egocentric authority ('I do want to.') in his word and action in this healing. In this sense he is set apart from his disciples and those OT figures who performed miracles with authority not inherently their own (e.g., 1 Kings 18:36f; 2 Kings 2:21, 3:16, 4:43). While Jesus' disciples and the OT figures can be regarded as secondary authors or channels of miracles, Jesus in Matthew's presentation is the true and proper author of this miraculous act.

Matthew identified Jesus as the Lord through 3:3. That is a conceptual and proper understanding of Jesus. However, Matthew elaborates what the Lordship of Jesus consists of through the narratives of Jesus' teachings in the Sermon on the Mount and his acts of healing and power after the sermon. Here, in the first miracle of healing presented by Matthew, Jesus' word and action witness to his own authority and hence his inherent Lordship.

Even though Matthew clearly presents Jesus as the author of this act of healing, it is implicit that this healing action is also the action of God. In the order of Matthew's presentation, at this point he does not explain how the action of Jesus the Son can also be implicitly seen as the action of God the Father. This explanation he reserves until 11:25-30 after the presentation of Jesus' words and actions in chapters 5-9 and the disciples' mission in chapter 10 is completed. Mt. 11:25-30 clearly attributes the works of Jesus (and his disciples in their mission) to God - 'Father, ..., you have hidden these things from the wise and learned, and revealed them to little children.' Also, it is in the context of Jesus' close and unique communion with the Father that the Father is revealed through the Son's work (11:27, the non-linear concept of revelation). Or, through the Father's communion with his Son, the Father partakes in the work of his Son and reveals himself through his Son. In that sense, the work is both the Father's work as well as the Son's. John 14:10 expresses the same idea - 'Don't you believe that I am in the Father and the Father is in me? The words I say to you are not just my own. Rather, it is the Father, living in me, who is doing his work.' There is a concurrency between the Father and the Son in the Son's work. In particular, Matthew presents Jesus' authority as his very own (hence his egocentric authority), yet this authority is not exclusively his own because it also rightly belongs to his Father. Neither Matthew nor John makes explicit the exact nature or mechanism of this concurrency but they both point to its indispensable foundation in the Father's communion with the Son. However, some understanding can be gained by a consideration of the Spirit. It is legitimate to infer from the gospel of Matthew (and John) that the Spirit is involved in the communion between the Father and the Son, and hence that the Spirit is involved in the concurrency of the work of the Father and the Son.[8] Also, from Mt. 12:28 - 'But if *I* drive out demons by the Spirit of God, then the kingdom of God has come upon you.' - it is legitimate to infer that the Spirit is the executive power simultaneously of the Father and the Son in mighty acts, in particular in this miracle.[9] With this understanding of the relationships between Jesus, the Father and the Spirit, this miracle of healing the leper can be, and should be, appreciated and interpreted in this wider context. One thus sees that in healing this leper, Jesus exercises his compassionate will, his authority and the Spirit's power in unison and in fellowship with his Father through the same Spirit, thus revealing his Father and his unity with him. (Or, in the communing presence of his Father, he shares the one compassion with his Father and exercises the healing in and with him. A more detailed discussion of this non-linear concept of revelation will be given in chapter 6 on a Theology of the Trinity). The healing of this leper, when interpreted in the wider context of the gospel, is an example of Jesus' revelation of his Father who himself is Lord, who in his radicalism transcends every barrier and reaches out to those in need through his Son with his compassionate and undiscriminating love, which he shares with his Son through the Spirit. The non-linear concept of Jesus' revelation of his Father in Mt. 11:25-30 finds its concrete expression in this the first miracle presented in Matthew's gospel.[10]

---

8 To see how the Spirit is involved in the communion between the Father and the Son, see the exegesis of Mt. 11:25-30 in chapter 2 and further considerations in chapter 6.

9 The idea that the Spirit is the executive power of Jesus the Son, or that Jesus is the Lord of the Spirit, will be considered in greater details in chapter 5. Even here, it can be seen that in Jesus' exercise of his Lordship he is presented as more than a human being inspired by the Spirit.

10 The above interpretation of the miracle shares the basic features with interpretations found in commentaries on Matthew, e.g., Jesus breaking the taboo of touching a leper, but it differs from these interpretations in the following ways. Here, firstly the radical nature of Jesus' act of compassion is emphasised in consonance with the radical nature of Jesus' teaching on undiscriminating love (5:45-48). Secondly, Jesus' egocentric authority and sovereign Lordship is highlighted in consonance with his radicalism, i.e., his radicalism is not bereft of authority but accompanied by his

1.2 Healing of the Centurion's Servant (Mt. 8:5-13)

When Jesus had entered Capernaum, a centurion came to him, asking for help. 'Lord,' he said, 'my servant lies at home paralysed and in terrible suffering.' Jesus said to him, 'I will go and heal him.' The centurion replied, 'Lord, I do not deserve to have you come under my roof. But just say the word, and my servant will be healed. For I myself am a man under authority, with soldiers under me. I tell this one, "Go," and he goes; and that one, "Come," and he comes. I say to my servant, "Do this," and he does it.' When Jesus heard this, he was astonished and said to those following him, 'I tell you the truth, I have not found anyone in Israel with such great faith. I say to you that many will come from the east and the west, and will take their places at the feast with Abraham, Isaac and Jacob in the kingdom of heaven. But the subjects of the kingdom will be thrown outside, into the darkness, where there will be weeping and gnashing of teeth.' Then Jesus said to the centurion, 'Go! It will be done just as you believed it would.' And his servant was healed at that very hour.

Matthew's presentation of Jesus' authority, radicalism and undiscriminating love is already evident in the first of the miracles. In the second miracle, Matthew continues with these themes about Jesus and in some way heightens the theme of his authority and radicalism. A centurion whose servant is in great need comes to Jesus for help.[11] The centurion is implicitly a gentile in this narrative.[12] Jesus responds to him by saying, 'I, having come, will heal him.'[13] Because a Jew would become unclean if he visits a gentile's house, some scholars have interpreted Jesus' response to the centurion as a question, expressing his

---

sovereign authority. Thirdly, this miracle is interpreted in the wider context of Matthew's gospel where the concept of revelation in 11:25-30 and the concept of the executive power of the Spirit in 12:28 help to illuminate the involvement of the Father and the Spirit in the action of Jesus. Commentaries by their very nature often deal with the verses in a passage locally and deals with passages linearly, i.e., one passage after another, such that theological connections and themes between different passages are difficult to make. However, the above interpretation makes use of these connections and themes to put Jesus' act in the context of his Lordship (3:3), his teaching on radical love (5:43-48), and his relationship with his Father through the Spirit (11:25-30), all of which are proper to the gospel of Matthew. The themes of Jesus' Lordship, radicalism and his relationship with his Father will be further pursued in the studies of the next two pieces of narrative.

11 The one in need could be the centurion's son instead of his servant, see Hagner, *Matthew 1-13*, p. 204. And in Luke 7:1-10, the centurion does not come to Jesus himself but sends some elders of the Jews to plead with Jesus. But these make no difference to the thrust of this narrative.

12 See Hagner, *Matthew 1-13*, p. 203.

13 Ἐγὼ ἐλθὼν θεραπεύσω αὐτόν. Translation by Hagner, *Matthew 1-13*, p. 204.

surprise at the centurion's request.[14] But Matthew is probably portraying Jesus' readiness to go to the centurion's house without any hesitancy so that Jesus' response here is a statement of intent rather a question (see the parallel in Luke 7:1-10 where there is no hint of Jesus' hesitancy).[15] He is quite prepared to go to the centurion's home himself and heal his servant even though it means that he will incur the risk of being accused of breaking Jewish customs and rendering himself ritually unclean. His boldness in transcending this ritual barrier for the sake of reaching out to the needy is of a piece with his boldness in touching the unclean leper in the previous miracle. In both miracles, he wills not to let any barrier stop the undiscriminating love of God from touching the lives of those in need.[16] In Matthew, he as the Lord has the authority to overcome the barrier and make this radical move in a public manner.

However, the centurion seems to understand the inconvenience (of ritual uncleanliness) that such a visit will cost Jesus. He therefore requests Jesus merely to utter the words of healing, believing that will be sufficient for his servant's healing. His reasoning is that as the soldiers under him are subjected to his authority and word of command, so Jesus has the authority over the power of sickness and therefore can overcome it by a word. Jesus marvels at the centurion's faith in him which even supersedes those of the Israelites. Matthew, apart from portraying Jesus' authority in teaching and in transcending Jewish customs, here highlights Jesus' egocentric authority in healing - he can exercise healing at his own will and merely by his word with palpable

---

14 See France's *Matthew Commentary*, p. 154, where this interpretation is cited.

15 Hagner, *Matthew 1-13*, p. 204. Jesus' readiness to heal the centurion's servant by his word (presented later in the narrative) contradicts the suggestion that Jesus has any hesitation about healing a gentile's servant. For the discussion of Jesus' and the disciples' ministry amongst the Jews and gentiles, see Hagner, *Matthew 1-13*, pp. 270-1, France, *Matthew Commentary*, pp. 177-8. In Mt. 15:21-28, Jesus was apparently reluctant to heal the Canaanite woman's daughter. However, the real point of that pericope is about the gentile woman's faith - 'Woman, you have great faith' (v. 28). A gentile's faith is also prominent in the present pericope about the centurion. Through these two pericopes, Matthew may be presenting the greater faith of these gentiles, compared to the Jews, to his Jewish readers so that their faith may be aroused. Therefore, these two pericopes are not about Jesus' reluctance to reach out to gentiles, which is also contradicted by his great commission to make disciples of all nations at the end of the gospel.

16 Jesus' radicalism is evident and consistent in much of Jesus' teachings and actions in Matthew. Taking Jesus' word here as a statement rather than a question is consistent with his radicalism in the gospel. See, e.g., another of Jesus' radical acts in Mt. 9:9-13 which will be dealt with shortly. This is another justification for the interpretation adopted here.

result, even at a distance from the patient.[17]

If Jesus manifests his radicalism by showing no hesitancy in visiting a gentile's house, his radicalism in breaking the gentiles/Jews divide is heightened to a shocking degree in his comments about the Messianic banquet.

> The imagery [of 9:11] is that of the Messianic banquet (cf. 26:29; Luke 14:15; 22:30), a prominent theme in Jewish eschatological expectation, derived from Isaiah 25:6, but narrowed down in both apocalyptic and Rabbinic writings to be an exclusively Israelite blessing, under the presidency of the Hebrew patriarchs, Abraham, Isaac and Jacob.[18]

The subjects/sons of the kingdom (v. 12) are the Jews while their corresponding contrast, the 'many' from the east and the west, are meant to refer to the gentiles. The offence of Jesus' statement comes in twofold. Firstly, the sons of the kingdom, the Jews, will be excluded from the joyful celebration of the victory of God at the end times while the gentiles are admitted as the people of God.[19] Secondly, a Jew will contract ritual defilement if he sits at a table with a gentile; here Jesus envisages the Israelite patriarchs, Abraham, Isaac and Jacob, to sit with gentiles as fellow guests at the Messianic banquet. Apparently, all this will happen in accord with the will of the God of Israel! If Jesus' readiness to visit a gentile's house is a sign of his radical move to break down the gentiles/Jews divide, his words here escalate that sign of his radicalism to an explicit, offensive and astonishing level. But he shows no scruple in uttering this radical and offensive statement to the Jews in Capernaum; he prefaces this statement with 'I tell you the truth' (Ἀμὴν λέγω ὑμῖν') in verse 10, followed by 'I say to you' (λέγω δὲ ὑμῖν) in verse 11. As in the Sermon on the Mount, here he exercises his Lordship, freedom and egocentric authority when he categorically utters what is radical and new in the kingdom of God - that God's love will cross every boundary and barrier to those who have faith in his Son

---

17 The centurion's words of faith include 'For I myself am a man under authority.' This might raise the question of what authority Jesus is under. Accordingly, some Old Syriac version have instead 'a man with authority' to mitigate this question. However, this alteration is unnecessary since the centurion's main point is not about his being under authority, but about others under his authority. And Matthew uses the centurion's word here not to raise the question of the source of Jesus' authority, but to highlight the authority Jesus himself possesses. See France, *Matthew Commentary*, p. 155.

18 France, *Matthew Commentary*, p. 156.

19 The criteria of entry into the banquet, in the context of this passage, is of course faith, not race, whether gentiles or Jews.

Jesus (cf. the healing of the leper above and 5:43-48). His Lordship and radicalism in his word and action again are vindicated by the result of healing: the servant was healed at that very hour.

It is clear here, as elsewhere, in Matthew that Jesus knows his Father's radical will intimately through their communion (11:27). And being in consonance with his Father's mind and will, he faithfully reveals his Father through his radical words and actions of undiscriminating love. Yet, in Jesus' revelation of his Father's radical love, Matthew does not present a Jesus who is utterly dependent on his Father such that he has no authority of his own. The narrative here presents a Jesus who possesses his own authority and who freely exercises that authority to heal and pronounce the new things in God's kingdom at his will. He is the Son of the Father, obedient to him, and at the same time the Son himself is Lord. Barth recognises this Lordship of the Son when he interprets this particular miracle, and all other Jesus' miracles.

> Those who believe in Jesus Christ have to do *ipso facto* with the *Lord of heaven and earth*, i.e., with the One who can dispose in the whole realm of reality distinct from God, and who does actually dispose always and everywhere. ... The faith which (according to Mt. 8:5f) Jesus did not find in Israel, but in the Gentile centurion of Capernaum, is that confidence in Him in which the centurion begs Him to speak only a word and his servant will be healed, just as he himself says to one of his soldiers, Go, and he goeth; and to another, Come, and he cometh; and to his servant, Do this, and he doeth it. But at this point we should really refer to *all* the accounts in the gospels which show us that *Jesus really possessed this power and freely exercised it*; that He found faith, i.e., this trust in His power, in all kinds of hopeless sufferers, and that these people simply counted on the fact that He could help them if He were *willing* to do so. ... What would the four gospels be without this *constant reference to the possession and exercise of power by Jesus*, and without the constant appeal to believe in Him as the Bearer of this power? [20]

But this raises the question of the relationship between Jesus' Lordship and his Father's Lordship, and the concomitant question of concurrency, the sharing or unity of authority and will between Jesus and his Father. These will be considered in chapter 6 on a theology of the Father, Son and Holy Spirit.

---

20 *CD* III.1, p. 35. Italics mine.

1.3 Jesus and the Sinners (Mt. 9:9-13)

As Jesus went on from there, he saw a man named Matthew sitting at the tax collector's booth. 'Follow me,' he told him, and Matthew got up and followed him. While Jesus was having dinner at Matthew's house, many tax collectors and 'sinners' came and ate with him and his disciples. When the Pharisees saw this, they asked his disciples, 'Why does your teacher eat with tax collectors and "sinners"?' On hearing this, Jesus said, 'It is not the healthy who need a doctor, but the sick. But go and learn what this means: "I desire mercy, not sacrifice." For I have not come to call the righteous, but sinners.'

The leper was excluded from his community because of his uncleanliness. The gentile centurion was excluded from close fellowship with the Jews because of his race. Such exclusions were hardly due to their own deliberate faults; they were the results of their physical ailment or natural birth. Jesus in his radical love and Lordship overcame these barriers and exclusions and reached out to them. While the leper and the gentile centurion were innocent and victims of exclusions, the tax collectors and other sinners were certainly responsible for their own behaviour, which had led them to be excluded from fellowship with their fellow Jews. Should these deliberate sinners and traitors receive favour from Jesus which was entirely unmerited? The barrier to fellowship here is not one of an involuntary ailment or race; it is one of deliberate sin. Should God break and transcend this barrier of sin and have fellowship with sinners and tax collectors who have deliberately turned their back on society, their own countrymen and God? This question is implicit in Matthew's presentation of this narrative. In the immediately preceding narrative where Jesus forgives the sin of the paralytic and heals him, Matthew presents Jesus and thus God as willing to forgive sin. Here, the question of Jesus' and God's attitude to sinners is taken one step further: is Jesus and thus God willing to have fellowship with sinners? This critical question, implicit in this narrative and explicit in the words of the Pharisees to Jesus' disciples, finds a radical answer from the mouth of Jesus which lies at the heart of his ministry (and of Christianity), but which is offensive and scandalous to those who are 'righteous'. Here lies one of the crucial points of Matthew's gospel and its force should not be evaded or dulled by the church's familiarity with it in the last two millennia.

The account of Jesus' call to Matthew in v. 9 is brief but the main point is that Jesus wills to choose to call a tax collector to be one of his disciples. The tax-collectors are people who have betrayed their own countrymen by working for the foreign Romans and extorting unfair taxes from them.[21] Tax collectors are despised and hated by their countrymen for being extortionate traitors, who are also ritually unclean (see last footnote). Their exclusion from decent society is the result of their deliberate choice of a profession which is inevitably tainted with greed and sin. The Jews' attitude towards them is quite understandable. Jesus' radicalism is revealed in the fact that he does not hate and despise them as other Jews do, that he draws near and comes personally to one of these - Matthew - and gives him the opportunity to be one of his disciples! It is clear that Matthew has not come to Jesus himself or acted in any way that would earn him such an invitation from Jesus (if that is possible). It is Jesus' own initiative to call this tax collector to be his disciple. Matthew accepts Jesus' invitation and in turn invites him to a dinner at his house where the attendants include yet more tax collectors and sinners.[22]

Table fellowship in the Jewish culture is an important symbol of closeness, indeed the oneness, of those participating.[23] Those who are sitting at the table with Jesus, apart from his disciples, are traitors and outcasts of the society. Yet Jesus, knowing what this table fellowship would imply, draws close to them, has fellowship with them in an act of acceptance and identification, apparently displaying no discomfort or signs of bad conscience. He as the Lord is willing not only to forgive sin (9:1-8) but also to have close fellowship with sinners. Here lies the

---

21 'The prevailing method of tax collection afforded collectors many opportunities to exercise greed and unfairness. For centuries force and fraud had been constantly associated with the revenue system of Palestine (*Nedarim* 3:4). Hence *telonai* [tax collectors] were hated and despised as a class. Strict Jews were further offended by the fact that the tax collector was rendered unclean through continual contact with Gentiles, and because his work involved breaking the sabbath.' *NIDNTT*, vol. 3, p. 757. 'A Jew entering the customs service cut himself off from decent society. He was disqualified from being a judge or even a witness in court, and excommunicated from the synagogue. The members of his family were considered to be equally tarnished (*Sanhedrin* 25b). Because of their exactions and extortions, customs officials were in the same legal category as murderers and robbers (*Baba Kamma* 113a), thieves (*Tohoroth* 7:6), the robbers and money-changers (*Derek 'eres* 2), and counted among ... the common herd (*Bekhoroth* 30b). Money handled by tax collectors was tainted and could not be used, even for charity (*Baba Kamma* 10:1), for to touch the wealth of a man who obtains it unlawfully is to share his guilt.' *Ibid.*, p. 756.

22 "Sinners" is 'a term which could apply to ... the common Jewish people who could not or would not keep the scribal rules of tithing and purity (among them the tax collectors were prominent), but is used more widely of the immoral (Luke 7:37ff), heretics (John 9:16f) and Gentiles (Gal. 2:15), as well as tax collectors.' France, *Matthew Commentary*, p. 167.

23 Hagner, *Matthew 1-13*, p. 238.

scandal of his radical act; here lies the offensive nature of his love which transcends not only the ritual barrier of uncleanliness (cf. the leper and the centurion) but also the ultimate barrier of sin. In this love, Jesus reveals the radical and unconditional love of his Father who accepts and draws close to sinners as Jesus does (cf. 5:43-48). But the Pharisees can hardly interpret Jesus' act as a revelation of God's unconditional love; they interpret it as undermining Jesus' credibility as a teacher from God and therefore ask, 'Why does your teacher eat with tax collectors and "sinners"?' The implied answer in the mind of the Pharisees can only be a negative one.

Jesus responds to their question with a proverbial saying about the sick, not the healthy, needing a doctor.[24] The sick alludes to the sinners, the healthy to the righteous, of the last sentence of this narrative. The doctor alludes to Jesus himself. The doctor has come to bring relief to the patients/sufferers of sin, not to alienate them and condemn them as the Pharisees do.[25] Alienating the patients can only lead to a deterioration of their condition; what they need is not alienation but fellowship and help. The teacher, whose credibility is far from being undermined, now gives a piece of OT Scripture (from Hosea 6:6) for the Pharisees to learn.[26] What God desires is not an outward adherence to rules or external piety which the Pharisees are quite capable of offering, but a heart of mercy, forgiveness, acceptance and unconditional love (cf. the first, fifth and sixth antitheses of the Sermon on the Mount). The teacher, far from contravening God's Torah, is himself fulfilling it and embodying God's radical will in his concrete words and actions amongst the tax collectors and sinners. In this, Jesus reveals the good news of the mercy of God not only to sinners in Israel but to all nations of the world. However, the 'righteous', the self-assured Pharisees do not seem to appreciate Jesus' words of wisdom here. To them surely the righteous, not the unrighteous, should be called and favoured, and Jesus' teaching and practice cannot be God's will. Their determination to oppose Jesus grows as Jesus' radicalism continues to unfold in his forthcoming ministry of words and actions. In the end, they believe that eliminating Jesus and his dangerous teachings from Israel is to remove a stumbling block to the coming of the kingdom of God - a responsible service to God.

---

24 See Hagner, *Matthew 1-13*, p. 239 for a similar saying by Diogenes in the fourth century B.C.

25 John 3:17, 'For God did not send his Son into the world to condemn the world, but to save the world through him.', expresses the same idea of God's mercy.

26 Hosea 6:6 is not quoted in the parallels in Luke and Mark. Its presence here serves to highlight the notion of God's mercy, and consequently our mercy, to sinners; this notion is already evident in the pericope and characteristic of Jesus' ministry.

Matthew presents Jesus speaking here, as elsewhere in his gospel, with his characteristic native authority, wisdom, freedom and Lordship. Even though his word and action here amount to an infringement of Jewish beliefs and customs to an astonishing level, he shows no hesitancy in uttering his radical word, he gives no apology for his revolutionary action. From the manner of his word and action, we can infer he is certain that he is acting according to God's radical will and thus revealing him. Mt. 11:25-30 informs us that this certainty is based on his intimate knowledge of or communion with his Father who has committed all things (about God's revelation) to him. Despite this apparent dependence on his Father and his receiving of all things from his Father, Jesus feels able to exercise authority and Lordship freely as his very own - he himself is the *subject* who has come to call sinners (9:13) to follow him (9:9).[27] His sense of egocentric authority and Lordship seems to co-exist without difficulty with his sense of dependence on his Father. This co-existence of dependence and egocentricity will be further considered in chapter 6 on the theology of the Father, Son and Holy Spirit.

2.0 Comments on Jesus' Liberating Acts and Radical Teachings

Limited space in this book has allowed only a selective treatment of Jesus' liberating acts and his radical teachings. As well as the Sermon on the Mount, much more could be said about the other four discourses attributed to Jesus by Matthew. And the other eight miracles by Jesus presented in chapters 8 and 9 could be studied to heighten further his relentless, insuperable and egocentric authority/Lordship over nature, demons, sin, other diseases and finally death. Furthermore, the clash between his radical love and righteousness and the Pharisees' legalism can be further highlighted by studying his interchange with the Pharisees (and the teachers of the law) over the issues of fasting (9:14-17), observing the Sabbath (12:1-14) and food laws (15:1-20). However, the limited and selective treatment of Jesus' words and actions presented above is a reasonable representation of the fuller picture of Jesus portrayed by Matthew - Jesus in his sovereign Lordship teaches the radical unconditional love of God, and fulfils this his radical teaching in his life and ministry by reaching out to the needy, the excluded, the marginalised, the hopeless and the outcasts, freely transcending and overcoming every ritual barrier and every human boundary with his uncompromising authority, Lordship, freedom and radical love. In all these radical teachings and actions, Jesus is not

---

27 'For I have not come to call the righteous, but sinners' (οὐ γὰρ ἦλθον καλέσαι δικαίους ἀλλὰ ἁμαρτωλούς) (9:13). 'Follow me' (Ἀκολούθει μοι) (9:9).

speaking and acting on his own because he knows that he is fulfilling the will of his Father who is with him. Despite all the serious confrontations and controversies with the religious leaders, and their accusations and threats, Jesus shows no sign of compromise or retreat but finds rest in his Father's presence as he unites himself with his Father's will in these actions (11:28-30). This rest in his Father is particularly manifested in the fearless manner in which he speaks and acts as he in his radicalism challenges the traditions and beliefs held dear by the religious leaders. His relationship with his Father not only affords him rest in the face of hostility, but it is the basis of his revelation of his Father (11:27). Through their fellowship/communion in the Spirit, he shares the will and mind of his Father, he has the same compassion and love for the suffering and needy as his Father has. In this consonance with his Father in heart and mind, in this unity with his Father in will and spirit through the Spirit, the Son of God on earth corresponds to his Father in heaven and thereby reveals his Father who is now to be understood as the God of this radical undiscriminating love seen in Jesus, contrary to the beliefs of many religious leaders and ordinary Jews of the day.[28]

---

28 However, Jesus' revelation of God's acceptance and love for sinners does not mean that he and his Father condone sin. His equally radical teaching against sin in the six antitheses and elsewhere (e.g., 18:6-9, which uses the language of maiming parts of the body) makes certain his demand for righteousness. How can his 'liberal' attitude to sinners be reconciled with his 'absolute' demand for righteousness? This question can be answered only from the perspective of his mission associated with his name, which is to save the people from their sins (1:21). There are at least three elements in Jesus' saving work. Firstly, the sick (sinners) are not able to heal themselves and lift themselves out of sin. They need the loving acceptance of the doctor/saviour who comes alongside them, teaches them, shows them by example the way of love and righteousness, urges them to repent and follow him in seeking God's kingdom and righteousness, trusting in the Fatherhood of God and finding rest in him. Secondly, Matthew presents Jesus as giving his life as a ransom for many (20:28) for the forgiveness of sins (26:28). In Jesus, sin is dealt with as his identification with sinners is completed in his death on the cross, accomplishing the loving saving purpose of his Father. Thus those who are guilty can now draw near to God and call out to him as their Father without the burden of guilt and fear of condemnation but with the assurance of God's acceptance and unconditional love. Thirdly, Jesus as the resurrected Lord will continue to be with his disciples, to assist and guide them, as they seek to teach and obey his commands (28:19). These are the three elements found in Matthew of how Jesus saves the people from their sins, according to the loving and saving purpose of his Father. On one hand, his disciples are to follow Jesus to do their utmost to fulfil God's righteousness with the help of the presence of the resurrected Lord; on the other hand, they are assured of God's forgiveness, acceptance and Fatherly unconditional love. This is how Jesus' and his Father's drastic demand for righteousness and their unconditional love co-exist. In Matthew,

It has been pointed out in 3.3 of chapter 3 that Jesus' relationship with his Father is not only the basis of his revelation of his Father, but it is also part of the content of this revelation. That is, on that basis, Jesus reveals not only his Father, but also his relationship with his Father. In Jesus' radical liberating acts presented above, one can discern from his words and actions some aspects of his relationship with his Father, as already hinted above. Firstly, despite the unconventional, controversial and radical nature of his words and actions, the manner of Jesus' words and actions witnesses to the fact that he has absolute certainty he is speaking and acting in full harmony with his Father's will. This is possible only if he knows his Father's will intimately, and in obedience speaks and acts according to that will (Mt. 11:27). Secondly, the courage that he shows in his fearless confrontations with the religious leaders witnesses to his unwavering trust and rest in his Father who loves him and reigns sovereign over all things, even in these confrontations (Mt. 10:28-30; 11:28-30). Therefore, Jesus in revealing the radical nature of his Father's unconditional love also reveals his intimate relationship with his Father, which at the same time is the basis of his revelation of his Father (11:27). This is to be expected because if his relationship with his Father is central to his life and thoughts, this relationship will be manifested in one way or another in his words and actions. And this relationship is characterised by knowledge, obedience, trust and rest in the Father's love. It is in the context of this relationship, and in his own Lordship, that the Son is like the Father and reveals him.

Matthew in 4:23-25 gives a condensed summary of Jesus' ministry of words and actions in Galilee, followed immediately by Jesus' teachings on the Sermon of the Mount in chapters 5 to 7. Chapters 8 and 9 present mainly Jesus' acts of healing and exorcism, and his exchange with the Pharisees on the questions of eating with sinners and his disciples' fasting. At the end of chapter 9 (vv. 35-38), Matthew gives another condensed summary of Jesus' ministry, which with the first summary forms an inclusio bracketing the details of Jesus' ministry of words and actions. In this second summary, the inner feeling of Jesus in his ministry of words and actions towards the people - compassion - is explicitly referenced while it needed to be inferred from his words and actions in the narratives within the body of the inclusio (such inferences are vindicated by this summary). Jesus not only teaches about love in the Sermon on the Mount but he also speaks and acts in his ministry with the spirit of love and compassion. Given Jesus' teaching, speech,

---

Jesus thus saves the people from their sins through his teaching, life, death and resurrection, that is, through the whole span of his earthly existence and his post-resurrection Lordship, and it is not limited to his death as in much evangelical theology.

act and his spirit of compassion in Matthew's presentation of Jesus, one comes to know him as a whole person - not only outwardly in terms of words and actions or only inwardly in terms of attitude/spirit, but as a whole person outwardly and inwardly united and consistent in his own person. This consistency between his teaching, speech, act and attitude, which is evident in chapters 5 to 9, witnesses to the integrity of the person of Jesus Christ, the unity of his thoughts, words and actions, and the truth which is found in him (cf. the fourth antithesis on truthfulness: his 'yes' is 'yes', 'no', 'no').[29]

Barth devotes a subsection to an insightful discussion of Jesus' compassion for the crowd (Mt. 9:36) in 'The Royal Man' in *CD* IV.2. In 'The Royal Man', he also speaks of Jesus' unique presence, radicalism, Lordship, his correspondence to God and reflection of God. It is worth listening to his insightful comments and his powerful rhetoric, as a complement to the exegeses above.

2.1 Barth's Comments on the Presence of the Royal Man in His Words and Actions

Barth in *CD* IV.1 treated 'the humiliation of the Son of God' with his 'going into the far country'; in *CD* IV.2 he counter-balances this downward movement of the Son of God with the upward movement of 'the exaltation of the Son of Man' and gives a substantial treatment on the earthly life, ministry and death of Jesus Christ, whom he calls the Royal Man, which is the title of that subsection. He uses materials mainly from the synoptic gospels to portray a dynamic picture of Jesus in these sections of the *Church Dogmatics*. Even though the exegeses and presentation of Jesus above make use only of the first of the synoptic gospels while Barth uses three, it will be seen that his comments are in effect consistent with the above presentation and indeed give it greater breadth.[30] It is therefore appropriate to include his comments here.

Barth begins 'The Royal Man' by presenting the presence of Jesus in his earthly life, which can only be called a unique presence. This is a Christological treatment of the gospel narratives, focussing on the person and presence of Jesus Christ who is the exalted Lord (*CD* IV.2, pp. 156-66). Then he considers Jesus' correspondence to God in some details (pp. 166-192). This is Barth's attempt to understand Jesus Christ not only Christologically, but also in the context of his revelation or

---

29 Barth has much to say about the unity of the person of Jesus in his body and soul, in his inner and outer moments of existence, see *CD* III.2, pp. 325-44, 'Jesus, Whole Man'.

30 Or rather, the exegeses and presentations above have been influenced by Barth.

reflection of his Father. Therefore, there is a binitarian shape to his treatment there. He then considers the words and actions of the Royal Man in a rather conceptual manner (see Introduction to the last chapter) before ending with the Passion of the Royal Man. For the purpose of this chapter, Barth's treatments of the unique presence of Jesus and his correspondence to God will be of particular relevance.

2.1.1 THE UNIQUE PRESENCE OF THE ROYAL MAN IN HIS WORDS AND ACTIONS: JESUS THE EXALTED LORD

Barth comments on four important aspects of Jesus' unique presence which pertain to his Lordship. Firstly, Jesus' presence in his teachings and acts was an amazing presence to the people around him and many were drawn to him. He points out that in the gospels one often finds people are amazed, surprised or astonished by Jesus' presence, as has been shown in the exegeses of Jesus' teachings and actions above.

> The descriptions of His appearance resemble those of the effects of an earthquake or some other natural catastrophe. ... Blessed were the eyes and ears which were privileged to see and hear what was then seen and heard! For this was something unique. ... He Himself was a source of amazement and even alarm to the people. He was an absolutely alien and exciting *novum*. This was how He was seen by His community. This was How He was present to them.[31]

Secondly, Jesus' presence to the people demands a decision from them concerning him. His presence in his words and actions constitutes a judgment on the world which is then called to a critical decision either to follow him or reject him.[32] Thirdly, his presence is an unforgettable presence such that this unforgettable presence dominates and shapes the recollection of him by his community (his recollection is now found in the New Testament). Typically, Barth writes with a burst of verbalised exaltation.

> [H]e was among His fellow-men as the *Lord*, the royal man. To be sure, He was a man as they were. He did not enjoy or exercise divine sovereignty or authority or omnipotence. But all the same He was its full and direct witness. And as such He was unmistakably marked off from other men. He was a *free* man. Neither on earth nor in heaven (apart from His Father) was there anyone or anything over Him. For He was wholly *free to do the will of His Father*. He was not bound by any man, by any

---

31 *CD* IV.2, p. 157.

32 See the other quote from *CD* IV.2, p. 157 in 3.3 of chapter 3, 'Conclusions from the Antitheses'.

power of nature or history, by any destiny, by any orders, by any inner limits or obstacles. He did not stand or fall with any of these things, nor did He need to fear them. For Him there was only one imperative. Subject to this one imperative, and therefore not arbitrarily if not under any outward compulsion or constraint, He came and went with absolute superiority, disposing and controlling, speaking or keeping silence, always exercising lordship. This was no less true when He entered and trod to the end the way of His death and passion. Indeed, to those who looked back, it was even more plainly true on this way. The presence of the man of Nazareth meant the presence of a kingdom - the kingdom of God or the kingdom of heaven the tradition calls it. This is what made Him absolutely unique and unforgettable.[33]

Barth helpfully emphasises the Lordship and freedom of Jesus in his unforgettable presence. His Lordship is exercised and revealed in the way he came and went with absolute superiority, disposing and controlling, speaking or keeping silence right to the end of his earthly life. Barth also refers to Jesus' 'unforgettable lordliness and His irrevocability which bursts and transcends all the limits of His life and its time.'[34] Indeed, in the gospel narratives this Lordship is characterised by his peace and composure, his courage, his amazing wisdom, his remarkable freedom and Lordship, his constant authority, his being always in control, knowing what to say and how to act in every situation, even to the very end. Jesus thus reveals himself as the Lord not merely by reference to a name or title, but by concretely confirming in words and actions the name or title - Lord (3:3) or Immanuel (1:23) - which are rightly appropriated to him by Matthew (cf. 'Jesus as the Coming Lord' in chapter 2). Barth's understanding of Jesus' Lordship here is of a piece with Barth's treatment on God's revelation and the Trinity in *CD* I.1 where one of his favourite phrases is 'God reveals himself as the Lord' - here Jesus reveals himself as the Lord.[35] It is evident that the above exegeses on passages in Matthew (his teachings and his actions) have been influenced by Barth's understanding of Jesus' Lordship.

Fourthly and finally, Barth comments that Jesus' earthly presence is irrevocable in that nothing can change the community's memory of him, not even his death. Furthermore, after his resurrection and ascension they continue to relate to him as he was present to them before.

---

33 *Ibid.*, p. 161. Italics mine.
34 *Ibid.*, p. 165.
35 In so doing, Jesus also reveals the Father's Lordship (cf. '4.0 Jesus' Lordship and His Revelation of His Father's Lordship' in chapter 3).

The Lord whose memory they enshrine is not a dead Lord. He is not only *unforgettable* for the community, but it thinks of Him as the One who still is what He was. It is not the community, but He Himself who sees to it that He is not forgotten. He was *present irrevocably* - in a way in which His existence was not compromised or broken by His death. He was present to it. He lived in His community, and His community lived with Him. He was also future to it. It did not think of Him without expecting to see Him as the One of whom it thought.[36]

Taking Barth's four points together, Jesus Christ reveals himself as the Lord whose amazing presence imprints the unforgettable memory of himself on his disciples who continue to experience his irrevocable presence amongst them.

2.1.2 JESUS' CORRESPONDENCE TO GOD

Having focused on the presence and Lordship of Jesus Christ, Barth moves on to considering how Jesus corresponds to God and reveals him. This section on Jesus' correspondence to and thereby revelation of God is of particular interest to this book.[37]

The royal man of the New Testament tradition is created "after God" (κατὰ θεόν). This means that as a man He exists *analogously* to the mode of existence of God. In what He thinks and wills and does, in His attitude, there is a *correspondence*, a *parallel* in the creaturely world, to the plan and purpose and work and attitude of God. He *reflects* God. As a man He is His εἰκών (Col. 1:15). In the human sphere He is τέλειος in the same sense, directed to the same goal, as His Father is in the heavenly (Mt. 5: 48). In Him the will of God is done on earth as it is in heaven (Mt. 6:10).[38]

Barth discusses four aspects of Jesus' correspondence to God, only some of which need to be presented here in detail for the purpose of this chapter (some of his lengthy exegeses cannot be covered here). Firstly, Jesus' lowliness corresponds to God's lowliness. God is 'the One who is ignored and forgotten and despised and discounted by men.'[39] Despite Jesus' unique and amazing presence, Jesus likewise is also ignored, despised and discounted by men. Secondly, Jesus identifies with the

---

36 *Ibid.*, p. 163. Italics mine.

37 Jesus' correspondence to and thereby revelation of God has been discussed conceptually in chapter 2 and highlighted with specific examples in Jesus' ministry in the last and present chapters.

38 *Ibid.*, p. 166. Italics mine.

39 *Ibid.*, p. 167.

poor as God does. Effectively, here Barth is reiterating, but briefly, the same point that he makes in 'The Way of the Son of God into the Far Country' in *CD* IV.1 at considerable length. This point will be dealt with under the section on the passion of Jesus later. Thirdly, Jesus is not bound by world orders or values as God is not bound. 'The conformity of the man Jesus with the mode of existence and attitude of God consists actively in what we can only call the pronouncedly revolutionary character of His relationship to the orders of life and value current in the world around him.'[40] This point about Jesus' radicalism has been stressed in the above interpretations of gospel narratives which have also been influenced by Barth in this respect. Barth shows at some length how Jesus transcends the world orders and values regarding the family, the Temple and the Law, the economic and industrial orders, the political and judicial orders. He concludes this discussion by the following burst of warning and reminder.

> [W]e have first had to set Jesus against man and his cosmos as the poor man who if He blessed and befriended any blessed and befriended the poor and not the rich, the incomparable *revolutionary* who laid the axe at the root of the trees, who pitilessly exposed the darkness of human order in the cosmos, questioning it in a way which is quite beyond our capacity to answer. We do not know God at all if we do not know Him as *the One who is absolutely opposed to our whole world which has fallen away from Him* and is therefore self-estranged; as the Judge of our world; as the One whose will is that it should be *totally changed and renewed.* If we think we know Him in any other way, what we really know (in a mild or wild transcendence) is only the world itself, ourselves, the old Adam. In the man Jesus, God has separated Himself from this misinterpretation. And we have had to copy this divine separation in all that we have said so far. But again, we do not really know Jesus (the Jesus of the New Testament) if we do not know Him as this poor man, as this (if we may risk the dangerous word) partisan of the poor, and finally this *revolutionary.* We have to be warned, therefore, against every attempt to interpret and use Him as a further and perhaps supreme self-manifestation and self-actualisation of the old Adam.[41]

What Barth is pointing out here is that the decisive point at which Jesus corresponds to God is his utter contradiction to the world because God Himself contradicts with man and opposes human orders in quite an absolute manner. Jesus has to be absolutely different from the world if

---

40 *Ibid.*, p. 171.
41 *CD* IV.2, pp. 179-180. Italics mine.

he is to correspond to God his Father, according to Barth.[42] Barth does alert one to the fact that Jesus in his attitudes, words and actions was radically different from the people around him, especially the religious leaders.[43]

Fourthly and finally, Jesus corresponds to God and thereby reveals God in that Jesus is for us as God is for us. If Jesus' radicalism and contradiction to the world might signify his and God's judgment of the world, Barth immediately counter-balances these with a powerful and lengthy presentation of Jesus 'for us' as God is for us. If the third aspect of Jesus' correspondence with God is his 'No', then the fourth aspect is Jesus' and God's emphatic 'Yes'.

> The word which is really the first and the last word is undoubtedly that the man *Jesus, like God Himself, is not against men but for men* - even for men in all the impossibility of their perversion, in their form as the men of the old world of Adam. The decisive point to which we now turn is that the royal man *Jesus is the image and reflection* of the divine Yes to man and his cosmos. It is God's critical Yes. ... [I]t is a Yes and not a No, even though it includes and is accompanied by a powerful No. *It is the image and reflection of the love in which God has loved, and loves*, and will love the world; of the faithfulness which He has sworn and will maintain; of the solidarity with it into which He has entered and in which He persists; of the hope of salvation and glory which He has given it by giving no less than Himself. The man Jesus is the royal man in the fact that He is not

---

42 One may wonder if it is strictly necessary to express the difference between God and his creation - the world - in Barth's absolute terms. In Barth's assessment of this difference in absolute terms, we may well be hearing echoes of his struggle against the theology which too easily aligned itself to the kingdom of this world - in his experience the German state - which was the cause of so much suffering and atrocities in the First World War. He is extremely vigilant in separating God and man, true theology and natural theology, kingdom of God and kingdom of man, God's self-revelation and human religion (or self-dialogue, or self-manifestation), the new Adam and old Adam. This motif finds frequent expression in his treatment on the Word of God in *CD* 1.1 especially on the possibility of knowing the Word of God. With this appreciation of Barth's background and experience, one can understand his picture of God in absolute and rather violent reaction against human worldly orders. However, he also speaks of Jesus' passive conservatism in relation to the world, i.e., Jesus accepted and took part in the customs and practices in the world (of the Jews).

43 The appreciation of this fact may help the church to better understand the astonishing significance and meaning of Jesus' life and ministry and thus the radicalism of God, which should have a crucial impact on the life and ministry of the church, whose radicalism would then enable her to be the distinctive salt and light of the world, bringing honour to the Father in heaven (5:13-16).

merely one man with others but the man for them (as God is for them), the man in whom the love and faithfulness and salvation and glory of God are addressed to man in the concrete form of a historical relationship of man to man: and this in spite of their own adamic form; and therefore in spite of their own estrangement ... ; in spite of their attempted safeguards against Him; and above all in spite of the misery to which they necessarily fall victim in this estrangement and error and the establishment of these safeguards. The divine Yes echoed by the royal man Jesus is the divine Word of comfort for this very misery, ... God grapples with sin as He has mercy on the men who suffer in this way as sinners. His weapon against it is the Gospel, the good news of the end of their misery and the beginning of their redemption, the coming of His kingdom as the kingdom of peace on earth, the reconciliation of the world with Himself. *The man Jesus is decisively created after God in the fact that He is as man the work and revelation of the mercy of God, of His gospel, His kingdom of peace, His atonement, and that He is His creaturely and earthly and historical correspondence in this sense.*[44]

Note how Barth relates Jesus Christ closely with God by using the terms 'like God', 'image and reflection', 'echoed', 'after God', 'revelation' and 'correspondence'. Furthermore, when he writes 'the solidarity with it into which He has entered and in which He persists; of the hope of salvation and glory which He has given it by giving no less than *Himself*', this 'He' or 'Himself' could equally refer to God or Jesus Christ or both. This is how tightly Barth couples Jesus with God but it would be incorrect to suggest that he has a modalistic tendency here, because he does clearly see Jesus as distinct from God, being his earthly and historical correspondence.

It has been mentioned above that Mt. 9:35-38 is a concluding summary of Jesus' ministry of words and actions in Galilee. In showing how Jesus and God are for us, Barth comes to expound on the meaning of the important verse of Mt. 9:36 on Jesus' compassion to some considerable depth.[45]

Jesus, went through all the towns and villages, teaching in their synagogues, preaching the good news of the kingdom and healing every

---

44 *CD* IV.2, pp. 180-1. Italics mine.

45 Mark portrays Jesus' compassion early on in his gospel, in the healing of the leper (1:41). Interestingly Matthew does not explicitly mention, or he omits, Jesus' compassion in the parallel narrative in 8:1-4, which is the first miracle presented in detail by Matthew. However, at the summary and conclusion of Jesus' ministry in Galilee in 9:35-38, Matthew explicitly presents Jesus' compassion. Mark and Matthew both portray the compassion of Jesus, but each in their own ways.

disease and sickness. When he [Jesus] saw the crowds, he had compassion on them, because they were harassed and helpless, like sheep without a shepherd. (Mt. 9:35-36)

But when he saw the multitudes, he was moved with compassion on them, because they fainted, and were scattered abroad, as sheep having no shepherd. As we have already read in Luke 1:78 about the σπλάγχνα of God, we now read about an ἐσπλαγχνίσθη expressly attributed to the man Jesus of Nazareth as He journeys through the towns and villages of Galilee, teaching and preaching and healing. The expression is a strong one which defies adequate translation. He was not only affected to the heart by the misery which surround Him - *sympathy in our modern sense is far too feeble a word - but it went right into His heart, into Himself,* so that it was now His misery. It was more His than that of those who suffered it. He took it from them and laid it on Himself. In the last analysis it was no longer theirs at all, but His. He Himself suffered it in their place. The cry of those who suffered was only an echo. Strictly speaking, it had already been superseded. It was superfluous. Jesus had made it His own. To the mercy of *God* which brings radical and total and definitive salvation there now *corresponded* the help which *Jesus* brought to men by His radical and total definitive self-giving to and for their cause. In this self-giving, by the fact that His mercy, in this sense, led Him to see men in this way, *He was on earth as God is in heaven.* In this self-giving He was the kingdom of God come on earth.[46]

'He took it from them and laid it on Himself. ... He Himself suffered it in their place. ... Jesus had made it His own.' These sentences are reminiscent of the theme of Jesus' identification and solidarity with men, which he expounds at length in 'The Lord as Servant' in *CD* IV.1, where the culmination of this solidarity is Jesus' atoning death. Here Barth brilliantly makes the observation that Jesus' identifies with men not only in his coming as man and dying for men, not only in his baptism, not only in his physical presence and ministering to the needy people, but also in his fellowship with them in his (*inner*) life and emotion, in his sharing with them of their griefs and sufferings, such that his solidarity with them is a true, comprehensive and integrated one. He is not one whose presence is only in outward form and whose inner

---

46 *Ibid.*, p. 184, Italics mine. Barth also refers to Mt. 9:36 and Jesus' compassion in 'The Community for the World' in *CD* IV.3, p. 774. He similarly expounds on the related word for compassion, σπλάγχνα , and mentions Mt. 9:36 in 'Jesus, Man for other Men' in *CD* III.2, p. 211. It is clear that Mt. 9:36 and the associated understanding of Jesus' compassion are very important to Barth. Matthew also refers to Jesus' compassion in 14:14,15:32, 20:34.

thought is aloof, uncaring and alienated from the people, but he is one who stands in the midst of the people and stands in oneness with them even in their miseries and emotions. Barth's observation here throws light on the understanding of Jesus' unity with men - his being men's representative and substitute in his death on the cross, and Jesus' earnest desire to be *with us* and *for us* in his life and death (not death alone), from the beginning to end. This earnest desire of Jesus ultimately reveals God's compassion and his earnest desire to be *with us* and *for us*. Barth spends considerable effort on expounding the nature of the objects of his compassion, which brings out the unconditional nature of his love. Barth highlights Jesus' compassion for the crowd with the following three observations concerning the crowd, the object of his compassion. The first is to do with the crowds' ignorance, the second their unbelief and the third their sins.

Firstly, the crowds, in their confused and harassed existent, are ignorant of their true need, the great gap in their existence which can only be filled by the Shepherd. But their failure to see does not alter Jesus' compassion for them.

> [I]t is striking that the Gospel records show very little interest in the palpable gracelessness of the ὄχλοι [crowds]. Their failure to see did not alter their misery and their actual suffering of this misery. It did not affect the great gap in their existence. Even less did it make any difference to the fact that the One had come and was present who was to fill this gap, to be their head and therefore their σωτήρ, the true Shepherd who did not think that the flock was there for His benefit but He for theirs, the truly royal man whose compassion reflected the compassion of the God who had sworn fidelity to man and was now finally and conclusively to prove it. The people's failure to see did not alter in the very least the true and deep and strong union and solidarity of Jesus with this people, and of this people with Jesus.[47]

Barth's point is that Jesus' and God's earnest compassion for the crowds persists despite the crowds' ignorance of their true need and the presence of one who alone can meet that need. Jesus' and God's love for the people is often a one-sided affair and independent of man's knowledge or the lack of it - ignorance.

Secondly, Barth observes that the crowds are not necessarily his disciples but Jesus has compassion for them just the same.

> In the strict sense, no one was not included. ... The crowd as it comes before us in the Gospel scenes, sometimes accompanying the disciples,

---

47 *Ibid.*, p. 187.

sometimes the publicans and sinners, sometimes the scribes and Pharisees (and always including these, not excluding them). ... [T]his is the multitude which when He saw it moved Jesus to compassion. ... It is never said in any general way that the people believed on him. There could be no question of that. The disciples who believed were people, but the people as such were not disciples. They were not the community. They do not normally believe. ... It has to be accepted as the serious view of the tradition that, although the ὄχλοι [crowds] did not believe as such, although they did not become his disciples, they were themselves brought into a very real union with Jesus by the fact that He was moved with compassion when He saw them.[48]

Thirdly, Barth further strengthens his point - effectively Jesus' unconditional love - when he comments on Jesus' miracles of healing and observes that those who are healed are above all sinful men.

There is another remarkable and almost *offensive* feature of the miracle stories which has been continually obscured, i.e., painted over in ethical colours, in so much well-meaning exposition (especially in the Western Church). This is that in these stories it does not seem to be of any great

---

48 *Ibid.*, p. 185. To further substantiate Barth's point about the unconditional nature of Jesus' compassion, it can also be added that, in Luke 17:11-19, Jesus healed ten lepers and only one came back to thank him. Of all the people loved and healed by Jesus, not all of them necessarily became his disciples or came back to thank him. Also, of all the healing miracles that Jesus performed in the four gospels, not even once did he set up a condition of commitment to be his disciple or gratitude to him before he healed them. He taught and healed them because they were suffering, harassed and helpless, like sheep without a shepherd and Jesus had compassion for them. It is interesting and important to observe that this description of Jesus' compassionate ministry in Galilee in Mt. 9:35-36 is starkly contrasted with the negative response of the people of Capernaum, Korazin and Bethsaida where most of Jesus' miracles had been performed (11:20-24). Jesus denounced them for their lack of repentance rather than praising them for their commitment. However, this does not detract from the fact that Jesus had compassion for them in their miseries and sufferings and had come to their aid (which is firmly given in the preceding passage of 9:35-36). Jesus' compassionate ministry for the people is not dependent on the expectation/prospect of favourable response to him or other conditions. This point is highlighted by Matthew's redactional work on Jesus' miracles compared to Mark. 'Matthew insists that Jesus performed a miracle for *all* who needed it, or that *all* the sick were brought to him (Mt. 4:23-24; 8:16; 12:15; 14:35; 15:37).' In 'Miracles and Miracle Stories', *Dictionary of Jesus and the Gospels*, p. 553. Jesus then fulfilled his own teaching in the fifth antithesis where he taught his disciples to 'give to the one who asks you, and do not turn away from the one who wants to borrow from you' (5:42). His compassionate ministry was therefore not driven by some higher principle other than compassion itself.

account that the men who suffer as creatures are above all sinful men, men who are at fault in relation to God, their neighbours and themselves, who are therefore *guilty* and have betrayed themselves into all kinds of trouble. No, *the important thing about them in these stories is not that they are sinners but that they are sufferers.* Jesus does not first look at their past, and then at their tragic present in the light of it. But from their present He creates for them a new future. He does not ask, therefore, concerning their sin. He does not hold it against them. He does not denounce them because of it. *The help and blessing that He brings are quite irrespective of their sin. He acts almost (indeed exactly) in the same way as His Father in heaven, who causes His sun to shine on the good and the evil, and His rain to fall on the just and the unjust.*[49]

Barth continues with his exposition of God's mercy to man through Jesus Christ,

He is interested in him [man] as this specific cosmic being. He has not given him up. He maintains His covenant with him. He is always faithful to him. He takes his sin seriously. But He takes even more seriously, with a primary seriousness, the fact that he is His man even as a sinner, and above all that He Himself is the God even of this sinful man. The fact that God takes man seriously in this direct divine way finds concrete realisation when Jesus' proclamation of His kingdom, His *coup d'état* in the miracles, takes the form of his direct comforting of the sad, this free liberation of the poor, these benefits which come so unconditionally to man; when in this form it consists quite simply in the fact that oppressed and therefore anxious and harassed men can breathe and live again, can again be men.[50]

To sum up Barth's points, even though (i) many amongst the crowd are ignorant of their true state of needs and the true identity of Jesus, (ii) they might not commit themselves to be Jesus' disciples (despite Jesus' favour for them) and (iii) they are sinners, Jesus in his unconditional love sees their needs and miseries, has compassion for them, teaches them and heals them. This is how Jesus and God are *for us.* This is Barth's incisive understanding of the love of God revealed in Jesus Christ in his teaching (5:43-48) and in his actions.

The exegeses above on Jesus' healing of the leper, the centurion's servant and his eating/fellowship with tax collectors and sinners, which have been influenced by Barth, all witness to Jesus and God's radical, unconditional and undiscriminating love which transcends every

---

49 *Ibid.*, pp. 222-3. Italics mine.
50 *Ibid.*, p. 224. See also p. 225.

boundary and barrier, even that of sin, to reach out and touch those who are suffering, struggling, lost, hopeless, crying and in need. This is how Jesus reveals his Father's heart for the people; this is how Jesus reveals his Father's spirit of compassion for them. And in this radical love of God, the third aspect of Jesus' correspondence to God - revolution or radicalism - coincides with the fourth aspect of correspondence - Jesus *for us*. The radicalism of Jesus and of God is revealed precisely in his unconditional love for all people and sinners.[51] But this radicalism of Jesus, which challenges the beliefs and practices cherished by the religious leaders, heightens the tension between Jesus and the religious leadership, to the extent that they think their attempt to eliminate Jesus is a service to God. Paradoxically, their murderous action, which is fuelled by Jesus' radicalism, is the very avenue through which the nature and full extent of Jesus' and God's radical love is revealed.

From the above quotes from 'The Royal Man', it can be seen that Barth is keen not only to present a dynamic picture of Jesus Christ but also to remind his readers frequently of Jesus' revelation of God in his words, actions and attitudes. Apart from using the language of correspondence (e.g., pp. 181, 184) in describing this revelation, he also uses the language of conformity (pp. 169, 171, 172), reflection (pp. 166, 180-181, 187), parallelism (pp. 166, 193), image (pp. 180, 192), likeness (p. 193), agreement (p. 192) and fellowship (p. 169). And he applies Mt. 5:48 to Jesus who is then the perfect Son on earth like his Father in heaven (pp. 166, 222-3). Barth in portraying Jesus as the Royal Man attempts to present him in the context of his relationship with his Father - Jesus in conformity and correspondence to God reflects and thereby reveals God. However, the notions of conformity, correspondence, reflection, parallelism, image, likeness and agreement, proper and necessary as they are in describing Jesus' relationship with his Father, have very similar meanings but do not quite capture the idea of fellowship or communion between Jesus and his Father. In the whole of 'The Royal Man', he only uses 'fellowship' once (on p. 169) to describe Jesus' relationship with his Father while he uses other descriptions such as conformity or reflection much more frequently. Coincidentally, he mentions the Spirit in relation to Jesus only once (p. 167).[52] The rarity of the mention of the Spirit in 'The Royal Man' may

---

51 However, Barth does not make this connection explicitly.

52 'As the Son of God He is obedient man, who is not only filled and impelled by the Spirit, but exists in the activity of the Spirit, establishing His work, incorporating Him in Himself as the capacity to receive the grace of God and its influence in the creaturely world.' *CD* IV.2, p. 167. On pp. 193 and 248, the Spirit is mentioned in relation to Jesus as the exalted Lord, not in the context of his earthly life and ministry.

be linked to the comparative rarity of the notion of fellowship or communion there, because the Spirit is the Spirit of fellowship/communion, as Barth clearly affirms elsewhere (see below). The comparative rarity of the notion of fellowship/communion could entail the rarity of reference to the Spirit, and vice versa.

In other contexts of Barth's writings, the Spirit of fellowship is more evident. For example, in speaking about the divine Son of God going into the far country to become man in *CD* IV.1, Barth discusses the distinction in God and the relationship between the Son and his Father through the Spirit. In this conceptual discussion of the Trinity, the role of the Spirit becomes more prominent. 'Jesus Christ is the Son of God who became man, who as such is One with God the Father, equal to Him in deity, by the Holy Spirit, in whom the Father affirms and loves Him and He the Father, in a mutual fellowship.'[53] 'The One who eternally begets is never apart from the One who is eternally begotten. Nor is the latter apart from the former. The Father is not the Father and the Son is not the Son without a mutual affirmation and love in the Holy Spirit.'[54] Further references to the Spirit of fellowship can be found, e.g., in *CD* I.1 where Barth deals conceptually with the doctrine of the Trinity. It is interesting to note that the Spirit of fellowship is more in view when Barth discusses Jesus' relationship with his Father, or the Trinity, conceptually. And when Barth discusses Jesus' relationship with his Father with reference to the gospel narratives, the Spirit of fellowship is much less in view. This could be partly explained if one considers the nature of the gospel narratives. The person of Jesus Christ is the central figure of the gospel story; he is the most visible figure, compared with the Father and the Spirit. It is most natural to read the gospel story Christologically, and that is proper. However, it requires a greater conscious effort to bear in mind the Father and the notion of Jesus' revelation of his Father through his life-act and attitudes when one is studying the gospel narratives. And it is a credit to Barth that he both (i) brilliantly interprets the unique, amazing, unforgettable, radical and gracious presence of Jesus, and (ii) frequently reminds his readers of Jesus' correspondence to and revelation of his Father. What he has achieved requires a strong understanding of the concept of revelation, which he surely has (see *CD* I.1). Now, if the Father is less visible than Jesus in the gospel narratives and it requires a strong understanding of revelation and a conscious effort to see the Father more clearly in the gospels, perhaps the Spirit and Jesus' communion with his Father through the Spirit are even less visible in the gospel narratives (even though they are there, as Barth would concur) and requires an even

---

53 *CD* IV.1, p. 204.
54 *Ibid.*, p. 209.

greater conscious effort to see these. However, in a conceptual study of the Trinity, the problem of the relative invisibility of the Father and the Spirit in narratives disappears and the three can be equally in view. This may partly explain the comparative rarity of reference to the Spirit of fellowship in Barth's study of the gospel narratives in 'The Royal Man'. But since he has taken the step of reminding his readers the reality of the Father through the notion of Jesus' revelation of him, he could have taken the further and justifiable step of reminding his readers of Jesus' fellowship with his Father through the Spirit, which is vitally important in this process of correspondence, conformity, parallelism and revelation, as has been seen in the non-linear concept of revelation, and shall be seen in chapter 6 on a theology of the Trinity. It is therefore possible that there may be other factors apart from the one above which could further account for the comparative rarity of the references to the Spirit and Jesus' fellowship with his Father through the Spirit in his treatment of gospel narratives (see later in chapter 6).

In the treatment on Jesus' revelation of his Father in words and actions in the last and present chapters, the Lordship of Jesus has been emphasised in the exegeses of the passages from Matthew, so has his correspondence to his Father in his radical righteousness and unconditional love. It is clear that the exegeses have been influenced by Barth who emphasises both Jesus' Lordship and his correspondence to his Father. However, the exegeses have also endeavoured to bring out more clearly Jesus' fellowship with his Father (through the Spirit) as the basis of correspondence and revelation, and as part of the content of revelation.

3.0 The Climax of Revelation: The Passion of Jesus

3.1 Continuity in Jesus' Life and Death: Solidarity with Humanity

In view of Jesus' authority and Lordship revealed in his words and works of power, it is not self-evident that the journey of Jesus should end in the suffering and shame in the cross. Jesus' disciples certainly found it difficult to understand and accept Jesus 'disastrous' ending as predicted by himself. Also, Jesus' cry on the cross, 'My God, my God, why have you forsaken me?' (Mt. 27:46) raises the question of the appropriateness of this ending, the question of the continuity of Jesus' ministry of power in Galilee and his passion in Jerusalem, the question of the possibility of a catastrophe which burst unexpectedly into His life. This is the question Barth addresses in the last section of 'The Royal Man'. He maintains that there is a strong continuity between Jesus' ministry in Galilee and his passion in Jerusalem.

[I]n His suffering and dying He is still the same as He always was, although in another form. The passion is not an alien element in His work as a whole. From the very first, and with decisive significance, all that He did was done under this sign. This emerged clearly in the death and passion, but it was there all the time. And the Gospels see this because they see the whole story in the light of Easter. We should have to adopt a different standpoint from that of the Gospels even to envisage - let alone investigate - it as an alien element. The Gospels do not allow the attentive reader to indulge in abstract considerations of that contrast or speculations on the problems to which it gives rise. There is no place for an approach of this kind. We should still have to say this even if we could forget for a moment the Easter story with which they all conclude. We should still have to say it only in view of the remarkable coherence, the non-dramatic directness, with which they link together what took place in Galilee and what took place in Jerusalem (Luke uniting them by his account of the great journey, and all the Synoptists by the so-called predictions of the passion, which are common to all the accounts, in spite of the variations in detail, and especially in relation to the words actually used by Jesus). For all its glaring contrast, the story is seen by them as a single whole. And in spite of the change of setting, the approach and occurrence of the passion do not involve any basic change in the narrative, not even a change of narrative style.[55]

With this conviction of the continuity between Jesus' ministry and death, Barth in *CD* IV.2, pp. 250-63, spends considerable effort in linking Jesus' life and ministry at Galilee and his passion in Jerusalem. He understands the relationship between the two as the following.

Jesus was not led to this place [the cross], nor did He go to this place, in contradiction of the fact that He was the royal man. On the contrary, it was in a sense His *coronation* as this man. The fact that His way issued in this darkness does not mean that what we have said about His existence and relationship to God and His life's work is in any way weakened or qualified, or has to be retracted. The very opposite is the case. What we have said finds its *true climax* and *glory* in the fact that - however hard this may sound - He finally hung on the gallows as a criminal between two other criminals, and died there, with that last despairing question on His lips, as One who was condemned and maltreated and scorned by men and abandoned by God. The story of His passion is all the more emphatically, although not very obviously, linked with what precedes, forming a single *whole*, because the latter is not at all denied or questioned by it, but finds in it its *fulfilment*. In His passion the name of

---

55 *CD* IV.2, p. 251.

the God active and revealed in Him is conclusively sanctified; His will is done on earth as it is done in heaven; His kingdom comes, in a form and with a power to which as a man He can only give a terrified but determined assent. And in the passion He exists conclusively as the One He is - the Son of God who is also the Son of Man. In the deepest darkness of Golgotha He enters supremely into *the glory of the unity of the Son with the Father. In that abandonment by God He is the One who is directly loved by God.*[56]

Barth uses the words 'coronation', 'climax', 'fulfilment', 'conclusively' and 'supremely' to describe the relationship between Jesus' passion and his ministry - Jesus' ministry is supremely and conclusively fulfilled in the climactic coronation in his passion.[57] This is how God's kingdom has come. This is how one sees the glorious unity of Jesus and his Father even though he was forsaken and alienated. But in what sense were Jesus and his Father united when he was forsaken? This question will be answered later. But here briefly, in Jesus' passion one sees how he, united with his Father in will, purpose and action, climactically reveals his Father. It may be added that the passion is also a point where his alienation and abandonment by his Father reveals paradoxically the close communion that he enjoys with his Father hitherto (Mt. 11:27): his cry of dereliction and forsakeness on the cross implies a state of non-forsakeness or close communion with his Father before encountering the state of abandonment on the cross.

Barth's point regarding the continuity between Jesus' life/ministry and his death is extremely helpful for it indirectly exposes the inadequacy of those theologies which either emphasise only Jesus' life or only his death (see Excursus A). The continuity that Barth insists in *CD* IV.2 is also found in his writing in *CD* IV.1 , 'The Obedience of the Son of God' in 'The Lord as Servant', where the theme of the identification of the Son of God with humanity is consistently maintained throughout Jesus' life and death (see 3.2 of chapter 2 on Jesus' identification with humanity). To fully appreciate the meaning and significance of his death, it is not sufficient therefore to look at Jesus' death on its own. It is necessary to look at his death in the light of his life of identification with humanity so that his death in solidarity with sinners can be seen as the climax or coronation of his life. Furthermore, by looking at Jesus' life and death as a whole, one can appreciate his consistent commitment to walk towards the cross

---

56 *Ibid.*, p. 252. Italics mine.

57 The point that Barth has been expounding in 'The Royal Man' - the humiliated Son of God is the exalted Son of Man, the Lord who is the Servant and vice versa - finds its supreme expression and confirmation in Jesus' passion.

throughout his whole life so that his constant and steadfast love for sinners in his life, witnessed by that consistent commitment, is manifested or revealed climactically in his death. With such an understanding of Jesus' constant and steadfast love in his life and death, one can also appreciate better the Father's constant and steadfast love for humanity. The Father, in unity and communion with his Son in this love for sinners, wills for his Son to maintain this love in unity with him from the beginning to the end, that his Son will unswervingly walk towards the cross overcoming all temptations and accomplish the forgiveness of sins and salvation for humanity, so that 'in the deepest darkness of Golgotha He [the Son] enters supremely into the glory of the unity of the Son with the Father.' The Father wills for his Son to share with him his commitment and steadfast love for humanity, the Son who in obedience to his Father perseveres in his path to the cross not only reveals his own commitment and steadfast love for humanity but also that of his Father. And in all these, Jesus' relationship with his Father, characterised by knowledge, obedience, trust, love and unity is also revealed. The presentation in the whole of section 3 of this chapter will elaborate on the continuity between Jesus' life and death (beginning at his baptism), his steadfast love throughout his life and death and the climax of Jesus' revelation of his Father. This presentation is based on Barth's notion of the continuity of Jesus' life and death (or Jesus' inexorable approach to the cross), and the notion of the unity of Jesus and his Father, which Barth highlights in the last quotation.

The baptism of Jesus (Mt. 3:13-17) in the context of Mt. 2-4 is a visible sign of Jesus' identification/solidarity with Israel (see 3.2 of chapter 2). Barth makes close connections between Jesus' identification with Israel, his baptism and death.

> His first public appearance is that of a penitent in unreserved solidarity with other penitents who confess themselves to be such in the baptism of John, and can look only for the remission of their sins in the coming judgment (Mt. 3:15) - a clear *anticipation of the story of the passion*, towards which the narrative in all the Evangelists hastens with a momentum recognisable from the very first, and at the climax of which Jesus is crucified between two thieves (Mt. 27:38).[58]

---

58 *Ibid.*, p. 165, Italics mine. Quoted in chapter 2. Oscar Cullmann also makes the same observation concerning Jesus' solidarity with the people in his baptism and death. 'At the moment of his Baptism he receives the commission to undertake the role of the suffering Servant of God, who takes on himself the sins of his people. ... This means that Jesus is baptised in view of his death, which effects forgiveness of sins for all men. For this reason Jesus must unite himself in solidarity with his whole people, and go down himself to Jordan, that "all righteousness might be fulfilled."'

The cleansing or forgiveness of sins, symbolised by baptism, is to be effected by Jesus' death in solidarity with the people. Although baptism does symbolise Jesus' death, it should not be limited to that alone because Jesus' solidarity with Israel, signified by his baptism and Mt. 2-4, ranges over his life as well as his death. In Jesus' life and ministry, his solidarity with the people is consistently maintained despite the temptations to do otherwise. The following discussion will elaborate on this important point.

Barth interprets Jesus' temptations in the wilderness after his baptism as a test of his fidelity to the commitment he made in the baptism - solidarity with humanity.

> There is a thread which runs through them all and confirms their identity in substance. In none of the three temptations is there brought before us a devil who is obviously godless, or dangerous or even stupid. And in none of them is the temptation a temptation to what we might call a breaking or failure to keep the Law on the moral or judicial plane. In all three we have to do "only" with the counsel, the suggestion, that He should not be true to the way on which He entered in Jordan, that of a great sinner repenting; that he should take from now on a direction which will not need to have the cross as its end and goal.[59]

Jesus' resistance to these temptations thus means that he wills not to use his power for his own convenience and for building an earthly kingdom for his own gain.[60] He is determined not to amass wealth or power for himself. Rather, he chooses to remain in a state of lowliness; in a spirit/Spirit of humility (Mt. 11:29) he wills to stand in solidarity with people of lowliness and need. He does not commit himself to the

---

Baptism in the New Testament, (London: SCM Press, 1950), p. 18. Cullmann studied the relationships between Jesus' baptism, his death, believers' baptism and their righteousness using other passages such as Mark 10:38, Luke 12:50, Rom. 6:3 and 1 Cor. 1:13. He treated Jesus' baptism as a reference to his death. The reference to the servant in Isaiah 42:1 - 'with him I am well pleased' - in the Father's word to Jesus in his baptism identifies Jesus as the suffering servant who ultimately dies for the sins of the people (Isaiah 53). E. Schweizer also understands that in Jesus' baptism he is presented as the suffering righteous one, *TDNT*, vol. VIII, p. 380. However, Luz states that it is eisegesis to associate Jesus' passion with his baptism, as Schweizer and Cullmann have done (G. Bornkamm is also implicated, see Luz, *Matthew 1-7* , p. 179). But Luz does not explain how these scholars have committed eisegesis while the text of Mt. 3:17 clearly alludes to the death and suffering of the servant in Isaiah 53 via Isaiah 42:1 (see also Matthew's reference to the suffering servant in 8:17 and the servant again in 12:18-21).

59 *CD* IV.1, p. 261.
60 See 5.0 of chapter 3, 'Jesus' Humanity in Knowing His Father's Will'.

kingdom of this world but he is committed to the kingdom of his Father for which he will have to suffer unto death in order to save the people from their sins (Mt. 1:21). The temptation episodes show that Jesus does not waver in his solidarity with and steadfast love for Israel/humanity, that he will keep this course of obedience to his Father to the end.

Barth likewise links Jesus' temptation in the Garden of Gethsemane with his baptism and his temptations in the wilderness.

> Jesus Himself - in prayer to God - raises the whole question [of his death] afresh. He prays that 'if it were possible, the hour might pass from him' (Mark 14:35 [Mt. 26:39 par]). ... But had not His whole way from Jordan been a single march - which Satan could not arrest, not even in the form of Peter (Mt. 16:23) - to this very hour, a single and determined grasping of this cup of the divine wrath (Isaiah 51:17)? [61]

> [I]n this prayer of Jesus there took place quite simply the completion of the penitence and obedience which He had begun to render at Jordan and which He had maintained in the wilderness. Had not His whole resistance in that temptation, the No which He had victoriously opposed to it, aimed at the different but no less victorious Yes which He said to the will of God in this hour? [62]

Jesus' words of prayer to his Father - 'Yet not as I will, but as you will.' - show his resolute will to complete the journey from Jordan, to persevere in this solidarity with man and to maintain the unity and consonance of will with his Father to the end.

Jesus' life and ministry are bracketed by his temptations in the wilderness and Gethsemane. Within this pair of brackets which signify his solidarity with needy humanity, in his life and ministry he has also consistently maintained this solidarity.[63] He does not forsake humanity in need; he draws close to them; he stands by their side to be *with them*; he stretches out his hand to help them because he is *for them*; he is amongst them; he understands them, identifies with them and has compassion for them.[64] From these considerations of solidarity and the

---

61 *CD* IV.1, pp. 264-5.

62 *Ibid.*, p. 272.

63 See Barth's discussion of Jesus and God *for us* in his ministry of compassion above and the exegeses of the Matthean passages in sections 1.1 to 1.3.

64 'Mt. 11:28f ... Whom does He call to Himself? Not those who are religiously, morally, politically and socially vital and exalted and triumphant in this world, but the "weary and heavy-laden", those who are retiring in their relation to God and men, those who are at an end of their own resources in both respects, those who are at their wits' end in both respects. The affinity of Jesus is not with the former class, but the

discussion of Jesus' Lordship in chapter 2, the following narrative/literary pattern has emerged.

X: Immanuel - God with us (Mt. 1:23)
> Y: Jesus identified with the Lord (Mt. 3:3)
>> A: Jesus' baptism at Jordan,
>>> B: His Temptations in the wilderness,
>>>> C: Jesus' ministry,
>>> B': His Temptation at the Garden of Gethsemane,
>> A': Jesus' passion and death.
> Y': Jesus' universal Lordship (Mt. 28:18)

X': Jesus' universal presence with his disciples (Mt. 28:20)

It has been shown so far that the five narratives of ABCB'A' all have to do with Jesus' solidarity with humanity which witnesses to the unwavering love of Jesus and his Father.[65] From this narrative pattern, one can learn three important points regarding three kinds of unity. Firstly, the narrative pattern witnesses to Jesus' unity with humanity. Jesus has consistently, faithfully and truthfully stood in solidarity *with* needy humanity in his baptism, temptations, ministry, life and death. Secondly, because of Jesus' consistent unity with needy humanity in this narrative pattern from beginning to end, there is a unity in Jesus' life and death, that Jesus' death in Jerusalem is not an unexpected ending but the climax, fulfilment and coronation of his life. Thirdly, the narrative pattern also shows that despite the struggles of temptations which presumably are present not only in the wilderness and Gethsemane but also in his ministry (e.g., to be made king in John 6:14-15) to deflect him from his course to the cross, Jesus' will has always been aligned and united with his Father's will through his obedience, that they have always shared in their communion this purpose of salvation towards sinful but needy humanity, that they together in unity have unswervingly held fast their faithful love for them to the very end. Putting the three points regarding unity together, there is a unity throughout Jesus' life and death in which he has consistently stood in oneness *with* the people, and remained one with his Father in their loving will and purpose *for* the people.

If the narratives of Jesus' baptism, temptations in the wilderness and ministry (ABC) witness to his *with us* and *for us*, his love and his desire

---

latter.' *CD* IV.1,p. 179.

65 Each of the two pairs of brackets, AA' and BB', is called an inclusio in narrative critical terms but Barth identified this pattern before narrative critical terms were used in literary approach to the Bible.

to stand with us in order to heal and save us, then his *with us* and *for us*, his steadfast love and his earnest desire to save us, which are held in unity with his Father, are climactically revealed in the passion narrative following his entry into Jerusalem. Only a summary description of the passion narrative can be given here but that will be sufficient to demonstrate this climax of Jesus' revelation of his Father. The following interpretation of Jesus' passion is evidently influenced by Barth's point that Jesus is consistent in his resolute and earnest desire to go to the cross for humanity.[66]

3.2 The Passion of Jesus

From a certain perspective, Jesus' response to the pressure put on him in his trials and suffering was a passive one. For example, he made no attempt to free himself from the danger and suffering; he passively accepted the verdict and sentence of the religious and political leaders; he received all the insults without any retaliation; he made no struggle against the unjust penalty of crucifixion. But the absence of all these is of great importance in understanding the passion of Jesus (and will be highlighted in the following). This absence should be seen in the positive light as the testimony of his earnest desire not to extricate himself from suffering but to endure his sufferings for sinners. The absence of this extrication from suffering, with the presence of what Jesus did and said, constituted his whole action which was the fulfilment of his own teaching on non-retaliation and unconditional love (or the *absence* of retaliation and the *presence* of unbreakable love) in the fifth and sixth antitheses. This whole action of Jesus witnesses to his unwavering love for needy humanity, his unflinching desire and commitment to be identified with humanity and to be united with his Father's will which is to save the people from their sins.

The determination of the religious leaders to oppose Jesus grows as Jesus' radicalism, in consonance with God's radicalism, unfolds in his ministry of words and actions which challenges the beliefs and practices cherished by the religious leaders. His radical outspokenness 'against'

---

66 Similarly, in grasping the meaning of Jesus' death and our forgiveness, W. Herrmann also was not content with looking at Jesus' death on its own and was interested in Jesus' attitude and life leading up to his death. What Herrmann was looking for was not a formula for forgiveness, which was not sufficient for the assurance of forgiveness that he desired. He was looking for an assurance of God's forgiveness by seeking God's motive and Jesus' attitude towards us in his path leading to the cross, particularly in the Last Supper. See Wilhelm Herrmann, *Systematic Theology* (London: G. Allen & Unwin, 1927), p. 120f.

the law,[67] his 'impious' move amongst tax collectors and sinners, his unconventional and free acts 'against' the Jewish observance of the Sabbath (12:1-14) and food laws (15:1-20), his allegedly irreverent stance against the temple (26:61), his uncompromising criticism of the Pharisees and the teachers of the law (chapter 23; 5:20) are more than sufficient to bring him into severe tension with the Pharisees, the teachers of the law and high priests. This tension grows to such an extent that the leaders decide that the author of this 'dangerous' radicalism is to be removed (12:14; 26:3-4), thinking that their attempt to eliminate Jesus is a service to God. Paradoxically, their murderous action, fuelled by their legalism and Jesus' radicalism, is the very avenue through which the full extent of Jesus' and God's radical love is climactically revealed.

As Jesus' ministry at Galilee draws near to a close, he takes his disciples to Caesarea Philippi and begins to teach them about his coming suffering (16:13-28). He repeats it on a number of occasions (17:12; 17:22-23; 20:28; 26:12, 26-29; 21:38-39). Knowing that his Father loves him (cf. his Father's words in 3:17 which is repeated at his transfiguration after Caesarea Philippi), he obeys his Father and gives himself to fulfil his role as the suffering servant. In his ministry, he has taught his disciples and the crowds the righteousness of God by words and examples, now he is going to realise and fulfil that righteousness to the climactic end. He has given himself to love his disciples and the people in his ministry, now he is going to give himself totally for them. He is not unaware of the danger from the religious leaders in Jerusalem but he boldly, publicly and triumphantly enters Jerusalem, riding on a donkey (21:1-11), knowing full well that the end of this journey will be a fatal one. He begins to openly lay claim to his Messiahship by this symbolic act of riding on a donkey which was prophesied in Zechariah 9:19 concerning the Messiah. His claim seems to have been understood by some who shouted, 'Hosanna to the Son of David!' But his gentleness and non-violence, symbolised by the donkey rather than a war horse, might not have been appreciated by them.[68] The king and Messiah will fulfil his mission not by a show of military power but by a humiliating death, in accordance with his Father's will and his own commitment which he made in his baptism and maintained throughout

---

67 Mt. 5:17 - 'Do not think that I have come to abolish the Law or the Prophets.' - implies that it is possible to understand him that way and some Jews, Pharisees or teachers of the law might have interpreted him in such a way regarding his radical teaching. In Mt. 21:23, Jesus was questioned by the leaders concerning the authority of his teaching which presumably had some conflict with their interpretation of the law. In John 18:19, during his trial the high priest questioned his teaching.

68 France, *Matthew Commentary*, pp. 298-9.

his ministry. His action of purifying the temple - by overturning the tables of the money changers and the benches of those selling doves (21:12-13) - further strengthens his claim to Messiahship.[69] Inevitably, these public claims and 'outrageous' actions in the temple heighten the tension and confrontation between Jesus and the religious leaders. Subsequently, his authority is questioned by the chief priests and the elders (i.e., representatives from the Sanhedrin, 21:23), he is tested by the Pharisees and Sadducees with questions to trap him (22:15-28). But none succeeds in their attempts.

He continues to teach in the temple courts in Jerusalem (26:55). Again he predicts his death as the Passover draws near (26:1-2). He accepts the anointing by the woman in Bethany as a preparation for his burial (26:6-13). He does not turn back and withdraw from Jerusalem; he remains faithful to his Father's will and to his words to his disciples. Knowing that his Father loves him and his appointed time of suffering is near (3:17; 17:5), he celebrates the Passover with his disciples (26:18).[70] He has clearly understood that his death will not be an accident, not a failure on his part, but it has been intended for the forgiveness of sins for many. This is how Jesus comes to save the people from their sins (1:21). By giving his disciples the bread and the wine, he continues to affirm his commitment to the path of the cross which his Father has set for him. But this affirmation of his commitment is not without its challenge and test because of the scale of the suffering to come. In the Garden of Gethsemane, his soul is overshadowed with sorrow to the point of death (26:38). There is genuine temptation for him to give up his path to the cross. Immediately before the beginning of his ministry, he was tested in the wilderness concerning his commitment to his Father's will and came through with obedience to his Father. The temptation at Gethsemane, which with those in the wilderness forms an inclusio, is also centred on the same issues. Will he renounce his power to save/serve himself? Will he renounce the earthly kingdom and give himself completely for the kingdom of God? Will he entrust himself totally to the sovereign hand of the Father? Even though the issues involved are much the same, the temptation at Gethsemane is more

---

69 *Ibid.*, p. 300. Jewish expectations included the belief, based on the visions of Ezek. 40-48, and focused by Zech 6:12-13, that the Messiah would renew and purify the temple. See also B. Gärtner, *The Temple and the Community* (Cambridge: Cambridge University Press, 1965), pp. 105-11.

70 "While they were eating, Jesus took bread, gave thanks and broke it, and gave it to his disciples, saying, 'Take and eat; this is my body.' Then he took the cup, gave thanks and offered it to them, saying, 'Drink from it, all of you. This is my blood of the covenant which is poured out for many for the forgiveness of sins.'" Matthew 26:26-28.

severe than in the wilderness because of the looming, imminent 'disaster' and suffering which will surely come. He turns to his Father and pray, 'My Father, if it is possible, may this cup be taken from me. Yet not as I will, but as you will'(26:39). He does this three times, expressing his genuinely human sorrow and anguish even though he knows that his Father has only one will for him. There is a genuine temptation for him to turn away from the will of his Father as his words to his disciples also witness - 'Watch and pray so that you will not fall into temptation'(26:41). By seeking his Father earnestly, by praying to his Father with his face to the ground (26:39), he makes his resolve to deny himself and persevere to unite his will with his Father's will. He remains faithful to his call, he remains true to the commitment he made throughout his life and ministry, he keeps the words he has spoken to his disciple concerning his suffering and the giving of his life as a ransom for many. He continues to love and obey his Father with all his heart, soul and mind (22:37), and continues to love his neighbours as himself (22:39), in fact more than himself.

When his betrayer and the soldiers come to arrest him in the Garden, he refrains from violence or self-protection. He could have called twelve legions of angels from his Father to save him but he submitted to his Father's will so that the Scripture would be fulfilled (26:53-54). He is tried before the Sanhedrin and many false witnesses come forward to accuse him.[71] They even accuse him of speaking against the temple (26:60-61).[72] But he refrains from self-defence; he does not plead his innocence, nor argue with them about the correctness of the details of their accusations. He could have defended and saved himself from the looming crucifixion but he is willing to give himself into the hands of these evil men. When asked by the high priest Caiaphas if he is the Christ, the Son of God (26:63), he openly confesses that he is but immediately defines his identity as the one 'seated on the right hand of the mighty one' and 'coming on the clouds of heaven,'[73] putting himself in a unique and exalted relationship with God. He does not deny this truth in order to save himself; he makes no compromise with his identity to extricate himself from this danger. When he is charged with

---

71 Mark 14:56 adds that their statements do not agree.

72 Matthew's 'two witnesses' seem to imply that the minimum number of agreeing witnesses required for a legal condemnation to death is reached. See Num. 35:30, Deut. 17:6, 19:15.

73 The first description he has already used for himself in 22:44 where he quoted Psalm 110:1. The second description is related to the son of man figure in Daniel 7. Jesus' claims seem to constitute 'an offensive encroachment on the prerogatives of God.' D.R. Catchpole, *The Trial of Jesus* (Leiden: Brill, 1971), p. 126 and see pp. 126-48 for a full discussion of the question of blasphemy involved.

blasphemy by the high priest for his claims, he again makes no effort to quarrel with him about the appropriateness of this charge. When the Sanhedrin condemn him as worthy of the death penalty (26:66), he does not argue with their decision. When they (the guards) strike him with their fists, spit in his face, slap him, mock him and insult him, he does not retaliate (cf. the fifth antithesis). He does not repay harm with harm, insult with insult. He fulfils his own teaching and truly denies himself (16:24), walking unswervingly and humbly on the path towards the cross in unity with the will of his Father. His attitude and composure before Pilate is much the same. When he makes no attempt to reply even to one single charge put against him, Pilate is greatly amazed (27:14). But the angry crowd keep shouting to Pilate against Jesus, 'Crucify him!' In the end, Pilate under the crowd's pressure sets free a notorious prisoner, Barabbas, instead of Jesus. He has Jesus flogged and hands him over to be crucified (27:26).[74] Pilate's soldiers put a scarlet robe on him, crown him with thorns and mock him, calling out to him, taunting him as 'king of the Jews'. They again spit on him, repeatedly strike his head and pour contempt upon him. Again, he does not retaliate; he does not repay violence with violence, contempt with contempt. Without resistance, he is led away to a place called Golgotha to be crucified (27:27-31). There, Jesus is nailed and hung on the cross. Darkness comes over the land from the sixth to ninth hour (27:45). The chief priests, teachers of the law, the elders and others continue to mock him (27:40-44), 'He saved others but he can't save himself! He is the king of Israel! Let him come down now from the cross, and we believe in him. He trusts in God. ...'[75] But the God he trusts, the Father whom he loves and obeys, this time does not draw near to him. In dereliction and abandonment, he cries, 'My God, my God, why have you forsaken me?'[76] Soon after, Jesus cried out in a loud voice and gave up his spirit.

Looking back at the narrative from his entry into Jerusalem, there are a number of occasions where Jesus could have extricated himself from his enemies and spared himself the suffering of crucifixion - by not entering Jerusalem, by not arousing the hostility of the leaders and high priest with his cleansing of the temple, by saying 'No' to his Father's will at Gethsemane, by actively defending himself against the unjustified charges, by compromising his identity before the high priest,

---

74 The flogging used a lash with sharp bits for tearing the flesh and was commonly administered to a person before crucifixion, perhaps to hasten death on the cross. See D.A. Hagner, *Matthew 14-28* (Dallas, Tex.: Word Books, 1995), p. 828 for further references.

75 Ironically, some of the mocking statements are true in Matthew's story.

76 This is the only time in Matthew where Jesus addresses his Father by calling him 'God', not 'Father'. This may well be a sign of his forsakeness.

by actively appealing to Pilate that he was innocent. But Jesus, knowing his Father loves him and remaining in unity with his Father's will, denied himself every opportunity to free himself from this danger, humiliation and this suffering of crucifixion. In his unwavering love for his Father, his neighbours and enemies, he wills to deny himself of every opportunity for freedom for the sake of others' freedom, he wills to drink this cup of suffering, he wills to tread this humble and humiliating path to the bitter end, he remains true to his commitment in his baptism, temptations and ministry, and true to the promise he made to his friends. At no point does he retract himself from this path of humility, faithfulness, truth and self-giving love, despite the very great cost he has to pay and the temptations to do otherwise. One cannot detect in him any hint of self-pity in his whole journey to the cross, nor is there any trace of heroism or self-aggrandisement, nor any ulterior motives or hypocrisy. His will is to do his Father's will, to be united with him in this will, to love his neighbours and enemies unconditionally, to be united with sinful humanity and save the people from their sins by giving himself as a ransom, by having his body broken and his blood poured out for many.

Jesus not only denies himself the opportunity to extricate himself from the shame and pain of crucifixion. When he is subjected to such pain and shame, he also refrains from retaliating against his enemy. There are no less than three occasions where the people insult, mock or spit at him, and inflict physical violence and injuries upon him - at the trials before the high priest and Pilate, and at Golgotha. He is insulted, hated and the crowd shout for his crucifixion and death. The ugly violence of sinful men is inflicted upon him. The faces of hatred and the voices of taunting pierce into him. Yet he refrains from retaliating (fulfilling the fifth antithesis), he wills not to fight back, he wills to accept their injuries, not wishing the worst for them, but enduring all these pains, shames and injuries for their sake, for the sake of paying their ransom, for the sake of opening the way of forgiveness of their sins. This is what Jesus wills to do, and has consistently willed to do, that he stands in solidarity with sinners, takes away their sins and take them upon himself, giving himself as a ransom for many (those who in enmity against him crucify him are not excluded, fulfilling the sixth antithesis in Mt. 5:44-48). This is the Christ presented in the gospel of Matthew, this is the one who loves without condition, this is the perfect Son of God (5:48), this is the enduring love of God, the suffering love of God. This is how Jesus Christ the Son of God climactically reveals himself and how in unity and consonance with his Father in this love climactically *reveals his Father* (5:48), who wills his beloved Son to go through all these for precisely the same cause, for the same sinful humanity, for the sake of forgiving their sins, for the sake of cleansing their guilty conscience and removing their shame so that they might approach and call upon him as their Father with the same assurance of his love and acceptance as Jesus Christ his Son does. For their sake, he did not intervene to thwart the evil plan of the leaders to murder his Son (12:14, 26:1-5). He did not send legions of angels to rescue his Son when he was arrested. He let his beloved Son be accused, insulted, beaten, flogged and hounded by the authorities. He watched how they vented their anger and hatred upon him. He allowed the soldiers to nail his beloved Son on the cross. Finally, he himself had to abandon his beloved Son in Golgotha, he had to cast him into utter darkness and agony, causing him to cry out to him in desolation and dereliction. It is true that Jesus suffered on the cross but it is also true that his compassionate Father suffers with the Son as he suffers the loss of his Son (see below). Paradoxically, in the Father's abandonment of the Son, the Father and the Son are strangely united in their suffering of the cross for the sake of sinful humanity.

3.3 The Climax of Jesus' Revelation of His Relationship with His Father

In 3.1, it has been shown that the baptism, life and ministry of Jesus are continuous with and anticipate his death. In the former, i.e., Jesus' baptism, life and ministry, his love and his Father's love for Israel/humanity have already been manifested in his solidarity with them, his *with them* and *for them* (see 1.0 and 2.0). But when one considers his passion and death - the manner of his suffering, the manner of his self-denial and self-sacrifice, the manner of his enduring the taunts, hatred, ugly violence and painful injuries by evil men without retaliation, the manner of his drinking this cup from his Father and experiencing his abandonment, the manner of his giving himself willingly into the hands of evil men for the sake of their forgiveness and salvation, his passion and death must be seen as the climax, fulfilment, coronation and culmination of his life and ministry, as Barth has correctly observed; and his passion and death is the climax of Jesus' revelation of his unconditional love, of himself and of his Father who has the same unconditional love. However, apart from being the climax of Jesus' revelation of his Father, the cross is also the climax of Jesus' revelation of his relationship with his Father, as Barth remarks, 'In the deepest darkness of Golgotha He enters supremely into the glory of the unity of the Son with the Father. In that abandonment by God He is the One who is directly loved by God.'[77] The cross is where the unity and

---

77 *CD* IV.2, p. 252. 'Darkness' is clearly dialectically related to 'glory', and 'abandonment' to 'directly loved by God'. Barth holds these dialectical elements together.

love between the Son and the Father is supremely revealed. Barth leaves his readers to ponder on the nature of this unity and love between the Father and the Son on the cross. The following aims to explore more on this revelation of unity and love in the paradoxical event of the Father's abandonment of his Son, in terms of Jesus' knowledge, obedience and trust.

In the previous chapter, it has been remarked that Jesus' knowledge of his Father's radical righteousness and unconditional love is vital in Jesus' revelation of his Father in words (Mt. 11:27). In this chapter, it has been shown that Jesus in obedience to the Father practises the radical righteousness and unconditional love that he himself teaches, even though it means serious controversies and repeated confrontations with the religious leaders. Despite the dangers that such controversies and confrontations inevitably bring, Jesus trusts in his Father to fulfil his purpose through his words and actions and even through the oppositions of the religious leaders. As the oppositions, confrontations and dangers escalate after his entry into Jerusalem, there is no sign that Jesus' knowledge of his Father's will for him, his obedience to and trust in his Father are weakened by the escalated scale of confrontations and dangers.[78] Rather, his courage rises to the occasion. The escalation of oppositions, confrontations and dangers, and Jesus' courage on these occasions, only serve to heighten the revelation of the fact that Jesus is fully certain of his Father's will and in resolute obedience he submits to his Father's will to the end, trusting that his suffering and death will ultimately accomplish his Father's purpose within his sovereign rule. It is true that Jesus' knowledge of his Father's righteous will, his obedience to and trust in his Father have already been revealed in his life and ministry, but in view of the facts (i) that the situations after his entry into Jerusalem - the intensified confrontations, persecutions, arrest, trials, floggings, beatings, insults, humiliation and finally crucifixion - call for a heightened degree of *conviction* of the Father's will, *obedience* to and *trust* in the Father on Jesus' part, and (ii) that Jesus has fully met this call, it is proper to claim that Jesus' knowledge of his Father's will, his obedience to and trust in his Father have been climactically revealed in his persecutions, suffering and death in Jerusalem. But this means that Jesus' unity with and love for his Father, expressed in terms of knowledge, obedience and trust, have also been climactically revealed in his suffering and death.

The above considerations bring out from Jesus' perspective his unity with his Father in his suffering and death, despite, paradoxically,

---

78 For Jesus' conflict with the religious leaders and its escalation in Matthew, see chapter 7, 'The Antagonists of Jesus' in J. D. Kingsbury, *Matthew as Story* (Philadephia: Fortress, 1988).

experiencing his abandonment. The following question arises from such considerations: from the Father's perspective, could the Father be united with his Son and continue to love his Son as he abandoned him on the cross? The Father was certainly united with his Son in their loving purpose to save the people from their sins. But does the unity also include his love for his abandoned Son? Can Barth's statement - 'In that abandonment by God He is the One who is directly loved by God.' - be substantiated? It seems that the narrative pattern identified above may shed some light on this important question. It has been shown that Jesus' baptism and his death form an inclusio, and that his baptism can be interpreted as a prefiguration of his death. Therefore, the two have the closest of connections. The latter may be better understood in the light of the former. In Jesus' baptism (the first bracket of the inclusio), the Father spoke to his Son, 'This is my Son, whom I love; with him I am well pleased'(Mt. 3:17). These words are a combination of Psalm 2:7 and Isaiah 42:1. Jesus is God's beloved Son and his suffering servant. This is not only true at his baptism (the first bracket) but also true at his cross (the second bracket) just as it is true that Jesus identifies himself with sinners both in his baptism and on the cross. God's love for his Son is irrevocable (cf. God's love for Israel is irrevocable; Rom. 11:28-29). God's love for his Son, which was made explicit at the prefiguration of his death - baptism, remains faithful and true to the end at the fulfilment of that prefiguration - his death on the cross. Therefore, Barth is correct in stating that the suffering Son on the cross is directly loved by God. But what does this mean? Does it mean that the Father maintains his loving communion with his Son even on the cross? Jesus' words of dereliction on the cross reveals the answer to this question to be the negative one: Jesus could only know his Father's love as a matter of conviction, not as an experience of his Father's loving communion at that point. And even this knowledge of his Father's love cannot contain the immense excruciating pains he suffers on the cross, both the pain of physical suffering and the pain of abandonment, which in his genuine humanity burst through and are expressed in the words of dereliction. The cross is the singular point where the communion between the Father and the Son through the Spirit, or Jesus' experience of rest in his Father's presence (11:27-30), is cut off even though the Father does love his Son and the Son knows his Father's love even there. The question raised above - does the unity between the Father and the Son include the Father's love for the Son? - can therefore be answered in the affirmative. Given this answer to the question, there emerges another aspect of the unity between Jesus and his Father - suffering.

One can infer the Father's love for his Son on the cross by identifying the baptism-death literary pattern (inclusio) in Matthew as above. But other than this, the text is almost silent on the Father's attitude towards his suffering Son. Does the Father suffer the loss of his Son as the Son suffers the abandonment by his Father on the cross? Barth certainly thinks so.

> It is not at all the case that God has no part in the suffering of Jesus Christ even in His mode of being as the Father. No, there is a *particula veri* in the teaching of the early Patripassians. This is that primarily it is God the Father who suffers in the offering and sending of His Son, in His abasement. The suffering is not His own, but the alien suffering of the creature, of man, which He takes to Himself in Him. But He does suffer it in the humiliation of His Son with a depth with which it never was or will be suffered by any man - apart from the One who is His Son. And He does so in order that, having been borne by Him in the offering and sending of His Son, it should not have to be suffered in this way by man. *This fatherly fellow-suffering of God is the mystery, the basis, of the humiliation of His Son*; the truth of that which takes place historically in His crucifixion.[79]

Barth's understanding of the Father's suffering might have influenced J. Moltmann's similar understanding in *The Crucified God*.[80] How can Barth's and Moltmann's understanding be justified from the gospel narratives? Only by inference. An important text for such an inference is Jesus' compassion for the lost and suffering crowds in Mt. 9:36, which Barth expounds at great length and depth. Now if Jesus' compassion reveals his Father's compassion for the lost sinners who are suffering because of their own sins, then it is in the spirit of Matthew to say that the Father is compassionate towards his obedient Son who is suffering on the cross because of others' sins, even though on the other hand he

---

79 *CD* IV.2, p. 357, italics mine; see also pp. 84-5. J. Thompson, in *The Holy Spirit in the Theology of Karl Barth* (Allison Park, Pa: Pickwick Publications, 1991), p. 23, points out Barth's understanding of the Father's suffering of the cross, which preceded Moltmann's understanding.

80 'In that case one will understand the deadly aspect of the event between the Father who forsakes and the Son who is forsaken, and conversely the living aspect of the event between the Father who loves and the Son who loves. The Son suffers in his love being forsaken by the Father as he dies. The Father suffers in his love the grief of the death of the Son. In that case, whatever proceeds from the event between the Father and the Son must be understood as the spirit of the surrender of the Father and the Son, as the spirit which creates love for forsaken men, as the spirit which brings the dead alive. ... [W]e have not just seen one person of the Trinity suffer in the event of the cross, as though the Trinity were already present in itself, in the divine nature. And we have not interpreted the death of Jesus as a divine-human event, but as a trinitarian event between the Son and the Father.' J. Moltmann, *The Crucified God* (London: SCM Press, 1974), p. 245.

has to abandon his Son also because of sins. The sin of humanity, which Jesus bears as the suffering servant, is the cause of both God's abandonment of his Son and his compassion for his Son; i.e., the Father has compassion for his obedient Son who suffers abandonment because of sin. If in Barth's interpretation of compassion in Mt. 9:36, 'sympathy in our modern sense is far too feeble a word - but it went right into His heart, into Himself, so that it was now His misery,' then Jesus' misery and suffering of abandonment does affect his compassionate Father who takes his Son's misery and suffering into his Fatherly heart. One might infer from these that in the Father's abandonment of his Son on the cross and in his compassion for his Son, the Father himself experiences the misery and suffering of this abandonment. One has to assume a Father to be apathetic, impassible, uncaring, indifferent and even cruel if he does not suffer the abandonment of his own Son, and one has to give an explanation of what kind of compassion Jesus reveals of his Father in his ministry. It is true that the above interpretation of the Father's suffering compassion for his Son on the cross is an inference which Matthew does not give explicitly and some biblical scholars will object to this kind of interpretation. But a dogmatician, encouraged by narrative criticism to responsibly fill in the gaps of narratives according to the indications shown to the readers, may be more inclined to make the above interpretation.[81] And the Father's attitude towards Jesus and sin on the cross may thus be understood as wrath against sin - hence abandonment - but compassion for his suffering Son - hence his own suffering.[82] If the inference of the Father's compassion for his Son is

---

81 See Mark Powell's *What is Narrative Criticism?* pp. 52-3 about 'showing', and pp. 18, 21 about gap.

82 This understanding of the Fatherhood of God, rather than the one where only the wrath of God on Jesus is in view with no signs of understanding and compassion for him, may have significant negative pastoral consequence and implications for the church, and the whole understanding of God. Tom Smail writes in *The Forgotten Father,* pp. 138-9, 'Many of us have known a sin-soaked guilt-ridden evangelicalism where there has been a great deal of talk about the cost of our atonement in the blood of Christ and very little upon the free and loving grace of the Father who in his intense desire for the homecoming of sinners gave his Son. The God people have been shown is the righteous judge who requires the propitiation which Jesus alone can offer, and who in response to it can just manage to restrain his wrath against us provided those redeemed by Christ continue to behave in a moral and religious way. In such a context which is of course parody, but one that many people have absorbed as gospel, the ability to answer the grace and freedom of God's forgiveness with a free and joyful heart, of which Forsyth speaks, was one that to put it mildly did not come easily, and their confidence and expectation towards God was about as great as that of a man who expected a life sentence but has been put on probation for life instead. In such a context atonement has the smell of law fulfilled rather than of

taken into account, then the Father is united with his Son in his love for the Son and in his own suffering of the cross - both the Father and the Son love and suffer.

If from Jesus' perspective he is united with his Father through his knowledge of his Father's will, his obedience, his trust in and his love for his Father, then from the Father's perspective the Father is united with his Son through his love for his Son and his suffering of the cross with his Son. Even though the Son on the cross was abandoned by the Father, paradoxically the cross can be interpreted as the supreme revelation of the relationship between the Father and the Son - unity and love. To conclude, Jesus' suffering and death is not only the climactic revelation of his Father, but also the climactic revelation of his relationship/unity with his Father.[83]

4.0 Concluding Summary

Jesus in freely exercising his own insuperable and relentless authority in his ministry of words and actions, without even invoking the name of his Father or the inspiration of the Spirit, revealed himself to be the Lord in his own right. However, he came not only to reveal himself but also his Father in his words and actions. His ability to reveal his Father did not merely rest on his equality with his Father but also on his unity with his Father. In the non-linear concept of revelation, his relationship/unity with his Father was both the basis and part of the content of his revelation - in addition to his revelation of his Father (Barth's point) he also revealed his relationship with his Father (a point complementing Barth's). His unity with his Father was characterised by intimate knowledge of the Father, obedience, trust, rest and love. This unity was revealed not only in his compassionate ministry amongst the people, but also in his fearless confrontations with the religious leaders as he fulfilled the radical righteousness and unconditional love that he preached, breaking and transcending the ritual and other legalistic

---

grace poured out.'

83 Even though the unity between the Father and the Son on the cross did not include their communion (because of abandonment), the cross still revealed the close communion/unity between the Father and the Son in his life - Jesus' cry of dereliction and forsakeness on the cross implies a state of non-forsakeness or close communion with his Father before encountering the state of abandonment on the cross. His cry of dereliction confirms and corroborates with Mt. 11:25-30 in witnessing to his experience of the Father which he enjoyed in his earthly life through the Spirit - rest in his Father's communing presence. Paradoxically, Jesus' separation from his Father in his death revealed Jesus' intimate communion with his Father in his life.

barriers of their Jewish religion. As Jesus' conflicts with the leaders escalated and reached the climactic point in Jerusalem, so did his revelation of his Father and his revelation of his unity with his Father climax in Jerusalem. Paradoxically and dialectically, as Barth suggests, the Father's abandonment of the Son on the cross simultaneously and supremely revealed 'the glory of the unity of the Son with the Father'.[84] Given Jesus' Lordship and his unity with his Father as revealed in his life, ministry and death, the next question to consider in detail is his relationship with the Spirit, which is the subject matter of the next chapter.

---

84 *CD* IV.2, p. 252.

Excursus A

Emphasis on Jesus' Life Only or on His Death Only:
Schleiermacher and Calvin

Churches of the liberal persuasion tend to major on Jesus' life while the conservative branch tends to major on his death. See Hendry, *The Gospel of the Incarnation*, for a criticism of neglecting Jesus' life and ministry. It is interesting that while Schleiermacher concentrated on the life and ministry of Jesus (146 out of the 185 sermons on the synoptic gospels deal with the period between Jesus' baptism and arrest)[85], Calvin seemed to have put his emphasis on the birth and passion of Jesus (though he must have covered the life and ministry of Jesus in the last four and a half years of his career, see below). For Schleiermacher, the death of Jesus was not central in man's reconciliation with God, as Calvin would insist. There needs to be no doctrine of atonement for Schleiermacher to understand such reconciliation. What is needed is the impression that Christ makes on the hearers through the proclaimed word, the spiritual self-presentation of Christ which draws them into Christ's power of God-consciousness. Such presentation does include Jesus' submission unto death on the cross but it does not have the atoning significance that Calvin ascribed to the cross. On the other hand, it is noteworthy that Calvin gave a sustained series of sermons on the four gospels only in the last five years of his life (1559-1564, on harmony of the Gospels). Calvin started his regular preaching career in 1536 when he consented to remain in Geneva where he shortly later became pastor. There is only scant information about his preaching and the texts covered from 1536 to 1549, after which time more information is available.[86] From 1549, the records show that Calvin preached twice every Sunday and once every weekday of the alternate weeks. From 1549 to 1558, he preached from Old Testament books, Acts and Epistles from the New Testament. (See the Chronological Chart in Parker, *Calvin's Preaching*.) The exceptions are those sermons preached in the Holy Week, Easter Day and Christmas. The texts for these church festivals in Easter and Christmas were taken from the gospels - the passion and resurrection narratives, and Luke 2 respectively. It was only in July 1559 to February 1564 that he preached a very sustained series of Sunday morning sermons on the gospels (and their harmony). This can be partly explained by the fact that he had completed the writing of

---

85 See D. DeVries, *Jesus Christ in the Preaching of Calvin and Schleiermacher* (Louisville, Ky.: Westminster John Knox Press, 1996), p. 79.
86 See T. H. L. Parker, *Calvin's Preaching* (Edinburgh: T. & T. Clark, 1992), p. 62.

his commentary on the harmony of the gospels only a few years before in 1555. (See DeVries, *Jesus Christ in the Preaching of Calvin and Schleiermacher* p. 26.) Of the sermons preached in that series, unfortunately only those sermons on Mt. 1-5:12, Mark 1 and Luke 1-4 (65 sermons in all) and nine other sermons on the passion and resurrection were published in Calvin's lifetime. And only these sermons from the series were included in the collection of Calvin's Work, *Calvini Opera*. These sermons cover from the birth of Jesus to the earliest phase of his ministry, and his passion and resurrection. One wonders why the sermons covering the life and ministry of Jesus, presumably preached in those four and a half years, were not published. Was this pattern merely a coincidence with no significance? But this pattern is very much echoed by his Geneva Catechism. In this Catechism, the question: 'Why do you leap at once from his birth to his death, passing over the whole history of his life?' was answered, 'Because nothing is treated of here but what so properly belongs to our salvation, as in a manner to contain the substance of it'.[87] This suggests Calvin's pattern of preference of Jesus' birth and death to his life and ministry. And this suggested pattern echoes Wright's complaint of the neglect of the life and ministry of Jesus in conservative theologies and preaching. See Wright, *Jesus and the Victory of God*, p. 14-5, quoted in 3.0 of chapter 1.

---

87 *Joannis Calvini Opera Selecta* (Monachii: C. Kaiser, 1926-1962), 1:82.

CHAPTER 5

Christ and the Spirit

Summary: Is the divinity of Jesus in any sense derived from inspiration by the Holy Spirit? The view of J.D.G. Dunn (and T.W. Manson) on this issue will be considered. By examining the paucity of references to the Spirit in the synoptic gospels and possible redactional activities, particularly in Luke, it becomes evident that the evangelists were much more interested in presenting Jesus at the centre stage of the gospel story than the Spirit, though at the same time Jesus gives the Spirit the highest honour. Jesus is consistently presented as the true author of his words and actions even though he is always full of the Spirit. Jesus' relationship with the Spirit as presented by the evangelists is one of Lordship, i.e., akin to the Father's relationship with the Spirit. Various suggestions to account for the paucity of references to the Spirit in the synoptic gospels will be evaluated. An alternative suggestion will be proposed which takes into account the readers of the gospels and the evangelists' communicative strategy.

An important element in the first century Jewish expectation of God's decisive intervention (the coming of God's kingdom, see 1.0 of chapter 2) was that God would inaugurate a new covenant with his people where, apart from the forgiveness of sins, God would pour out his Holy Spirit on to the people. The Spirit would cleanse the people and enable them to keep the Torah from their hearts (Jer. 31:31f, Ezek. 11:19f, 36:22-32, Joel 2:28, Isa. 32:15, Zech. 12:10).[1] Along with this, there was

---

1   Wright, *The New Testament and the People of God*, p. 301.

also the expectation of a Messiah, the anointed one, endowed with the power of the Spirit to liberate the people from their bondages.

> A major strand of Judaism anticipated a Messiah mightily endowed with the Spirit as *both* the Spirit of prophecy (affording unique wisdom and knowledge of the Lord as the basis of his dynamic righteousness and 'fear of the Lord') *and* the Spirit of power (i.e., of the 'might' by which he asserts liberating rule against opposition). The model is first David, then more especially the 'Davidic' figure of Isaiah 11:1-4, endowed with the Spirit of wisdom, knowledge and might. The Targum renders Isaiah 11:1-2, 'And a king shall come forth from the sons of Jesse, and the Messiah shall be exalted from the sons of his sons. And upon him shall rest the spirit of prophecy, a spirit of wisdom and understanding, a spirit of counsel and might, a spirit of knowledge and the fear of the Lord.'[2]

The expected figure of the Messiah was himself not a divine person and his power to act and liberate the people came from God through the bestowal of the Holy Spirit on him. In that sense, the expected human Messiah was to be dependent on the Spirit. However, the New Testament writers were not strictly bounded by every element of such an expectation; they were free to present a Messiah who was both continuous and discontinuous with this expectation. For example, the Messiah of the New Testament was the divine Lord (see 3.1 of chapter 2) which was not claimed by the expectation - discontinuity, while at the same time he was a genuine human being - continuity. Also, the New Testament presents a Messiah who was filled with the Spirit of God (cf. Jesus' baptism) and by the Spirit healed and set the people free from their bondages. In a general sense, this aspect of the Spirit-filled Messiah was continuous with the expectation. However, the New Testament gives more details about the Messiah's relationship with the Spirit. An important question to be put to the New Testament is: what is the nature of Jesus' relationship with the Spirit? In particular, in what sense was the Spirit the *source* of power for his life and ministry? These important questions have been considered by some theologians and New Testament scholars in their conceptions of Spirit Christology.[3] Many feel that the traditional Logos Christology does not do full justice to the role of the Spirit in Jesus which is portrayed in the New Testament. In traditional dogmatic theology, even though the distinctive role of procession between the Father and the Son is attributed to the Spirit in the immanent Trinity, in the life and ministry of Jesus in the economy

---

2 Turner, *The Holy Spirit and Spiritual Gifts*, p. 17.

3 See, e.g., R Del Colle, *Christ and the Spirit* (New York; Oxford: Oxford University Press, 1994), for a review.

the Logos played such a dominant role that little room is left for the Spirit. One of the reasons for this is that the dominance of the Logos in the economy would ensure the divinity of Jesus, while a Spirit Christology might have the opposite effect. However, in the conception of the immanent Trinity, where the divinity of Jesus is not under threat, the role of the Spirit between the Father and the Son can be quite clearly acknowledged. It seems that the inadequate space given to the Spirit in the economy is closely related to the understanding of the humanity and divinity of Jesus Christ. There seem to be two sources of divine action in Jesus, the Logos and the Spirit. How is it possible to stress both at the same time? Does not one make the other redundant? If the Logos is emphasised, little room may be left for the Spirit. If the Spirit is emphasised, little room may be left for the Logos and the divinity of Jesus, who would become like the human Messiah expected by the Jews. The dichotomy between Logos Christology and Spirit Christology is not an easy problem to solve. But this problem needs to be faced in a study of the economic Trinity, the conception of which will have implications for the conception of the corresponding immanent Trinity. This is the problem to be addressed in this chapter and the next, with the help of the results obtained in the previous two chapters and some further study of the gospel narratives on this particular question of Jesus' relationship with the Spirit.

The Spirit Christology of J.D.G. Dunn will be presented and evaluated first, followed by the problem of the paucity of references to the Spirit in the synoptic gospels. Possible solutions to this problem will be evaluated by a specific examination of the gospels of Matthew and Luke before a proposal is made at the end of this chapter. The discussion in this chapter naturally leads on to the next chapter on a theology of the Father, Son and Holy Spirit.

1.0 Jesus and the Spirit

1.1 J.D.G Dunn

Dunn wrote two of the most significant books on pneumatology in the last century - *Baptism in the Holy Spirit: A Reexamination of the New Testament Teaching on the Gift of the Spirit in Relation to Pentecostalism Today* (London: SCM Press, 1970) and *Jesus and the Spirit* (London: SCM Press, 1975). His view on Jesus' relationship with the Spirit is expressed in these two books. A summary of his view can also be found in his *Christology in the Making: A New Testament Inquiry into the Origins of the Doctrine of the Incarnation* (London: SCM Press, 1989). He attributes Jesus' teaching and mighty works, *both* in terms of authority and power, to the inspiration and empowerment of the Holy Spirit.

> The eschatological kingdom was present for Jesus only because the eschatological Spirit was present in and through him. In other words, it was not so much a case of 'Where I am there is the Kingdom', as *'Where the Spirit is there is the Kingdom.'*[4]

> His consciousness of a spiritual power so real, so effective, so new, so final, was the wellspring of *both* his *proclamation* of the presentness of the future Kingdom and his *authority* in deed and word.[5]

> Here we see coming to clear expression Jesus' sense of the awfulness, the numinous quality, the eschatological finality of the power which *possessed* him.[6]

According to Dunn, Jesus was then so possessed and inspired by this spiritual power that he was enabled to proclaim the presentness of the Kingdom of God, speak and act in authority. The presence of the Kingdom is ultimately attributed to the Spirit's presence, not Jesus' presence. Speaking about the authority of Jesus' preaching, Dunn wrote,

> Again, it is perhaps significant that the authority of his preaching can be said to *derive* from his sense of being Spirit-inspired, but also from his sense of Sonship (Mt. 11:27). *'Father' as much as 'Spirit' spells 'authority'.*[7]

Dunn augmented the Spirit as the source of Jesus' authority with the Father as the source, leaving a void in the Son's own authority. He again repeated this external source of Jesus' authority.

> He was a charismatic in the sense that he manifested *a power and authority which was not his own*, which he had neither achieved nor conjured up, but which was *given to him, his by virtue of the Spirit*/power of God upon him. The power did not possess him and control him so that he was its instrument willing or unwilling. But *neither was he the author of it; nor was he able to dispose of it or ignore it at will.* ... It is in terms of this consciousness of power and authority his own and yet not his own, *this inspiration immediate and direct from beyond*, that Jesus can be

---

4   *Jesus and the Spirit* , p. 48. Italics mine.
5   *Ibid.*, p. 54. Italics mine.
6   *Ibid.*, p. 53. Italics mine.
7   *Ibid.*, p. 66. Italics mine.

called a charismatic.[8]

Even though Dunn very briefly mentions the authority as Jesus' own, this authority is actually not his own because it came from beyond him and to him through the Spirit's inspiration. Dunn can comfortably write, 'The Spirit was the "divinity" of Jesus.'[9] Dunn's subordination of Jesus to the Spirit can be further understood at the following crucial point. Jesus is the *object* inspired and possessed by the Spirit; he is therefore dependent on the Spirit. In his understanding, Jesus cannot be the *subject* who possesses the Spirit and cannot be the ultimate and true *author* of his action in the Spirit.

T. W. Manson trod a similar line before Dunn when he considered the authority in Jesus' teaching. He contrasted Jesus' authority with that of OT prophets.

> A single phrase, the frequent and emphatic ἀμὴν λέγω ὑμῖν , 'Verily I say unto you', is enough to set Jesus as a teacher apart from either prophets or scribes. When the prophet spoke with authority, it was as the messenger of God: and the message which he had to deliver was properly introduced by the formula, 'Thus saith the Lord'. When the scribe spoke authoritatively, it was to declare what Scripture or tradition had to say. When Jesus speaks with authority, the formula is 'I say unto you'. ... [T]he only ultimately satisfactory explanation of the authority of Jesus is that which sets the foundation of it in his unique spiritual experience.[10]

He rightly observed that an OT prophet's authority was a 'delegated authority' derived from religious experience,[11] but he effectively put Jesus into the same class as the OT prophets when he wrote, 'With Jesus likewise, the source of his authority is to be sought in the experience at Jordan which initiates his public activity.'[12] As the OT prophets received their delegated authority in their religious experience, so Jesus received his delegated authority in his spiritual experience at the Jordan. Like Dunn but before him, he attributed Jesus' authority to his Sonship and the Spirit's inspiration which are two important aspects of Jesus' baptism at the Jordan. And he concluded, 'The complete dependence on the Father carries with it the astonishing independence of men: and the conviction of constant possession by the Spirit justifies the substitution

---

8   *Ibid.*, p. 87. Italics mine.
9   *Ibid.*, p. 325
10 T. W. Manson, *The Teaching of Jesus* (London: Cambridge University Press, 1931), p. 106
11 *Ibid.*, p. 107
12 *Ibid.*

of "I say unto you" for "Thus saith the Lord".[13] For Manson as it is for Dunn, there is a christological vacuum as far as the source of Jesus' authority is concerned.

1.2 Response to Dunn (and Manson)

Although Manson's argument seems acceptable at first sight, it is in fact incoherent. His argument for Jesus' distinctive use of the phrase 'I say unto you' compared to the OT prophets' use of 'Thus saith the Lord' hinges on the fact that Jesus' spiritual experience, particularly at the Jordan, is unique and distinct from the prophets' experience. Somehow Jesus' unique experience of his Father and the Spirit at Jordan is the source of his unique authority. But one wonders if Jesus' unique spiritual experience does afford him the right to use a different formula from the OT prophets, 'I say unto you', given the fact that in Manson's understanding the authority both of Jesus and the prophets *wholly* comes from an external source - God himself. According to Manson, the authority both of Jesus and the prophets is *wholly* delegated by God, i.e., Jesus does not have his own authority. In that case, Jesus should align himself with the self-effacing prophets and declare the source of his authority by using the phrase 'Thus saith the Lord' (or 'Thus saith my Father') as the prophets did; Jesus, despite being the Father's Son and having had a unique experience of (or even a unique relationship with) his Father, is not entitled to use the phrase 'I say unto you' because the use of this phrase demands a self-owned authority on the part of the speaker, and those who do not have this self-owned authority should advisedly use the alternative formula, as the self-effacing prophets clearly did. According to Manson, Jesus lacks this self-owned authority. The conclusion he should draw - but did not - is that Jesus should not use the authoritative formula. Therefore, starting with Manson's premise of Jesus' unique spiritual experience at the Jordan, we have found ourselves unable to arrive at his conclusion that Jesus can properly use the unique formula 'I say unto you'. Manson's argument is thus deemed to be incoherent. Another approach to Manson's argument is the following: how conceivable is the scenario which corresponds to his argument? How conceivable is it that Jesus' authority was *wholly* derived from his Father and yet repeatedly used the 'I say to you' formula? That is as conceivable as the OT prophets who received their authority *wholly* from God and yet repeatedly used the formula 'I say to you' in their addresses to Israel. But these are inconceivable scenarios.

Similarly, Dunn's argument that Jesus' experience of the Spirit's inspiration and the Father is the basis of his authority in teaching (and

---

13 *Ibid.*

healing) cannot stand. Although he does refer to Jesus' 'emphatic ἐγώ' and 'Amen' as a 'style of speaking expressing a consciousness of transcendent authority', and quotes W. Barclay's comment on Jesus as 'a teacher who needed no authority other than his own', he does not bring these observations to bear on his assertion that Jesus' authority is derived from his experience in the Spirit.[14] One of Dunn's crucial errors lies in this mishandling of the authoritative sayings of Jesus, whose ultimate significance he is reluctant to draw, possibly because it will become the antithesis of his thesis. One should also note that despite the gospels' portrayal of the Spirit in Jesus, they do not in any way attribute his authority to the Spirit. Dunn's thesis is not actually found in the gospels as he would wish. It will be shown in 2.0 that the reverse, Jesus being Lord of the Spirit, is what the evangelists intended to portray.

However, it may be argued that in view of the Father's committing all things to the Son (Mt. 11:27), there is a real sense that the Son's authority proceeds from the Father. But the fact that the Son invokes his Father's name neither in his teachings nor in his mighty acts, but typically invokes his own name, calls for a careful consideration of the issue of authority. Even though the Son's authority is in some sense derived from his Father, at the same time one finds in the narratives that he himself also has his inherent authority, which he exercises as his own in his typical sayings and mighty acts. Therefore, his authority is in some sense delegated, but it is *not wholly delegated* (as is in the case of the prophets) because of the rightful authority of his own. Dunn and Manson have interpreted this rather complicated issue of authority too simplistically, effectively bringing the Son to the level of the prophets and attributing the Son's authority to the Father and the Spirit, but not to the Son. This book aims to look for a more nuanced and satisfactory solution to this issue. The Son's Lordship and authority raises the

---

14 Dunn, *Jesus and the Spirit*, p. 79. He also writes on the same page, 'It is this charismatic nature of Jesus' authority, the immediacy of his sense of authority together with the conscious self reference of so much of his teaching, which seems to set Jesus apart from other men of comparable significance in the history of religions.' In saying this, he quotes H.F. von Campenhausen, 'Again and again the only discernible backing for his words and actions is himself and his own decision; and for this there seems to be no appropriate name nor standard of comparison.' *Ecclesiastical Authority and Spiritual Power in the Church of the First Three Centuries* (London: Adam and Charles Black, 1969), p. 4.. But Dunn does not square these comments of the incomparable egocentric authority of Jesus with his assertion - Jesus' authority was derived from the Spirit. And he dithers earlier on p. 79 on Jesus' authority, 'His authority was charismatic also in the sense that it was immediately received from God, or rather was the immediate authority of God.' The data push him towards the latter but he makes no further use of it, committing himself to the source of the Spirit.

questions of (i) his unity with the Spirit and (ii) his unity with his Father. These questions will be treated in chapter 6 on a theology of the Trinity. But for now it is sufficient to maintain the fact that Jesus did use the authoritative formula, which implies that Jesus' authority was *not wholly derived* from a unique spiritual experience and he was therefore genuinely in a different class from the OT prophets. To explain his use of such authoritative formula, one has to conclude either that Jesus did not use the formula appropriately, i.e., he has no inherent authority and used the formula presumptuously, or that Jesus was not a Son wholly bereft of his own authority. Max Turner writes,

> While Jesus is presented as the giver of foundational teaching, the authority of the content is presented as his own ('I say to you ...'), rather than attributed to the Spirit.[15]

Next, Jesus' authority will be considered in the context of his revelation of his Father.[16] If he is to reveal his Father's sovereign authority on earth in person, he must possess/own the same sovereign authority and exercise it freely as his own, as his Father would exercise it, so that he in the exercise of such sovereign authority truly corresponds to his Father and thereby reveals him *in person*. If he was bereft of his own sovereign authority and spoke with a wholly delegated authority, he would have to efface himself and speak as the prophets spoke. In that case, he would not have corresponded to his Father in this respect of sovereign authority and would have failed to reveal him in person in that respect; the disciples' encounter with Jesus Christ (and for that matter the reader's encounter with him as well) would not then be a genuinely unimpaired encounter with God. But this is not the picture that Matthew presents.

Dunn is keen to emphasise that Jesus' baptism at the Jordan initiates the new covenant and the new epoch, and sees him as the first of many entering eschatological sonship.[17] He understands Jesus' experience of sonship and relationship with the Spirit at the Jordan as the archetype for Christians.[18] He can entertain the thought that 'divinity' could be interpreted as an unusually high degree of inspiration (to the nth degree) such that the disciples of Jesus are not qualitatively different from Jesus, only quantitatively.[19] Similarly, Manson has effectively put Jesus in the

---

15 Turner, *The Holy Spirit and Spiritual Gifts*, p. 33.

16 Cf. 4.0 of chapter 3, 'Jesus' Lordship and His Revelation of His Father's Lordship'.

17 '[T]here is a sense in which he only becomes Messiah and Son at Jordan.' Dunn, *Baptism in the Holy Spirit*, p. 28.

18 *Ibid.*, p. 32.

19 *Jesus and the Spirit*, p. 91.

same class as OT prophets in his use of delegated authority in teaching. It is understandable that Dunn and Manson have made such moves, because there are genuine similarities between Jesus and the disciples, between Jesus and the prophets, in their relationship with the Spirit - the same Spirit moves in them all. But the fact that the same Spirit moves in them all does not necessarily cast them into the same, monolithic, relationship with the Spirit. Indeed, E. Schweizer warns of the over-simplistic picture of Jesus as the first example of a pneumatic,

> The community experienced the gift of the Spirit as the sign of God which stamped it as the people of the last time. It realised that this rested solely on the coming of Jesus and faith in him. For a long time, however, it was unable to formulate this belief clearly. On the other hand, by *avoiding so consistently the solution of simply portraying Jesus as the first pneumatic*, it displayed with astonishing clarity an awareness that Jesus was not making it the people of the last time either as a pneumatic Example or as a Teacher. The one essential point is that in Him God Himself encountered His people. All the Spirit-statements concerning Jesus simply underline His uniqueness, His eschatological position, the fact that in Him God Himself is really present as He is not present anywhere else.[20]

Turner, in discussing the Spirit on Jesus in Luke, also warns of such a simplistic approach.

> The clear emphasis on the Spirit as the Messiah's endowment should also warn us against too quickly assuming Luke presents Jesus as a pattern for all other Christians' experience of the Spirit. Both the timing of his reception of the Spirit and the *nature of his endowment* with the Spirit might be anticipated to have *unique* elements corresponding to his unique mission.[21]

An understanding of Jesus' relationship with the Spirit needs to be more nuanced than that Dunn and Manson have provided. It is difficult to see the divinity of Jesus Christ in their understanding of Jesus' utter dependence on the Spirit and the Father. An inspired man other than Jesus but adopted by the Spirit can conceivably play Jesus' role in their schemes. Yet the gospel narratives and the NT as a whole do not tolerate such schemes. And a dilution of the sovereign majesty and divine authority of Jesus Christ amounts to a damaging dilution of the decisive finality in which he reveals his Father's sovereign majesty and divine authority on earth (Barth's point). What then is the nature of

---

20 *TDNT,* vol. VI, pp. 403-4. Italics mine.
21 Turner, *The Holy Spirit and Spiritual Gifts,* p. 35. Italics mine.

Jesus' relationship with the Spirit and the nature of Jesus' authority in relation to his Father's? Does the study of the passages from the gospel narratives in Matthew conducted in chapters 3 and 4 yield any clue?

1.2.1 JESUS' AUTHORITY IN TEACHING AND MIGHTY ACTS IN MATTHEW

In considering Jesus' humanity in the temptations in the wilderness (see 5.0 of chapter 3), it was proposed that Jesus, when meditating and pondering over the OT Scripture, received in greater details his Father's will for him in his coming mission, and that the Spirit's role of leading Jesus in the wilderness could be interpreted as conveying his Father's will to him. After receiving the new law from his Father during the forty days and forty nights, Jesus delivered this new law to the people and his disciples in the Sermon on the Mount. (This interpretation uses Moses as a typology for Jesus.) That Jesus received his Father's righteous will at some stage was a necessary process in his preparation for ministry, for one could not assume that he had known his Father's will from birth (such an assumption is inconsistent with Luke 2:52 which is about Jesus' growth in wisdom). In taking seriously the humanity of Jesus, it was suggested that Scripture and the Spirit played significant roles in Jesus' knowing his Father's will.

In Mt. 11:25-30, in the midst of speaking of the Father revealing himself to little children, Jesus acknowledged that this revelation of the Father - 'all things' in 11:27 - 'have been committed to me by my Father.' The subsequent sentence about Jesus' unique mutual relationship with the Father elaborates this point - the Father in that intimate relationship with his Son is known by the Son who thus is able to reveal the Father. This means that there is a definite conveying of the Father's self to the Son in the Son's revelation of him. It was proposed that the Spirit, despite the lack of explicit reference in Mt. 11:25-30, implicitly plays the role of conveying the Father to the Son.

If these interpretations are correct, then the Father and the Spirit are the source of the *content* of Jesus' teaching. On this point, one can agree with Dunn,

> His own experience of God, of divine power and inspiration, made clear to him what parts of OT prophecy were applicable to and descriptive of his ministry, and what were not.[22]

But one cannot agree with Dunn and Manson that Jesus was bereft of his own authority and that his *authority* as well as the *content* of his teaching were *both* wholly derived from the Father and the Spirit. For

---

22 Dunn, *Jesus and the Spirit*, p. 61.

the data in the synoptic gospels do not concur with this, as has been seen in the narrative studies in chapters 3 and 4 on Jesus' teachings and mighty acts. In the exegeses of the antitheses of the Sermon on the Mount, one finds that Jesus did not invoke any authority other than his own - he did not invoke his Father's authority nor the inspiration of the Spirit. By the repeated use of his formula - 'But I say to you ...' - he exercised his own, egocentric, authority (see 3.2 of chapter 3). Jesus' characteristic egocentric authority in his teaching is not only found in the six antitheses alone, or the Sermon on the Mount, or the gospel of Matthew, it is a ubiquitous feature of his sayings in the four gospels (see 3.3 of chapter 3). Such constant and consistent use of egocentric authority on Jesus' part contradicts the notion of a derived authority. Someone with a derived authority is bound to signify his source by using the formula 'Thus saith the Lord' but Jesus did not use this formula to invoke the name and authority of his Father. The same egocentric authority exercised by Jesus can also be clearly discerned in his acts, as was seen in the exegeses of his acts in 1.1 to 1.3 of chapter 4. Again, Jesus characteristically healed the leper, the centurion's servant and moved freely amongst tax collectors and sinners as the Lord, radically contradicting Jewish traditions and practices with his own authority. In none of these and his other activities in Matthew, did Jesus invoke the name of his Father or the inspiration of the Spirit *in his acts*. He might have mentioned the involvement of the Spirit in exorcism in Mt. 12:28, but that occurred within a verbal exchange in his controversy with the Pharisees, not in an act of exorcism, and the involvement of the Spirit in no sense weakened his authority (see next section). Matthew also mentions the involvement of the Spirit in 12:18, but it occurs in Matthew's own comment on Jesus' fulfilment of Isaiah 42:1-4, again not on Jesus' lips in the context of an act of teaching or healing by Jesus. And the Spirit's involvement mentioned there does not relate directly to Jesus' authority or imply that Jesus' authority is a purely derived one. In sum, regarding Jesus' words and actions, Matthew never presents Jesus invoking his Father's name and authority in the act of teaching or healing by using formulae such as 'thus saith the Lord' or 'in the name of the Lord', nor precedes Jesus' teaching and healing with such phrases as 'Filled with the Spirit, Jesus ...'[23]

Jesus might have indeed received the *content* of his teaching from the Father through the Spirit, but in his delivery he attributed the *authority* of his teaching neither to the Father, nor to the Spirit, but to himself - hence the term 'his egocentric authority'. He unmistakably made himself the subject of his speech and the subject of the authority of the

---

23 Luke does use phrases like this in three places, 4:14, 18 and 10:21. These will be looked at in the next section.

speech by attributing the teaching to himself, saying, 'I say to you ...' One may question him on the appropriateness of his egocentric *authority* in view of the source of the *content* of his teaching, but he made no apology for it, he did not pronounce these teachings in a weak or uncertain manner, or with a diluted or delegated authority. He did not speak as the OT prophets did by saying 'Thus saith the Lord.' He did not speak in the manner of the New Testament apostles who explicitly confessed their authority as deriving from God or Jesus Christ.[24] But Jesus, whose uniqueness and exaltation can be seen in the way he is contrasted with the figures in the Old and New Testament, decisively and repeatedly stamped his own sovereign authority on his new teaching, even against the Torah given by Yahweh, and on his radical mighty acts of unconditional love even when these broke Jewish customs and ritual boundaries. Matthew's gospel, and for that matter the other three gospels also, present a Jesus who speaks with his characteristic wisdom, certainty, intensity and egocentric sovereign authority, calling the people to believe and follow him, who acts and heals in his radical unconditional love with his own Lordly sovereign authority. R. Banks, when concluding his study in *Jesus and the Law in Synoptic Tradition*, writes,

> Other endeavours to find similarities between the form of Jesus' teaching and that of rabbis indicated that, while verbal parallels sometimes do exist, ..., substantial differences occur in the instruction that is given and the *authority* with which it is conveyed. Most significant is *the culmination of Jesus' instruction in the command to follow him*, a call to a life of discipleship for which no real parallel can be found in the rabbinic writings. His was a unique ministry expressing itself in a unique teaching and stemming *from a unique authority*. ... Jesus cannot be viewed merely as the mouthpiece of the absolute and eschatological will of God, for the call to personal discipleship indicates that something more is involved than this.[25]

Jesus Christ cannot be considered merely as a Spirit-inspired man who acted 'as the mouthpiece of the absolute and eschatological will of God' as Dunn would wish. *He* spoke and acted with the relentless sovereign authority of God and called people to devote their lives to *him* who will reward them according to how they have responded to *him* (Mt. 16:24-

---

24 For example, Paul in Rom 1:5 wrote, 'Through him [Jesus Christ] and for his name's sake, *we received grace and apostleship* to call people from among all the Gentiles to the obedience that comes from faith.' See also the opening greetings in the epistles: 1 Cor. 1:1; 2 Cor. 1:1; Gal. 1:1; Eph. 1:1 ...

25 Banks, *Jesus and the Law in Synoptic Tradition,* pp. 262-3. Italics mine.

27). These are the distinctive features of Jesus Christ with which one has to contend in understanding his relationship with the Spirit and in appreciating his relationship with his Father. Any Spirit Christology, which, like that of Dunn, neglects these unmistakable features of the gospel narratives, cannot do justice to the person of Jesus Christ and risks losing touch with Jesus' divine Lordship and the decisive finality in which he revealed his Father. However, the Spirit is given a definite role in Jesus' human existence (in his conception Mt. 1:20), in his life and ministry (indicated at his baptism). Also, Jesus' exercise of authority cannot be conceived of as being apart from his Father. The evangelists were in no way presenting a unitary understanding of God in Jesus Christ. But the unique and insuperable authority that Jesus exercised raises intricate questions of Jesus' relationship with the Spirit and his relationship with his Father, particularly in terms of authority. These questions need to be further addressed and will be attempted in the rest of this chapter and the next.

An important observation raised by C. K. Barrett in his book, *The Holy Spirit and the Gospel Tradition* (London: SPCK, 1947), is the paucity of references to the Holy Spirit in the gospels. Consistent with this observation is the fact that even though one may deduce Jesus' communion with his Father in Mt. 11:25-30 as through the Spirit, the Spirit is not actually explicitly mentioned in that passage. And even though one may deduce the implicit role of the Spirit in making the Father's will known to Jesus in the wilderness of temptations (as in 5.0 of chapter 3), none of the evangelists made this explicit in their presentations. There seems to be a reluctance on the evangelists' part to portray Jesus as over-dependent on the Spirit in his knowledge of and communion with his Father. Yet they did not deny the definite role of the Spirit in Jesus' existence and life. It seems that they were dealing with a delicate issue and were extremely cautious in their approach. Modern approaches to Spirit Christology may gain much by studying how they negotiated this intricate path of balancing Christ and the Spirit in their presentations in the gospel narratives.

2.0 Jesus and the Spirit in Matthew and Luke

This section will start with Barrett's observation of the paucity of references to the Spirit in the gospels, followed by his theory and those put forward by others. Then the evangelists' handling of the Spirit in Matthew and Luke will be closely examined in relation to Jesus' exorcism. Some conclusions will be drawn that could be useful for clarifying Jesus' relationship with the Spirit as presented by the evangelists.

2.1 The Paucity of References to the Spirit in the Synoptic Gospels:
C. K. Barrett

The following is a survey of the references to the Spirit in Matthew and Luke. In both gospels, the Spirit played the crucial role of the conception of Jesus in Mary (Mt. 1:18, Luke 1:35) and the Baptist prophesied that Jesus would baptise the people by the Spirit (Mt. 3:11, Luke 3:16). The Spirit also featured in Jesus' baptism where the Spirit descended on him like a dove (Mt. 3:16, Luke 3:22). It was the same Spirit who led Jesus into the wilderness of temptations (Mt. 4:1, Luke 4:1). Luke includes Jesus' proclamation of his manifesto based on Isaiah 61:1-2 in his home town of Nazareth (4:14f), while Matthew omits it (but Matthew's beatitudes have close parallels with it, in particular God's help to the poor). In this manifesto, Jesus openly declares that the Messianic prophecy in Isaiah 61:1-2, 'The Spirit of the Lord is on me because he has anointed me', has been fulfilled in him. That is the only incidence in the whole of Luke where Jesus himself speaks directly of his relationship with the Spirit. Luke in his editorial comments likewise relates Jesus directly with the Spirit only once (see below). Even though Luke refers to the Spirit much more than Matthew and Mark in his first four chapters, i.e., before the main body of Jesus' ministry, these references mostly concern figures other than Jesus himself - John the Baptist, Mary, Elizabeth, Zechariah, Simeon and probably the prophetess Anna. Interestingly, the growth of Jesus' wisdom at a young age (Luke 2:40, 52) is not attributed to the Spirit even though the Messiah was thought to be filled by the Spirit of wisdom (Isaiah 11:2). After Jesus' giving his manifesto at Nazareth, Luke only once mentions the Spirit in Jesus, i.e., after the disciples' return from their mission, Jesus, full of joy through the Holy Spirit gives praise to the Father. Jesus' teaching on praying for the gift of the Spirit in Luke 11:13 concerns his disciples, not himself. The comparison between the blasphemy against the Holy Spirit and speaking against the Son of Man in Luke 12:10 does not connect Jesus directly with the Spirit in their relationship. Again, the mention of the Spirit in Luke 12:12 concerns the Spirit enabling the disciples to defend themselves before rulers and authorities; it is not about Jesus' relationship with the Spirit. That is the last direct mention of the Spirit in Luke, at about the midpoint of his gospel, though the reference to the disciples being 'clothed with power from on high' in 24:49 should also be counted. After Jesus' directly relating himself to the Spirit in his manifesto at Nazareth, Luke mentions the Spirit only five times, of which only one is related to Jesus - his praise to the Father - and that only incidentally.

In Matthew, after Jesus' baptism, the Spirit is related directly to Jesus only twice. In Mt. 12:18, the evangelist reiterates that Jesus fulfils the servant's role in Isaiah 42:1f and that God puts his Spirit on him (cf. the Father's words at his baptism and the decent of the Spirit on him, Mt. 3:16-17). In Mt. 12:28, it is said that Jesus casts out demons by the Spirit of God. These words are on Jesus' lips and it is the only time Jesus mentions his relationship with the Spirit in the whole of Matthew. Apart from these two references to the Spirit after Jesus' baptism, there are four other references all of which are not directly related to Jesus. The two references of speaking before rulers and authorities in the Spirit (10:20) and blaspheming against the Spirit (12:31-32) are shared with Luke. One reference concerns David speaking by the Spirit and calling his son 'Lord' (22:43). The last reference appears in the baptismal formula invoking the name of the Father, Son and Holy Spirit (28:19).

To summarise, the references to the Spirit in Matthew and Luke after the introduction to Jesus' ministry are few, and only one out of five such references in Luke is to do with Jesus' relationship with the Spirit, while in Matthew the ratio is two to six. C. K. Barrett clearly highlighted the question of the paucity of references to the Spirit in the synoptic gospels in his book *The Holy Spirit and the Gospel Tradition,* although he did not present the data in the above form. After surveying Jesus' baptism, temptations, exorcism, miracles and prophetic teachings, Barrett concluded,

> There is no doubt that these 'pneumatic' traits are to be found in the Synoptic Gospels; but it is also true that they are not found unless they are looked for. They are not set out by the Evangelists as they have been set out in the last few pages. The word πνεῦμα itself occurs but rarely in the Synoptic Gospels, and this is an index of the attitude of the Evangelists which we have already observed on several occasions with regard to deeds of Jesus which were, or which might have been, ascribed to the Spirit. Jesus ... lays no stress on his visions, and he hardly ever speaks of himself as a prophet. The 'pneumatic' features of his character and of the narrative are mentioned occasionally and incidentally. Yet it would be wrong to say that they were suppressed. If those who handed on and at the same time moulded the Gospel tradition had intended to get rid of all traces of spiritual phenomena from the matter with which they were dealing, they would no doubt have done so more successfully than appears to have been the case. For the traces are there in the Gospels to be found.[26]

There appears to be this rather strange feature concerning the evangelists' references to the Spirit - the Spirit is there but not clearly portrayed to be there. The same pattern is found in Mark as in Matthew

---

26 Barrett, *The Holy Spirit*, p. 117.

and Luke. This is the most important feature which one has to contend with in appreciating Jesus' relationship with the Spirit. Barrett was not the first scholar to observe it and he quoted others who had made such an observation and given their hypotheses to explain it.[27] Barrett himself essentially gave three reasons for the paucity of references to the Spirit in the synoptic gospels. Firstly, the evangelists did not wish to emphasise that Jesus was merely a 'pneumatic' even though some of the evidence indicates that Jesus was such a person. '[H]e seems to have exercised the same control over spiritual conditions which other exorcists employed. ... Moreover, there is at least the suggestion that he was also a visionary (the temptations and Luke 10:18). Yet these facts, strangely enough seem to be depreciated by the Evangelists. They are in themselves not stressed, and no pains are taken to describe Jesus in impressive terms as a potent bearer of the Spirit of God. ... It is only by reading between the lines of the Gospels that we discover Jesus was a

---

27 E. F. Scott, *The Spirit in the New Testament* (London: Hodder & Stoughton, 1923), pp. 77-80, commented that the pre-Christian understanding of God in Judaism had become so transcendent (or holy) that a hierarchy of spiritual intermediaries such as angels was necessary to span the gulf between God and his creation. But Jesus, in bringing the people to a more direct relationship with the Father, stood opposed to this kind of idea and the Spirit was not exempted. To him, 'an idea like that of the Spirit removed God to a distance, or put an abstract power in place of him.' *Ibid.*, p. 79. But Barrett replied that Jesus did accept the current belief in spiritual intermediaries and 'it is unlikely that he would have believed in these minor beings and yet disliked speech about the Spirit of God, which has a secure place in the OT, simply because the Spirit stood between God and man.' *The Holy Spirit*, p. 141. In *The Holy Spirit*, the Headingley Lectures, 1937, pp. 53-5, Vincent Taylor based his hypothesis on form criticism: since the communities were confident that they possessed the Spirit, no one disputed the presence of the Spirit and there was no need to prove it by the words of Jesus when they handed down the traditions. But Barrett, *The Holy Spirit*, p. 141, commented, 'an evangelist in selecting his material might have chosen what was agreed and omitted controversial subjects. Barrett also cited Luke 1:1 concerning 'the things most certainly believed'. And contrary to Taylor, there was controversy on the subject of the Spirit (Acts 18:24-28; 19:1-7). R. N. Flew, in *Jesus and His Church* (London: Epworth, 1938), pp. 70f, linked the slim references to the Spirit to the Messianic secret. The disciples' understanding of the Spirit based on the OT was not sufficient in Jesus' judgment and speech about the Spirit might mislead them as much as speech about his Messiahship. 'The whole conception of the Spirit in the OT must needs to be baptised into the death of Christ. Calvary was the only gateway to Pentecost.' But Barrett, *The Holy Spirit*, pp. 142-3, commented that since Jesus had begun to teach his disciples, and repeated his teaching, about his own Messiahship and suffering from Caesarea Philippi onward, he could also have taught them about the Spirit. But Jesus did not teach them more about the Spirit after Caesarea Philippi. Reticence about the Spirit and the Messianic secret do not seem to be coupled.

"pneumatic" person.'[28] The evangelists were much more interested in the person and mission of Jesus than his being merely an inspired pneumatic.

> Their faith rested upon the Messiahship, the divine mission and status of Jesus of Nazareth. Hence, in comparison with the actual presence of the Lord's Anointed, and the operation of the powers of the Kingdom of God, the commonplace phenomena of prophetic and other inspiration were insignificant and irrelevant. The writers of the NT are never content merely to align Jesus with the OT prophets, strongly as he resembled them in many aspects, and they distinguish clearly between him and the other exorcists and miracle-workers of his day. The ancient world contained as many 'spiritual' men as it wanted, and the church had no motive in depicting Jesus as another of them.[29]

Barrett's point here needs to be qualified. The evangelists could have stressed the pneumatic or inspired nature of Jesus' work without putting him into the same category as other spiritual men or thaumaturges because Jesus' mighty acts were paralleled and interpreted by his teaching on the inbreaking of the Kingdom of God and his significance in the Kingdom (cf. Barth's point regarding the intimate relationship between Jesus' words and acts, see beginning of chapter 2). Jesus' teachings and his self-referencing authority would have made him distinct from other spiritual persons. Also, Jesus performed many healing miracles and exorcisms openly (Matthew emphasises Jesus healed all) and the pneumatic nature of these acts was not as hidden as Barrett assumed. Yet, his observation is correct that the evangelists made no attempt to present Jesus as 'a potent bearer of the Spirit of God' in the midst of all his mighty acts. The reason Barrett gave for this is also sound - 'the actual presence of the Lord's Anointed, and the operation of the powers of the Kingdom of God' through Jesus were more significant to the evangelists than the nature of his inspiration. One may qualify Barrett's point by commenting that even though this aspect of Jesus' inspiration is less significant than Jesus' presence and the kingdom's presence, it is nevertheless an important aspect which the evangelists would wish to retain and did retain. The critical question here concerns the comparative significance of the two, not the unimportance of Jesus' inspiration. The evangelists might be aware of

---

28 Barrett, *The Holy Spirit*, p. 68.

29 *Ibid.*, p. 157. 'When Philostratus wrote the life of Apollonius of Tyana he was wise enough to make him a philosopher as well as a thaumaturge; and when Lucian wanted to poke fun at the oriental cults (including Christianity) he portrayed their representative as a "pneumatic" pure and simple.' *Ibid.*, p. 117.

the possibility that over-emphasising the Spirit's inspiration of Jesus might eclipse the significance of Jesus and the kingdom's presence through him. Thus they balanced their presentation of Jesus and the role of the Spirit accordingly. This important point will be taken up later.

The second reason Barrett gave for the lack of references to the Spirit was, like Flew's explanation (see footnote 27 above), linked with the Messianic secret. Flew's point was that Jesus taught his disciples as little about the Spirit as he did about his Messiahship. Barrett's point was that because of the association between the Spirit and the Messiah (the anointed one), for Jesus to keep his identity as Messiah secret from the public until after his death he had to avoid claiming a pre-eminent measure of the Spirit and act under the same constraint. Barrett's argument, apparently plausible, is actually not sound on close examination (see Excursus B of this chapter for a rather involved discussion).

The third reason Barrett gave for the lack of references to the Spirit in the synoptics was that Jesus had mistaken the times of the consummation of the Kingdom. This reason does not directly concern our interest in the Spirit in Jesus but the arguments against it are presented in Excursus C of this chapter.

In accounting for the paucity of references of the Spirit in the gospels, one must remember that not only was Jesus reticent, but the evangelists also made very few editorial comments about the Spirit or even removed some of them (Barrett seemed to have noticed the former concerning Jesus, but not the latter concerning the evangelists). For example, Luke wrote in 5:17, 'the power of the Lord was present for him to heal the sick' and in 6:19, '... the people all tried to touch him because power was coming from him and healing them all.' These are Luke's editorial comments and he could have referred to the Spirit rather than 'power' in relation to Jesus but he did not. This double feature, reticence about the Spirit on Jesus' lips and in the evangelists' comments, needs to be accounted for. Barrett tried in his second and third reasons to account for reticence on Jesus' lips but not for the reticence in the evangelists' editorial comments; and these reasons have been found unconvincing. However, his first reason is more to do with accounting for the evangelists' reticence and is worth reiterating. 'The actual presence of the Lord's Anointed, and the operation of the powers of the Kingdom of God [through Jesus]' were more significant to the evangelists than the nature of his inspiration.[30] Could the same reason account for the reticence on Jesus' lips, i.e., Jesus was more concerned with speaking about the kingdom and his relationship with it rather than the kingdom and the Spirit? The reason for not emphasising the Spirit in

---

30 Barrett, *The Holy Spirit*, p. 157.

Jesus might be christological, i.e., to stress Jesus' presence and the kingdom's presence through him (though the role of the Spirit is by no means discounted in the kingdom, see Mt. 12:28).

In this respect, the suggestion by H. Windisch that was mentioned by Barrett but dismissed might be useful, and the discussion was as follows. H. Leisegang submitted that 'the Holy Spirit as a concept bound up with the life and teaching of Jesus, and the myths and speculations attached to it, are foreign elements within the Synoptic gospels, which crept into the narratives of the deeds and sayings of the Saviour from Hellenistic thought and belief.'[31] There is therefore little continuity between the gospels and Jesus in terms of his deeds and sayings in relation to the Spirit. Windisch intended to keep the Hellenistic influence on the gospels regarding the Spirit but also keep the continuity between the gospels and Jesus in this respect.

> There was, Windisch thinks, a double process in the history of the tradition. At first, many incidents and sayings which revealed Jesus as a 'spiritual' person were suppressed in the interests of a 'higher' Christology; later the Church read back its own experience and doctrine of the Holy Spirit into the empty space which had been left in its account of Jesus. In this way are explained both the fewness of the explicit references to the Spirit which is so striking a feature of the tradition, and the late and Hellenistic character of those which do occur.[32]

Barrett contradicted Windisch by pointing out that the data do not correspond to Windisch's theory, i.e., the reintroduction of the scarce references to the Spirit does not match the importance of the role of the Spirit in the life of the church.[33] If the church intended to reintroduce the Spirit into the gospel, it could have made a much more successful attempt. Also, the idea of a late Hellenistic source for the Spirit needs to be questioned. As Barrett observed, the Spirit has a secure place in the Old Testament.[34] There is no need to invoke a foreign source for its appearance in the gospels.[35] Indeed, there was a strand of Jewish expectation that God would pour out his Spirit on to the people in the

---

31 H. Leisegang, 'Pneuma Hagion', *Studies in Early Christianity* (New York & London: Century Co., 1928), S. J. Case (ed.), p. 140.

32 Barrett, *The Holy Spirit*, p. 3. Windisch's article, 'Jesus und der Geist nach synoptischer Ueberlieferung', can be found in *Studies in Early Christianity*.

33 Barrett, p. 117.

34 *Ibid.*, p. 141.

35 Barrett decisively contradicted Leisegang's assertion that Jesus' conception by the Spirit was influenced by Hellenistic elements. *Ibid,* pp. 10-14.

end time and the Messiah would be anointed by the Spirit.[36] The question of a Hellenistic source of the Spirit does not arise in more modern writings, such as those by J.D.G Dunn, M. Turner and R. Menzies (see below). Despite these two counter-arguments against Windisch, his suggestion of the concern of a 'higher' Christology in the church is worth contemplating because the evaluation of Barrett's own arguments has shown that the evangelists, and presumably the church too, were comparatively more interested in the presence of the figure of Jesus Christ and the presence of the kingdom through him in the narratives than Jesus' inspiration by the Spirit. As one surveys the gospel narratives, one has to admit that the central figure portrayed by the evangelists in these narratives is the person of Jesus Christ, and to a lesser extent the Father, and to an even lesser extent the Spirit. (See the exegeses of narrative passages in chapters 3 and 4, and 2.1.2 of chapter 4 on how Barth manages to link the Father to Jesus through the concept of revelation in his exposition but less so with the Spirit.) However, the presence of the Spirit in Jesus is inerasably there through his conception and his baptism. The evangelists seemed to be seeking a way to present Jesus and his relationship with the Spirit in a manner which was most proper to the church's understanding and need. That task was not easy but all the three synoptists seemed to have adopted a very similar strategy. Their strategy is the important subject of the next two sections and may helpfully inform any modern conception of Spirit Christology, as well as answering the question of the paucity of references to the Spirit in the synoptic gospels.

2.2 The Pneumatology of Matthew

In the book *The Holy Spirit: Growth of a Biblical Tradition* (New York: Paulist Press, 1976), G. T. Montague entitled the chapter on Matthew 'The Discreet Pneumatology of Matthew'. His point is that Matthew's gospel is not adorned with extravagant references to the Spirit. Matthew's exposition of the Spirit in Jesus during his ministry is inevitably limited to Mt. 12:15-21 (Jesus as the fulfilment of the Spirit-filled servant of Isaiah 42) and Mt. 12:22-32 (the exorcism controversy and blasphemy against the Spirit) because these are the only passages available for this purpose. But these passages do clearly affirm the role of the Spirit in Jesus' ministry and echo Jesus' baptism episode, which involved the Spirit and the Isaiah passage.[37]

---

36 Turner, *The Holy Spirit and Spiritual Gifts*, pp. 2-18.

37 Montague's comment that Matthew 'emphasises Jesus' possession of the Spirit manifested in his charismatic activity' (*The Holy Spirit*, p. 310) may be an overstatement because only two references to the Spirit in Jesus are made throughout

When analysing the relationship between Jesus, the Spirit and the church, Montague finds that Jesus plays a much more dominant role than the Spirit in relation to the church. While Jesus clearly has the Spirit, the disciples sent out by *Jesus* for the mission in Mt. 10 receive *Jesus'* authority to heal every disease and sickness, to drive out evil spirits (Mt. 10:1) and to proclaim the message of the kingdom as they have learned from *Jesus* himself (Mt. 10:27). There is no mention of the gift or empowering of the Spirit; only the authority and the teaching of Jesus are involved. While Jesus is said to cast out demons by the Spirit of God, the disciples exorcise in the authority and name of Jesus (cf. 7:22). Also while Luke emphasises the power of the Holy Spirit in the church in Acts after Jesus' resurrection and ascension, in Matthew it is the presence and power of the risen Lord Jesus himself living and acting in his church (Mt. 28:20). Even though Jesus is said to baptise the people with the Holy Spirit and with fire (Mt. 3:11), there is no Pentecost in Matthew.[38] The only place where the Spirit is said explicitly to be at work in the disciples is when they are called to witness before authorities and rulers (Mt. 10:21).

To summarise, the Spirit is clearly in Jesus in his ministry but this fact is by no means stressed by Matthew, while the Spirit is even less prominent in relation to his disciples, with Jesus himself giving them his authority for their mission and himself mediating his own presence in the church with his sovereign authority. Jesus, rather than the Spirit, is Lord of the church. Montague does not explain the paucity of references to the Spirit in Jesus but he does give an explanation regarding the similar feature in relation to the church.

> Matthew's central discerning sign is Jesus himself. It is upon him that the Spirit rests (3:16; 12:18). If the church has the Spirit, it is only because she has Jesus. Or, to put it another way, it is not because of the Spirit that she has Jesus (Luke's view). ... [W]e recall the crisis of false prophecy Matthew had to deal with and the probability that some Christians were, under pretence of inspiration by the Holy Spirit, promoting a relaxation of the ethic of Jesus. ... Rooting the Spirit totally in Jesus was a way of excluding any possibility of meaningful charismatic activity outside the community that is gathered around Jesus as Lord.[39]

It is possible that some false prophets were operating in the Matthean community and these so called Spirit-inspired prophets must not be

---

his whole ministry (12:18, 28).
38 *Ibid.*, p. 308.
39 *Ibid.*, pp. 308-9.

given licence to cause confusion and sin in the community.[40] The way to identify true and false prophets is by their fruit (Mt. 7:16), which is to be measured by Jesus and his teaching on righteousness, not by their degree of so-called inspiration. For Matthew and his community, it is safer to speak in terms of Jesus and his presence mediated through his teaching by his disciples (28:20) than in terms of the Spirit's inspiration and his direct presence. Hence, the person of Jesus is much more prominent than the Spirit in the church in Matthew - Jesus is the Lord of the church.

Central to this chapter is Jesus' relationship with the Spirit as portrayed by the evangelists of the synoptic gospels. To answer questions raised by Dunn, *one has to consider whether the evangelists present the Spirit as the source of the divinity of Jesus. Is the Spirit the Lord of Jesus or is Jesus the Lord of the Spirit*? Is the Spirit the subject who possesses Jesus or is Jesus the subject who possesses the Spirit? This question can be partly addressed by the comparative authority/honour/priority/importance/prominence given to Jesus and the Spirit by the evangelists. If Jesus consistently has a higher authority and priority than the Spirit, or Jesus and the Spirit are equally presented, then Dunn's argument is undermined. So far, in terms of the disciples' mission during Jesus' earthly life and in terms of his presence in the church after his resurrection, it is Jesus not the Spirit who is the central figure and Lord of the church in Matthew. From the narrative study in chapters 2, 3 and 4, it has been seen that Matthew presents Jesus as the Lord of freedom who, despite the barriers and oppositions from religious leaders, exercises his sovereign and relentless authority to speak and act in his radical righteousness and unconditional love, reaches out to the poor and needy in his compassionate ministry. He does these without even invoking the name of his Father or his inspiration in his egocentrically authoritative speech and powerful acts. Jesus rather than the Spirit is clearly presented as the central, prominent and lordly figure in his ministry. This brief recapitulation throw doubts on Dunn's position. In relation to the church after his resurrection, Jesus' prominence, rather than the Spirit's, is consistent with Jesus' prominent Lordship, freedom, radicalism and unconditional love in his ministry. In Matthew, Jesus is consistently presented as the Lord in his life, death, resurrection and sovereign rule. But is Jesus' Lordship and authority in any way diluted or undermined by the fact of the Spirit's presence in Jesus himself?

The Spirit in Matthew is indeed given a very high status in relation to

---

40 'Watch out for false prophets' (Mt. 7:15). 'Many will say to me on that day, "Lord, Lord, did we not prophesy in your name, and in your name drive out demons and perform many miracles? ...' (7:22).

Jesus. It was the Spirit who acted in the conception of Jesus, who in Jesus' baptism came upon him from the Father for the empowering of his mission, who led Jesus in the wilderness of temptations, and it was by the Spirit that Jesus drove out demons and ushered in the Kingdom of God. Moreover, blaspheming against the Holy Spirit is more serious than blaspheming against the Son of Man. The Spirit in Matthew is given very high honour indeed, probably at least that of the Son of Man. Is it possible that the Spirit truly is the divinity in Jesus Christ, that his divinity is functionally derived from the Spirit as Dunn subscribed? (Or, equivalently, is the Spirit the Lord of Jesus?) This question must be addressed carefully in view of the serious consequence of the answer. It will be approached from the perspective of Jesus' exorcism, his disciples' exorcism and his inherent relationship with the Spirit.

Firstly, does the Spirit or Jesus (or the Father) feature more prominently in Jesus' exorcism? This question is answered by studying Mt. 12:25-32.

> Jesus knew their thoughts and said to them, 'Every kingdom divided against itself will be ruined, and every city or household divided against itself will not stand. If Satan drives out Satan, he is divided against himself. How then can his kingdom stand? And if I drive out demons by Beelzebub, by whom do your people drive them out? So then, they will be your judges. But if I drive out demons by the Spirit of God, then the kingdom of God has come upon you. Or again, how can anyone enter a strong man's house and carry off his possession unless he first ties up the strong man? Then he can rob his house. He who is not with me is against me, and he who does not gather with me scatters. And so I tell you, every sin and blasphemy will be forgiven men, but the blasphemy against the Spirit will not be forgiven. Anyone who speaks a word against the Son of Man will be forgiven, but anyone who speaks against the Holy Spirit will not be forgiven, either in this age or in the age to come.

(The question concerning the phrase 'the Spirit of God' in Matthew and 'the finger of God' in Luke will be addressed in the next section and does not affect the discussion here.)

The concentration of the references to the Spirit in Mt. 12 (three times, including 12:18) is noteworthy in view of its sparseness elsewhere. Matthew quite clearly intends to portray Jesus healing and exorcising in the power of the Spirit (12:15-18, 28). And Jesus' exorcism by the Spirit of God is an important sign of the inbreaking of the long-awaited kingdom of God. Dunn understands Jesus' identity in his exorcism as God's instrument filled by the Spirit.

> [I]t was an *awareness* of *otherly* power working through him, together

with the *conviction* that this power was *God's* power. In his action God acted. When he spoke or stretched out his hand *something happened* - the sufferer was relieved, the prisoner freed, the evil departed; this could only be the power of God. Here, we may already conclude, is the source of Jesus' authority - the sense that God's Spirit was ready to act through him, the knowledge that God would use him to heal, to overcome demons when they confronted him.[41]

The real author of the acts of exorcism, accordingly to Dunn, is the Spirit or God himself. Jesus, who is *used by God* for this purpose, *derives* his authority from his *awareness* of this *otherly* power - the Spirit's inspiration or empowering. Jesus is then subordinate to the Spirit in his exorcism, entirely dependent on the Spirit's empowering and having no authority of his own to exercise the power of the Spirit (for according to Dunn the authority Jesus has is an authority derived from the Spirit). Dunn cannot accept the view that in the period of Jesus' ministry Jesus is already Lord of the Spirit;[42] in his view he is only the uniquely anointed Man of the Spirit.[43] His position amounts to acknowledging the Spirit as the Lord of Jesus.

But when one studies the text more carefully, one finds that the subject of exorcism in 12:28 is clearly Jesus himself - 'But if *I* drive out demons by the Spirit of God' (εἰ δὲ ἐν πνεύματι θεοῦ ἐγὼ ἐκβάλλω τὰ δαιμόνια).[44] The word of Jesus is not 'the Spirit enables me to exorcise' or 'God enables me to exorcise by the Spirit'. The egocentricity of Jesus is still manifested in this saying and it is of a piece with his other egocentricity manifested in his authoritative teaching and healing (see chapters 3 and 4). Jesus clearly sees himself as the *author* of his authoritative action of exorcism, while at the same time acknowledging the unmistakable involvement of his Father through the Spirit. In his exorcisms, Jesus exerts his own egocentric authority which is a consistent feature throughout his ministry. Jesus is not reduced to merely an instrument in God's hand who has no authority of his own. Analysis of the following verses throw further doubts on Dunn's interpretation.

---

41 Dunn, *Jesus and the Spirit*, p. 47.

42 Jesus being 'Lord of the Spirit' means he can exercise the power of the Spirit with freedom and authority.

43 *Ibid.*, p. 46. Even though Dunn arrives at this conclusion in relation to Luke, his view would most probably be the same for Matthew because his view is expressed here in the context of the study of Luke 11:20 and Mt. 12:28.

44 Dunn argues that the most likely original for Luke 11:20 lacks εγώ (*Ibid.*, p. 373, footnote 25), but the verb, εκβάλλω, already indicates firmly that Jesus is the 'I', the subject of the action of exorcism.

Verses 29-30, 'Or again, how can anyone enter a strong man's house and carry off his possession unless he first ties up the strong man? Then he can rob his house. He who is not with *me* is against *me*, and he who does not gather with *me* scatters', are christocentric. In the short parable in v. 29, Jesus is represented by the stronger man, the *subject* who binds the strong man and rob his house. 'The main point is again *christological*: Jesus is stronger than the strong one (cf. Isa 53:12) and is hence able, as the *subject*, to raid his kingdom at will and deliver those who are oppressed in a variety of ways. In this basic sense the ministry of Jesus is the beginning of eschatological deliverance, the turning point of the aeons.'[45] In v. 30, 'he who is not with me' may refer to the exorcists on the side of the Pharisees (v. 27).[46] 'Gather' could mean eschatological harvest (Hagner, *Matthew 1-13*, p. 344) but in this context may mean taking the spoils from the strong man's house with Jesus, i.e., exorcism in Jesus' name and with his authority (10:1). Verse 30 then amounts to a call to the people to become disciples of Jesus, not disciples of the Pharisees. 'The threefold occurrence of the pronoun ἐμοῦ, 'me', in relation to which the true character of a person's work is finally evaluated, points again clearly in the direction of *Christology*. Of the highest importance is the person of Jesus and one's relationship to him. This verse is therefore in effect a "call to decision."'[47] The christocentricity, already manifest in v. 28 (ἐγώ) is heightened by v. 29 (Jesus the stronger man) and v. 30 (to Jesus one is to plead one's allegiance) where clearly the central figure concerned is Jesus, not the Father, nor the Spirit.

This christocentricity is the clue to understanding the uniqueness of Jesus' exorcism compared to others and the clue to understanding the very presence of the kingdom of God. In the eyes of Jesus, it is not the mere fact of the operation of the Spirit that signifies the inbreaking of the kingdom of God, for *in Jesus' understanding* (while it may not be within the grasp of the Pharisees' understanding) the exorcists on the side of the Pharisees also exorcise by the Spirit of God.[48] The coming of the kingdom of God has to do with Jesus himself (and his proclamation

---

45 Hagner, *Matthew 1-13*, p. 344. Italics mine.

46 *Ibid.*

47 *Ibid.* Italics mine.

48 Jesus' question, 'if I drive out demons by Beelzebub, by whom do your people drive them out?', implies that the source of their power of exorcism cannot be from Beelzebub but from God. If Jesus understands their power of exorcism is from God, he must have understood it as from 'the Spirit of God', as it is true in his case. How else can it be *in Jesus' understanding*? However, this role of the Spirit of God may not be clearly grasped by the Pharisees as 'no available Jewish sources directly connect exorcisms with the Spirit.' Turner, *The Holy Spirit and Spiritual Gifts*, p. 30.

of the kingdom) and the free manner in which he exorcises demons by the Spirit of God, rather than merely the Spirit inspiring Jesus (Dunn's view).[49] It has to do with the way he authoritatively binds Beelzebub and sets free, in a *wholesale* manner, prisoners under his bondage, so much so that others can join him in releasing the oppressed *in his name* (not the Spirit's name or even the Father's name, 7:22; c.f. Luke 10:17).[50] It is his amazing presence in authority and remarkable *free* exercise of the Spirit's power as the *subject* that signify the coming of God to help and liberate his people and establish his reign. And it is the people's response to him that determines their fate in (or outside) the kingdom. Such is the Lordship and freedom of Jesus (cf. 3:3); such is the power of his name. It is only by a stretched imagination that one could see Jesus as merely an inspired instrument of God, an inspired man devoid of his own authority. If that is the case, he is merely more inspired than the exorcists of the Pharisees and could be properly called a prophet, even a mighty prophet but he could not have been the Lord to whom one has to plead allegiance and whose name can be invoked for exorcism. The evangelists consciously refuse to present such a lowly picture of Jesus and set him apart from all of them as the Lord (cf. 3:3). (The important question of how his authority and Lordship relates to his genuine use of the Spirit's power will be dealt with later.) In the gospels, the Lordship, freedom and authority of Jesus is a constant and inerasable feature, as shown in chapters 2 to 4. This is also clearly shown in the way he commissions his disciples during his earthly ministry.

---

49 Barrett commented on Jesus' uniqueness amongst other exorcists including Jewish Rabbis, 'The narratives themselves, with nothing further, are enough to show that Jesus was a "pneumatic" person; but this is by no means enough to make him unique. The striking fact is that his power over demons is held to be a sign of the Kingdom of God, and it is *the particular Messianic nature of the spiritual power wielded by Jesus that distinguishes him.* Consequently, if we are rightly to understand the exorcism narratives, we must consider also the sayings explanatory of them.' *The Holy Spirit*, p. 57. Italics mine. Barth relates Jesus' healings and exorcisms closely to his person, his teaching and the Kingdom of God and distinguishes his activities from others by these, 'As they are recounted and attested in the Gospels, they are absolutely new and different in *their unity with the good news, the teaching, the proclamation and therefore the existence of the man Jesus*, from all other human or cosmic occurrence, usual or unusual, ordinary or relatively extraordinary.' *CD* IV.2 , p. 215, Italics mine.

50 'Josephus saw an exorcist drawing out a demon through a victim's nostrils by applying herbs of a kind described by Solomon, who had secret knowledge of spells (*Ant.* 8, 45ff). All such exorcisms, whether effective or not, are complicated and second-rate compared with the instant authority of Jesus and his disciples in their *wholesale* assault on the kingdom of Satan wherever they met it.' *NIDNTT*, vol. 3, p. 476, Italics mine.

Then he said to his disciples, 'The harvest is plentiful but the workers are few. Ask the Lord of the harvest, therefore, to send out workers into his harvest field.' *He* called his twelve disciples to him and *gave them authority* to drive out evil spirits and to heal every disease and sickness. ... These twelve Jesus sent out with the following instruction ... (Mt. 9:37-10:5)

As observed before, Jesus gives authority to his disciples to heal and exorcise without mentioning the Spirit. However, because he clearly knows that he exorcises (and heals) by the Spirit of God, he would have understood that the power that his disciples use for exorcism also comes from the Spirit (note the parallel nature of Jesus' own work and the disciples' mission[51]). While dealing with an almost parallel passage in Luke 10, where Jesus gives the disciples authority to trample on snakes and scorpions and to overcome all the power of the enemy (10:19), Bultmann attributed this saying to the exalted Lord, not the earthly Jesus.[52] The reason was probably that Bultmann could not accept the earthly Jesus could exercise such a high authority, an authority which enables him to *delegate authority* to his disciples to exorcise and heal in the power of the Spirit. Dunn defends the authenticity of this saying of Jesus by citing other parallels or similar passages in the synoptic gospels (Mark 3:15; 6:7; Luke 10:2-12; Mt. 9:37f; 10:5-16).[53] He clearly notices that Jesus' delegation of authority requires authority on Jesus' part but he does not submit a sound explanation of this special authority of Jesus.

The sense of authority which must lie behind such a delegation of authority hardly needs any comment; it is the statement of one who not merely trusts implicitly in God, but who also knows himself to be distinguished by divine authority as the agent of the end-time rule of God (cf. Mt. 12:28/Luke 11:20).[54]

---

51 Schweizer, *The Good News According to Matthew*, p. 233.

52 R. Bultmann, *The History of the Synoptic Tradition* (Oxford: Blackwell, 1963), p. 158. Similarly, Conzelmann, *The Theology of St. Luke*, p. 179, suggested that Jesus was 'not yet empowered to bestow the Spirit during his lifetime'. However, even in Luke, as in Matthew, Jesus already gave authority to his disciples to cast out demons during his earthly ministry (10:17-20) and the power for exorcism delegated or bestowed by Jesus was the power of the Spirit (11:13). See later treatment on Luke's pneumatology on this point.

53 Dunn, *Jesus and the Spirit*, p. 78.

54 *Ibid.*

By quoting Mt. 12:28 and Luke 11:20 regarding Jesus' exorcism by the Spirit (see his treatment of these in 1.1), Dunn is locating Jesus' special authority to delegate the authority of the Spirit to his disciples in his inspiration by the Spirit and his Sonship to the Father, but not his own authority.[55] That is, Jesus' authority to delegate is itself a *wholly* delegated authority. It is true that he receives authority from the Father to delegate but it has to be pointed out (from Mt. 10:1) that he himself also has authority to delegate, just as while the Father entrusts him with the teaching of the kingdom of God, he also exercises his own authority in delivering the teaching. When Jesus delegates the power of the Spirit to his disciples ('*He* called his twelve disciples to him and *gave them authority* to drive out evil spirits'), he neither invokes the authority of the Father nor the inspiration of the Spirit but his own authority - a pattern which is also consistently found in his teachings and his mighty acts. Furthermore, if Jesus has the authority to delegate the power of the Spirit to his disciples, then he is in a real sense already Lord of the Spirit within his life and ministry and his authority is not dependent on the Spirit.[56] E. Schweizer, while commenting on Luke, also arrives at the conclusion that Jesus is Lord of the Spirit within his life and ministry.

> Luke, then, avoids the idea that the Spirit stands over Jesus. The OT view of the power of God coming upon men does not satisfy him. Jesus becomes the *subject* of an action in the Holy Spirit. He is not a pneumatic, but the *Lord of the πνεῦμα.*[57]

To delegate the authority of the Spirit to others, to be Lord of the Spirit, requires nothing less than equality with God, no matter how plainly and non-dramatically the evangelist presents Jesus in this move in Mt. 10:1 (and similar verses in Mk. 3:14-15, 6:7; Lk. 10:19).[58] Jesus' equivalence with God can also be seen in the context around Mt. 10:1. It is no coincidence that after presenting God, the Lord of harvest, as the one who sends out workers into his harvest field in 9:38, Matthew shortly parallels this sending by God with Jesus' sending of the twelve in 10:5 (and also 10:16). And Jesus does not invoke his Father's

---

55 '"Father" as much as "Spirit" spells "authority". ... In short, Spirit and sonship, sonship and Spirit, are but two aspects of the one experience of God out of which Jesus lived and ministered.' *Ibid.*, pp. 66-7.

56 Cf. Jesus who gave the Spirit to the church at the Pentecost in Acts 2 was thereby revealed as 'Lord of the Spirit', see Turner, *The Holy Spirit and Spiritual Gifts*, pp. 175-8; 'The Spirit of Christ and Christology', especially pp. 180-1, 183-4, 188-90.

57 *TDNT*, vol. VI, pp. 404-5. Italics mine.

58 See Turner, *The Holy Spirit and Spiritual Gifts,* pp. 175-8, where he is treating the case of the Pentecost.

authority in sending his disciples to mission but his own though the former is implicit (see Mt. 10:40). Matthew is therefore presenting Jesus taking the place of God, or paralleling his Father, in sending the workers into the harvest field (Luke uses the same parallelism in 10:2-3). With such an understanding of Jesus' relationship with his Father, the sovereign Lordship of Jesus manifested in his delegating the authority of the Spirit to his disciple can be readily understood. And Jesus' equivalence with God in his sovereign Lordship here, and elsewhere in Matthew,[59] is of a piece with the Lordship that Matthew ascribes to Jesus at the beginning of his gospel (3:3) and at the end (28:18-20, see chapter 2 on Jesus' Lordship).[60]

Dunn's assertion, the Spirit is the divinity of Jesus, if accepted has serious implications for orthodox understanding of Christology, atonement, Jesus' revelation of his Father and the Trinity, all of which are based on the inherent divinity of Jesus Christ whether on earth or in heaven.[61] By looking at Jesus' exercise of the Spirit's power in exorcism in Mt. 12:28, it has been shown that despite the real power of the Spirit in Jesus, (i) he is presented as the genuine author and subject of the action of exorcism with his characteristic egocentric authority; (ii) the crucial element of the coming of the kingdom of God is Christological and only pneumatological when seen in the context of how *freely* Jesus exercises the Spirit in exorcisms compared to others; and (iii) it is the people's response to *him* that decides their fate in (or out of) the kingdom of God. Therefore, the fact of the Spirit in Jesus in no way detracts Jesus from the centrality of the gospel narratives. He is still the Lord who has come (3:3); he is the Lord of his own actions. He is even the Lord of the Spirit as he commissions his disciple to exercise in his name the power of the Spirit in their mission (7:22; cf. Luke 10:17; Mark 3:14-15, 6:7). And he is the Lord, even as the Father, the Lord of harvest, is the Lord. With such a picture of Jesus' Lordship presented in Matthew's narratives, which is shared by Luke (and Mark), Dunn's assertions that (i) the Spirit is the divinity of Jesus and (ii) Jesus' authority is derived *wholly* from the Spirit and the Father, which really makes him no Lord at all, is put into grave doubt. A final repudiation of Dunn's assertions, especially (i), is to be made by taking a broad perspective of Jesus' relationship with the Spirit in his life and ministry

---

59 See France, *Matthew: Evangelist and Teacher*, pp. 308-17.

60 Unfortunately, commentators generally do not draw out the parallelism between God and Jesus in Mt. 10, and the crucial significance of Jesus' delegating authority to his disciples to heal and exorcise in the power of the Spirit. However, these two aspects are mutually reinforcing.

61 'As the Spirit was the "divinity" of Jesus, so Jesus became the personality of the Spirit.' Dunn, *Jesus and the Spirit*, p. 325.

as presented in Matthew's narratives.

Jesus was conceived by the Holy Spirit (Mt. 1:20).[62] His existence cannot be divorced from the Holy Spirit. The very nature of his existence demands that his life and movement in the Spirit is a function of his existence. It is inconceivable that Jesus is without the Spirit, or that the Spirit conceived him then left him and returned to him at his baptism. The Spirit is not an extra and late factor added on to his existence. The Spirit is *inherently* in him. When he lives and moves in the Spirit, he lives and moves in his very own existence and atmosphere. There is nothing alien or external to him about the Spirit. He sees and experiences the Spirit very much as part of his existence. Yet, he is not identical with the Spirit; he is in a mysterious sense distinct from him.

Jesus' visionary experience of his Father and the Spirit at the Jordan is the Father's expression of love to him and the Father's commissioning of the Messianic task to him. The Spirit is the very power he will exercise in the fulfilment of his Messianic task but the Spirit and the power are not something new or unknown to him for he has moved in the Spirit from the very moment of his conception. (Jesus' growth in wisdom and power of the Spirit from childhood is not denied here - see treatment in Luke later, what is denied is that the Spirit and his power are extrinsic to him.) It has always been in his nature and existence to move and live in the Spirit. And it has always been in the Spirit that he experiences his Father's holy and loving presence; it has always been in the Spirit that he lives and moves in communion and unity with his Father (Mt. 11:27-30). He did not experience this presence of his Father only from the Jordan onward, for the Spirit through whom he has communion with his Father has always been with him. Through and in the Spirit, he has known his Father (again growth from childhood in this aspect is not denied). And it may well be that during his time in the wilderness he, through the Spirit, discerns his Father's will for his forthcoming mission and resists other dangerous options.[63] When he comes to deliver his Father's will on the new righteousness in the Sermon on the Mount, however, he makes no mention of the Spirit and exercises his egocentric and relentless authority in delivering God's new law to the people. He may well have spoken in the power of the Spirit and in communion with his Father but he invokes neither of their authorities - he invokes his own. When he comes to heal the people of their sickness and cast the demons out from the possessed, unlike other exorcists who call and depend on a higher power to deliver, he exercises his own will freely, exerting and wielding

---

62 This is a crucial conceptual element for understanding Jesus' relationship with the Spirit. See below.

63 See 5.0 of Chapter 3, 'Jesus' Humanity in Knowing His Father's Will'.

the power of the Spirit *at his own will*, neither invoking the name of his Father (or God) nor the inspiration of the Spirit (see, e.g., his action and short conversation with the leper in 8:3 - 'I am willing.' - and his free exercise of his authority to heal the centurion's servant in 8:5-13; see chapter 4). And his exercise of the power of the Spirit has a decisive effect on those who suffer. When he lives and moves in the Spirit, he lives and moves in his very own existence and atmosphere. When he heals and exorcises in the power of the Spirit, he heals and exorcises with the power which he experiences and sees as his very own, which he can exert and wield at his own will. He is the subject, the Lord, who possesses the Spirit. There is nothing alien to him about this power for there has not been a time where the Spirit and his power were not with him - the Spirit is inherently in him. His very existence is in the Spirit and he experiences and exercises the power of the Spirit as his very own. Yet he does not dishonour the Spirit or take him lightly but gives him the highest honour, proclaiming that his name should never be blasphemed (12:31-32). Whilst honouring the Spirit, he does have the authority to delegate the power of the Spirit to his disciples, seeing himself as Lord of the Spirit who sends out workers into the harvest field and equips them with the Spirit. This he does with the plainest of words and movement, understanding this momentous act as an act most natural to him, an act not usurping his Father's authority but fully consonant with the will of his Father in heaven. This is how Jesus relates to the Spirit, one in unison and yet somehow mysteriously distinct, being his Lord and yet giving him the highest honour, exercising the Spirit's power as his own power yet acknowledging the Spirit's power in him. This is the mystery of Jesus' inherent relationship with the Spirit. (The above presentation of Jesus' relationship with the Spirit can be understood as a *conceptualisation* based on (i) the conceptual element of Jesus' conception by the Spirit found in the narratives (Mt. 1:20) and (ii) the narratives of his life and ministry. Cf. McGrath's comments on the dynamic relationship between conceptualisation and narratives in 3.0 of chapter 1.)

One certainly does not see in this relationship the kind of subordination that Jesus allegedly experiences under the Spirit according to Dunn. Jesus is never the object of possession by the Spirit.[64] Rather, Jesus is the subject who possesses the Spirit, who is the true author, or co-author with his Father and the Spirit, of his action in the Spirit.[65] Schweizer writes,

---

64 Dunn alleges that the Spirit is the power which possessed Jesus. *Jesus and the Spirit* , p. 54. See also p. 87.

65 Dunn alleges that Jesus was not the the author of the Spirit's power; nor was he able to dispose of it at will. *Ibid.*, p. 87.

Jesus becomes the subject of an action in the Holy Spirit. He is ... the Lord of the πνεῦμα. ... As one who is born of the Spirit, Jesus is from the very first a possessor of the Spirit and not just the Spirit's object, like the pneumatic.[66]

By trying to make Jesus the archetypal example of sonship for Christians, Dunn shows a tendency to reduce Jesus to the level of his disciples.[67] But in doing so, he has confused Jesus' unique and intrinsic Sonship to the Father with the disciples' sonships through adoption; he has neglected the fundamental difference between Jesus' inherent relationship with the Spirit (through conception) and the disciples two-stage relationship with the Spirit, where there was a time in which they did not have the Spirit.[68] Concerning Jesus' distinctive relationship with the Spirit, Schweizer, while commenting on Luke, also writes,

> The fact that the baptism in the Jordan and the story of Pentecost were in no way assimilated to one another is a possible indication that for Luke the endowment of Jesus with the Spirit lay on a different plane from that of the community.[69]

It has been noted in 1.2 that Dunn's mishandling of Jesus' authoritative sayings led him astray in his understanding of Jesus' identity and his relationship with the Spirit. Here, he has mishandled Jesus' conception by the Spirit.[70] He has actually neglected this important intrinsic aspect of Jesus' relationship with the Spirit completely in *Jesus and the Spirit,* where no reference is made to Mt.

---

66 *TDNT*, vol.VI, p. 405.

67 Dunn has the tendency to see that Jesus is merely quantitatively and uniquely more inspired. See *Jesus and the Spirit,* p. 91. See also Turner's interpretation of Dunn's position, *The Holy Spirit and Spiritual Gifts*, pp. 19-20, 23-5. Turner interprets Dunn's position as 'Jesus only began to experience what Dunn means by "new covenant" existence and eschatological "sonship" with his reception of the Spirit in or after his baptism' (p. 25). Thus, Christians also go through this experience after the pattern of Jesus.

68 'The allusion to, if not complete citation of Ps. 2:7, suggests that the gift of the Spirit was understood to be Jesus' *adoption* as Son - "You are my son, this day I became your father."' Dunn, *Jesus and the Spirit*, p. 65. Dunn's adoptionist tendency here is more pronounced than in *Baptism in the Holy Spirit,* which was written earlier.

69 *TDNT*, vol. VI, p. 405.

70 Turner criticises Dunn for this, *The Holy Spirit and Spiritual Gifts*, pp. 24-5, 29. And Dunn has conceded that he did not take adequate account of Luke 1:35, see his 'Baptism in the Spirit: A Response to Pentecostal Scholarship on Luke-Acts', *Journal of Pentecostal Theology,* 3 (1993), p. 17.

1:20 or Luke 1:35.[71] That is why Dunn can think of Jesus' relationship with the Spirit only in extrinsic terms and tends in the direction of adoptionism. In failing to grasp Jesus' intrinsic or inherent relationship with the Spirit, he fails to grasp the notion of Jesus as the subject and the author of his actions in the Spirit; he can only consider Jesus as the object of possession by the Spirit. Dunn's way of seeing Jesus merely as 'the uniquely anointed Man of the Spirit' but not Lord of the Spirit (*Jesus and the Spirit*, p. 46) and his tendency to walk down the road of adoptionism (*Jesus and the Spirit*, p. 65) amounts to a serious dilution of the divinity of Jesus Christ, or even a denial of it, which has a whole host of implications and consequences for Christian life and experience, church doctrines, such as atonement and the Trinity, worship and prayer, and the sense of the decisive finality of God's revelation in Jesus Christ. By upholding the Spirit above Jesus Christ, it also contradicts the Spirit's desire to help us to confess 'Jesus as Lord' (1 Cor. 12:3).

Matthew presents Jesus, not the Spirit, at the centre stage of his gospel: Jesus is the Lord (even of the Spirit) in his words and actions; Jesus is the subject of his free actions in the Spirit. Luke is the evangelist who heightens the profile of the Spirit most amongst the synoptists. It remains to see how he treats Jesus' relationship with the Spirit.

2.3 The Pneumatology of Luke

The pattern of the references to the Spirit in Luke has already been given in 2.1. Most of the references are concentrated in the first few chapters of the gospel. Particularly, most of these are to do with Mary's conception of Jesus and her giving birth to Jesus. The characters inspired by the Spirit are John the Baptist, Mary, Elizabeth, Zechariah, Simeon and probably the prophetess Anna. And most of them were inspired by the Spirit to give praise to God. 'We are really faced with a liturgical drama in which Luke is clearly up to something quite different than what he portrays during the rest of his gospel. It sounds as if the small circle around Mary have already experienced Pentecost!'[72] However, with respect to Jesus, the growth of his wisdom at his young age (Luke 2:40, 52) and his awareness of his Father (2:49) are not

---

71 Luke 1:35 is mentioned by Dunn in *Baptism in the Holy Spirit* (written in 1970) four times. By 1975 when *Jesus and the Spirit* was written, Dunn had focused his attention more on Jesus' baptism and his experience of the Spirit and the Father; there he relinquished the idea of Jesus' intrinsic relationship with the Spirit via his conception - Luke 1:35 was not mentioned at all.

72 Montague, *The Holy Spirit*, p. 268. He interprets these as a 'prologue to the ecclesiology of Acts'.

attributed explicitly to the Spirit. Jesus' relationship with the Spirit becomes much more prominent at his baptism and immediately afterward. Luke 4:1, compared to Mt. 4:1, emphasises that Jesus was 'full of the Holy Spirit' when he was 'led in the Spirit' to the wilderness. Here, πλήρης denotes abiding fullness of the Spirit in Jesus, which is distinct from επλήσθη (being filled, used for other people, e.g., Elizabeth in 1:41 and Zechariah in 1:67).[73] And Jesus is led in, not by, the Spirit into the wilderness.[74] Luke adds another πνεῦμα in 4:14 - 'Jesus returned to Galilee in the power of the Spirit' - and sets the portrayal of Jesus as a *possessor* of spiritual power above all that follows.[75] Luke 4:18 - 'The Spirit of the Lord is on me because he has anointed me to preach good news to the poor' - (which is peculiar to Luke) also emphasises the abiding of the Spirit on Jesus.[76] Jesus' unique possession of the Spirit is therefore different from others being moved or filled by the Spirit.

Considering the increased factor of the power of the Spirit in Jesus after his baptism in Luke, one may not dispute the possibility of Jesus' progressive growth in his possession of the Spirit's power, and the growth in his knowledge of his Father and wisdom (Luke 2:49, 2:40, 52) through the Spirit.[77] Even his baptism could be an important step in completing that growth. But what we do dispute with Dunn is that, once Jesus is clear of his mission and is about to embark on the mission that requires authority on his part, whether he is continuously dependent on the Spirit's inspiration for his authority. Even though the Spirit plays an important part in the progressive process of his knowledge of his unique identity as the Son of God, his knowledge of his mission and his knowledge of his unique authority, once his inherent identity as the Son of God is known, this identity is by no means dependent on the Spirit's inspiration. Likewise, *his inherent authority, once it is known, is by no means dependent on the Spirit's continuous inspiration.* Dunn has attributed to the Spirit *both* Jesus' *knowledge* of his authority and the *right* to own and exercise that authority. The former can be attributed to the Spirit but the latter, Jesus' intrinsic right, cannot. By attempting to find a major role for the Spirit in Jesus, Dunn has overstepped the boundary in an approach and concept too simplistic to correspond to the data in the gospel narratives.

After the five references to the Spirit in Jesus from his baptism to his

---

73 *TDNT*, vol. VI, p. 405.

74 *Ibid.*, see also Turner, *The Holy Spirit and Spiritual Gifts*, p. 30.

75 *Ibid.*

76 *Ibid.*

77 John Owen certainly subscribed to this view. See G. McFarlane, *Christ and the Spirit* (Carlisle: Paternoster, 1996), pp. 160-1.

declaration of his manifesto in Nazareth, such references completely disappear from the rest of Luke, except an incidental mention in 10:21 on Jesus' spontaneous praise to the Father. Barrett's attempt to explain this remarkable feature has been dealt with in 2.1 where we agree with one of Barrett's reasons, which will be taken up later. Here, the approaches of E. Schweizer and R. Menzies, and M. Turner's response to them, will be discussed.

2.3.1 E. SCHWEIZER, R.P. MENZIES AND M. TURNER

Turner and Menzies have very different approaches to the study of the Spirit in Luke. Menzies stands close to Schweizer and develops his view.[78] Schweizer understands that the Spirit in Luke is essentially the Spirit of prophecy which is a typical Jewish understanding. Schweizer and Menzies suppose that Luke does not attribute to the Spirit either the miracles of healing or the effects of ethical righteousness in the life of the believing community.[79] Rather, the Spirit of prophecy gives revelation or wisdom and thus inspires or empowers *preaching* and witness by the community.[80] Schweizer observes that in Luke-Acts miracles 'are never ascribed to the Spirit'. 'Healing power is associated with the name of Jesus, with faith in Jesus, with Jesus Himself, with prayer ..., or more simply the δύναμις [power] of Jesus.'[81] He also points out that in Jesus' answer to the Baptist's question in Luke 7:22, there is no mention of the Spirit in Jesus' (the Messiah's) healings. To substantiate his view that for Luke the Spirit is the Spirit of prophecy as in Jewish understanding, he gives a list of people who were inspired by the Spirit to speak (Luke 1:41 (Elizabeth), 1:67 (Zechariah); Acts 2:4 (disciples speaking in tongues); 11:28 (Agabus); 13:9 (Paul)), and those who were prompted by the Spirit for action (Acts 8:29; 10:19; 11:12; 13:2,4; 16:6f; 20:22).[82] And a particularly important, in fact primary, work of the Spirit of prophecy is empowering the disciples' preaching and witness (Luke 12:12; Acts 1:8).[83] In view of these observations by Schweizer about the role of the Spirit being limited to prophecy or

---

78 For E. Schweizer's view, see his article in *TDNT*, vol. VI, especially around p. 409. For R. Menzies' view, see his *The Development of Early Christian Pneumatology* (Sheffield: JSOT, 1991).

79 *TDNT*, vol. VI, p. 409. Turner, *The Holy Spirit and Spiritual Gifts*, p. 13, notices that the English translation of Schweizer's article mistranslates him.

80 See Turner, *The Holy Spirit and Spiritual Gifts*, pp. 13-4.

81 *TDNT*, vol. VI, p. 407. The references to Jesus' power are Luke 5:17; 6:19.

82 But against Schweizer's observation of Acts 13:9, the prophetic statement made by Paul in Acts 13:9-11 cannot be divorced from its miraculous effect on the Jewish sorcerer in verse 11.

83 *Ibid.*, pp. 407-9.

wisdom inspiration in Luke-Acts, the paucity of the references to the
Spirit in Jesus' ministry could possibly be explained.

However, while it is true that Jesus' disciples in Acts and several
figures around Mary in the early chapters of Luke are inspired by the
Spirit of prophecy to speak and act, Turner observes that Luke does not
ascribe to Jesus any of the prototypical gifts of the Spirit of prophecy
(these are revelation, guidance, charismatic wisdom, invasively inspired
speech or praise, see Turner, *The Holy Spirit and Spiritual Gifts*, pp. 6-
12), except on one occasion - invasive doxology (10:21).[84] Turner notes,

> [T]he Synoptics are surprisingly reticent to speak of Jesus receiving
> revelation (contrast the paucity of such references in Luke (only 3:21,22,
> 10:18? and 10:22) with the numerous occasions on which *disciples*
> receive revelations in Acts), and *this is never specifically attributed to the
> Spirit.*[85]

It may be added that Jesus' answer to the Baptist in Luke 7:22 not
only includes healing miracles but also preaching to the poor, and yet
the Spirit's role is not mentioned in relation to Jesus' preaching. This is
also true of Jesus' other preaching occasions, except in Nazareth (4:18).
Contrary to Schweizer's suggestion, the distinctive work of the Spirit of
prophecy is rarely, if ever, presented explicitly by Luke in relation to
Jesus' preaching, life and charismatic experience. These counter-
observations against Schweizer and Menzies put their theory into
question. The following observations reinforce this doubt.

Turner manages to expand the gifts of the Spirit of prophecy to
include the power of healing and ethical righteousness by adducing
some evidence from the OT and Jewish literature.[86] In relation to the
synoptic gospels, he works hard to attribute the power in Jesus to heal
and exorcise to the Spirit by linking the Spirit-anointed Messiah with
the New Exodus theme of liberation in Isaiah.[87] It may be added
explicitly that the programmatic statement made by Jesus in his
manifesto at Nazareth clearly links his works of liberation (which as the
gospel unfolds include healings and exorcisms) with the Spirit.[88] Even

---

84 Turner, *The Holy Spirit and Spiritual Gifts*, p. 34.
85 *Ibid.*, p. 33. Italics mine.
86 *Ibid.*, pp. 14-18. Dunn has also dealt with Menzies' restriction of the role of the
  Spirit in Luke-Acts to prophecy in his 'Baptism in the Spirit: A Response to
  Pentecostal Scholarship on Luke-Acts', pp. 7-16.
87 *Ibid.*, pp. 30-32. Turner's argument is convincing despite the fact that 'no available
  Jewish sources directly connect exorcisms with the Spirit nor do they explicitly
  interpret exorcisms as evidence of the arrival of the kingdom'.
88 This link between healings and the Spirit cannot be easily set aside by a mere

Schweizer himself acknowledges δυνάμις/power and πνεῦμα/Spirit are synonyms.[89] Both terms are used to describe Jesus' ministry of healings and exorcisms in Acts 10:38, so that where it is said Jesus has the power to heal, the Spirit can be also be *inferred*. Concerning the role of the Spirit in effecting ethical righteousness, Turner *infers* that during Jesus' temptations in the wilderness the Spirit grants Jesus 'new depth of charismatic wisdom and insight, which is the basis of the hoped-for Messiah's redoubtable righteousness. (*1 Enoch* 49:2-3; *Pss. Sol.* 17:37; 18:7; ...)'[90] Here Turner does *infer* the prototypical gifts of the Spirit of prophecy exercised by Jesus and links such gifts to ethical righteousness. All in all, it seems possible and reasonable to draw *inferences* of and *links* with the Spirit in Jesus' miraculous works and spiritual experiences in Luke's gospel. It would be inappropriate to limit the work of the Spirit in Jesus only to prophecy, as Schweizer and Menzies do.

Given (i) Jesus' conception by the Spirit, (ii) the Spirit explicitly descending upon Jesus as the Father commissions him to his Messianic task and (iii) the references of Jesus' having the Spirit in abiding fullness (4:1, 14), there can be little doubt that Jesus lives and moves in the Spirit, he heals and exorcises in or by the Spirit (of power), and he has communion with the Father and knows his Father's will through the same Spirit (of prophecy). It will be difficult to accept Schweizer's and Menzies' suggestion that somehow the Spirit in Jesus is dormant when he heals and exorcises, and somehow the Spirit in Jesus is active again when he proclaims the message of the kingdom. Such compartmentalising of Jesus' life and ministry in the Spirit is difficult to conceive. It will not be appropriate for us, then, to use Schweizer's and Menzies' theory to explain the paucity of the references of the Spirit in Jesus.

Against Schweizer and Menzies, Turner has pointed out the lack of explicit reference to Jesus receiving or exercising the prototypical gifts of the Spirit of prophecy in Luke. However, his and other *inferences* of the work of the Spirit within Jesus' ministry, although reasonable and sound, are nevertheless inferences based on passages where the Spirit is not explicitly mentioned. It is still true that the Spirit in relation to Jesus within his ministry, after the introduction in the first few chapters, is not presented explicitly in Luke. Turner has not explained why *Luke refrains from ascribing the prototypical gifts of the Spirit of prophecy to Jesus explicitly and why Luke is reluctant to delineate clearly the role of the Spirit in Jesus' healings, exorcisms, his visionary experiences and*

---

mention of 4:23, as Schweizer does.
89 *TDNT*, vol. VI, p. 407.
90 Turner, *The Holy Spirit and Spiritual Gifts*, pp. 29-30. See also p. 35.

his ethical righteousness. This problem, which has been raised by Barrett and others but not satisfactorily resolved, is to be addressed in the following section.

2.3.2 JESUS' RELATIONSHIP WITH THE SPIRIT AND HIS DISCIPLES' RELATIONSHIP WITH THE SPIRIT

The problem of Luke's reluctance to speak about the Spirit in Jesus' ministry is to be tackled by revisiting Jesus' exorcisms as referenced in Luke 11:20 and Luke 9:42-43. Inevitably the issue concerning the phrase 'the Spirit of God' in Matthew and 'the finger of God' in Luke requires close attention. Dunn has a brief review of the discussion as to which is the original in Q.[91] He finds it difficult to reach a decision but the considerations seem to 'tip the scales in favour of the Spirit'.[92] Turner accepts that Luke has changed 'the Spirit of God' to 'the finger of God' but he will not concur with those (e.g., Schweizer and Menzies) who advocate that Luke made this change because he could only regard the Spirit as the Spirit of prophecy and not also the Spirit of miraculous power.[93] His explanation for this change is that 'the finger of God' (a clear reference of Exo 8:19) relates more closely to Luke's prophet-like-Moses Christology but still refers to the Spirit. Thus according to Turner, Luke sacrificed a reference to the Spirit in Jesus in order to strengthen his prophet-like-Moses Christology.[94] Most earlier scholarship considered the Lukan form is the original.[95] The reason was that Luke, who had a keen interest in the Spirit, was unlikely to sacrifice such a valuable reference.[96] However, 'all the more recent studies that have focused attention on this matter conclude that Luke is the one who has altered the text.'[97] Briefly, some of the reasons are (i) Luke has also omitted the Spirit in 21:15 and 20:42 compared to Mark 13:11 and 12:36, (ii) Matthew cannot be shown to have added 'the Spirit of God', (iii) Luke also uses other anthropomorphisms, namely 'the hand of God' (1:66; Acts 4:28, 30; 7:50) and 'the arm of God' (1:31; Acts 13:17) and (iv) the reason given by Turner. Barrett's observation of the paucity of

---

91 Dunn, *Jesus and the Spirit*, pp. 45-6.

92 *Ibid.*, p. 46.

93 Turner, *The Holy Spirit and Spiritual Gifts*, p. 31. For Menzies' view, see his *The Development of Early Christian Pneumatology*, pp. 186-9.

94 But could Luke not strengthen his prophet-like-Moses Christology by other means in another context while preserving this reference to the Spirit of God, if it is precious to him, in this context? Turner's explanation is not yet satisfactory.

95 John Nolland, *Word Commentary: Luke* (Dallas: Word Books, 1989-1993), p. 639.

96 Dunn, *Jesus and the Spirit*, p. 45.

97 Nolland, *Word Commentary: Luke*, p. 639. References of scholars who hold this view are given there. Barrett also holds that 'the Spirit of God' in Matthew is original, *The Holy Spirit*, p. 63.

references to the Spirit in both Matthew and Luke suggest that neither is keen to include the Spirit in the narratives more than strictly necessary. It is most probable that the one with 'the Spirit of God' is the original; otherwise, their introduction of the Spirit is contrary to their overall practice. The same argument can be applied to Luke 10:21 where the reference to Jesus as full of joy through the Holy Spirit could well be original but omitted by Matthew.

Luke's redaction in 11:20 is further closely followed by another. Luke moves the verses on the saying of the blasphemy against the Holy Spirit, which are clearly there in Matthew (12:31-32) and in Mark (3:28-29) in the context of the exorcism controversy, to Luke 12:10, which reads 'And everyone who speaks a word against the Son of Man will be forgiven, but anyone who blasphemes against the Holy Spirit will not be forgiven.'[98] This second redaction has an important implication for the interpretation of the last redaction. In the Matthean context, this saying is a consequence of Jesus' assertion that it is by the Spirit of God that he drives out demons: to attribute to Beelzebub the exorcism wrought through the power of the Spirit by Jesus is blasphemy against the Holy Spirit, which is unforgivable. The presence of this saying therefore *confirms* Jesus' assertion about the role of the Spirit in his exorcisms. It is highly probable then that Luke, by changing 'the Spirit of God' to 'the finger of God' and moving the blasphemy saying to another context, intends to create a distance between Jesus' exorcism and the power of the Spirit in him. Menzies attributes these redactional moves of Luke to his prophetic pneumatology, i.e., Luke conceives of the Spirit only in prophetic terms but not in terms of power of healings or exorcisms.[99] However, even though this is a plausible explanation, it is by no means the exclusive one.

The content of the blasphemy saying gives exceedingly high, or the highest, honour to the Spirit compared with Jesus. In the original context where this saying is *coupled* with the explicit reference to 'the Spirit of God' as the power of Jesus' exorcism, the profile of the Spirit is *doubly* heightened such that in some readers' interpretations the honour of Jesus might possibly be eclipsed by the Spirit. It is here

---

98 See Menzies, *The Development of Early Christian Pneumatology*, pp. 190-1 on the details of the redaction.

99 Menzies, *The Development of Early Christian Pneumatology*, pp. 194-5. He also tries to interpret Luke's blasphemy saying (12:10) in its new context, giving it a prophetic slant. Blasphemy against the Spirit is committed by Christians: 'it is their failure to heed the voice of the Spirit and bear witness to Christ in the face of persecution.' (p. 193) However, it is doubtful if any interpretation of this verse, wrenched from its original context of the exorcism controversy, can ever be truly satisfactory.

proposed that Luke's double redactions are aimed at preserving Jesus' high profile and honour, which are consistent with the Lordship of Jesus presented in his gospel (Luke 3:4; cf. exegesis of Mt. 3:3 in chapter 2). This proposal, alternative to Menzies', needs to be further substantiated. It needs to be shown that when this proposal is further developed it is more coherent than Menzies' proposal. And it needs also to be shown why Matthew is willing to accept the double references to the Spirit in Q without worrying about its implications, while Luke is unwilling to do so. To address both issues, Jesus' teaching his disciples to pray for the the gift of Holy Spirit in Luke 11:11-13 needs to be carefully studied.

> Which of you fathers, if your son asks for a fish, will give him a snake instead? Or if he asks for an egg, will give him a scorpion? If you then, though you are evil, know how to give good gifts to your children, how much more will your Father in heaven give the Holy Spirit to those who ask him.

The Matthean parallel in 7:9-11 has the contrast of bread and stone instead of Luke's egg and scorpion while they share the contrast of fish and snake. Also, Matthew has the promise of 'good gifts' instead of Luke's 'Holy Spirit'. These two differences between Matthew and Luke are significant in the following manner. 'Snake' and 'scorpion' have been used by Luke as metaphors for evil spirits in 10:18-20 in the context of the disciples' mission of preaching, healing and exorcism. In the context of prayer in Luke 11:11-13, snake and scorpion as metaphors for evil spirits may well be contrasted with the Holy Spirit or 'good spirit'.[100] Jesus is then reassuring his disciples, who may be unsettled by allegations that they have cast out demons by evil spirits, that the Father has given them the Holy Spirit, not evil spirits, to perform exorcisms in their earlier mission (10:17-20).[101] This interpretation involving others' allegation and Jesus' reassurance is supported by the immediately succeeding passage on *the exorcism*

---

100 Some manuscripts have 'good spirit' instead of 'Holy Spirit', see Max Turner, 'Prayers in Gospels and Acts', in *Teach Us to Pray: Prayer in the Bible and the World* (Exeter: The Paternoster Press and Baker Book House, c1990), D. A. Carson (ed.), p. 68. See also Nolland, *Word Commentary: Luke*, p. 630.

101 Not only Jesus but his disciples are also accused of casting out demons by the power of Beelzebub. See Turner, 'Prayers in Gospels and Acts', p. 68, or pp. 113-5 of his Ph.D thesis, 'Luke and the Spirit: Studies in the Significance of Receiving the Spirit in Luke-Acts' (Cambridge University, 1980). Matthew 10:25 clearly implies this, 'If the head of the house has been called Beelzebub, how much more the members of his household.'

controversy which also negates the use of evil spirits in (Jesus') exorcisms.

From the above interpretation, Luke is making clear that *at least on the part of the disciples*, exorcisms are effected by the good gift of the Holy Spirit in response to prayer to the Father, even though Jesus' association with the Spirit in this respect is veiled by the reference to 'the finger of God' instead of 'Spirit of God'.[102] *This interpretation of 11:11-13 thus contradicts Menzies' suggestion that Luke understands the Spirit purely in prophetic terms and not in terms of power for healings and exorcisms.*[103]

An important point emerging out of the above interpretation of 11:11-13 is that while Luke emphasises, in comparison with Matthew (by redacting Q, see Nolland, *Word Commentary: Luke*, p. 631), the need of the disciples to pray for the gift of the Holy Spirit in the context of mission, which involves preaching as well as healings and exorcisms (9:1-6; 10:13-20), he deliberately *veils* Jesus' exercising the power of the Spirit in his mission, as can be seen in his double redactions in the passage on the exorcism controversy. Luke's deliberate intention to make this contrast between Jesus and his disciples can be seen in the three redactions that he made in very close proximity in order to consistently achieve this very purpose. Although Luke is extremely keen to raise the profile of the Spirit and present the work of the Spirit prominently in Jesus' disciples in Acts and the figures around Mary in the early chapters of Luke, he sets Jesus quite apart from them such that the Spirit is relatively *veiled* in his life and work.[104] In Luke's presentation, Jesus' relationship with the Spirit is different from the disciples' relationship with the Spirit. The Spirit dwells in Jesus in abiding fullness while the disciples need to pray for the power of the Spirit regularly (the preceding context of 11:11-13 is the Lord's prayer which involves daily asking God for provisions). Jesus has the authority to grant them the power of the Holy Spirit for preaching, healing and exorcism (9:1-2; 10:17-20). In this real sense, Jesus is already Lord of

---

102 It is veiled but not totally hidden because in the OT, 'the hand of God', which is a parallel term of 'the finger of God', was interpreted as the Spirit of God, e.g., Ezek. 8:1-3 and 1 Chr. 28:11-19. See R.G. Hammerton-Kelly, 'A Note on Matthew 12:28 par. Luke 11:20', *New Testament Studies*, 11 (1964-65), pp. 167-9.

103 Understandably, in treating Luke 11:11-13 Menzies does not make any connection between this passage on prayer for the Holy Spirit and the immediately succeeding passage on the exorcism controversy. He interprets Luke 11:11-13 only in prophetic terms by referring to other passages in Luke-Acts which serve his purpose but without a thorough exegesis of this passage in its local context.

104 But it is certainly not totally hidden, see his baptism, his temptations and his sermon at Nazareth.

the Spirit even in his earthly life and ministry. He is the Lord (cf. 3:4) who sends his disciples out to mission even as they pray to the Lord of the harvest (God) to send out workers (10:2-3) - such tight proximity of the former (Jesus sending) to the latter (God sending) in Luke is remarkable (in Matthew they are more separated, 9:38 and 10:5). Jesus and his disciples, though both acting in the power of the Spirit in their missions, are not comparable and their relationships with the Spirit are also distinct. Jesus is not merely a Spirit-inspired or Spirit-empowered man as his followers are. Jesus as Lord of the Spirit is not subservient to the Spirit as his disciples are. This point becomes even clearer if we invert Luke's double redactions on the exorcism controversy.

If, after emphasising (through redacting Q) the disciples' need to pray for the gift of the Holy Spirit in 11:11-13, Luke presents Jesus claiming explicitly to exorcise by the Spirit of God, which is followed by the saying concerning the forgivable sin of speaking against the Son of Man and the unforgivable sin of blaspheming against the Holy Spirit, the accumulated effect of these three passages might lead some readers to ponder upon the possibility that the Spirit is the Lord of Jesus who is no different from his disciples and needs to regularly pray for the Spirit's enabling for his ministry, particularly exorcisms. In this picture, Jesus is just another pneumatic, perhaps a more inspired one, and the Spirit rather than Jesus is to be honoured. But this is the picture that Luke painstakingly tried to avoid in his gospel. Rather, Jesus is the Lord to whose name the demons submit and in whose name the demons are cast out (10:17-18). Luke's distancing Jesus from the disciples in his relationship with the Spirit and in his acts of exorcism can be confirmed by a further redaction by Luke.

Matthew (17:14-23), Mark (9:14-32) and Luke (9:37-45) all have the episode of Jesus casting out an evil spirit from an epileptic boy after his transfiguration. The details of how the disciples failed to drive out the evil spirit and how Jesus came to the father's help and drove out the spirit are similar in the three accounts.[105] But after the point where the boy was freed, the accounts diverge. Matthew and Mark both have the disciples asking Jesus the reason for their failure to drive out the spirit. Jesus' answer in Matthew was their lack of faith (17:20), while in Mark (9:29) Jesus replied, 'This kind can come out only by prayer.' In Luke, no such question was raised and therefore no answer was necessary. Luke instead parallels Jesus' exorcism in v. 42 with 'the greatness of God' in v. 43. The answer related in Mark might possibly give the impression that Jesus received power from God in answer to his prayer so that he was empowered to cast out demons. Matthew avoids this

---

105 The endings of the three accounts are also similar - a reiteration of the coming suffering of the Son of Man.

possible impression by presenting a different answer by Jesus - the disciples' failure is to do with their lack of faith, prayer was not directly mentioned. Luke deals with this possible impression by omitting it altogether even though Jesus' prayer is of special interest to Luke.[106] Interestingly, Luke does have Jesus praying on the Mount of Transfiguration before the incidence while Matthew and Mark do not. The intention of Luke's omission of the disciples' question and Jesus' answer can be gleaned by surveying the consequence if he had followed Mark by including Jesus' reply that prayer was necessary for exorcism. It would then appear that Jesus, having prayed on the Mount of Transfiguration, was enabled by God to cast out the evil spirit and so taught his disciples to follow his example of praying for power. *If this portrayal of Jesus in chapter 9 is coupled with the almost identical theme of Jesus teaching his disciples to pray for the Holy Spirit in their exorcisms and mission in chapter 11, immediately followed by Jesus' casting out demons by the Spirit of God and the saying of blasphemy against the Holy Spirit (which could be interpreted to mean the Spirit is of higher honour than Jesus), the accumulated force of all these is that Jesus could be interpreted as a mere example for the disciples, who behaves in a manner subservient to the Holy Spirit, whose authority is derived from the inspiration by the Spirit as a result of prayer, who cannot dispose the power of the Spirit at his own will, who is therefore at the mercy of the Spirit.* Such an interpretation of Jesus is very close to Dunn's picture of Jesus and the Spirit but it is not the one that Luke desires to portray. In fact, he deliberately mounts a concerted effort to avoid this picture: *he is quite prepared to (i) sacrifice a valuable reference to Jesus' prayer in the episode of the epileptic boy despite his interest in Jesus' prayer, (ii) edit out the reference to 'the Spirit of God' in his source and replace it with 'the finger of God' despite his keen interest in the Spirit and (iii) remove the saying of blaspheming against the Holy Spirit and place it in a rather awkward context.* Luke is willing to make valuable sacrifices and expend great effort to avoid putting Jesus into the same category as the disciples and portraying him merely as another Spirit-inspired man. But a question remains to be answered. Granted that Matthew, as Luke does, also avoids including Mark's

---

106 Turner, 'Prayers in Gospels and Acts', pp. 59-64. Luke includes references to Jesus' prayers into his narratives (in contrast to Matthew and Mark) and underscores Jesus' prayer life, e.g., 3:21, 5:16. W. Liefeld, *The Expositor's Bible Commentary* (Grand Rapids: Regency Reference, 1984), vol. 8, p. 930, comments on Luke 9:43, 'We might have expected Luke to dwell on the role of prayer, given his interest in it.' A similar observation is made by Luke Johnson, *Sacra Pagina Series*, vol. 3, *The Gospel of Luke* (Collegeville, Minn.: Liturgical Press, 1991), p. 158.

reference to prayer in the epileptic boy episode, why is he willing to sustain a triplet of references to the Spirit in relation to Jesus all within the short space of Mt. 12 (vv. 18, 28, 31-32), while Luke can only sustain one reference in relation to the disciples' praying for the gift of the Spirit from the Father?

A threefold attempt will be made to address this question. Firstly, while it cannot be said that Matthew in any way emphasises the Spirit (see 2.2), he does seem to enjoy comparatively greater freedom than Luke in relating Jesus to the Spirit, despite the fact that Luke's interest in the Spirit's relationships with Jesus' disciples (in Luke-Acts) and the figures around Mary (in Luke) outweighs Matthew's interest in the Spirit's relationship with Jesus' disciples. It should be remembered that Matthew has no Pentecost - Jesus *himself* is present with his disciples after his resurrection (28:20), nor a kind of mini-Pentecost that Luke has in the early chapters of his gospel (see the beginning of 2.3). But it is precisely this feature, Matthew's lack of emphasis of the Spirit in Jesus' disciples or other figures, that gives Matthew this comparatively greater freedom to be slightly more explicit than Luke concerning the Spirit in Jesus. While Luke has greater need than Matthew to maintain a high profile for Jesus to *distinguish him from many other Spirit-filled figures* present in Luke-Acts, Matthew has relatively less of this concern because there are very few such Spirit-filled figures, if any, other than Jesus in his narratives. This point about distinction from other inspired figures will be taken up later in looking at the context of the audience/community of the gospel.

The second reason is to do with Luke's critical introduction of praying for the specific gift of the Spirit in 11:13. Matthew's first of the three references to the Spirit in chapter 12 concerns a different matter - fulfilment of Isaiah 42:1-4. Matthew's double references to the Spirit later in that chapter do not imply that Jesus is dependent on prayer for the Spirit's power in exorcisms; Jesus' exorcisms with the power of the Spirit merely witness positively to his fulfilment of Isaiah 42:1-4. However, once Luke has introduced prayer for the gift of the Spirit in 11:13, he may have found it more difficult to avoid the picture of Jesus merely as a Spirit-inspired man whose prayer for this gift has been answered if he maintains the further two references to the Spirit. Luke therefore has greater pressure than Matthew to remove the two references to the Spirit in the exorcism controversy, especially in the light of his greater need to distinguish Jesus from other Spirit-inspired figures (cf. the first reason).

The third reason for Matthew retaining three references to the Spirit in chapter 12 is that all three synoptic evangelists are certainly not opposed to referring to the Spirit in Jesus - they desire to portray an appropriate relationship between Jesus and the Spirit. This is a delicate task and is not as simplistic as some modern scholars presume. It seems that within Matthew's overall presentation of Jesus and the Spirit in his narrative, which has a strong Christological focus, and with the high Christology (12:29-30, see 2.2) introduced between the two references to the Spirit in the exorcism controversy, together with Jesus as the egocentric/Christocentric subject of the action by the Spirit in 12:28, Matthew has found it satisfactory to make these references to the Spirit in relation to Jesus for the purpose of highlighting his theme of fulfilment, without the worry of upsetting his overall plan or strategy of presentation. It is true that Luke also shares these allowances of high Christology with Matthew. However, for Luke, once the redaction of prayer for the gift of the Spirit is introduced, and with the need to distinguish Jesus from other Spirit-inspired figures, he has found himself unable to retain these two further references to the Spirit without worrying that his picture of Jesus and the Spirit may be disturbed.[107]

In the above discussion, the notion of the delicate nature of the evangelists' task of presenting Jesus and the Spirit has emerged. It is to the nature of this specific task of the evangelists and their strategy for this task that we now turn.

3.0 The Evangelists' Communicative Strategy

One certainly cannot deny, rather should affirm positively, that the evangelists intend to present Jesus as the Messiah who is anointed by God with his Holy Spirit. However, their task is not merely to present a human Messiah who is God's agent and inspired by the Spirit, as in Jewish expectation. In all three synoptic gospels (but not in John), the word of fulfilment of Isaiah 40:3 is deliberately taken away from the lips of the Baptist and the LXX translation of Isaiah 40:3 is altered to reflect that the straight paths are prepared for Jesus. These two moves allow the evangelists to identify Jesus with Yahweh in Isaiah 40:3 - Jesus is equivalent with God his Father or Jesus is everything the name of Yahweh represents (see 2.1 of chapter 2, 'Jesus as the Coming Lord'). The evangelists therefore have a *twofold* task - to present Jesus as the divine Lord (who is equal with God his Father and one with his Father) and Jesus as the Spirit-anointed Messiah. This is a delicate task: how can a Spirit-anointed man, the Messiah, be the divine Lord who is

---

107 In his presentation, Mark has little concern with the Spirit in Jesus. Although he has the saying of blasphemy against the Spirit (3:28-29), the explicit reference to the Spirit of God in Jesus' exorcisms is absent and needs to be inferred, as in Luke. And that is the only reference to the Spirit in relation to Jesus in the whole of Jesus' ministry in Mark.

equal with God? Stressing the former might give the impression that the latter is not true and vice versa. Anyhow, they attempted this delicate task not only by attributing these titles to Jesus but also by the words and actions of Jesus in the narratives.

Accordingly, they present Jesus as speaking with constant and relentless sovereign authority, without even invoking the name of the Father or the Spirit, but not denying their honour and their implicit involvement in his life and work. Also, they present Jesus as acting with the same insuperable egocentric authority and exercising divine power to heal and exorcise at his own will. They even present Jesus as delegating authority to his disciples to preach, heal and exorcise in the power of the Spirit. Jesus is then presented even as Lord of the Spirit who sends out and equips his workers for harvest. Furthermore, the evangelists portrays Jesus as always in control in every situation, speaking or keeping silent, acting or refraining from action, always manifesting his supreme wisdom and freedom as the Lord. Barth ascribes to Jesus the phrase 'his unforgettable lordliness'.[108] But the evangelists do not present Jesus as such an exalted Lord that he is aloof or his Lordship blows people away from his path. They portray Jesus at the same time as the humble and gentle one, associating with lowly and needy people, standing in solidarity with them in their sufferings and pains, stretching out his compassionate hand to touch and liberate them, and in the end giving his own life in utter humiliation and agony for them. The evangelists indeed present Jesus as the divine and exalted Lord but at the same time they present him as the humble and suffering servant.[109] Also, implicitly in all these Jesus speaks and acts in his Lordship not in isolation from his Father, but in the strictest unity, consonance and communion with his Father.

As regarding the Spirit in Jesus as the Messiah, the synoptic evangelists have all adopted the strategy of presenting the Spirit descending on Jesus in his baptism which is verified by the Father's voice to his Son, declaring him as the Davidic Son of God (Psalm 2:7) and the Spirit-anointed servant (Is. 42:1). They all have the Spirit leading the Messiah into the desert for temptations. Luke in particular chooses to highlight the fullness of the Spirit in Jesus at this point (4:1). He further heightens this fact by his redactional notice in 4:14 where Jesus returns from the temptations 'in the power of the Spirit', and by including Jesus' programmatic manifesto at Nazareth (4:18-19), where Jesus declares his mission will include preaching to the poor and liberating the prisoners and oppressed in the power of the Spirit of the

---

108 *CD* IV.2, p. 165.

109 Barth entitled chapter 14 in *CD* IV.1 'Jesus Christ, the Lord as Servant' and chapter 15 in *CD* IV.2 'Jesus Christ, the Servant as Lord'.

Lord. This programmatic statement is probably meant by Luke to cover the whole of Jesus' forthcoming ministry, including preaching, healings and exorcisms. Jesus' baptism and temptations in all three synoptics, his conception by the Spirit in Matthew and Luke, and his programmatic statements in Luke all appear in the early chapters of the gospels. It is probable that this concentrated introduction of the Christ anointed by the Spirit in the early chapters is meant by the evangelists to *induce* into the reader's understanding the Spirit's involvement in Jesus' life and ministry following the introduction. In literary terms, this introduction is called a 'preparation', which is to be elaborated or unpacked in the rest of the story.[110] In this connection, Jesus' baptism is a preparation which is unpacked in the gospel story as his life, ministry and death in solidarity with Israel (see 3.0 of chapter 4). According to this preparation, the notion of the presence of the Spirit in Jesus is also unpacked in his life, ministry and death.

After this concentrated introduction of the Messiah anointed with the Spirit, and the associated induction of the notion of the Spirit in Jesus into the reader's mind in all three synoptic gospels (especially heightened and concentrated in Luke), within the narratives covering Jesus' ministry and death the evangelists make very few references to the Spirit, and still less in direct relation to Jesus, i.e., in Jesus' life and activities. After Jesus' baptism and temptations, the centre of attention is primarily focused on the person of Jesus Christ - his exercise of Lordship in his ministry of words and actions through which the kingdom of his Father has come. The evangelists' communicative strategy seems to be this: (i) they are satisfied that they have given the reader the *background* knowledge of the Spirit-filled Messiah and his Sonship by the inductive statement in Jesus' baptism and other events in the early chapters, and (ii) they now intend to bring the person of Jesus Christ, rather than the Spirit, even more to the *foreground* of the reader's attention and focus, presenting him as the Lord of authority, power, compassion, gentleness, humility, integrity, wisdom and freedom (see chapters 3 and 4), and *as the subject and Lord of the Spirit* (see above). At the same time, the evangelists also intend to relate Jesus to God his Father. In this respect the Johannine thunderbolt in Mt. 11:27 and Luke 10:22 is also *inductive* (as Jesus' baptism is inductive regarding his relationship with the Father and the Spirit) in the sense that this statement is meant to induce this aspect of Jesus' intimate relationship with his Father into the reader's mind as he reads and reflects on the rest of the gospel. With these background inductive statements given by Jesus' baptism (and other events) and Mt. 11:27 (par. Luke 10:22), the reader is left by the evangelists, or given the

---

110 See Powell, *What is Narrative Criticism?*, p. 33.

openness, to ponder on the relationship between Jesus, his Father and the Spirit as he reads the gospel narratives.

One of the reasons for the evangelists' installing these inductive statements in the background is that bringing the Spirit into the foreground in Jesus' ministry might have created multiple centres of attention and detracted Jesus from the centre stage of the gospel story. More importantly, as especially illustrated by Luke's redactions above, the evangelists might have been concerned that too high a profile of the Spirit in relation to Jesus in the foreground could have been misinterpreted to imply a merely human Jesus inspired by the Spirit, like other *Spirit-filled figures in the gospels and the OT*. Barrett's point is valid here, 'Their faith rested upon the Messiahship, the divine mission and status of Jesus of Nazareth. Hence, in comparison with the actual presence of the Lord's Anointed, and the operation of the powers of the Kingdom of God, the commonplace phenomena of prophetic and other inspiration were insignificant and irrelevant.'[111] However, one should not use the strong words 'insignificant and irrelevant' to denote the Spirit in Jesus. But it is still true that *the evangelists' principal objective is to present the divine Lordship, sovereign majesty and humility of Jesus, who being in unity and communion with God is present as God his Father is present, who acts as his Father acts, who thus brings his Father's kingdom, inaugurates his reign, reveals the Father and saves the people from their sins.*

The need to present the centrality and the divine Lordship of Jesus is heightened in a context where the disciples/community are active in their spiritual lives and spiritual experiences, particularly in their use of prophetic gifts. This is the case in Matthew (7:15,22; 10:41; see 2.2 above) and even more so in Luke-Acts. (E. Schweizer observed that to a certain extent it is also true in the letter to the Colossian church where there is 'a shrouding of the doctrine of the Spirit' compared to the emphasis on Christ.[112]) If the centrality and the divine Lordship of Jesus are not emphasised in such contexts, some 'disciples', 'prophets' or 'Spirit-inspired figures' of the community may boast of their 'spiritual experiences' such that they could claim superiority over the teaching of Christ and override the authority of Jesus with the claimed authority of the Spirit's inspiration. (The last paragraph deals with Jesus' distinction from Spirit-inspired figures in the gospel story and the OT, here the distinction is in relation to Spirit-inspired figures in the community.) The evangelists need to guard against such kind of spiritualism or

---

111 Barrett, *The Holy Spirit*, p. 157.

112 E. Schweizer, 'Christus und Geist im Kolosserbrief', in *Christ and the Spirit in the New Testament* (Cambridge: Cambridge University Press, 1973), B. Lindars and S. Smalley (eds.), p. 313.

mysticism afforded by a Christological vacuum. The way to achieve this is to heighten the centrality of Jesus, his authority in teaching and healing, i.e., to stress the Lordship of Jesus who is not merely a Spirit-inspired man at a level comparable to the other so-called 'prophets' in the community, but who is the *objective and concrete* expression of the authority of God, the Lordship of God and the will of God. Stressing the Lordship of Jesus in the community then involves not threatening Jesus' Lordship in the gospel by reducing him merely to a mouthpiece or the object of possession of the Spirit but presenting him as the subject and Lord of the Spirit who therefore has higher (the highest) authority than any disciples merely inspired by the Spirit. This is what the evangelists are at pains to do. In the light of this, one may appreciate why Luke especially amongst the three evangelists is so keen to go to great lengths to raise the profile of Jesus with respect to the Spirit to a level not less than the Spirit, and even present him as Lord of the Spirit, while also giving the highest honour to the Spirit (12:10). The reason is that he, amongst the evangelists, has the greatest need to *distinguish Jesus as the Lord of the Spirit from (i) the Spirit-inspired disciples in the community* and (ii) Spirit-filled figures in the narratives. He needs to balance his encouragement to the community to lead fully Spirit-filled lives, which involve frequent use of the prophetic gifts (see Acts), with the centrality of Jesus. Spiritual enthusiasm without the Christological centre amongst fallible human beings can only lead to chaos, exploitations and sins. For Matthew, this need to install the Christological centre is clearly there (see the prophetic activities in 7:15, 22; 10:41) but perhaps not as urgent as Luke's (for there seem to be fewer prophetic activities in Matthew's community), hence his treble concentrated references to the Spirit in relation to Jesus in Mt. 12 is quite acceptable to him while a similar concentration is not acceptable to Luke.[113] However, he has also been careful not to break the delicate balance, as seen in the paucity of references to the Spirit in his whole gospel.

Windisch's observation that some references to the Spirit in the synoptic gospels may have been suppressed is possible, but it is uncertain how much of the paucity of the references to the Spirit is due to suppression (in the passing on of traditions and in the evangelists' redactions) and how much is due to Jesus' reticence.[114] But what one can be sure of is that the pattern of reticence is both portrayed on Jesus' lips and the evangelists' editorial comments. The following are a few more examples of this trend. Prominent is the Transfiguration account. This account appears in all three synoptic gospels (Mt. 17:1-9; Mark

---

113 This is another reason, in addition to the three given in the last section, why Matthew can accept the treble references to the Spirit in Mt. 12.

114 Barrett, *The Holy Spirit*, p. 3.

9:2-9; Luke 9:28-36) and bears close similarities to Jesus' baptism: a voice from the cloud parallels the voice from heaven and the contents are very similar (both involving Isaiah 42:1 and Psalm 2:7). It is the Father's words concerning his Son and his mission, but the Spirit who descended upon Jesus in his baptism is not mentioned here - only the Father (or his voice) and the Son are in view. Similarly, in the mutual knowledge between the Father and the Son in Mt. 11:27; Luke 10:22, there is no explicit mention of the Spirit and his role has to be deduced from the inductive statement represented by Jesus' baptism which depicts a clear role for the Spirit. Again, Jesus' temptations in the wilderness involve visionary experiences and probably his exercise of some charismatic gifts of the Spirit (wisdom in particular), but the role of the Spirit in these experiences of Jesus is not explicit at all and needs to be deduced even though the Spirit is mentioned (see 5.0 of chapter 3, also Jesus' vision in Luke 10:18). Also, in Jesus' struggle with temptation at Gethsemane, the Spirit is not mentioned at all, but an angel is (Luke 22:43). Moreover, the growth of Jesus' wisdom at young age (Luke 2:40, 52) is not attributed to the Spirit even though the Messiah was thought to be filled by the Spirit of wisdom (Isaiah 11:2). Jesus' post-resurrection presence to the disciples which is not mediated by the Spirit in Matthew, and Luke's suppression of the Spirit in Jesus' exorcisms only serve to heighten this trend in the synoptic gospels. Nevertheless, the evangelists' stamp of the Spirit in Jesus is inerasable through Jesus' conception by the Spirit (only in Matthew and Luke), his baptism and temptations. While Windisch attempted to explain this phenomenon by a two-stage process, i.e., (i) references to the Spirit were suppressed in the interest of a higher Christology and (ii) later the church read back its own experience of the Spirit into the empty space left in its account of Jesus, it is proposed here that the present pattern in the gospels is the result of a more straightforward and consistent process: Jesus was more concerned with speaking about his Father's kingdom and with revealing its presence through his authoritative teachings and his mighty works rather than speaking about the Spirit in him, and this pattern was perpetuated in the traditions and by the evangelists. Accordingly, the evangelists chose to adopt a background-foreground communicative strategy to present Jesus' relationship with the Spirit in an inductive manner. In Windisch's scheme, the church was first concerned with high Christology at the expense of pneumatology and then tried to remedy this neglect of the Spirit (see Barrett's criticism of Windisch in 2.1: the church had made a poor attempt at this remedy). Here, the evangelists (following the traditions that they received) had concern both for Christology (foreground) and pneumatology (background) *at the same time*, and devise their communicative strategy to accommodate both *simultaneously* in their gospels, while bearing in mind the distinct identity of Jesus Christ compared to other Spirit-inspired figures in the gospel story and how that identity and its centrality can positively impinge on a Spirit-filled community.

Schweizer and Menzies assert that Luke has retained the Jewish understanding of the Spirit of prophecy and thus has precluded the Spirit from Jesus' healings and exorcisms. But their thesis has been seriously questioned. Turner points out that some OT and Jewish literature does include the concept of power in their understanding of the Spirit of prophecy.[115] He counter-argues against Schweizer and Menzies that the Spirit's power in Jesus' exorcisms and healings can be *inferred* by linking the Messiah with the Isaianic New Exodus theme. One may add that Jesus' manifesto at Nazareth, which does contain the reference to the Spirit in his ministry of liberation, serves as a background *inductive* statement (in addition to his baptism) to remind the reader of the Spirit's involvement as he reads about Jesus' healings and exorcisms. Furthermore, the exegesis of Luke 11:13 on the disciples' praying for the gift of the Spirit shows that J*esus' disciples do need the Spirit to perform exorcisms* in their own mission. Lastly, Luke does not explicitly ascribe to Jesus any of the prototypical gifts of the Spirit of prophecy (revelation, guidance, charismatic wisdom, invasively inspired speech or praise) except on one occasion (10:21). All these counter-arguments put Schweizer's and Menzies' thesis - the work of the Spirit is solely in prophecy but not in mighty acts - into serious doubt. But what has been established at this point is that one can *infer* the Spirit in *Jesus'* mighty acts (implicit) but one finds no such explicit reference in Luke, whereas one can be quite *sure* that the *disciples* exorcise by the power of the Spirit. This pattern of *implicitness* in the Spirit's relationship with Jesus and *explicitness* in the Spirit's relationship with the disciples surfaces again in the exercise of the prototypical gifts of the Spirit of prophecy by Jesus and his disciples. One can only infer the *implicit* role of the Spirit in affording Jesus wisdom and insight in the wilderness temptations, but the exercise of prototypical gifts of the Spirit by his disciples is very *explicit* in Acts and Luke (e.g., Luke 12:12). A pattern thus has become clear: Luke is implicit (relying on inductive statements in the early chapters to frame the background) in portraying Jesus' relationship with the Spirit both in his prophetic activities and his mighty acts, whereas he is virtually explicit in presenting the Spirit in the disciples' mission and exorcisms in Luke

---

115 Turner, *The Holy Spirit and Spiritual Gifts*, p. 24 also points out that in Luke 1:35 concerning the conception of Jesus, the Spirit is the *miraculous power* of new creation and even Menzies, *The Development of Early Christian Pneumatology*, pp. 127-8, concedes this point.

(11:13) and explicit in their prophetic activities in Luke-Acts.[116] Instead of delineating the gifts of the Spirit into prophetic gifts and gifts of power, and limiting Luke's usage to the former as Schweizer and Menzies do, one should apply a delineation to distinguish Jesus himself from Jesus' disciples and understand how Luke relates these various works of the Spirit to them differently - implicitly and explicitly respectively. Although Schweizer's and Menzies' delineation may first appear to be Luke's concern, on closer examination it is the latter delineation - distinguishing Jesus' relationship with the Spirit from the disciples' relationship with the Spirit and thereby highlighting the centrality and Lordship of Jesus in the story - that is truly Luke's concern and hence his communicative strategy. In this respect, the fact that Luke has at least on one occasion (Luke 21:15) sacrificed a prophetic pneumatological reference for a Christological one further confirms this Christological concern of Luke and contradicts the hypothesis of Schweizer and Menzies that Luke has a special concern for prophetic pneumatology.[117] Again, for the reasons discussed above, Luke's concern is to present a balanced picture of Jesus' relationship with the Spirit which is decidedly different from the disciples' one. Jesus is different from his disciples because he is the divine Lord who is everything the name of Yahweh represents (3:4), who speaks as his Father speaks, who acts as his Father acts, who is present as his Father is present, who inaugurates his Father's kingdom and reign, who effects the liberation of the people from their sufferings and sins, who as the Lord is at the same time the servant, who as the Lord of the Spirit relates to the Spirit as God his Father does. The last sentence, especially the last clause, brings us to a dogmatic consideration of the Father, Son and Holy Spirit.

---

116 It remains to account for the role of the Spirit in healings and exorcisms in Acts. See Excursus D for a brief discussion.

117 In Luke 21:15 in the eschatological discourse, Luke has Jesus speaking 'For I will give you words and wisdom that none of your adversaries will be able to resist or contradict', whereas the parallel in Mark 13:11 has the Spirit enabling them to speak. See Nolland, *Word Biblical Commentary: Luke*, p. 639. This again confirms Luke's Christological concern rather than his alleged purely prophetic pneumatological concern.

Excursus B

Barrett's Second Reason for the Paucity of the References to the Spirit

Direct emphasis upon the Spirit had to be avoided also because Jesus was keeping his Messiahship secret; to have claimed a pre-eminent measure of the Spirit would have been to make an open confession of Messiahship. ... [I]t was not merely that a secret had to be kept. Jesus acted under the necessity of a divine constraint. Lack of glory and a cup of suffering were his Messianic vocation, and part of his poverty was the absence of all the signs of the Spirit of God. They would have been inconsistent with the office of a humiliated Messiah. ... Even his miracles, though it is not hard to detect the marks of 'pneumatic' thaumaturgy upon them, are not compelling signs, but are of significance and value only to the elect, and not to those who are without.[118]

Barrett's assertion of the coupling of the Messianic secret with Jesus' restraint in claiming the Spirit needs to be evaluated.

Did Jesus exercise the power of the Spirit under a divine constraint? Was there the absence of all the signs of the Spirit in him in his ministry? Did his ministry always lack glory? His fate in Jerusalem was indeed 'lack of glory and a cup of suffering' but his ministry in Galilee was far more 'glorious'. In the narratives, Jesus performed many miracles which pointed to Jesus' Messiahship and the Spirit in him even though the responses to him did vary (see, e.g., Luke 7:20-23). The feeding of the five thousands is a notable example where the crowd, not only the elect as suggested by Barrett, understood its Messianic significance and had the desire to make Jesus king.[119] The miracles were signs of Jesus' Messiahship and the Spirit in him; whether these signs were accepted or not is another matter. It would be inappropriate to suggest that Jesus curbed his miracles performed through the Spirit in order to maintain the Messianic Secret, because he did not do so.[120]

---

118 Barrett, *The Holy Spirit*, pp. 158-9.

119 J. G. Dunn, 'The Messianic Secret in Mark', in *The Messianic Secret* (Philadelphia; London: Fortress Press; SPCK, 1983), C. Tuckett (ed.), pp. 122-3, 126.

120 Wrede's original thesis and his original meaning associated with 'Messianic Secret' are now not generally accepted and modified into many different forms. See C. Tuckett, 'The Messianic Secret', *Anchor Bible Dictionary* (New York; London: Doubleday, 1992), vol. 4, pp. 797-800. His original collections of Messianic Secret passages are now treated rather more in a piecemeal manner, with different

Instead of speaking of the Messianic secret in Wrede's sense, it is better to speak of Jesus' progressive self-unveiling of his identity through his life, ministry (including miraculous acts) and death. There were real signs in Jesus' ministry that he was the Messiah (Luke 7:20-23) and that the Spirit was in him, though it is true that he made no explicit claim for the title of Messiah. However, he did make explicit and strong claims that he had the Spirit in him on two separate occasions (Luke 4:18; Mt. 12:28) - these were not passing comments but bear serious weight (see below). Therefore, Barrett's assertions that (i) Jesus did not claim to have a pre-eminent measure of the Spirit in him in order to keep the Messianic secret and (ii) Jesus did not perform miracles which could serve as signs of his Messiahship (and the Spirit in him) to the people are incorrect. His assertions then cannot be used to explain the lack of reference to the Spirit in the synoptic gospels. However, one wonders if it is possible to relax Barrett's assertions in order to accommodate Jesus' progressive self-unveiling through his life and ministry. That is, as Jesus' Messiahship was progressively revealed through his words and mighty acts, the presence of the Spirit in him was correspondingly revealed, so that the progressive nature of Jesus' self-revelation or unveiling accounts for the scarcity, not total absence, of Jesus' explicit references to the Spirit in him. In other words, Jesus' reference to the Spirit is to be proportionate to his progressive self-unveiling as the Messiah through his words and deeds (even though he did not directly claim the Messiahship). But this modified hypothesis also runs into difficulty.

Against such a hypothesis, one can use Barrett's criticism against Flew to point out the same problem with this proposition.[121] The fact that after Caesarea Philippi Jesus taught his disciples about his suffering as the Messiah without giving them more explicit claim and teaching about the Spirit in himself shows that a progressive unveiling of his

---

explanations given for different passages. The phrase 'Messianic Secret' therefore needs to be carefully qualified. Contrary to Wrede who alleged that Jesus' disciples, or the church, created miracle stories and attributed these mighty acts to him in a veiled manner, some scholars think Jesus did perform mighty acts in his life and ministry but refused to claim the title of Messiah in order to avoid the misapplication of this misunderstood title and concept to him before his crucifixion. After crucifixion, the nature of his Messiahship was made known so that the title could be applied to him without the risk of misunderstanding (see Dunn, 'The Messianic Secret in Mark', pp. 122-130). Instead of understanding the Messianic Secret in Wrede's sense, one should understand it as a continuous unfolding or unveiling of the *content* of Jesus' Messiahship in his life, ministry (including healings and exorcisms through the Spirit) and death, with the *title* unveiled to his disciples at Caesarea Philippi, and to the world after his resurrection.

121 For Barrett's criticism of Flew, see Barrett, *The Holy Spirit*, pp. 142-3.

Messiahship did not need to be coupled with a progressive teaching of his relationship with the Spirit.[122] For Jesus, the two issues were quite distinct and not linked as Barrett has suggested. It may be that Jesus' reticence about the Spirit in him was for a rather different reason and this reticence sometimes happened to coincide with Jesus' veiling of his Messiahship while at others times such coincidence was absent.[123] It seems that *Jesus' central concern is the proclamation of the presence of the Kingdom of God, which is inaugurated by his presence.* The nature of his Messiahship, though important, is not at the top of his teaching agenda, probably and mainly because the Jewish expectation of the Kingdom of God is more prominent and more important than the expectation of a Messiah (see Jewish expectations of the Kingdom of God and the Messiah in 1.0 of chapter 2), partly because Messiahship is a problematic subject for him to speak on before his crucifixion. Still less central to his teaching concern was the Spirit in him, as reflected by only two such explicit references. As the proclamation of the Kingdom and its presence through him took the centre stage of his teaching, Jesus was comparatively reticent in speaking about Messiahship and the Spirit in him. This gives the apparent link between Jesus' reticence on his Messiahship and his reticence on the Spirit in him but such a link, being apparent and lacking consistency, is not the material link as suggested by Barrett.

---

122 Barrett tried to explain the decoupling, after Caesarea Philippi, of the Messianic secret from Jesus' claim to have the Spirit by his third reason which called for a rather drastic and unconvincing measure. He was required to submit a reason for this decoupling after Caesarea Philippi because he had linked them before Caesarea Philippi. But if he had not linked them before Caesarea Philippi, his drastic measure taken in the third reason would have been unnecessary.

123 It was not that Jesus wished to speak more about his relationship with the Spirit and that his wish was capped by the Messianic secret. If it were so, Jesus could have spoken more about his relationship with the Spirit after Caesarea Philippi. It may well be that Jesus had no wish to speak too much about his relationship with the Spirit; rather he was more inclined to speak of his relationship with his Father.

Excursus C

Barrett's Third Reason for the Paucity of the References to the Spirit

> He did not prophesy the existence of a Spirit-filled community, because he did not foresee an interval between the period of humiliation and that of complete and final glorification. He did not distinguish between his resurrection and parousia, and accordingly there was no room for the intermediate event, Pentecost.[124]

According to Barrett, Jesus thought his resurrection would be followed immediately by the kingdom's consummation, with him coming on the clouds of heaven, so that there was no need to teach his disciples about the Spirit in the church in an interim period, even after Caesarea Philippi where Jesus' Messiahship was explicitly unveiled to the disciples. Against this Barrett's third reason for the paucity of the references to the Spirit, it can be said that he did concede (and confirmed his concession later) that 'If Mark 13:32 is genuine, Jesus himself refused to date the time of his vindication; but his followers probably expected it to take place immediately after his death.'[125] That means his own comment on p. 160, 'he did not foresee an interval between the period of humiliation and that of complete and final glorification', is inconsistent with his possible admission of Mark 13:32. According to Barrett's possible admission of Mark 13:32, only the disciples (not Jesus) committed this error of seeing no gap between Jesus' death and vindication. Jesus then could have foreseen a period where his disciples would need the Spirit (which could necessitate Jesus' teaching them about the Spirit). Barrett's argument is weakened because of his possible acknowledgement of Mark 13:32, which, once acknowledged, provides the space between Jesus' death (or resurrection) and the final consummation which could necessitate Jesus' teaching on the Spirit. Even if his admission of Mark 13:32 is dropped so that his argument is not contradicted by that admission, it is still problematic. The eschatological discourses in all three synoptic gospels all refer to times of wars and famines before the return of the Son of Man (Mark 13, Mt. 24, Luke 21). Barrett's suggestion would require a major truncation of long and important sections from the three synoptic gospels or attributing them to the church, which some modern scholars will not

---

124 Barrett, *The Holy Spirit*, p. 160. In Barrett's interpretation, Jesus understood resurrection, vindication, parousia and final glorification to be the same event.
125 *Ibid.*, p. 155. Repeated on p. 157.

accept.[126] Barrett submitted such a drastic suggestion to explain the decoupling after Caesarea Philippi of Jesus' unveiling of his Messiahship and his teaching of the Spirit in the church. But such a drastic measure is not necessary if one does not maintain such a tight link between Jesus' reticence about his Messiahship and his reticence about the Spirit before Caesarea Philippi, i.e., there was no coupling in the first place. Again, the centre of Jesus' teaching was the presence of God's kingdom and, after Caesarea Philippi, how the kingdom would decisively come through his death. Jesus was much less occupied with teaching his disciples either about the Messiah explicitly, even after Caesarea Philippi (the term Son of Man was used instead), or with teaching about the Spirit in him or in the church. The centre of attention remained with the Son of Man, his coming suffering and the coming of his Father's kingdom.

---

126 There are scholars who oppose this truncation, e.g., G. Ladd, E. E. Ellis, I, H. Marshall, W. G. Kümmel, see 'Apocalyptic Teaching' in *Dictionary of Jesus and the Gospels*, p. 21. See also D. Wenham, *The Rediscovery of Jesus' Eschatological Discourse* (Sheffield: JSOT Press, 1984).

Excursus D

Jesus and the Spirit in Healings and Exorcisms in Acts

E. Schweizer observes that in Luke-Acts miracles 'are never ascribed to the Spirit. Healing power is associated with the name of Jesus, with faith in Jesus, with Jesus Himself, with prayer, ... or more simply the δύναμις [power] of Jesus.'[127] His observation is correct but it does not necessarily mean that his hypothesis about Luke's prophetic pneumatology is a proper and the only explanation. Turner has tackled this question by inferring the Spirit in the disciples' miraculous act from the Spirit in Jesus' mighty acts in Luke.[128] However, more can be given to counter Schweizer's suggestion. Limitation of space can allow only a brief discussion here. All the miracles or exorcisms performed explicitly in Jesus' name or with explicit reference to him were performed to *outsiders*, i.e., non-believers (or not yet believers). The Christological references in these circumstances are crucial for only these references can distinguish these Christian acts of power from others. Invoking the name of God or the power of the Holy Spirit is not sufficient and specific enough because these could be understood by outsiders merely as Jewish, not Christian. It is interesting that in two miraculous acts performed within the *Christian community*, the name of Jesus is not specifically invoked (in contrast to Acts 3:6) - the healing of Tabitha, a believer, in Acts 9:36-41; the death of Ananias and Sapphira in Acts 5:1-11 where the Spirit is more prominent. Again in a *Christian community* context (Acts 15:28), the Holy Spirit's prominence is heightened. It seems that within a Christian community context, invoking the name of the Spirit causes no misunderstanding because it is understood that the Spirit has been sent by the risen Lord Jesus and his Father and is therefore their representative. However, in a context of witnessing to outsiders/non-believers, e.g., through works of healing and exorcism, the Spirit is not yet understood as the representative of Jesus and Jesus' name needs to be specifically invoked to stamp his mark on those miraculous works. In these cases, it seems that the Spirit is not involved in the mighty acts but that is only an apparent perception.

Luke seems to be consistently safeguarding against a Christological vacuum in both his gospel and Acts. In Luke's gospel, the divine Lordship of Jesus is maintained and in some way heightened (through his redactions) to avoid any Christological vacuum in a Christian

---

127 *TDNT*, vol. VI, p. 407.
128 Turner, *The Holy Spirit and Spiritual Gifts*, p. 44.

spiritually enthusiastic community or in the thought of a non-Christian reader. In Acts, the Christological (rather than pneumatological) reference and focus is aimed at the outsiders for soliciting their faith in the correct object/subject - Jesus Christ, so that a Christological vacuum is again avoided. This is a valid explanation of the miraculous acts performed in Jesus' name in Acts. Furthermore, the programmatic statement in Acts 2:17-21 about the work of the Spirit includes both prophesy and signs and wonders. It is most unnatural and unlikely that the disciples understood this only in prophetic terms.

CHAPTER 6

A Theology of the Father, Son and Holy Spirit

Summary: The question of the compatibility of Spirit Christology and Logos Christology will be addressed with reference to J.D.G. Dunn, G. Lampe, E. Irving and K. Barth. The issue of the double Lordships of Jesus and his Father, and the associated issue of filioque, will also be considered. The resolution of these question and issues points to and requires the unity of the Trinity. The unity of the Trinity is further explored by developing a refined non-linear concept of revelation which makes use of three senses of the word 'spirit'.

1.0 Issues Raised in Previous Chapters

One important problem which Dunn's Spirit Christology raises is that his form of Spirit Christology does not allow sufficient room for acknowledging the divinity of Jesus Christ. It will be seen that there are other forms of Spirit Christology, as expounded by Geoffrey Lampe and Edward Irving, which also try to see a major role of the Spirit in Jesus. While it is important to affirm the work and presence of the Spirit in Jesus, the question is: how is it possible to hold Spirit Christology and the divinity of Jesus, or Logos Christology, together? Do the two forms of Christology not postulate two sources of divinity in Jesus Christ? How can the two be compatible with each other in the one person of Jesus? This will be one of the key questions to be answered in this chapter.

An analogous question to the one above concerns the Lordship of

Jesus (see chapters 2 to 5) and the Lordship of the Father presented in the gospel narratives. The narratives do present Jesus exercising sovereign authority and Lordship in his words and actions as his very own, yet the authority is not exclusively his own as the Father implicitly also has this authority and Lordship. Even if one can resolve the compatibility issue of Spirit and Logos Christology, the issue of the dual Lordships of Jesus and his Father still remains. These are the two issues relating to the unity of the three persons of the Trinity to be tackled in this chapter. Another issue closely related to the dual Lordships of the Father and the Son is the controversial issue of *filioque* with regard to the Spirit. Do the gospel narratives offer any possible solutions to these issues? And how do the possible solutions gained from the narratives of Jesus' life and ministry impact on our understanding of these issues in the immanent Trinity?

Lastly, the concept of divine communion within the Trinity will be further explored and the role of the Spirit in the dynamic unity of the Trinity will be considered in this chapter, with special attention given to the three senses of the word Spirit/spirit. The resulting concept of spiritual communion between Jesus and his Father will be exploited to give a refined version of the non-linear concept of Jesus' revelation of his Father which was first explored in chapter 2. The refined concept of revelation may also throw some light on the question of compatibility between the humanity and the divinity of Jesus Christ in his one person.

2.0 A Theology of the Trinity

2.1 Logos Christology or Spirit Christology

2.1.1 J.D.G. DUNN

The question of the relationship between Spirit Christology and Logos Christology is an intricate one when one tries to understand Dunn's perspectives on these. There is no question of his subscribing to the former, as evidenced by his *Jesus and the Spirit* (1975) and an earlier paper presented to the Faculty of Theology in Manchester on the subject 'Rediscovering the Spirit'.[1] However, in 1981 when he presented a paper at the annual conference of the Society for the Study of Theology, he seemed to have retracted some of his extreme views concerning Spirit Christology.[2] After quoting the summary of his earlier paper, he

---

1   This earlier paper was published as 'Rediscovering the Spirit', in *Expository Times*, vol. 84 (1972-73), pp. 7-12, 40-44.

2   The conference was held at Ashburne Hall, University of Manchester, March - April, 1981. His paper was subsequently published as 'Rediscovering the Spirit - 2' in *Expository Times*, vol. 94 (1982), pp. 9-18.

wrote, 'This summary now seems to me too loose and imprecise; it suffers from the fault of trying to explain the mystery of Christ solely in terms of the Spirit. The Spirit cannot be simply identified with the divinity or deity of Christ.'[3] Tom Smail remarked, concerning Dunn's apparent change of position:

> Professor James Dunn, who once on his own confession flirted with Spirit Christology as an alternative to incarnation Christology, has now happily withdrawn from that position. In one of his more recent writings he criticises a christology concerned to understand Jesus exclusively as a man filled with the Spirit. 'It suffers from the fault of trying to explain the mystery of Christ solely in terms of the Spirit. The Spirit cannot simply be identified with the divinity or deity of Jesus.' ... He warns us against 'blurring the distinction between a Spirit Christology and a Logos Christology, between a Christology of inspiration and a Christology of incarnation: *these are distinct Christologies and both should have a place in any dogmatic synthesis which claims canonical authority.*' In the New Testament, he explains, 'A Christology of inspiration was supplemented by, but also retained alongside a Christology of incarnation.'[4]

However, this chapter will show how he manages to hold Spirit Christology and Logos (and Wisdom) Christology together in his *Christology in the Making* (London: SCM Press, 1989), i.e., by diluting Logos (and Wisdom) Christology. One of the key questions concerning his Christology is the question of the pre-existence of Christ, but he consistently handles this question negatively.

Dunn disputes with the scholars' consensus that the Christ hymn in Phil. 2:6-11 speaks of a divine pre-existent being who humbled himself and became a man. Rather, he interprets it purely in terms of the parallel between Adam and Jesus - Adam Christology - in such a way that the notions of pre-existence and therefore divinity of Christ can be done away with.[5] According to Dunn, in the hymn Jesus in the form of God (εν μορφῇ θεοῦ) means Jesus was merely a man in the image of God. But one of the most serious difficulties with this interpretation is the question: when did this *man* choose to become a *man* (as the rest of humanity are) and how did this happen? The other difficulty is his

---

3 Dunn, 'Rediscovering the Spirit - 2', p. 14.

4 T. Smail, *The Giving Gift* (London: Hodder and Stoughton, 1988), p. 93. Quotes taken from Dunn's article, 'Rediscovering the Spirit - 2', pp. 14-16. Italics mine.

5 J.D.G. Dunn, *Christology in the Making* (London: SCM Press, 1989, 2nd edition), pp. 114-21. He is not the first to suggest this interpretation; e.g., J. Murphy-O'Connor, 'Christological Anthropology in Phil 2:6-11' *Revue Biblique* 83 (1976), pp. 25-50, preceded him in this interpretation.

mishandling of μορφῇ θεοῦ (the form of God) which should be in direct parallel with μορφὴν δούλου (the form of servant). This parallel means that Jesus is as much in the form of God as he is in the form of a human servant.[6] If Dunn insists Jesus is a man (a human servant), then the text requires him to insist as much that Jesus is divine. There is a list of scholars who acutely question him on these aspects of his interpretation and reject them.[7]

Dunn also disputes the scholar's opinion that the Wisdom Christology in the epistles (e.g., 1 Cor. 1:24, 30; Col. 1:15-20) and in the gospels (e.g., Mt. 11:25-30, see exegesis in chapter 2) presents the aspect of the pre-existence of Christ.[8] Again, Dunn's position is questioned by many.[9] He maintains that Phil. 2:6-11 and Wisdom Christology in the NT have been used to speak of Christ's pre-existence only as a result of a misunderstanding of the original meanings of these passages.

> In expressing this conviction in Wisdom language, as when he [Paul] used the Adam language of the Philippian hymn, he introduced into christology phrases and terminology which when read apart from the original context of Wisdom and Adam christology would be understood as ascribing to Christ himself pre-existence and a role in creation. But there are insufficient indications that this was what Paul himself had in mind. What we may say with greater confidence is that in the Philippian and Colossian hymns we see *language in transition*, with a meaning that probably grew as the original context and thought *culture* changed.[10]

---

6 G. Hawthorne, *Word Biblical Commentary: Philippians* (Waco: Word Books, 1983), p. 82.

7 *Ibid.*, pp. 79f, especially p. 82. A.T. Hanson, *The Image of the Invisible God* (London: SCM, 1982), pp. 62-6, see also the whole of chapter 3. N.T. Wright, ἁρπαγμός and the Meaning of Phil 2:5-11', in *Journal of Theological Studies*, 37 (1986), p. 335. Howard Marshall, 'Incarnational Christology in the New Testament' in *Christ the Lord*, p. 6. See also the traditional interpretation by S. Kim, in *The Origin of Paul's Gospel* (Tübingen: J.C.B. Mohr, 1984), chapter 6.

8 Dunn, *Christology in the Making*, pp. 176-209. It is interesting and surprising that in the 1981 paper he wrote to the contrary concerning Matthew, '... for Matthew it is quite proper to speak of Jesus while on earth as the incarnation of divine Wisdom (Mt. 11:19, 25-30, 23:34-9).' 'Rediscovering the Spirit - 2', p. 15.

9 See again Hanson, *The Image of the Invisible God,* chapter 3; Marshall, 'Incarnational Christology in the New Testament'; France *Matthew: Evangelist and Teacher*, pp. 302-6; John Balchin, 'Paul, Wisdom and Christ' in *Christ the Lord*, pp. 218-9.

10 Dunn, *Christology in the Making*, p. 255, Italics mine. We do not dispute with Dunn that Jesus is 'the climactic embodiment of God's power and purpose - his life, death and resurrection understood in terms of God himself reaching out to men.' *Ibid.* But

Wisdom Christology (and Phil. 2:6-11), therefore, does not imply Jesus' pre-existence in Dunn's understanding in his 1989 *Christology*. How about Logos Christology?

> Towards the end of the first century in a religious climate where it was possible to experiment with the idea of a pre-existent heavenly figure coming to earth, the meaning of Wisdom Christology (and Adam Christology in Phil. 2:6-11) evolved to include the notion of pre-existence.[11]

How did this happen? Apparently when the fourth Evangelist used Wisdom/Logos Christology in his prologue, he applied the Logos-Son concept to Jesus only as *imagery* depicting God's action in creation through the Logos or his Wisdom, but not meaning the Logos or Wisdom as the pre-existent divine being who became a man.[12] However, the Evangelist's original intention was quickly misunderstood in a cultural evolution or transition in the use of such language such that his prologue was thought to ascribe true pre-existence to Jesus. And it may be that 'our modern conception of "person" (a being self-consciously distinct from even though related to other beings) imposes *a category on John which he never intended.*'[13] Thus according to

---

we maintain that Wisdom and Logos Christology are saying something more than this, i.e., about Christ's inherent identity which makes such functional embodiment or fulfilment possible. See Balchin, 'Paul, Wisdom and Christ', in *Christ the Lord*, pp. 218-9.

11 *Ibid.*, pp. 259-61.

12 Dunn wrote, '"Incarnation" means initially that God's love and power had been experienced in fullest measure in, through and as this man Jesus, that Christ had been experienced as God's self-expression, the Christ-event as the effective, re-creative power of God.' *Christology*, p. 262.

13 The following is a fuller explanation by Dunn on this misunderstanding. 'The danger for a monotheistic faith, however, lies in an over-simplification or over-elaboration of the way in which the relation between God and Jesus illuminates the personal in God. The impersonal is no problem . ... But the personal relationship of Father and Son, particularly when the Son is the person Jesus, is much more of a *problem*. It may be of course that our modern conception of 'person' (a being self-consciously distinct from even though related to other beings) imposes *a category on John which he never intended*. ... It could be said that the Fourth Evangelist was as much a prisoner of his *language* as its creator; or more precisely, that his formulation suffered from the *'cultural evolution'* of thought in which it played such an important part. That is to say, perhaps we see in the Fourth Gospel *what started as an elaboration of the Logos-Son imagery applied to Jesus, inevitably in the transition of conceptualisation coming to express a conception of Christ's personal*

Dunn, we have consistently misunderstood Paul and John (and possibly Matthew too) if we interpret their writings as witnessing to a Jesus who was pre-existent. Dunn's own interpretation requires the reader to go behind the texts of Paul and John (and possibly Matthew too) to fumble for a different meaning which he cannot see in the texts; Dunn is effectively alleging that the texts are ambiguous and the reader should seek the more hidden meaning. But this contradicts any sensible rule of exegesis.

We have now come to understand how Dunn could hold Wisdom/Logos Christology and his form of Spirit Christology together as suggested by his paper delivered in 1981 and published in 1982. The former is severely compromised so that the truth content that one normally associates with it - pre-existence and divinity - is virtually emptied. He holds this same view on Wisdom/Logos Christology in his 1980 and 1989 editions of his *Christology*. However, within this period in 1981, in his address to the Society for the Study of Theology, surprisingly he allegedly held the true form of Logos Christology.

The only form of Christology that Dunn truly embraces in his two editions of *Christology* is Spirit Christology in its two phases corresponding to the earthly and exalted Jesus. However, even his Spirit Christology, with the second phase of Christ's exaltation and identification with the Spirit in the experience of the disciples, could have prompted Dunn to widen his Spirit Christology to embrace a true Logos Christology.

> Where the pre-Easter Jesus could be understood straightforwardly as 'man of the Spirit', as a result of Easter such a proposition or any immediate corollary could evidently no longer serve. ... Instead of the obvious contrast , 'The first Adam became a living soul; the last Adam became a living spirit', we have, 'The last Adam became a life-giving Spirit.' Christ has become not simply the first spiritual man but has become somehow for the believer identified with the Spirit of God as the giver of life (Rom. 8:9-11, 1 Cor. 6:17, 12:4-6). ... *[W]hy should he who was but a prophet, albeit the eschatological prophet, albeit the first*

---

pre-existence which early Gnosticism found more congenial than early orthodoxy. To put it another way: perhaps what we see in John is *the clarification of the nature and character of God* which Christ afforded brought to the point where the available categories of human language are *in danger of simplifying the conception both of God and of Christ* too much. It is a danger inherent in a writing which can speak so effectively to the simple believer ...' *Christology in the Making*, p. 264. Italics mine. But in his 1981 paper, he wrote to the contrary, 'And certainly there can be little question that the Fourth Evangelist thinks of Christ on earth as the incarnate Logos (John 1:14).' 'Rediscovering the Spirit - 2', p. 15.

> *resurrected man, why should he be identified with the life-giving Spirit of*
> *God?* The evidence indicates that it was their experience which pushed
> Christian thinking in this direction. They experienced the Spirit in a
> 'Christ-shaped' way - the Spirit of sonship inspiring the characteristic
> prayer of Jesus ...'[14]

Indeed, their experience of the Spirit in a 'Christ-shaped' manner might
help to prompt them to identify the Spirit with Jesus, but it does not
answer the question raised by Dunn himself in a fundamental sense -
'Why should he who was but a prophet, albeit the eschatological
prophet, albeit the first resurrected man, why should he be identified
with the life-giving Spirit of God?' His suggested answer, given in the
last two sentences of the quote, is merely the effect of Jesus becoming
identified with the Spirit in the disciples' experience, i.e., Jesus'
presence is really experienced through the Spirit. But this suggested
solution of effect does not answer the more fundamental question of
why Jesus himself could be identified with the Spirit in the first place,
which is the very question that he set himself. A more thorough and
careful answer to his own question might have led Dunn to ponder on
the limitation of the category of prophet, even the category of the
eschatological prophet, and open up the possibility of widening and
revising his Spirit Christology to truly embrace Logos Christology, so
that a proper answer acknowledging Jesus' *divinity* could have been
given to the question of why the exalted Jesus could be identified with
God's divine Spirit. But this did not happen. The following two further
aspects of the exalted Christ are also opportunities for Dunn to
recognise Christ's divinity. Firstly, Turner argues that Jesus' exaltation
and his sending of the Spirit to the disciples requires that Jesus is Lord
of the Spirit and therefore divine.[15] But even when Dunn can see Jesus

---

14 Dunn, 'Rediscovering the Spirit - 2', p. 16. Italics mine.
15 Discussed in 2.2 of chapter 2. See M. Turner, 'The Spirit of Christ and "Divine"
   Christology', in *Jesus of Nazareth* (Grand Rapids: Carlisle: Eerdmans; Paternoster
   Press, 1994), Green and Turner (eds.), or 'The Spirit of Christ and Christology', in
   Christ the Lord. More briefly in *The Holy Spirit and Spiritual Gifts*, pp. 175-8. Dunn
   acknowledges that Luke and John present the exalted Christ as the Lord of the Spirit
   but does not draw the conclusion of Christ's divinity as Turner does, see
   Christology, p. 142-3. He rather emphasises his assertion that Paul in contrast to
   Luke and John hesitated to present the exalted Christ as Lord of the Spirit, i.e., as the
   one who bestows the Spirit on others, pp. 143-4. He also refuses to identify the Spirit
   as the dynamic power of Christ; only of God (2 Cor. 3:7-18). But his interpretation
   of this passage is suspect because the immediate context for 'the Lord is the Spirit'
   in v. 17 is Christ in v. 14, and 'transformed into his likeness' in v. 18 clearly refers to
   Christ (cf. Rom. 8:29). For a lists of scholars who also contradict his interpretation,
   including Schweizer, Davies and Bultmann, see his footnote 74. According to these

in an exalted state after his resurrection, in his understanding Jesus' exalted status is not divine - the power of the Spirit does not belong to Christ, only to God; Jesus' equivalence with the Spirit is only apparent in the believers' experience but not inherent, and his Lordship only has an intermediate status (*Christology*, p. 147, see the last footnote). Secondly, in chapter 2 it is argued that the divine Lordship of Jesus was recognised in the context of worship offered to the exalted Jesus in the early church.[16] Wright has also commented, 'The idea that Christ, as a mere man, could ever have had the "right to be treated as if he were god" is hardly a notion which a Jew could grasp without asking at once whether, in that case, this man had in some sense always been God.'[17] But the topic of worship offered to Jesus is conspicuously absent in Dunn's writings.

The above three considerations of the exalted Jesus could have enabled Dunn to recognise Christ's inherent divinity which can truly account for his identification with the Spirit. But the recognition of Christ's divinity from these considerations did not materialise for him.[18]

---

scholars and the brief discussion there, the Spirit can be identified as the power of Christ himself, not only of God. However, Dunn can only accept that it is only *in the experience of the believers* that Spirit and Christ can be identified together (p. 146). What Dunn is driving at is that the exalted Christ is not the Lord of the Spirit and the power of the Spirit does not belong to him in Paul's thought, which is earlier than Luke and John and apparently is to be preferred. For Dunn the exalted Christ does not have divine status despite the clear fact that Jesus is Lord. 'In Paul's thought the exalted Christ assumes a uniquely *intermediate status*: before God he appears as firstborn Son, firstborn of a new family of resurrected humanity, first instalment of a new relationship between God and man; before man he appears as life-giving Spirit, not just the first instalment of that new relationship, but as the one who makes that relationship possible for other.' (p. 147). But this intermediate status of the exalted Christ is arrived at by (i) misinterpreting the relationship between the exalted Christ and the Spirit (in 2 Cor. 3:7-18) which drives a wedge between the believers' experience of Christ's equivalence with the Spirit and Christ' inherent relationship with the Spirit (i.e., the power of the Spirit belongs to Christ), (ii) by diluting the the meaning of 'Lord' clearly ascribed to the exalted Christ such that the power of the Spirit is beyond the realm of his Lordship and (iii) by misinterpreting Paul's writing in Phil. 2:6-11 where Christ's divinity and Lordship are clearly presented. Because of these, Dunn therefore cannot deduce Christ's divinity from his relationship with the Spirit in his exaltation and Lordship as Turner does.

16 See France, 'The Worship of Jesus: A Neglected Factor in Christological Debate?' in *Christ the Lord*, pp. 17-36; Bauckham, 'The Worship of Jesus in Apocalyptic Christianity', *New Testament Studies* 27 (1980-1), pp. 322-41; Hurtado, *One God, One Lord*, pp. 99-114.

17 Wright, ἁρπαγμός and the Meaning of Phil 2:5-11', in *Journal of Theological Studies*, 37 (1986), p. 335.

18 Dunn, *Christology*, pp. 141-51.

As shown in chapter 5, the divinity manifested in Jesus' authoritative words and actions in his earthly ministry was also not noted by him. Therefore, all the evidences for Jesus' divinity in his earthly ministry and in his exalted Lordship somehow have consistently been dissolved in Dunn's Christology. Dunn's Spirit Christology, both in the pre-Easter phase and the post-Easter phase, cannot accommodate Christ's divinity and therefore stands as a stumbling block to recognising his pre-existence. In that sense, his Spirit Christology is the stumbling block to true Logos Christology. For true Logos Christology, for true divinity and true pre-existence to be ascribed to Jesus Christ, Dunn's Spirit Christology must be revised so that the two Christologies can truly come together in the person of Jesus Christ.

Barth's dictum for his doctrine of revelation and the doctrine of the Trinity is 'God reveals himself to be the Lord'. In particular, Jesus the Son reveals himself to be the Lord. Barth would not accept a Christology which is only functional in character, e.g., Jesus only as the expression of God's creative activity in creation, without the ontological content of his sovereign Lordship and divinity. The contrast of Barth's Logos Christology and Dunn's Spirit Christology is seen very clearly in their identifications of the kingdom of God.

> The eschatological kingdom was present for Jesus only because the eschatological Spirit was present in and through him. In other words, it was not so much a case of 'Where I am there is the Kingdom', as *'Where the Spirit is there is the Kingdom.'* [19]

> It was quite unnecessary to ask concerning the time and manner of the coming of this kingdom, 'for, behold, the kingdom of God is among you.' *It is among them as Jesus Himself is among them* (Luke 17:21). For 'if I with the finger of God cast out devils ... no doubt the kingdom of God is come upon you' (Luke 11:20). The King and His kingdom, the Lord and His lordship, are one. As Origen puts it, He is the αὐτοβασιλεία. [20]

Still there remains the question of how Logos and Spirit Christology can be united together in the person of Jesus Christ. This question will be tackled later.

2.1.2 G. LAMPE

If Dunn explores Christ's relationship with the Spirit by looking into the Scripture which for him seems to bear canonical authority, Lampe exercised much greater liberty in interpreting the Scripture in his

---

19 Dunn, *Jesus and the Spirit* , p. 48.
20 Barth, 'The Royal Man' in *CD* IV.2, pp. 162-3.

understanding of Christ and the Spirit. While Dunn, once having decided the NT does not witness to the divinity of Jesus Christ, has to work hard to explain away or *minimise* the meaning of those passages of the NT which do portray Christ's pre-existence or divinity, Lampe did not need to struggle with the Scripture and its natural meaning in order to present his own ideas for he did not ascribe canonical authority to it. He therefore expressed his ideas much more freely and straightforwardly than Dunn in his *God As Spirit*. His Spirit Christology, sometimes so called, is also more radical than Dunn's in that he neither acknowledged the personal existence of the risen Christ nor the Spirit as a divine being distinct from God. His understanding of God therefore very much tended in the direction of unitarianism. However, his concept of Spirit, or Christ-Spirit, will be relevant to our later discussions about Christ's communion with his Father, and the disciples' fellowship with the Father through the Son in the Spirit. Therefore, he needs to be engaged with. First, his understanding of Christ and the Spirit will be presented.

Lampe did not attach great importance to the Jesus of history; what is important to him was the Christ of his faith.

> The 'Christ' in whom we find the supreme disclosure of divine grace and human faith cannot be identified with any single, real, historical figure. He is rather, a *mythical* embodiment of an ideal 'son of God', a notional 'second Adam' in whom there is represented, in the guise of a historical character, the *ideal* of 'sonship' which has never been realised perfectly in a single individual ...[21]

Lampe's position is very much like what Barth called 'the humanisation of a divine idea', i.e., the attractive idea of of the communion of deity and humanity (or God's condescension and self-manifestation) is expressed or personified in a human *symbol* - Jesus Christ. What is important in this approach to Christology is the attractive idea and symbol, not the concrete historical reality of the symbol Jesus Christ (see *CD* I.1, pp. 402-5). Christ as Lampe's mythical and notional ideal is subjected to changes and evolution in time.

> The Christ-event is not confined within the limits of the NT. ... The insights and experience of the generations which separate us from the world of the NT are included in the Christ whom we find to be uniquely revelatory of God and of man's response to God.[22]

---

21 G. Lampe, *God As Spirit* (Oxford: Clarendon Press, 1977), p. 103. Italics mine.
22 *Ibid.*, p. 108.

For example, Christ's sayings in the gospels are subjected to later interpretations which are allowed to reshape the idealistic Christ. Some portions of the gospels can be relinquished altogether in the light of further reflections, e.g., Jesus' pre-existence and post-Easter existence. Who then was the Jesus of history? He was the archetypal human *example* who, though fallible, *concretely* exhibited the indwelling presence of God as Spirit in the freely responding spirit of man.[23] But the historicity of the Christ-event has no great religious importance, what matters is that the words (and actions) of Jesus as given by the gospels 'touches the conscience and quickens the imagination of the reader.'[24] For Lampe therefore, Christ is not the same as Jesus: Christ is the idealisation of Jesus and the process of idealisation continues in time. However, Jesus is 'decisive' as being at the heart of the Christ-event or this idealisation; he is 'the central key point in God's dealings with man.'[25] This is so because Jesus is the concrete demonstration of the Spirit of God working in a freely responding man, and the Spirit of God in him can be identified as the Christ-Spirit who continues to guide his followers on beyond the Jesus of history into truth.[26]

There is some similarity between Lampe's understanding of the 'Christ-Spirit' and Dunn's understanding of the Spirit of Christ. For Dunn, 'Jesus became the personality of the Spirit' after his resurrection and exaltation in that the disciples' experience of the Spirit was characterised by the personality or character of the earthly Jesus whom they had met.[27] For Lampe, the work of the Spirit of God is stamped with the character or quality of Jesus so that it is proper even to refer to the Spirit of God as the Christ-Spirit. Christ, which is an idealisation of Jesus, becomes the principle or quality with which the Spirit of God works in Jesus' followers and in creation. Or conversely, Spirit should be used to express 'the totality of God in his creativity: in the whole process of his creative work which has its focus in Jesus Christ and continues now in believers.'[28] And the mark of this continuous presence of the Spirit of God in the believers is 'the "fruit of the Spirit", and at every stage in the process of the making of the human personality God's immanent presence is recognisable in the *Christlike qualities*, and pre-eminently in love.'[29] The work of the Spirit of God, though stamped with the character of Jesus, is not confined to believers of Jesus but

---

23 *Ibid.*, p. 114.
24 *Ibid.*, p. 106.
25 *Ibid.*, p. 113.
26 *Ibid.*, p. 113.
27 Dunn, *Jesus and the Spirit*, p. 325.
28 Lampe, *God As Spirit*, pp. 118-9.
29 *Ibid.*, p. 115. Italics mine.

embraces comprehensively 'the entire creative work of God throughout history'; it is a 'complex disclosure, focused upon Jesus but not confined to him, of God's dealings with men.'[30] In this sense, the Spirit of God, or the Christ-Spirit, worked in the Old Testament time and in this way constituted the pre-existence of Christ.[31] In the same sense, the Christ-Spirit continues to work and constitutes the post-existence of Christ.[32] Lampe has therefore replaced incarnation (pre-existence) and ascension/exaltation (post-existence) of a personal being with the continuous existence of some principle according to which the Spirit of God, the Christ-Spirit, works. This now brings us to the concepts of 'Wisdom' and 'Logos' and their relationships to 'Spirit' and 'Christ'.

> In Hebrew religious language 'Spirit' is one of those 'bridge' words which express the idea of God's outreach towards, and contact with the created world. These are terms which link transcendent deity with the realm of time and space, for they speak of God directing his thoughts towards his creation, purposing, willing, bringing into being, sustaining, guiding the cosmos and everything within it.[33]

> The concept of 'Spirit', like 'Word' and 'Wisdom' but to a greater extent, combines the idea of God's external outreach towards man with that of his immanent activity within the human personality, energizing it and working through its agency.[34]

Philo's concept of Logos, as God's pre-existent agent of creation, is similar to the Hebrew concept of Wisdom which also pre-existed as the blueprint for creation. In terms of God's work in a human person,

> [S]uch terms as "Word", "Wisdom" and "Spirit" are quasi-poetical words, expressive of a profoundly mysterious inner awareness of confrontation with transcendent personal grace, love, demand, judgement, forgiveness, and calling. In their original usage they are not metaphysical terms, analytically descriptive of the structure of deity itself; nor do they denote hypostatically existent mediators between God and the world. They refer, rather, to the human experience of being, as it were, reached out to and mysteriously touched and acted upon by transcendent deity.[35]

---

30 *Ibid.*, p. 104.
31 *Ibid.*, see chapter 5.
32 *Ibid.*, see chapter 6.
33 *Ibid.*, p. 35.
34 *Ibid.*, p. 47.
35 *Ibid.*, p. 37.

It is clear then by 'Spirit' Lampe did not mean a divine being distinct from God but it is a word to denote God's outreach and activities towards the world and especially in human experience of God. The Hebrew concepts of Wisdom, Word of God and the Greek concept of Logos played similar roles. How are these concepts related to Jesus and to Christ? God's Spirit has reached out to *Jesus* and through him decisively manifested the qualities or principle associated with the Spirit, Wisdom or Logos, i.e., in Jesus the content of these are manifested. And *Christ* is the idealised principle or qualities abstracted from Jesus who was filled by the Christ-Spirit, with love as the pre-eminent quality. Therefore Christ, Spirit, Wisdom and Logos are virtually synonymous but they are not hypostatised beings; they remain at the level of ideas, principles or ideals or qualities with which God works in human beings and creation.[36] When speaking of the presence of Christ in believers, which is the same as the indwelling of the Spirit, Lampe did not mean the experience of the presence of the personal Christ but he meant God's presence through his action - indwelling of the Spirit - with the characteristics of Christ.[37]

It is interesting to observe what the NT writers did with the concepts of Logos, Word and Wisdom, and what Lampe did with Jesus Christ. The NT writers *hypostatised* these concepts in the person of Jesus Christ such that the qualities, ideas, principles or God's action associated with these concepts are embodied in a real person (but the Spirit was not treated this way, there was no Spirit Incarnate, as Dunn observed in his 1981 paper[38]) - Jesus Christ is the Wisdom of God and the Word of God. Lampe effectively reversed this process accomplished by the NT writers and abstracted from the person of Jesus Christ qualities and principles which are referenced as Wisdom, Logos, Word, Christ or Christ-Spirit (according to which God's action is to be exercised in believers and in creation). It amounts to a process of *de-hypostatisation*, in which the reality of the person is much less important than the yield of these qualities, principles or ideas.

Another way of interpreting Lampe's approach makes use of the concept of 'spirit'. In Lampe's scheme, sometimes it is difficult to speak of Wisdom, Christ-Spirit and Logos solely in terms of content, i.e., in terms of qualities, ideas and principles, without also mixing them with God's action which is exercised according to these ideas and principles and therefore denoted by these same words.[39] The concept of

---

36 For the equivalence of Spirit, Wisdom and Logos, see *Ibid.*, pp. 115-116. And p. 118, '[T]his "Christ" is not other than the Spirit.'

37 *Ibid.*, pp. 117-118.

38 'Rediscovering the Spirit - 2', p.15.

39 Sometimes it is useful to refer specifically to the content, which can change in time

'spirit' helps to clarify the distinction between 'the content of God's action' and 'God's act' when such a distinction is necessary. By 'spirit' is meant the qualities, principles or ideas which are the content of God's action, e.g., the spirit of love. Therefore, in Lampe's understanding but put in different terms, *the Spirit of God acts according to the spirit of Christ and implants this spirit, or Christlikeness, in believers as they respond to God, granting them the presence of Christ, Spirit and God which are identical in Lampe's scheme.* Lampe's idealistic Christ then embodies the spirit of Christ (pre-eminently love) which is also the content of God's Wisdom. *What Lampe did to the Jesus of the gospels was to abstract the spirit of Jesus or Christlikeness from the person of Jesus and idealise it as the spirit of Christ,* after which he was quite willing to relinquish aspects of the Jesus of the spirit. He understood that the Spirit of God (or Christ-Spirit) had acted in Jesus and in the OT according to the spirit of Christ and continues to do so. The spirit of Christ can therefore be equated with God's Wisdom in the OT, and according to Lampe also equated to Wisdom or Logos (or their content) in the NT. The spirit of Christ is therefore the content of the work/action of the Spirit of God. And Christ is the idealistic or notional embodiment of the spirit of Christ.

Lampe's Spirit Christology without any question is unorthodox, even more so than Dunn's Spirit Christology. Dunn does retain the existence and exaltation of Christ in the post-Easter period, while Lampe only retained the existence of the spirit of Christ, the principle or qualities manifested in the Jesus of history. However, both would agree that Jesus was inspired by the Spirit of God (though Spirit of God has different meanings to them) and the Christian experience of the Spirit bears the character or spirit of Christ, i.e., Christlikeness. They would also agree that God had decisively acted through Jesus in history so that he is the pre-eminent expression of God's activities and purpose in the world; in that sense to them Jesus is also the Wisdom and Logos of God but not as the pre-existent Wisdom or Logos. Their Christologies are functional in that they both are reluctant to give a definite divine ontological identity, apart from his human identity, to match the important function that Jesus performed as Wisdom or Logos in God's action in the world. Compared to Dunn, Lampe exercised greater liberty/autonomy in his treatment of the NT but he gave a more informative and useful picture of the work of the Spirit in man than Dunn whose description remains at the more general level of 'inspiration', 'experience' or 'consciousness of a spiritual power'. Lampe's analysis of the Spirit of God and the spirit of man in chapter 2

---

according to human understanding, in order to distinguish it from the references to the action - Wisdom, Christ-Spirit or Logos - which do not change.

of *God As Spirit* is especially helpful. The following are only a few valuable examples of his insights.

> 'Spirit', ..., seems better able to express the truth that God's interaction with human persons, and the integration of human personality with God, takes place at every level, *involving not only the intellect but the will, the emotions, and the subconscious.* To use the concept of 'Logos' to express this communion between God and man, and to say that it is man's own *logos*, his rational faculty, which furnishes his link with the creative Logos of God, tends towards a restricted and *over-intellectualised conception of the divine-human encounter.* It may also suggest that divinity, almost equated with rationality, inheres by nature in the constitution of man and is less than the personal grace of God, that is to say, God's personal presence evoking from man a personal response of trust and love. It is, in fact, less easy to recognise love as the primary operation of the 'Logos' than as the chief fruit of the 'Spirit'; for the term 'Spirit' carries with it a greater connotation of freedom and of personal volition than 'Logos', and perhaps also than 'Wisdom', for 'the Spirit blows where it will'.[40]

> [F]or the most part in the Old Testament the Spirit is God in his outreach towards men, interacting with their created spirits and integrating their thoughts and emotions and wills with his own.[41]

> ... 'Spirit' ... his immanent activity within the human personality, energizing it and working through its agency.[42]

It is these notions of the dynamic work of the Spirit in Jesus Christ that will aid us in better appreciating the *activity* of *Jesus' communion with his Father* in the theology of the Trinity to be presented later. And the concept of 'spirit' as the *content* of the work of the Spirit developed above will also be of use in thinking more concretely about the content of Jesus' communion with the Father. Thus, by appreciating both the *activity* and *content* of Jesus' communion with his Father through the Spirit, one might develop a more concrete understanding of the economic Trinity - Father, Son and Holy Spirit. Also, Lampe's emphasis on abstracting the Christlike qualities from Jesus (i.e., the spirit of Christ) and understanding this as the continuous locus of the work of the Spirit are valuable for the believers' practical obedience to the Father through the Son in the Holy Spirit. However, despite his

---

40 *Ibid.*, p. 116. Italics mine.
41 *Ibid.*, p. 50.
42 *Ibid.*, p. 47.

valuable insight into *how* (the *process*) the Spirit of God might work in our spirits according to Christ in the here and now, his understanding of Christ (the *content*) is too fluid for the full power of the person of Jesus as given in the gospel narratives (and the rest of the NT) to be wielded by the Holy Spirit in the spirit of believers. Barth would agree with Lampe that the Spirit of God reveals God to us or imparts the knowledge of God effectively to us but he would insist that 'Jesus reveals himself to be the Lord' and the content of his revelation cannot be weakened to anything less than sovereign Lordship and divinity. Barth's doctrine of revelation (and doctrine of the Trinity) emphasises that it is with the divine content of Jesus' revelation that the Spirit imparts the true knowledge of God.

There is an important point on which Barth agrees with Lampe, that is, on the nature of the experience of encountering God's revelation. He understands that the event of the Word of God is an experience.[43] And this experience of God's Word involves the intellect, feeling, conscience and other anthropological centres of a person.[44] Even though Christian experience had been interpreted too much as feelings or moral conscience (e.g., by Herrmann, Schleiermacher and other liberal Protestant theologians), they should not for that reason be excluded as part of the Christian experience. The same is true for intellect or other anthropological centres. The important point is that God's Word is at work in and through these centres. This discussion of Barth pertains to human experience of the Word of God. But if we were to apply it to Jesus' knowledge of his Father despite the fact that Barth did not intend to do so - because that would intrude into the area of Jesus' experience of his Father in his inner life (cf. Herrmann) or consciousness (cf. Schleiermacher) - we would have a similar understanding to that of Lampe concerning God's interaction's with Jesus as the Spirit, i.e., Jesus' communion with God through the Spirit takes place at every level, 'not only the intellect but the will, the emotions, and the

---

43 *CD* I.1, p. 198

44 Against certain distrust or suspicion of their roles in the knowledge of God's Word, Barth writes, 'There is also no compulsion to invest certain anthropological centres with the fundamental distrust and suspicion that is often found in the history of theology ... The Word of God that determines human existence is strong enough to deal also with man as he determines himself in thought [intellect]. The same may naturally be said , and for the same reason, when attempts are made on the other side to discredit or exclude feeling or conscience as the locus of possible experience of the Word of God. If we have to reject it as more than a suspicious tyranny when Christian experience is interpreted expressly and preferentially as the experience of feeling or conscience, we obviously cannot assent to any exclusion of these anthropological centres.' *Ibid.*, pp. 202-3.

subconscious'.[45] In particular, the love between the Father and the Son does involve the rational (logos), but again it takes place at every level involving the intellect, will and emotions so that it is best to describe it as the *spirit* of love between the Father and the Son through the Spirit. This will have implications to our understanding of Jesus' experience of his Father.

It is probably true that Lampe's ideas are useful for understanding Jesus' communion with the Father through the Spirit as a man, even more useful than Barth's, but Barth is much firmer than Lampe in holding onto the divinity of Jesus Christ and the content of his divine revelation. *We need both Barth and Lampe to more fully appreciate Jesus and the Spirit, or to see how Logos Christology and Spirit Christology can come together in the doctrine of the Trinity.* This will be further explored later.

2.1.3 E. IRVING

Edward Irving was born in Annan in southwest Scotland in 1792. At the age of 17, he took his degree from Edinburgh University. He was then in part-time theological training for seven years before working as an assistant in a parish in Glasgow. In 1822, he moved to London to pastor the Caledonian Chapel in Hatton Garden (near Islington). It was in this period in London that his sermons and publications attained a real theological focus but it was also his controversial teaching in this period that caused him to be eventually excommunicated from the Church of Scotland in 1833. In the year following his excommunication, he died at the age of 42. One can only assume that the ecclesiastical hounding that he received was a factor in his early death. Ironically, the Church that condemned and excommunicated him brought him to rest in her cathedral in Glasgow in 1834.[46]

2.1.3.1 Irving's Theology

Irving was a contemporary of Schleiermacher but unlike Schleiermacher he put great emphasis on the doctrine of the Trinity in his theology and particularly focused his attention on Jesus' relationship with the Spirit. His theology has been studied by C. G. Strachan in *The*

---

45 The quote is from Lampe, *God as Spirit*, p. 116. A. Torrance, *Persons in Communion*, pp. 100f, criticises Barth for not giving sufficient consideration to Jesus as the recipient and respondent of God's Word.

46 These brief details of Irving's life are taken from Graham McFarlane (ed.), *Edward Irving: The Trinitarian Face of God* (Edinburgh: Saint Andrew Press, 1996), pp. 3-15. For a more detailed biography of Irving, see Arnold Dallimore, *The Life of Edward Irving: The Fore-runner of the Charismatic Movement* (Edinburgh; Carlisle: Banner of Truth Trust, 1983).

Pentecostal Theology of Edward Irving (London: Darton, Longman and Todd, 1973), and by C. Gunton and G. McFarlane in the recent renaissance of trinitarian theology.[47] He gave the premier place to the doctrine of the Trinity in Christian theology at a time when this doctrine was neglected.

> I do maintain that all doctrine whatsoever, concerning intercession, atonement, and mediation; concerning the creation, the fall, and regeneration; is truly, and verily, an indefensible doctrine, save by the presupposition of the doctrine of the Trinity, which, in all systems of sound faith, is advanced into the first and highest place.[48]

His doctrine of the Trinity is closely related to his doctrine of incarnation because for Irving the latter in God's economy reveals the immanent Trinity.

> Your Trinity is an idle letter in your creed; but it is the soul, the life of mine. Your Christ is a suffering God; I know it well: my Christ is a gracious condescending God, but a suffering man. In your Christ, you see but one person in a body: in my Christ I see the fullness of the Godhead in a body. My Christ is the Trinity manifested ...[49]

Christ for Irving is therefore the window into the Trinity. And it was his understanding of the person of Jesus Christ which both undergirded his doctrine of the Trinity and led to his tragic downfall. A careful examination of his doctrine of incarnation is therefore in order.

While Irving affirmed the orthodox doctrine that it was the divine Son, the second person of the Trinity who became flesh, he was keen to insist that the humanity that the Son of God took was true humanity.[50] And he emphasised the latter point to the extent that he asserted: the flesh that the Son of God took was the sinful flesh of fallen humanity, with all its undesirable weaknesses.[51]

---

47 C. Gunton, 'Two Dogmas Revisited: Edward Irving' s Christology', in *Scottish Journal of Theology*, 41 (1988), pp. 359-376. Graham McFarlane, *Christ and the Spirit: The Doctrine of the Incarnation According to Edward Irving* (Carlisle: Paternoster, 1996); see also his 'The Strange Tongue of a Long Lost Christianity: The Spirit and the Trinity' in *Vox Evangelica*, XXII, pp. 63-70.

48 Edward Irving, *The Collected Writings of Edward Irving, in Five Volumes* (London, Alexander Strahan, 1864-5), vol. V, Carlyle, G. (ed.), p. 431.

49 *Ibid.*, p. 170.

50 For the divinity of the incarnate Son, see *Ibid.*, pp. 438-9.

51 Barth read Irving on this point and quoted him favourably in *CD* I.2, p. 154.

> For he condescended to dwell in concert and communion with flesh; to look up through fleshy eyes; by fleshy senses to converse with the great wickedness of the earth; and through the faculties of the human soul, to commune with every impious, ungodly and blasphemous chamber of the fallen intellect and feeling of men.[52]

But at the same time, Irving insisted that the life of the incarnate Son, Jesus Christ, was completely sinless and holy.[53] How is it possible for a person with fallen human nature to live a sinless life? Irving's answer was that as the Son unites himself with fallen human nature, it was the Holy Spirit who sustained and upheld him against sin so that he remained pure and holy throughout his whole life.

> He was not merely filled with the Holy Ghost, but *the Holy Ghost was the author of His bodily life*, the quickener of that substance which He took from fallen humanity: or ... the Holy Ghost uniting Himself forever to the human soul of Jesus, in virtue and in consequence of the Second Person of the Trinity having united Himself thereto, this threefold substance, the only-begotten Son, the human soul and the Holy Spirit ... [T]he Eternal Son, therefore, humbling Himself to the human soul, the human soul taken possession of by the Holy Ghost, this spiritual substance (of two natures only, though of three parts) did *animate* and give life to the flesh of our Lord Jesus; which was flesh in the fallen state; ... but the soul of Christ, thus anointed with the Holy Ghost, did ever resist and reject the suggestions of evil. ... *Christ's soul was so held in possession by the Holy Ghost, and so supported by the Divine nature, as that it never assented unto an evil suggestion.*[54]

Irving affirmed the concurrence of the persons of the Trinity in the action *ad extra*. How is the Father involved in this action by the Spirit in the Son? He is the one who wills and purposes the Son's action.

> The Father's it is to will; the Son's to word what the Father hath willed; and the Spirit's it is to bring it into existence, as a thing separate and outward from the Creator. In the first form, it is a purpose [of the Father]; in the second, it is a covenant; in the third, it is a work of God

---

52 *The Collected Writings of Edward Irving*, vol. V, p. 269. Irving used the words 'sinful' and 'sin' to describe the flesh that the incarnate Son took, in *Christ's Holiness in the Flesh, the Form, Fountain Head, and Assurance to us of Holiness in the Flesh, In Three Parts* (Edinburgh: John Lindsay & Co., 1831), p. 36.
53 Irving, *Christ's Holiness in the Flesh*, p. 36.
54 Irving, *The Collected Writings of Edward Irving*, vol. V, p. 126. Italics mine.

accomplished.[55]

> In everything done in creation, in everything spoken in revelation, in
> everything acted in the incarnation, in everything suffered in the Church,
> and in everything to be executed in the kingdom; Christ is the doer, the
> Father is the willer, and the Holy Ghost the suggester of the will. ... Thus
> it is, because it is revealed that there is a trinity of persons in the
> Godhead. And thus the Son, in coming into action in the finite form, doth
> already possess the consenting goodness, the harmonious mind of *the*
> *three infinite personalities* of the Godhead, acting by the Son, in finite
> things; and this He is, from the first beginning to create, until eternal and
> eternal ages, during which He shall in finite form reveal the Godhead
> unto every creature.[56]

Thus for Irving the action of Jesus Christ is the window into the Trinity
for the three are involved in the one action of Jesus, each playing
distinctive roles. Further still, the Father and the Son are bonded in
unity through the activity of the Holy Spirit in this action.

> Now, how is this assent and concurrence of the three persons of the
> blessed Trinity secured, to his great undertaking of the Godhead? Here
> comes in the doctrine of the orthodox fathers concerning the Holy Ghost,
> as the *vinculum trinitatis*, the circle of communication between the Father
> and the Son, through whom the will of the Father expresseth itself to the
> Son, through whom the obedience of the Son expresseth itself back to the
> Father.[57]

This unity and oneness in the Trinity revealed in the economy is the
same unity through the bond of the Spirit in eternity.

> [S]o from the Father and the Son, in their harmonious union, proceedeth
> the Holy Ghost; through whom, before creation, in the depths of eternity,
> the Son expresseth unto the Father the perfect unity of His being, ... The
> self-existence of the Son, and the self-existence of the Father would
> constitute them twain in existence, as well as in personality, were it not
> for the procession of the Holy Ghost from both, in whose self-existing
> intercommunion they behold, and are satisfied, with their oneness. This is
> the idea of the Godhead before creation, their first work. ... For, the Spirit
> being originated both from the Father and the Son, must in His self-
> existent being represent the unity and harmony of these two self-existent

---

55 *Ibid.*, p. 408.
56 *Ibid.*, p. 406. Italics mine.
57 *Ibid.*

beings.[58]

Irving therefore appealed strongly to a dynamic pneumatological unity within the Trinity even as he did not deny the substantial unity (through sharing the same substance) in the Trinity. Thus, the Spirit plays two prominent roles in Irving's theology. In regard to Jesus' humanity, the Spirit sanctifies the sinful flesh that the Son assumed. In regard to the unity or communion within the Trinity, the Spirit is the dynamic bond, the *vinculum trinitatis*. Despite coming from the Western tradition, Irving had truly made use of the humanity of Jesus Christ in his doctrine and found significant roles for the Spirit in both Christology and Trinity, which are unusual in the West. Here is a theologian who had made some important contributions to Western theology, whose significance has been realised by Gunton and McFarlane, especially in view of the recent interests in the roles of the Spirit in the Trinity, the church and inter-personal relationships.

2.1.3.2 Evaluation and Critique of Irving
Irving's understanding of the immanent Trinity is undoubtedly orthodox, acknowledging the distinctness of the three divine persons and their oneness in the Godhead. His particular emphasis on the active role of the Spirit in the dynamic unity in the Trinity is to be welcomed, as is his insistence on the true humanity of Jesus, in which Barth also concurs (*CD* I.2, p. 154). However, his understanding of the processes involved in Jesus' sinless life and of Jesus' relationship with the Spirit in his mighty acts needs to be carefully evaluated for even though his understandings of these seems plausible, it is by no means complete or balanced. These two issues will be dealt with in the given order.

According to Irving, Jesus the Son did not overcome the sinful flesh by his own divinity (or divine power) but by the power of the Holy Spirit. More specifically, 'Irving *emphatically* holds to the belief that the Son assumes *a will in bondage* and in solidarity with fallen humanity,' and 'the Spirit establishes and upholds the humanity of the Son, maintains his human will against sin and establishes a new humanity.'[59] This state of affairs does not apply only for a moment but according to Irving it persists throughout Jesus' earthly existence. In that earthly existence,

> ... the heat of battle was then going forward, when the warrior is all soiled with sweat, and dust, and blood. He was wrestling with sin, in sin's own

---

58 *The Collected Writings of Edward Irving*, vol. 1, pp. 263-4.
59 First quote from McFarlane, *Christ and the Spirit*, p. 167, second quote from p. 168. Italics mine.

obscure dwelling-place, against the powers of darkness, in their dark abode: He was overcoming sin in the flesh. And therefore was it that He appeared not in the glorious raiment of a conqueror, or in the full majesty of a possessor, as He shall appear when He cometh the second time.[60]

In this struggle with sin and against the bondage of will, the powerful work of the Holy Spirit is seen 'accomplished in the feebleness of Jesus Christ'.[61] One wonders if the gospel narratives do present such a picture of Christ who, in his feebleness and with a will in bondage to sin, constantly requires the Spirit to help him to overcome this tyrannous assault by the flesh, and in the process being all soiled with sweat, dust and blood. This picture is of someone who barely survives the onslaught of temptations, who with considerable difficulties escapes the claw of sin, who does not look to be a convincing conqueror and who in his feebleness ought to thank God for his deliverance. This picture looks more like the disciples of Jesus than Jesus himself. One can agree that there were severe temptations to be contended with in Jesus' life, e.g., in the wilderness and in the Garden of Gethsemane, but one should recoil from the thought that he was under bondage to sin and was therefore feeble. There is not a shred of evidence in the gospel narratives, and indeed in the whole of the New Testament, that Jesus Christ was under such a bondage and that he should be thankful to God for deliverance. And his victory over the temptations in the wilderness was such that he did reappear as a conqueror, full of the power of the Spirit (ministering powerfully in Galilee, Luke 4:14-15), and indeed as a possessor of majesty as he, being subject and Lord of the Spirit, possessed the power of the Spirit and exercised this power with freedom and majesty (see chapter 5). The much more dynamic picture of Jesus found in the gospel narratives does not fit in the neat pattern of Irving's scheme where the battle between the Spirit and the flesh left the Lordship of Jesus out of sight. Barth, while acknowledging Jesus took the nature of fallen humanity, did not find it necessary to present a passive and needy picture of Jesus who was in bondage to sin. Rather, he presented Jesus in his 'unforgettable lordliness' and moving freely in the power of the Spirit (see later), notwithstanding the real temptations and challenges he faced.[62]

The New Testament affirms that Jesus faces temptations as humans do (Hebrew 2:18, Mt. 4:1-11) and perhaps much more severely than ordinary human beings experience (e.g., in Gethsemane). In these, one

---

60 McFarlane, *The Trinitarian Face of God*, p. 67. Quoted from *The Collected Writings of Edward Irving*, vol. V, p. 124.

61 *Ibid.*, p. 79.

62 'Unforgettable lordliness' found in *CD* IV.2, p. 165

comes to know that he has identified himself with humanity. But the New Testament does not teach that he has identified with humanity to the extent of falling into bondage to sin even though it is possible for him to sin and fall into that bondage. And the New Testament does not apologise for this unique presentation of Jesus who is free from this bondage and has remained free despite the severe temptations he faced. Who are we to say that it is unfair for Jesus not to be under bondage when he faced severe temptations and bore the burden of sins on the cross in a way and of a magnitude that we can barely imagine? Whatever notion one may have concerning Jesus' identification with sinful humanity, one should not take our simplistic notion which one might have experienced in one's powerlessness and bondage to sin as the norm for Jesus Christ. One should not impose one's simplistic notion on the biblical picture of Jesus even though dogmatically and logically it seems to be attractive and plausible, for in the end it will distort the picture of Jesus. Irving's position of an extreme form of the Son's identification with humanity was not consonant with Scripture, and his putting so much weight on this form of the doctrine of incarnation throughout his theology would inevitably entail imbalances, problems and criticisms. These problems will be attended to later. Here, the nature of the Spirit's involvement in Jesus' obedience to his Father must also be affirmed.

Irving is correct when he understood the Spirit as 'the *vinculum trinitatis*, the circle of communication between the Father and the Son, through whom the will of the Father expresseth itself to the Son, through whom the obedience of the Son expresseth itself back to the Father.'[63] There is in the Son's obedience to the Father a fellowship of communion through the Spirit. It is under the condition of Jesus' intimate communion with his Father, or Jesus experiencing the loving and holy *communing presence* of his Father through the Holy Spirit, that he *knew* his Father's good and perfect will and *chose* to unite his will with his Father's in resolute obedience.[64] This obedience of Jesus involving the Spirit will be elaborated here. As presented in '5.0 Jesus' Humanity in Knowing His Father's Will' in chapter 3, the Spirit did play the crucial role of conveying the Father's specific will to the Son (through his meditation of Scripture) in the wilderness which was one important element in his obedience. But that does not exhaust the nature of Jesus' obedience, for his obedience also involved and was supported by his knowledge of his own identity before God as the beloved Son, and the knowledge of his Father's mission for him (see Jesus' baptism

---

63 Irving, *The Collected Writings of Edward Irving*, vol. V, p. 406.
64 See 5.0 of Chapter 3, 'Jesus' Humanity in His Teaching', and the exegesis of Mt. 11:25-30 in 4.0 of Chapter 2.

before the temptation episodes). Arguably, this knowledge might also have come to Jesus from the Father through the Spirit, for the visionary experience that Jesus had in his baptism was one conveyed to him by the Spirit. Lastly, it was also the Spirit who conveyed his Father's holy and loving presence to him as he chose to do his Father's will (see the exegesis of Mt. 11:25-30 in 4.0 of Chapter 2). Thus, the Spirit worked in three ways in Jesus' obedience: conveying from his Father to him (i) his identity and the cognitive knowledge of his Father's love and mission for him (e.g., in his baptism), (ii) his Father's specific will for him when he faced the choices open to him in the desert and (iii) his Father's presence to him. But even these three aspects of the Spirit's work did not exhaust the nature of Jesus' obedience despite the fact that together they provided a firm and beneficial basis for it, for crucially it also took Jesus' conscious will and deliberate decision to unite his will with his Father's for his obedience to be truly effected.

Now concerning Jesus' will, Irving would hold that it was under bondage to sin so that, in addition to the work of the Spirit mentioned above, it also took the Spirit freeing Jesus from the bondage of will in order for him to obey his Father. But the New Testament does not acknowledge such a bondage in Jesus and his need for liberation, rather it presents a Jesus who had not sinned and remained free from sin - there is no evidence that his will was under the bondage of sin. In seeking to find a more significant role for the Spirit (as a kind of remedy to the Western tradition to which he belonged), Irving had taken the rather extreme position of attributing virtually everything to the Spirit in Jesus' obedience, even denying Jesus his own proper will. It is hard to see what active role Jesus himself had to play if he is 'animated' by the Spirit who is 'the *author* of His bodily life'.[65] He did not even soften his position by having the Spirit free Jesus from bondage and thus make Jesus free in his will to choose to obey his Father. His position is rather a simplistic and wholesale one stressing the work of the Spirit to an extreme degree. In any case, Irving's own interpretation of the cross invalidated his own argument. According to him, 'He [Christ] fell into the agony and the pangs of death; when the power of the Spirit, through which He had enjoyed the light of His Father's countenance, was for a season removed away ...'[66] *If* the Spirit indeed left Jesus on the cross (which is a contentious point), then in Irving's scheme the Spirit could not be there to sustain Jesus' will to obey his Father and it would be impossible for Jesus to obediently and willingly endure the pain of the cross - there could only be bitterness and reproach both to God and men. In that case, the atonement will be

---

65 *The Collected Writings of Edward Irving*, vol. V, p. 126.
66 *Ibid.*, p. 133.

invalidated by Jesus' disobedience.[67] Therefore, here Irving contradicted his own position that Jesus needed the Spirit's liberation in order to obey.

There has to be a clear role for Jesus in his obedience, that is, with a will which is not in bondage to sin he freely and consciously chose to unite his will with his Father's, trusting in his Fatherly love and sovereign rule; the Spirit did not perform this function of choice/decision for him.[68] The gospel narratives and the rest of the New Testament never attribute Jesus' will to obey to the Spirit, only to Jesus himself. One can illustrate this by looking at Jesus' temptations in the wilderness and his temptation in the Garden of Gethsemane.

Concerning the temptations in the wilderness, the evangelists are reticent about the precise role of the Spirit in Jesus' obedience, and this particular reticence is in the context of the general reticence about the Spirit in Jesus in the gospels, which is intended by the evangelists to make space for highlighting Jesus as the author of his own actions (see chapter 5).[69] While the role of the Spirit is not clearly portrayed in the temptations, it is clear that the evangelists present Jesus as the obedient Son of God, in contrast with the disobedient son of God - Israel - in the desert after the exodus from Egypt. Thus, the evangelists present Jesus the Son of God as the subject of obedience and never present Jesus as in bondage and being freed by the Spirit in the wilderness. The role of the Spirit is even more conspicuously quiet in the temptation that Jesus faced in the Garden of Gethsemane.

The Spirit was present in Jesus' baptism and the temptations in the wilderness, but in all three synoptic gospels *the Spirit is mentioned neither in Jesus' transfiguration nor in the Garden of Gethsemane*! The Evangelists, rather than presenting the Spirit as the enabler of Jesus' obedience (as Irving would imagine), lower the profile of the Spirit in the Garden of Gethsemane compared to the episodes in the wilderness and heighten Jesus as the Son who obeyed his Father. This is not to say that the Spirit was not present with Jesus in Gethsemane; rather, the

---

67 The cross shows that even without the intimate communion with the Father, Jesus on the cross still had the resolute will to obey the Father. Communion mediated by the Spirit is conducive to obedience but it is not strictly necessary although one has to affirm that, apart from the exceptional case of the cross, Jesus was in close communion with his Father (see exegesis of Mt. 11:25-30 in chapter 2).

68 Irving would say it was Jesus who obeyed but his bottom line would be Jesus was so empowered, animated and sanctified by the Spirit that he was freed from his bondage in sinful flesh to obey.

69 The role of the Spirit in Jesus' obedience has to be inferred in the study of the temptation episodes in '5.0 Jesus' Humanity in Knowing His Father's Will' of chapter 3.

evangelists are not portraying the Spirit in the *wholly* decisive and comprehensive role in Jesus' obedience as Irving imagined. *The Evangelists, by lowering the profile of the Spirit in Gethsemane, are making a clear space to present quite unambiguously and unequivocally the Son's own active obedience to his Father.* Irving's simplistic notion which attributes Jesus' obedience wholly to the Spirit does not stand up to closer scrutiny. Jesus is always presented by the gospel narratives as the true author of his obedience; he is the *central figure* on the centre stage of the gospels; he is the *Lord* and the *subject* of his own action.[70] Indeed, in Jesus' high priestly prayer he prayed, 'For them [his disciples] *I sanctify myself,* that they too may be truly sanctified' (John 17:19).[71] And even in Christian experience, the Spirit's sanctification does not exempt a disciple from his own conscious obedience no matter how much the Spirit grants him the knowledge of God's will, his identity as beloved son and the Father's presence to him - he himself has to make a conscious choice to obey or disobey.[72] To teach a doctrine which dilutes one's responsibility for the sake of highlighting the role of the Spirit is to teach an extreme position which the New Testament does not warrant and is bound to raise pastoral problems in the church.

To summarise, Jesus' sinless life and obedience involved the communion, or the mutual knowledge, between the Father and the Son through the Spirit, and, crucially the Son's own conscious willing to obey his Father which cannot be subsumed under the work of the Spirit. Irving tended to present Jesus' sinless life *too simplistically* - merely in terms of the Holy Spirit subduing the sinful flesh in Jesus, which was the key notion in his theology. His position concerning Jesus' will being in bondage to sin was extreme and unwarranted by Scripture. One can sympathise with Irving in his attempt to affirm the humanity of Jesus Christ and raise the profile of the Spirit in Western theology. Unfortunately, Irving's taking a simplistic notion too far and using it too

---

70 See many of his self-references (ego-references) throughout the gospels, e.g., in chapters 3 and 4 (and 5) of this book. His words and actions are properly attributed to him, not the Spirit.

71 See a similar statement by Athanasius in *Contra Arianos*, 1.46. Jesus' own deliberate decision in obedience can be seen very clearly in his purposeful approach and entry into Jerusalem, and his subsequent suffering and death, which involved his trust in the sovereign rule and purpose of his Father and a series of conscious and courageous decisions on Jesus' part (see the elaboration on this in 3.0 of Chapter 4, 'The Climax of Revelation - The Passion of Jesus').

72 Even in Rom 8:13 where it says, ' ... by the Spirit you put to death the misdeeds of the body', the conscious action of the one who obeys is crucially involved, notwithstanding the advantage of God's dwelling presence in him through the Spirit (Rom. 8:9-11).

often had its inherent imbalance and danger, and invited strong criticisms.

The roles of Jesus and the Spirit in Jesus' obedience have been discussed. Concerning the roles of Jesus and the Spirit in the mighty acts in Jesus' ministry, Irving's approach was virtually the same as above. Again, he stressed the role of the Spirit at the expense of the Son.

> Also, power super-human over animated nature ... all which are manifestations, not of the Divinity of the Son, but of the Father in the Man by the Holy Spirit; manifestations of the power and virtue of the anointing of the Holy Ghost which the Son of Man received at his baptism in order to reveal him Son of God.[73]

> That this [his power over diseases to heal them] belonged to him, not in virtue of his incommunicable divinity, but of his anointed manhood ...[74]

The mighty works of Jesus were attributed to both the Father and the Spirit, but not the Son. In Irving's thought, because the Son had taken human flesh, somehow the Son could not exercise his divinity - his divinity had to be inert/passive; whereas the Father and the Spirit, who had not taken flesh, can conjoin together in the divine mighty act in unity. Again, the divine Son had to limit himself in order to give 'space' to the Holy Spirit.[75] Even though Irving confessed the unity of God's action in the economy, his actual scheme of thinking does not do justice to the unity of the Trinity in the action *ad extra* because the Son does not play a truly active and constitutive role in the action despite the fact that this role of the Son is conceivable (see later). To evaluate Irving's thought about Jesus' mighty acts, one has to ask if his picture of Jesus' inert/passive divinity and his manhood anointed by the Holy Spirit in Jesus' mighty act does justice to the gospel narratives.

From the study in chapter 5 on Jesus and the Spirit (and chapter 4 on Jesus' healings), it was found that in the gospel narratives Jesus relates to the Spirit as the subject and Lord of the Spirit, having the authority to freely exercise the power of the Spirit and even the authority to delegate the power of the Spirit to his disciples. Jesus as the Lord is always presented as the true author of his mighty works. It is true that the Spirit is involved in his mighty works but he is not possessed by the Spirit such that he is subservient to the Spirit who becomes the true author of

---

73 McFarlane, *The Trinitarian Face of God*, p. 89.

74 *Ibid.*, p. 88.

75 The notion of opening a 'logical space' is used by McFarlane to interpret Irving's Christology and pneumatology. See, e.g., *Christ and the Spirit*, pp. 161-2.

the mighty works. Rather, he himself is the subject who has control of the power of the Spirit and exercises that power freely and *virtually as his own*. Athanasius, when dealing with Jesus' exorcism by the Spirit and the issue of blasphemy against the Spirit in the fourth letter to Serapion (section 19), maintained that the Spirit did not work through Jesus as through a prophet but that Jesus as the subject worked through the Spirit. The high point of Jesus' Lordship in relation to the Spirit is seen in his delegating the power of the Spirit to his disciples before Pentecost, without even invoking the name of his Father. Such sovereign exercise of Lordship, authority and freedom with regard to the Spirit can hardly be called the work of a man inspired or anointed by the Spirit or a divine person in a state of inert/passive divinity, and can only be attributed to a divine person in his active divinity. In chapter 5, it was shown that the Evangelists were very careful in distinguishing Jesus' relationship with the Spirit from the disciples' relationship with the Spirit, especially Luke who went to great lengths to avoid confusing the two. While the disciples could be properly called the *object* of the Spirit, inspired/anointed by the Spirit, the Evangelists elevated Jesus (the *subject* of the Spirit) to a different level, one which is above the disciples and one which can only be commensurate with the Father who is also Lord of the Spirit. Irving's understanding of Jesus' relationship with the Spirit is akin to Dunn's: there is no active divinity of Jesus as the Spirit acts in him. But both fail to appreciate the dynamic Lordship of Jesus and his active divinity in relation to the Spirit and effectively reduced him to the level of his disciples, which the gospel narratives forbid.

2.1.3.3 Analysis of Irving's Theology and Suggestions
After evaluating Irving's understandings of Jesus' sinless life and Jesus' mighty work, it is time to give an overall analysis of his theology and make possible suggestions. Irving was keen to insist on the humanity of Jesus and the active role of the Spirit. And he aimed to draw the close parallel between Jesus and his disciples so that Jesus' example could be relevant to his disciples.[76] These are admirable aims. But in order to achieve his aims, he had to suppress the active divinity of Jesus because

---

76 'What is of pivotal importance for Irving is not merely the belief that unless the Saviour has himself overcome that bondage then we have no assurance of freedom, but much more that the Saviour must overcome in the same way that we must, if there is to be any realistic assurance on our part. As we have seen, it is the Spirit who upholds the humanity possessed by the Son. It is the Spirit who upholds the human will against that which is the common oppressor of humankind, and through the risen and glorified God-man establishes a new dimension to human being.' McFarlane, *Christ and the Spirit*, p. 165.

he could not see how his active divinity could be compatible with his active humanity and the active work of the Spirit. Thus, in both Jesus' sinless life and his mighty works, the divinity of Jesus Christ had to be made inert/passive in order to make space for the Spirit working in humanity. But are these incompatibilities, between Jesus' active divinity and the active work of the Spirit, and between Jesus' active divinity and his active humanity, truly necessary as Irving imagined? Is it possible that Jesus' divinity, humanity and the Spirit (his so-called 'spiritual substance, of two natures only, though of three parts'[77]) can be active in Jesus Christ such that no violence is done to any and that Jesus' true humanity can be our real and relevant example? This will be looked at with respect to Jesus' mighty works and his sinless life.

In terms of Jesus' mighty works, his divinity is active at the same time as the Spirit - as the study of the gospel narratives in chapters 4 and 5 shows, *it is precisely in the way he freely exercises the power of the Spirit in mighty acts that his divinity is active and manifested.* The one who exercises the power of the Spirit in this manner has to be divine and his divinity has to be active. The active divinity of Jesus (Logos Christology) and the active work of the Spirit (Spirit Christology) are not mutually exclusive, as Irving thought; rather, they are complementary to each other - Jesus' activities in the Spirit witness to his divinity and his divinity explains these activities. And Jesus' humanity is also actively involved in these mighty acts - he uses his human voice and human touch to bring these mighty works into reality, and his compassion for the needy and weak is also regarded as a truly human one on earth which reflects and reveals his Father's compassion in heaven (see 2.1 chapter 4). Therefore, in Jesus' mighty works, his divinity (Logos Christology), humanity and the work of the Spirit (Spirit Christology) are compatible with each other, according to the gospel narratives.

In terms of Jesus' sinless life or his obedience to his Father, the active relationship between Jesus' divinity, his humanity and the Spirit is more intricate. How can the three be active together? David Coffey and Rahner provide some clue.

> Modern Christology, like, for example, that of Rahner, takes its cue from biblical Christology and sees Christ's *divinity* not as something separate or even distinct from his *humanity* but as its supreme actualisation under grace. ... The *Spirit*, through the answering love it evoked from him, enabled him to live his whole life in dedicated obedience to the Father's will.[78]

---

77 *The Collected Writings of Edward Irving*, vol. V, pp. 126.
78 David Coffey, *Deus Trinitas* (New York ; Oxford: Oxford University Press, 1999),

For Coffey and Rahner, it is possible to see the divinity, humanity and the Spirit active simultaneously (see chapter 7 for further discussion). Indeed, the NT does not seem to see Jesus' divinity and his humanity to be totally separate in such a way that there can be no compatibilities between the human and divine. It is true that Jesus' sovereign authority to speak and perform mighty works cannot be attributed to his humanity and can only properly belong to his divinity. But there are other areas, such as in his obedient sinless life, which could belong to his divinity and humanity at the same time. For example, the gospel narratives do not speak of a divine compassion of Jesus which is separate from the human compassion of Jesus, see, e.g., Mt. 9:36. The narratives speak of only one compassion of Jesus. As the narratives acknowledge him to be the divine Lord, this compassion of Jesus can be understood as his divine compassion. As the narratives also acknowledge him to be a genuine man, the representative of Israel (see 3.2 of chapter 2), his compassion is also a human compassion. As Jesus is human and divine at the same time, so is his compassion but according to the narratives there are no two distinct compassion in the one person of Jesus. And according to the narratives, as Jesus pro-actively obeys his Father and works out his compassionate ministry, the Spirit is also at work (e.g., Mt. 12:18). Thus, the gospels present a picture of Jesus where his divinity is actively (though not exhaustively) expressed in his perfect humanity which moves in the power of the Holy Spirit; Jesus' divinity (Logos Christology), humanity and the Holy Spirit (Spirit Christology) can be active together in Jesus' obedient sinless life as in Jesus' might works, contrary to Irving's assumption. (This important point will be further explored in 3.0 later.)

It seems that one of the fundamental problems of Irving's theology was that he saw divinity, humanity and the Spirit too *discretely* or too distinctly. His notion of Jesus' spiritual substance, of two natures only, though of *three parts* (quoted above) betrays this rather simplistic distinction, as if the part of Jesus' divinity is completely distinct from the part of his humanity and dynamically incompatible with the part of the Spirit in Jesus.[79] In his scheme, the part of Jesus' divinity can be

---

p. 37. Italics mine. Coffey also refers to Rahner's 'On the Theology of the Incarnation' in *Theological Investigation* (London: Darton, Longman and Todd, 1966), vol 4, pp. 105-120. Coffey's view is also presented in *Grace: The Gift of the Holy Spirit* (Manly: Catholic Institute of Sydney, 1979), e.g., p. 109.

79 When speaking of the three parts, Irving wrote, ' ... for we may not mingle the divine nature with the human nature, nor may we mingle the personality of the Holy Ghost with the personality of the Son.' *The Collected Writings of Edward Irving*, vol. V, p. 126. His intention not to mingle became his tendency to separate them too much.

neatly made inert/passive as if Jesus' active divinity is not taken up in his human obedience and communion with his Father, as if Jesus can exercise the power of the Spirit without also involving or invoking his active divinity.

His *discrete* approach is also manifested in his use of words to describe the Son and the Spirit in the Trinity. Apart from using the phrase 'three infinite personalities of the Godhead',[80] he wrote concerning the independent personality of the Son in his conception,

> And the instant that act of the Holy Ghost began, in the very beginning of it, in the instant of life quickened before the sight of God, did the Son, in his *independent personality*, once and forever join Himself to the holy thing.[81]

And he wrote concerning the independent personality of the Spirit in his work in Christ's human nature,

> The Father bestowed upon his human nature the power of the Holy Ghost, or, I should say, the Holy Ghost, in his *independent personality*, did condescend to inform that human nature ...[82]

It can only be assumed that the Father is another independent personality and there are three independent infinite personalities in the Trinity. Irving saw the three persons of the Trinity too independently. He did not see their unity as clearly as their distinctions. He therefore could not maintain the genuine functional unity between the Son and the Spirit in the economy - the Son has to be inert/passive in order to give space for the Spirit to work. But it has been shown in chapter 5 and above that the divinity of Jesus can be active with the Spirit together in unity. There can be a genuine unity of action *ad extra* by the Triune God - the Father *and* the Son acting through the same Spirit. But Irving can only have the Father and the Spirit working actively in the economy, as shown above. With the Son's inactive divinity, his trinitarian theology concerning the economy therefore violated the principle of the inherent unity of the Trinity despite his alleged adherence to this principle.

The real cause to Irving's discrete approach to Christology and Trinity as described above might well lie in his insistence on his basic notion that the Holy Spirit sanctifies the sinful flesh of Jesus Christ. For this notion to be sustained, he separated the divinity and humanity of

---

80 *The Collected Writings of Edward Irving*, vol. V, p. 406.
81 *The Trinitarian Face of God*, p. 66. Italics mine.
82 *The Collected Writings of Edward Irving*, vol. V, pp. 427-8. Italics mine.

Jesus and made them quite *independent* with the former inert/passive in Jesus, he also treated the divine Son and the divine Spirit as *independent* personalities so that the Spirit could act independently of the inert/passive Son. Thus the flaws in his Christology and Trinity, rooted in such independence, might have flowed from a basic insistence and conviction concerning the Spirit and the humanity of Jesus which was unfortunately over-simplistic (and dualistic in disallowing a third).[83] By using it too often and taking it too far (or taking a too extreme form of it) in his construction of theology, he stepped into imbalances and dangerous areas. In the end, criticisms, justified or not, would inevitably come.

Finally, when reading his sermons in his collected writings, one finds that he preached passionately and there is much one can learn from him about the Father, the Spirit, the church and even the immanent Trinity. However, when reading about Jesus in Irving's writings which emphasise his self-humbling or self-limiting, one does not receive the sense of the dynamic or 'unforgettable presence' (to use Barth's phrase) of Jesus who exercises his insuperable authority in his words and actions, which one receives when one reads the gospel narratives themselves or Barth's exposition of them. (In this respect, it is interesting that his sermons on Luke in his *Collected Writings* end with Luke 4 where the temptation episodes are found.) Often, Irving's sermons are like expositions of traditional doctrines, taking references from the gospels (or Scripture) without engaging intently with the story but using them for his doctrinal purposes. It seems that his doctrinal convictions steered his sermons and his use of Scripture in such a way that his doctrinal expositions hovered over but were not earthed in the foundation of Scripture. Inadvertently, his own doctrinal convictions had become the primary source of preaching. And the subtle errors in his doctrinal convictions were not corrected by Scripture but were propagated to the congregation. This reminds one of Herrmann's criticism of doctrinal legalism, or doctrinal confession without a face-to-face encounter with Jesus Christ.[84] One wonders if there has not been at least some benefits, despite their often negative and deplorable approaches and results, from the biblical criticism in the last two centuries where the Bible and its actual texts have been studied and examined more closely. This book therefore has sought to pay closer attention to the text and story of the gospel narratives (in chapters 2 to 5) in order to gain an understanding of the Father, Son and Holy Spirit

---

83 Dualistic in the sense that his Christology has the active pattern of Spirit-humanity and his Trinity has the active pattern of Father-Spirit. Both neglect a third element - the active divinity of the Son.

84 See his *The Communion of the Christian with God*, or his *Systematic Theology*.

and their intra-relationships.

2.1.4 K. BARTH

Barth read about Irving's doctrine of incarnation in H. R. Mackintosh's *The Doctrine of the Person of Jesus Christ* and quoted Irving favourably in *CD* I.2, p. 154.

> The point at issue is simply this: Whether Christ's flesh had the grace of sinlessness and incorruption from its proper nature, or from the indwelling of the Holy Ghost. I say the latter. ... It was manhood fallen which He took up into His divine person, in order to prove the grace and the might of Godhead in redeeming it.[85]

Apparently, Barth did not read Irving's original writings which also include the notions of Christ's will in bondage to sin and the inactivity of the divine Son which then calls for the sanctifying work of the Holy Spirit. Although Barth concurred with Irving on Christ assuming fallen human nature, he certainly did not concur with him on the inactivity of the divine Son. But that raises the question of the activity of the divine Son and the activity of the Holy Spirit in Jesus. Barth did not feel that there was any contradiction between the two in Jesus - the Trinity was involved in the acts and life of Jesus. When dealing with the issues of communion of natures in the incarnation in *CD* IV.2, he wrote,

> And again it is only another form of the one grace addressed to human essence in Jesus Christ that his humanity as that of the Son of God is determined by the fact that as the Son of Man he is fully and completely not only in the good-pleasure of God the *Father* but also in the presence and effective working of the *Holy Spirit* - fully and completely because in virtue of his origin, because as the *Son of God* he is also the Son of Man. ... As the Son, therefore, he is sustained outwardly by the inflexible Yes of the Father and his inexhaustible blessing, and enlightened and impelled inwardly by the comfort and power and direction of the *Holy Spirit*. For where the *Son* is, of the same divine essence there is also the *Father*, and again of the same essence the *Holy Ghost*. ... Godhead surrounds this man like a garment, and fills him as the train of Yahweh filled the temple in Is. 6. This is the determination of his human essence.[86]

However, concerning the weights he put on the divine Son and the Holy

---

85 *The Collected Writings of Edward Irving*, vol. V, p. 4. Quoted by H. R. Mackintosh in *The Doctrine of the Person of Jesus Christ* (Edinburgh: T. & T. Clark, 1912), p. 277.

86 *CD* IV.2, p. 94. Italics mine.

Spirit in their involvement in the Son of Man, it is fair to say that contrary to Irving he put his emphasis on the divine Son, rather than on the Spirit.

> He is totally unlike even the most saintly among us in the fact that his human essence alone is fully, because from the very outset, *determined by the grace of God*. This is the qualitatively different determination of his human essence, and of his alone as that of the One who as the Son of Man is also and *primarily the Son of God*. ... It is genuinely human in the deepest sense to live by the electing grace of God addressed to man. This is how Jesus Christ lives as the Son of Man. In this he is the Mediator between God and us men *in the power of his identity with the Son of God and therefore in the power of his divinity.*[87]

And concerning Jesus' resistance to temptations, the Son of God is truly responsible for obedience.

> He knew it [sinful action] even as a tempting question addressed to Himself, as emerges clearly enough in the gospels. But there could be no question of it ever becoming his act. Because and as he was man only as the *Son of God*, it was excluded from the choice of his acts. In virtue of this *origin of his being*, he was unable to choose it. Therefore he did not choose it. And he did not do it.[88]

Barth did not attribute Jesus' overcoming temptations to the Spirit as Irving did, but attributed it to the Son of God. Despite Barth's emphasis on the identity of the Son of God when thinking about Jesus Christ, he writes about Jesus' relationship with the Spirit in a profound manner when treating the subject of the manhood of Jesus in *CD* III.2.

> For Jesus does not have the Holy Spirit in the way in which it can be said of any man that he has the Spirit. He does not have Him only in virtue of an occasional, transitory and partial bestowal. He could not be without him, and would thus be subject to death and corruption. *Jesus has the Holy Spirit lastingly and totally*. He is the man to whom the creative movement of God has come primarily, originally and therefore definitively, *who derives in his existence as soul and body from this movement*, and for whom to be the 'living soul' of an earthly body and earthly body of a 'living soul' is not a mere possibility but a most proper reality. *He breathes lastingly and totally in the air of the 'life-giving Spirit'*. He not only has the Spirit, but *primarily and basically He is Spirit*

---

87 *Ibid.*, p. 89. Italics mine.
88 *Ibid.*, p. 93. Italics mine.

and He is soul and body. For this reason and in this way He lives. This is His absolutely unique relationship to the Holy Spirit.[89]

The author's interpretation/conceptualisation of Jesus' relationship with the Spirit in the gospel narratives in this book may have been significantly influenced by this passage written by Barth. The following interpretation/conceptualisation is very much related to this passage and has been used in chapter 5 (2.2). There is an inalienable and unbreakable relationship between Jesus and the Spirit, not only in Jesus' earthly existence and constitution but also in everyone of Jesus' movements - 'he breathes lastingly and totally in the air of the "life-giving Spirit"'.[90] The Spirit, or the Father's presence through the Spirit, is the natural atmosphere in which Jesus lives and breathes, in such a way that he has never experienced the Spirit or God's presence as something extrinsic to him, but as something inherent to him and in him throughout his earthly existence from the very beginning (conception).[91] Therefore, when he moves in the Spirit, he moves in the atmosphere native to his existence; when he acts in the Spirit and in the presence of his Father, the power of the Spirit is experienced as his native power - it is not an extrinsic power added to him at some point in time as it is to the disciples. There is *a mysterious identity/unity between Jesus and the Spirit*, as Barth says 'primarily and basically He is Spirit' even though they are *equally mysteriously distinct* (cf. John 14:15-18). 'This is His absolutely unique relationship to the Holy Spirit.' Therefore, even though there are many similarities between Jesus' relationship with the Spirit and the disciples' relationship with the Spirit - and Jesus in that sense can be their example - one must never confuse the two and set

---

89 *CD* III.2, p. 334. Italics mine.

90 For the inherent unity between Jesus and the Spirit as espoused by the Cappadocian Fathers, see Borris Bobrinsky, 'The Indwelling of the Spirit in Christ: "Pneumatic Christology" in the Cappadocian Fathers' in *St. Vladimir's Theological Quarterly*, vol. 28, no. 1, 1984, pp. 49-65.

91 (i) His conception was by the Spirit so that he had unity with the Spirit from the beginning of his earthly existence. This intrinsic unity in the economy reflects the intrinsic unity between the Spirit and the Son in eternity. Ralph Del Colle, *Christ and the Spirit: Spirit-Christology in Trinitarian Perspective* (New York; Oxford: Oxford University Press, 1994), p. 122, when presenting David Coffey's Spirit Christology, writes, 'The revelation of the office of "Christ" to which the anointing at Jordan attests does bespeak the inner *constitution* of the hypostatic union.' There is an inherent relationship between Jesus and the Spirit even in his earthly existence and constitution. (ii) On the cross, God's presence was withdrawn from him even though the Spirit may still be upon Jesus (Heb 9:14). Perhaps it could be said that in Jesus' crucifixion, the Trinity mutually *share* the sense of the non-presence of one another.

them to be identical. This is the flaw in Irving's theology: he was so keen to set Jesus as the prototypical example for Christians that he made the two identical and so functionally emptied the divinity of Jesus Christ.[92] From the study of the gospel narratives in chapter 5, it was found that the narratives present Jesus as the Lord of the Spirit even in his earthly life and ministry. From this observation, one might conclude that Jesus' relationship with the Spirit on earth is akin to his Father's relationship with the Spirit. This important observation will be taken up further in the discussion of *filioque* later.

It may be noted that the above interpretation is slightly different from Barth in that the Spirit's presence in Jesus is interpreted as the Father's communing presence to Jesus through the Spirit. This Barth may well admit given his insistence on the involvement of the Trinity in Jesus Christ (see above quote from *CD* IV.2, p. 94). But the fact remains that Barth does not often speak about Jesus experiencing the communing presence of his Father through the Spirit. In the analysis of Barth's presentation of the Royal Man from the synoptic gospels (*CD* IV.2) in chapter 4, it has been found that Barth can speak often of Jesus' correspondence to and conformity with God, reflection and revelation of God, but very rarely mentions the Spirit or Jesus' communion with his Father through the Spirit in his life-act. Also, in the passage above where the Spirit is indeed mentioned in relation to Jesus, the Father and his *presence* through the Spirit are not mentioned. This reticence can still be observed in *The Christian Life* (Edinburgh: T. & T. Clark, 1981) where his attention is very much focused on understanding God as Father. He can write, 'God and this man ... belong together as Father and Son, that they are indeed one to the extent that reciprocally they perfectly know and confirm and love one another.'[93] But he does not expound this mutual love and knowledge in terms of intimate fellowship or Jesus' experiencing rest in his Father's communing presence. Given his insistence on the presence of the Trinity in the life of Jesus, one wonders why he is reticent on this aspect of Jesus' experiencing his Father's communing presence through the Spirit. Could the answer lie in his reluctance to entertain the thought of the spiritual experience of Jesus which inevitably sounds like the note of Jesus' inner life (Herrmann) or his God-consciousness (Schleiermacher)? His dislike of the subjective approach of 19th

---

92 From the perspective of having life inherently, Jesus and the disciples are also different. Jesus the Son has 'life in himself' (John 5:26) and 'in him was life' (John 1:4) while others, including the disciples, do not have life in them inherently (John 6:53).

93 Barth, *The Christian Life,* p. 65.

century Liberal Protestantism is evident.[94]

> What we thus learn of the inner life of Jesus is certainly not little, but it is definitely not very much, and it falls short of all that we should like to know. ... There is obviously no attempt at a full portrait or even a characterisation; and certainly not the exhibition of an inner development. ... [W]e are only made aware that Jesus had a real human inner life. But we are given no guidance for reflection concerning it, and for forming a picture of this matter we are in fact offered no material at all.[95]

> Against the powerful and too spiritualised conception of the picture of Jesus in the 18th and 19th centuries, it was and is necessary to draw attention to this [the concrete word and deed of Jesus], especially in relation to the bodily aspect of the whole range of the mighty works of the New Testament.[96]

This may be one of the reasons why Barth seldom speaks of Jesus' communion with his Father through the Spirit when he deals with the gospel narratives (see chapter 4) even though he does acknowledge in principle this aspect of the life of the Son of God in the economy and in eternity in his dogmatic framework. Had he been willing to speak more of Jesus' inner dimension in terms of his experience of and communion with the Father which was facilitated through the Holy Spirit, his pneumatology might have been considerably strengthened. However, in *The Christian Life* which was written near the end of his life with the prominent theme of God's Fatherhood, there are some signs of the receding of his reticence concerning Jesus' communion with his Father.[97]

---

94 See Dorrien, *Theology Without Weapons: the Barthian Revolt in Modern Theology*, pp. 31-36, 42-46; and Bruce McCormack, *Karl Barth's Critically Realistic Dialectical Theology: its Genesis and Development 1909-1936* (Oxford: Clarendon Press, 1995), pp. 49-67, 111-125.

95 *CD* III.2, p. 329.

96 *Ibid.*, pp. 330-1

97 For example, Barth wrote, 'He is the Son of Man who lives and acts as the Son of God, and may be known as such, by being the executor of God's love in childlike obedience and service, in *childlike trust*, in the doing of his will, in unrestricted self-giving, and by glorifying him as his Father in this way. As man, *he loves God* in exact reflection, in full conformity to the love with which *God loves him* and in him the world.' *The Christian Life*, p. 74. Italics mine. Also, 'Father! It is obvious that this vocative points, but does so in a very special way, to a place where the one who calls on God knows that he himself, along with everything and all things, is absolutely dependent and conditioned. It points to this place too, so that there can be no contradicting Schleiermacher's definition of God as the "source of the feeling of

Barth's understanding of Jesus' intimate relationship with the Spirit - one of virtual identity - does not mean that Jesus is merely a man fully inspired and determined by the Spirit (as in Dunn's Spirit Christology). Rather the divine Son of God (or the divine Logos/Word) is the personal subject active in Jesus Christ, not inert/passive as in Irving's Christology.[98] Barth tends to see the active divine Son/Logos as the more fundamental/primary in Jesus than the Holy Spirit. He has been criticised for this (and defended).[99] However, despite clearly emphasising Logos Christology, Barth still maintains a very close relationship between Jesus and the Spirit as shown above. Instead of subjecting Jesus (and thus the divine Logos/Word) to the Spirit who possesses him, Barth seems to see Jesus as the Lord, subject and possessor of the Spirit. While commenting on the healing of the centurion's servant in Mt. 8, Barth writes,

---

absolute dependence." All the same, this definition is unsatisfactory because the source might finally be a neuter, an original "It" or "Something." For Schleiermacher this is what it actually was - an interpretation which, as we have seen, is ruled out by the personal address "Father." *Ibid.*, p. 57.

98 'By *anhypostasia* classical Christology asserted that in the *assumptio carnis* the human nature of Christ had no independent *per se* subsistence apart from the event of the incarnation, apart from the hypostatic union. By *enhypostasia*, however, it asserted that in the *assumptio carnis* the human nature of Christ was given a real and concrete subsistence within the hypostatic union - it was enhypostatic in the Word.' *Essays in Christology for Karl Barth* (London: Lutterworth Press, 1956), T. H. L. Parker (ed.), p. 16; see also *CD* I.2, p. 163. The divine Word is the personal subject in Jesus Christ; there is no other personal subject. For Barth this divine personal subject is active while for Irving the divine personal subject is passive in the human soul which is animated by the Spirit.

99 '... it is tenable that the fragmentary Spirit Christology, which Barth himself at times weaves into the *CD* as an auxiliary way of comprehending the Christ-event, could have afforded him a more adequate approach to the mystery of Christ if he had developed it at greater length. As it is, his exaggerated Logos Christology seems blatantly to bypass the biblically attested truth that Christ must be understood in the context of God the Spirit's continual interactions with man, all of which are aimed at the attainment of man's salvation. As soon as it is advocated that Christ be placed in a larger pneumatic framework, *the objection naturally comes to mind that this methodology can only result in a new expression of Adoptionism. A Pneuma-Sarx Christology is perpetually in danger of minimizing the uniqueness of Jesus by categorising Him as a special case of the Spirit-filled king, judge or prophet.*' Philip Rosato, *The Spirit As Lord: The Pneumatology of Karl Barth* (Edinburgh: T. & T. Clark, 1981), p. 174. Italics mine. But George Hunsinger defends Barth in 'Karl Barth's Doctrine of the Holy Spirit' in *The Cambridge Companion to Karl Barth*, pp. 177-94. In particular, a point for defence is that Barth did not have time to write before his death the doctrine of redemption where the Spirit would have featured more prominently, see p. 179.

Those who believe in Jesus Christ have to do *ipso facto* with the *Lord of heaven and earth*, i.e., with the One who can dispose in the whole realm of reality distinct from God, and who does actually dispose always and everywhere. ... The faith which (according to Mt. 8:5f) Jesus did not find in Israel, but in the Gentile centurion of Capernaum, is that confidence in Him in which the centurion begs Him to speak only a word and his servant will be healed, just as he himself says to one of his soldiers, Go, and he goeth; and to another, Come, and he cometh; and to his servant, Do this, and he doeth it. But at this point we should really refer to *all the accounts in the gospels* which show us that *Jesus really possessed this power and freely exercised it*; that He found faith, i.e., this trust in His power, in all kinds of hopeless sufferers, and that these people simply counted on the fact that He could help them if He were *willing* to do so. ... What would the four gospels be without this *constant reference to the possession and exercise of power by Jesus*, and without the constant appeal to believe in Him as the Bearer of this power? [100]

The power possessed by Jesus can be inferred to be the power of the Spirit. Jesus, who is Lord of heaven and earth, is then the subject and possessor of the Spirit who exercises the power of the Spirit freely at his own will. This can be the only relationship between Jesus and the Spirit in Barth's thought regarding Jesus' mighty works in the Spirit, given his very high Christology and the passionate manner in which he celebrates the Lordship of Jesus Christ. Regarding Jesus' obedient sinless life in the Spirit, Barth would insist that it is the Son of God who obeys (see quote above from *CD* IV.2, p. 93). But how is it possible to attribute obedience to the Son of God when he is 'impelled inwardly by the comfort and power and direction of the Holy Spirit'? [101] Barth does not seem to make an effort to answer this intricate question about the dual sources for obedience. Perhaps the following postulate or conceptualisation, based on the narrative studies in this book, may be consistent with Barth's high Christology.

Indeed, Jesus lives and breathes in the atmosphere of the Spirit, in the loving and holy presence of his Father which inclines him towards obedience, but as the Son of God he still needs to exercise his will to choose to obey his Father - this the Spirit cannot do for him (compare Mt. 4:1-11 and 26:36-46 where the Spirit is not mentioned; see 2.1.3.2). And as he *chooses* to do his Father's will in loving obedience and moves to act out this obedience (or moves to actualise his obedience in acts), he moves and actualises his obedient act in the power of the Holy

---

100 *CD* III.1, p. 35, quoted in chapter 4. Italics mine.
101 Quoted above, from *CD* IV.2, p. 94.

Spirit. Thus, it is the Son who obeys and the Spirit who empowers. However, as seen above there is such a unity between the Son and the Spirit of God that the power of the Spirit in which he moves and actualises his obedient act is experienced by him as his own power, and the power of his Father living in him.[102] *This is the unity and mystery of the Trinity.* This may be a way to see how, in the context of Jesus' obedient life, Barth's high and active Logos Christology can be compatible with and complementary to the form of Spirit Christology he subscribes to. This is the way this book sees how Logos Christology and Spirit Christology can come together.

Barth's Christology, then, differs from Dunn's and Lampe's Spirit Christologies in that the personal subject of Jesus Christ is the pre-existent divine Son of God; and differs from Irving's Christology in that the divine Son of God exercises the power of his divinity on earth, and as the subject of the Spirit *freely exercises* the power of the Spirit at his own will. Barth's Christology can be described as *primarily Logos Christology and secondarily Spirit Christology.* This book, as is already evident, concurs with Barth in this respect and asserts that these two Christologies are *compatible with each other with a given order.* In addition, it would assert that *it is precisely the way that he relates to and freely exercises the power of the Spirit that manifests and confirms his divinity.* Logos Christology and Spirit Christology, when appropriately understood, affirm one another. The fact that Jesus fully moves in the Spirit does not weaken the sense of his inherent divinity (contra Dunn) but rather expresses and affirms it. Furthermore, this book would emphasise that whenever the Spirit is mentioned in conjunction with Jesus Christ, the aspect of the communing presence of the Father to the Son through the Spirit should also be in view. The Spirit in Jesus is not merely his divine power in which he lives, moves and acts, the Spirit is the Spirit of fellowship between Jesus and his Father. It is in this spiritual fellowship/communion with his Father, it is in this spiritual presence of his Father through the Spirit that Jesus breathes, lives, moves, acts and finds rest in him.[103] Finally, Jesus knows his Father's love and his Father's will in this fellowship and he sets himself to unite his will with his Father's will in resolute obedience to the very end. This *will* of Jesus, his *capacity* to be *fully* in communion and consonance with the Father through the Spirit, and his *free exercise* of the power of the Spirit are the expressions and

---

102 'Jesus realised that power had gone out from him' (Mark 5:30) in the healing of the woman with bleeding illness is consistent with the notion that Jesus experienced the power of the Spirit as his own power.

103 For the aspect of Jesus' rest in the Father, see exegesis of Mt. 11:25-30 in chapter 2.

confirmations of his inherent divinity. How the divinity of Jesus is related to his obedient will and his capacity for communion will be further explored in the context of revelation later, but the issue of *filioque* will first be discussed in the light of the above discussion on Jesus' relationship with the Spirit in the economy.

2.2 Jesus' Lordship, His Father's Lordship and Filioque

Logos Christology, which emphasises the divinity of Jesus, and Spirit Christology, which emphasise the divine work of the Spirit in Jesus, apparently postulate two sources of divinity in Jesus Christ. But this apparent competition between these two sources of divinity has been resolved in the last section so that they can be seen to co-exist in the one person of Jesus Christ with the Logos as the personal subject. However, there is a third source of divinity fundamental to and implicit in all the above discussions - God the Father. If in the economy Jesus the Son of God is Lord of the Spirit and if the Father is Lord of the Spirit, how do these Lordships relate together to the Holy Spirit? And what is the significance of the answer to this question for our understanding of the immanent Trinity, in particular concerning the issue of *filioque*? Also, the issue of *double Lordships* occurs not only in the context of relating to the Spirit but also *in the context of Jesus' authoritative preaching*, where he freely exercises his Lordship without even invoking the name of his Father even though his Father's authority is implicit in all that he does. Basic to these two issues is the issue of the double Lordships/authorities of Jesus and his Father which will be considered in the following.

In chapter 2, it was shown that Matthew in 3:3 purposefully identifies Jesus as the coming Lord - Yahweh - of Isaiah 40:3, implying that Jesus is everything the name of Yahweh stands for. He presents Jesus' Lordship not only through the identification of this title - Lord - but the literary structure of his gospel is also designed to witness to Jesus' Lordship (e.g., Mt. 3:3 and Jesus' universal Lordship in Mt. 28:18 form an inclusio, see 2.1 of chapter 2). Furthermore, he elaborates Jesus' Lordship in terms of his ministry of authoritative words and mighty acts in the body of his narratives bracketed by the inclusio. There Jesus in his Lordship preaches with the sovereign authority and freedom of God (e.g., in changing the Torah), without even invoking the name of his Father nor the inspiration of the Spirit. His typical style of saying - 'I say to you' - appeals to his own personal authority so that he cannot be put into the category of prophets. Matthew thus presents Jesus as having his own inherent sovereign authority in preaching (see chapter 3). The picture in Jesus' mighty works is almost identical with the one of his preaching. In the same Lordship, he exercises the power of the Spirit freely in healings and exorcisms, and reveals his inherent sovereign authority in delegating the power of the Spirit to his disciples, again without invoking the name of his Father (chapters 4 and 5). But amidst Matthew's presentation of Jesus' sovereign authority in preaching, healings, exorcisms and giving of the Spirit, Matthew in 11:25-30 gives the reader the insight of Jesus' relationship with his Father which is the basis of all his preaching and mighty works, and thus the basis of his revelation of his Father.

> All things have been committed to me by my Father. No-one knows the Son except the Father, and no-one knows the Father except the Son and those to whom the Son chooses to reveal him. (Mt. 11:27)

'All things' should include not only the content of Jesus' revelation of his Father in his teaching and mighty works but it probably also includes the Father giving authority to the Son in all that he does. This is supported by a similar saying in Mt. 28:18 - 'All authority in heaven and on earth has been given to me.' - where Jesus' post-resurrection universal Lordship is in view. Even though Matthew presents Jesus' authority in preaching and his authority in his exercise of the power of the Spirit as his very own in the narratives, he in 11:27 is augmenting that understanding with the notion that Jesus' authority is *not exclusively his own* and in some sense he receives authority from his Father. This latter notion is already implicit in the narratives of Jesus' ministry because he was commissioned by his Father at his baptism to fulfil his task as the beloved Son of God. This implicit notion of the Father's authority in Jesus' ministry is made explicit in 11:27. But Matthew is not suggesting that the Son's authority is wholly derived from the Father, for that would contradict his presentation of Jesus' self-referencing inherent authority in the narratives where the authority of his Father is not invoked at all (see argument against Dunn and Manson in 1.2 of chapter 5).[104] The picture Matthew is presenting is therefore that Jesus has his own inherent authority but he also receives authority from his Father. But are there two separate authorities, one owned by the Father and one owned by the Son?

---

104 (i) If Jesus' authority is merely given by his Father, i.e., not inherently his own, then he is required to invoke his Father's authority in his preachings and mighty acts, and if he does not do so he is speaking presumptuously and acting in vain. (ii) Also, if Jesus did not have his own authority and Lordship, then he would not be able to truly and personally reveal his Father's authority and Lordship on earth. He could only speak indirectly and act indirectly as a prophet, deriving his authority from God, and not speaking and acting as the Lord who truly reveals the Lordship of God the Father. This is Barth's point: it takes God to truly reveal God.

It seems that in view of the second sentence of Mt. 11:27 on the mutual knowledge and communion between the Father and the Son there may well be one authority co-owned by the Father and the Son. There is such a mutual giving between the Father and the Son in the communion through the Spirit that what belongs to the Father is given to the Son by the Father, and what belongs to the Son is offered to the Father. At bottom, the authority of the Son and the authority of the Father cannot be separated strictly into two entities because the Father and the Son are united as one, and *in mutual knowledge and communion they hold the one authority* and exercise it *through the Son* who is on earth. Perhaps it is possible to speak of the *co-authority* of the Father *and* the Son which is *exercised in their mutual knowledge* and communion through the representative Son who on earth reveals the Father in heaven. This idea of co-authority of the Father and the Son is supported by John 16:15 - 'All that belongs to the Father is mine [the Son's].' In John, it is also true that the Son is in the Father and the Father is in the Son (14:11, mutual knowledge in Matthew) who reveals the Father on earth. The picture in the gospels seems to be this: *Jesus Christ in his Lordship freely exercises his own inherent authority on earth, knowing that he has the full approval and authority to do so from his Father in heaven as he unites his will with his Father's will in obedience and communion.* The Father in his pleasurable will has entrusted all things to his obedient Son (cf. Phil. 2:9-11).

When this understanding of co-authority is applied to the exercise of the power of the Spirit, the authority to act through the Spirit proceeds both from the Father *and* the Son for both the Father and the Son are Lord and one. But the authority to act through the Spirit also proceeds from the Father *through the Son* on earth as Mt. 11:27 clearly witnesses. This is equivalent to saying that the Spirit proceeds from the Father and the Son (*ex Patre filioque*) and the Spirit proceeds from the Father through the Son (*per filium*) *in the economy*. Barth discusses the issue of *filioque* in *CD* I.1, pp. 477f.[105] Barth clearly stands on the side of the West insisting that *filioque* is important for safeguarding the unity of the Trinity (p. 483), the Son's equality with the Father (p. 484) and the basis of communion between God and man (p. 480). He comments that the East 'does not contest the fact that this [*filioque*] is so in revelation. But it does not read off from revelation its statements about the being of God "antecedently in Himself"' (p. 480). Barth also accepts the Spirit proceeds from the Father through the Son (*per filium*, pp. 482, 484) and

---

105 For a history of this controversial issue between the East and the West, see J.N.D. Kelly, *Early Christian Creeds* (London: Longman, 1972), pp. 358-67, and *The Forgotten Trinity*, 2, pp. 37-40.

quotes Augustine for support.[106] But Barth would only accept it on the basis of *filioque*, not on its own (pp. 482, 484).[107] In dogmatic theology, the issue of *filioque* (and the associated issue of *per filium*) is often discussed in the context of the sending of the Spirit after Jesus' resurrection (in economy) or in the context of the immanent Trinity. *This study, however, seeks to find their meanings within Jesus' life and ministry.* How the Spirit proceeds from the Father and the Son *(filioque)* and through the Son *(per filium)* to the church after Jesus' resurrection, and how the Spirit proceeds from the Father and the Son in their mutual communion in eternity are not easy to imagine and appreciate purely because it is difficult to visualise how the Father and the Son act in their heavenly place of abode. But it is comparatively less difficult to understand how *Jesus Christ in his communion with his Father on earth freely exercises the power of the Spirit in his ministry as subject and Lord, and how the Father in granting his communing presence to his Son through the Spirit exercises the power of the same Spirit through his Son on earth.* From these pictures one is able to comprehend more concretely that it is in the crucial context of *communion* that the Spirit proceeds from the Father *and* the Son, and *through* the Son. (Therefore, this book insists that both *filioque* and *per filium* should be taken together.) Without the context of communion, the Spirit would be sent from two different authorities which is absurd, and the notion of *per filium* would be nonsensical. It is interesting that when Augustine spoke about the Spirit proceeding *principally* from the Father ('principally' embraces both *filioque* and *per filium*), he used the concept of the Father begetting the Son in this giving of the Spirit to the Son.[108] But it is not so easy, although not impossible, to imagine how this begetting effects the Spirit proceeding through the Son and principally from the Father. However, the discussion above based on the more tangible revelation of God in the economy, i.e., in Jesus' life and ministry, has identified communion as the more dynamic relation and context than begetting for appreciating how *filioque* and *per filium* can be effected together. This in turn may help us to appreciate more concretely and

---

106 *De Trinitate*, Book 15: 26, 47; 17:29.

107 A. Heron has an interesting and relevant discussion on these two aspects in 'The Problem of the Filioque', *Scottish Journal of Theology*, 24 (1971), pp. 149-66, especially pp. 164-6. For him, *filioque* is defensible but not necessary and it may be adequate to use the phrase 'from the Father through the Son'. But the author insists that both *filioque* and *per filium* should be taken together.

108 'And therefore I have added the word principally, because we find that the Holy Spirit proceeds from the Son also. But the Father gave Him this [the Spirit] too, not as to one already existing, and not yet having it; but whatever He gave to the only-begotten Word, He gave by begetting Him.' *De Trinitate*, Book 15: 29.

dynamically *filioque* in the immanent Trinity and *per filium* in the sending of the Spirit after Jesus' resurrection. This is one example illustrating why this book has focused so much attention on Jesus' relationships with the Father and the Spirit through studying the gospel narratives: the economic Trinity, especially as revealed in Jesus' life, ministry and death, is the ground for our understanding of the immanent Trinity though the latter is the ground for manifesting the former. It will be interesting to see how *filioque* and *per filium* seen in the context of Jesus' life and ministry might contribute towards ecumenical discussions on these issues between the East and the West.

The discussion above concerning the authority of the Father and the Son in exercising the power of the Spirit can be repeated for the authority of the Father and the Son in giving authoritative teaching, with minimum changes. A corollary of the above discussion is that the Son's relationship with the Spirit does not change after he has taken flesh - He is still the Lord who freely exercises the power of the Spirit in unity with his Father. This is not the case in Irving's understanding, where, because the Son has taken flesh, the divinity of the Son has to be inactive in order to make room for the Spirit to be active. But that was based on the unnecessary assumption that the activity of the divine Son and the activity of the Spirit are incompatible in the economy even though they are compatible in eternity. In practice, in Irving's scheme the economic Trinity does not truly reveal the immanent Trinity even though in theory he confessed to the contrary.

The apparently competing sources of divinity in Logos Christology and Spirit Christology was resolved in the last section - there is a unity between Jesus and the Spirit. In this section, the two apparently separate Lordships of the Father and the Son in exercising the power of the Spirit has been accommodated by seeing their unity in communion. The same is true of the Lordships in Jesus' authoritative preaching. Thus, both a binitarian and a tritheistic view of the Trinity have been avoided by appealing to the notions of unity between the Son and the Spirit and unity between the Son and the Father. And the expression of unity between the Father, Son and the Holy Spirit is in their mutual communion. It is to this topic of the book that we now turn.

3.0 Spirit as the Agent of Communion and 'spirit' as the Content of Communion

If, in presenting the Lordships of the Father and the Son, the Lordship of the Spirit seems to be eclipsed in the sections above, in this section the paramount importance of the role of the Spirit in the life of the

Trinity will be made abundantly clear.[109] It is the intention of this author to acknowledge a primary role of the Spirit in Christian theology, instead of seeing the Spirit as an addendum to main theological discussions, as is often the case in the West. This intention is already evident in the emphasis on the communion between the Father and the Son through the Spirit in the discussions in chapter 2, and in chapters 3 and 4 where attention was drawn to Jesus' revelation of his relationship/unity with his Father (not merely his revelation of his Father). Now, the nature of this communion facilitated by the Spirit in the Trinity will be further explored. The exploration will have implications for our understanding of (i) the non-linear concept of Jesus' revelation of the Father (see chapter 2) and possibly (ii) the expression of the divinity of the Son on earth. The *narrative* studies in this book, using the *conceptual* elements in Mt. 3:3, 11:25-30, 1:20 and others as interpretative framework, have witnessed to Jesus' Lordship, his unity with his Father and his relationship with the Spirit. These three aspects of the *narrative* studies will be brought together *conceptually* in a refined non-linear concept of revelation. This process of using conceptual elements found in the narratives as framework for interpreting the narratives, which then suggest refinement of the conceptual framework, is what McGrath calls 'dynamic oscillation between representation and concept' and 'dynamic interaction ... between doctrine and scripture'.[110]

3.1 The Meanings of Spirit

We begin this exploration of the nature of the communion between Jesus and his Father through the Spirit by recalling some of Lampe's ideas about the work of the Spirit of God. Even though one may not agree with him on the ontological identities of Jesus Christ and the Holy Spirit, his understanding of the work of God's Spirit in human person is very dynamic and profound and can be used in exploring the Father's communion with his Son through the Spirit.

> [W]hen the 'Spirit' is understood in a fully personal sense, it is peculiarly valuable as a way of speaking about God as he is experienced in intimate communion with rational human beings. In Hebrew and Greek, as in English, the same word can denote the human spirit, that is, man as a rational, feeling, willing personality endowed with insight, wisdom and

---

109 For the biblical witness to the divinity of the Holy Spirit, see Turner, *The Holy Spirit and Spiritual Gifts*, pp. 175-80.

110 See McGrath's comment on the relationship between conceptualisation and narratives in 3.0 of chapter 1.

moral sensitivity, capable of responding to God, and also the creative and life-renewing power of God which is nothing less than his personal presence. This in itself is a fact of great theological significance, for it points to the truth that revelation comes to men only in personal dialogue between their imaginative insight and God's creative power.[111]

Spirit therefore can refer to God's Spirit - God himself reaching out towards men and bringing them his personal presence - and man's spirit - man as a rational, feeling, willing personality endowed with insight, wisdom and moral sensitivity, capable of responding to God. In this book, instead of understanding Spirit as merely an expression of God's creative power and action (as in Lampe), we understand the *Spirit of God* as God's personal agent who reaches out to the *human spirit*, interacting with the created spirit, integrating man's thoughts, emotions and will with God's own. These two meanings of 'Spirit/spirit' can be augmented with a third sense of the word - i.e., spirit as the mind, attitude and thought of God, which is the content being conveyed by the divine Spirit to the human spirit. The phrase 'spirit of God' does bear this sense already in the OT. One of the meanings of 'the *rûah* of God' in the OT given by *TDNT* is God's inner nature - his will, attitude, thought or his mind, just as the '*rûah* in man' is the seat of emotions, intellectual functions and attitude of will.[112] And when intertestamental literature refers to the Spirit of God and his work in the receiving subject, often it is closely associated with God's inner nature or thoughts. For example, the Spirit is referred to as the 'spirit of holiness', 'spirit of righteousness', 'compassionate spirit' or 'spirit of wisdom and understanding'.[113] God implants his spirit - his own attitudes and thoughts of holiness, righteousness and wisdom - by his Spirit into the human spirit.[114] God communicates himself to the human spirit by his Spirit and the content of his self-communication is his thoughts, his will, his mind, his attitudes - his spirit. Likewise, in the NT, when the Spirit is referred to as the Holy Spirit or the Spirit of Christ, the attribute of holiness and the personality of Christ (Dunn) are closely associated

---

111 Lampe, *God As Spirit*, p. 44.

112 *TDNT*, vol. VI. See p. 361 for the spirit of man and p. 364 for spirit of God. Is. 40:13 can be translated as 'Who has understood the spirit of the Lord ...' or 'Who has understood the mind of the Lord ...' See also Is. 63:10; Ps. 106:33; Mich. 2:7.

113 See Turner, *The Holy Spirit and Spiritual Gifts*, pp. 16-18. Cf. Isaiah 11:2. See also Montague, *The Holy Spirit: Growth of a Biblical Tradition*.

114 See the Spirit as the Spirit of prophecy - prophecy understood generally as God's self-communication to man - in Turner, *The Holy Spirit and Spiritual Gifts*, pp. 5-18.

with the word 'Spirit'.[115] The thought of the *Holy* Spirit in a believer brings one's attention to the spirit of holiness that the Spirit imparts to a believer's spirit. The thought of the Spirit of Christ in his disciples highlights the fact that the Spirit of Christ implants the spirit of Christ into their spirits. In fact, πνεῦμα χριστοῦ can be translated as the Spirit of Christ or the spirit /attitude/mind/personality of Christ when it is permitted by the context. For example, the expression in Rom. 8:9 could be translated as either - 'And if anyone does not have the spirit (Spirit) of Christ, he does not belong to Christ.' The incorporation of both meanings for the phrase in this verse gives a more comprehensive sense of Christ's indwelling in the believers because the thoughts, the attitudes, the will and the mind of Christ - which represent his personal spiritual presence - can be grasped more concretely as the elements by which his presence is conveyed to and realised in the believers by the Spirit in them. This indwelling of Christ in a believer by the Spirit/spirit is probably what Paul understood as 'one with him [Christ] in spirit.'[116] There is a concrete sharing of thought, mind and spirit in the unity between Christ and his followers through the work of the Spirit. This might be what Archbishop Rowan Williams in his enthronement sermon called 'breathing his [Jesus'] breath, his Spirit' as his disciples 'stand where Jesus is'.[117] Also in. 1 Cor. 2:10-16 where Paul teaches that the Spirit of God conveys the thoughts of God to men, those thoughts are summarised as 'the mind of Christ', which could legitimately be understood as 'the spirit of Christ' because the 'mind/voῦν ' of v. 16 in the original context of Isaiah 40:13 is the 'spirit/*rûah*' of God. To summarise, the above discussion on the use of spirit in both OT and NT informs us of the legitimacy of holding both the senses of Spirit and spirit together in our interpretations.

What is being suggested above is that the Spirit of God, or the Spirit

---

115 '... Jesus became the personality of the Spirit.' Dunn, *Jesus and the Spirit*, p. 325.

116 '... he who unites himself with the Lord is one with him in spirit.' 1 Cor. 6:17.

117 Archbishop Rowan Williams' enthronement sermon, delivered on 27th February, 2003 in the Canterbury Cathedral, was on Mt. 11:25-30. The fuller section of the text of his sermon surrounding this quote is: 'So wherever he [Jesus] is, God is active, pouring out his gift, inviting our response. And this means we can't know fully who God is and what God gives unless we are willing to stand in the same place as Jesus, in the full flood of the divine life poured out in mercy and renewal. It's only in the water that you can begin to swim. We learn painfully quickly that we cannot hold our own there by our own strength; it is Jesus' gift in life and death and resurrection that makes it possible for us to stand with him, *breathing his breath, his Spirit*. Without the gift of the Spirit, we couldn't survive the presence of that absolute Truth, that unfading light which is God. But if we're not seeking to *stand where Jesus is*, all our talk about God remains on the level of theory; nothing has changed.' Italics mine.

·

of Christ, could bear these two senses - one as the Holy Spirit as the personal agent of revelation or communion, and the other as the spirit/mind/thought of God (or Christ) which is the *content* being conveyed by the Spirit to the human spirit. Thus, altogether 'spirit' takes on three meanings - the divine Spirit as the personal agent of communion conveys the spirit of God to the human spirit as God reaches out to him, integrates the human thoughts with his own, and grants him his personal presence. The spirit of God therefore represents God's own inner nature and thoughts which are the content of communion/revelation from God, or the content of God's self-communication, to man which is conveyed by the agency of the Holy Spirit. At bottom, in our understanding the agent of communion/revelation, the Holy Spirit, should not be divorced from the content of his work, i.e., the content of communion - the spirit/mind/thought of God.[118] In Lampe's scheme as already indicated in section 2.1.2, the content of the revelatory work of the Christ-Spirit can be interpreted to be the spirit of Christ which was supremely embodied by Jesus in history, the pre-eminent quality of which is love; and God has worked according to this spirit of Christ in the OT, in Jesus

---

118 The concept of Spirit/spirit understood as the agent and content of the Father's communion with Jesus is echoed by A. N. MacDonald, *The Interpreter Spirit and Human Life* (London: S.P.C.K., 1944). He entitled chapter 4 of his book as 'The Holy Spirit as Agent and Endowment' in which he differentiated the use of the term 'Spirit' in the New Testament with or without the definite article, the former corresponding to the reference to the Holy Spirit, the latter to the spiritual endowment or the condition of the man in the Spirit. In particular, he pointed out this dual usage of the Spirit in relation to Jesus, 'St. Luke's record of this incident is one of those key verses to which attention has been drawn: "And Jesus, full of Holy Spirit, returned from the Jordan, and was led by *the* Spirit in the wilderness during forty days, being tempted of the devil" (iv. 1-2). This *endowment* by the Spirit was expressly claimed by Jesus when he opened his mission in Nazareth: "Spirit of the Lord is upon me, because he anointed me to preach good tidings to the poor ... Today hath this scripture been fulfilled in your ears" (Luke iv. 18 and 21). As in the parallel passage of St. Matthew and St. Mark, the Spirit's action as an external guiding or leading agency distinct from Jesus himself is noted by the use of the article; but the *condition* of Jesus Himself - namely, that of a Spirit-inspired being, with a specially *endowed* human consciousness - is noted by the omission of the article. Because the stress, in the first half of the passage, is laid upon *the spiritual condition of Jesus*, the Holy Spirit is described, not as a personal agent, but as an endowment. Surely the writer must have had some definite reason for omitting the article in the one case and including it in the other? If his object was not to stress a contrast, why was it not omitted, or included, in *both* cases?' pp. 67-8. Italics mine. Here, the spiritual endowment in MacDonald's sense is equivalent to the content of the Father's communion to Jesus and is denoted not by the absence of the definite article but by the lower case spirit of communion.

Christ and his disciples up to now and into the future.

There is another important relationship between the Spirit of God and the spirit of God which needs to be considered. Lampe correctly emphasised that the Spirit of God in the OT is often understood as God's creative power and action towards his creation. But this creative power and action of God in his *outward* activities towards his creation is intimately connected with his *inner* nature or thought - the spirit of God. There is a direct relationship between *God's spirit* in himself and God's outreach and activities towards his creation which is denoted by *God's Spirit* in the OT. The Hebrew language therefore connects God's mind/thought and the expression of his mind in outward activities together through the word spirit - *rûah*. This relationship between mind/thought and action also appears when 'spirit' is used of man in the OT. When the OT refers to the spirit of man, it does not merely refer to man's inner thoughts or movements but also to his outward actions and behaviour. 'The thought implicit in *rûah* is that breathing, with the movement of air which this involves, is the *outward expression* of the life-force inherent in all human behaviour. ... [T]he spirit may be said to denote the direction in which a man's vitality flows, the *self-expression involved in his behaviour* - including ecstatic behaviour.'[119] Man's mind/thought and the expression of his mind in outward activities are also connected together through the word spirit/*rûah*. When God reaches out towards man, integrates man's thoughts with his and inclines man's action in a certain direction, the relationship of these four elements - God's thought and action, man's thought and action - can be understood in the following manner. *God's thought and movement in himself - his spirit - is expressed in his outward action through the Spirit toward man's spirit, which is thus energised and inclined by God's Spirit to act according to God's will/thought; man's spirit thus energised and inclined may in obedience be expressed in man's outward action which conforms to God's spirit and will.* While in the Hebrew language the word spirit/*rûah* can stand for both thought and action, thus linking them directly together, it seems that 'spirit' in the English language denotes more of the inner movement of man and less of man's outward action such that man's outward life-act is not so readily connected with his inner thought in the use of the word 'spirit'.[120] But in other languages, e.g., in Chinese, 精神/spirit can denote both thought and outward action together as in Hebrew. The NT also highlights the relationship between the two (see Mt. 12:34 and

---

119 *NIDNTT*, vol. 3, p. 691. Italics mine.

120 Although one may argue that there can be such a relationship, e.g., the spirit of sportsmanship as demonstrated in behaviour is ultimately linked to the spirit of the sportsman. Still, spirit is not often related to man's outwardly demonstrated action.

Mark 7:21-23 where 'heart' is used instead of 'spirit').[121] This link between thought and action via the notion of spirit may be important in conceiving Jesus' communion with his Father through the Spirit/spirit and his obedient action flowing from his obedient spirit, such that his life and action in the Spirit/spirit *reveals* God's inner nature/spirit/mind. This will be taken up in the next section on Spirit/spirit and revelation. It is possible that the author's understanding of this communion between Jesus and his Father in the Spirit/spirit and his revelation of his Father in the Spirit/spirit has been significantly influenced by the Chinese concept of 精神/spirit which links the outward and inner together as one.[122] The author is not suggesting that the Chinese concept in itself bears any canonical authority but that this concept, because it has its commonality with the Hebrew concept of *rûah*, might have helped him to better appreciate the biblical picture of Christ moving in the Spirit/spirit, which is understood both in terms of his outward words and actions *and* his inner communion with his Father in the spirit/Spirit. It is interesting to ask if there are other concepts or phrases in other cultures which could awaken one's understanding of the biblical concept of Spirit, Jesus' life-act and his spiritual communion with his Father. These concepts and phrases, if they exist, could be harnessed for speaking of the Trinity in concepts and terms which are indigenous to local cultures, thus possibly opening the horizon for relating the Trinity more meaningfully and closely to these local cultures. This could be an interesting area for future research.

One of Paul Tillich's telling comments in his *Systematic Theology* (Welwyn: James Nisbet, 1968), vol. 3, is to the effect that 'without an appreciation of the latter - i.e., lowercase spirit - it is impossible to speak of the divine Spirit (Uppercase). In fact, the fading of the symbol "Holy Spirit" from the living consciousness of Christianity is due in Tillich's view to the disappearance of the word "spirit" from the doctrine of the human.'[123] Tillich prefers to designate the Holy Spirit as

---

121 A man's action is closely related to his heart or his inner spirit. '... out of the overflow of the heart, the mouth speaks' (Mt. 12:34). 'For from within, out of men's hearts, come evil thoughts, sexual immorality, theft, murder, adultery, greed, malice, deceit, lewdness, envy, slander, arrogance and folly. All these evils come from inside and make a man "unclean"' (Mark 7:21-23).

122 In the 1996 Easter Conference of The Chinese Church in London, Rev. Philip Teng, the elderly scholar and pastor most respected amongst the worldwide Chinese church, spoke on the subject of the Holy Spirit. In one of his sermons, he said, '基督的靈向我們啟示基督的精神.' When translated to English, it reads, 'The Spirit of Christ reveals the spirit of Christ to us.' The author's thinking on the spirit of Christ has been influenced by this sentence of Rev. Teng.

123 Tillich's comment is summarised in this quote by Del Colle, *Christ and the Spirit*, p. 199. For Tillich's view, see his *Systematic Theology*, vol. 3, pp. 22f.

the 'Spiritual Presence' because this understanding unites the *'power of being'* with 'the *meaning* of being'.[124] It is indeed abstract to speak of the power of the work of the Spirit in human spirit when one does not have some notion of the meaning of life - i.e., the spirit of God, the content of the Spirit's work - which is being instilled into the human spirit. To merely speak in terms of the power of the Spirit could be a rather mechanical way of presenting the personal work of the Spirit. This way of speaking needs to be augmented with the meaning and content of the Spirit's revelatory work: when God does reaches out and conveys/reveals his personal spirit of holiness, love, truth and wisdom ... to the human spirit, the human person experiences this work of the Spirit as God's holy, loving and personal presence, a spiritual presence which energises the human spirit, draws him towards God and inclines him to thoughts and actions of holiness and love in obedience to God. This is a more concrete and tangible manner of speaking of the work of the Spirit.

The three senses of 'spirit' discussed above - the Holy Spirit as agent, the spirit as content of revelation or communion, the human spirit - witness to the fact that 'spirit' is indeed a bridge word between the divine and human, as Lampe correctly observed. Moreover, 'spirit' unites our understanding of inner nature and outward action, both in the human and divine realm. These understandings of 'spirit' have implication for our non-linear concept of Jesus' revelation of his Father.

3.2 Spirit/spirit and Jesus' Revelation of His Father: A Refined Non-Linear Concept of Revelation

Now the above understanding of 'spirit' and Lampe's dynamic understanding of the work of the Spirit are applied to Jesus Christ as a real man.[125] *The Father by the Spirit reaches out to Jesus and conveys his own spirit to him, granting him the Father's loving and holy communing presence, interacting with Jesus' spirit, integrating his thoughts, emotions and will with his (Father's) own.[126] Jesus Christ by the Spirit receives this spirit and personal presence of his Father and returns this spirit of love and holiness as the Son to his Father as he obeys his Father, keeping in step with his Father's Spirit/spirit of holiness and love, uniting his own thoughts, emotions and will with his Father, and expressing this spirit which he shares with his Father in obedient action.* This mutual giving and receiving in the Spirit/spirit, involving the content of the Father's holy and loving personal presence,

---

124 *Ibid.*
125 But insisting the divine identities of the Jesus Christ and the Holy Spirit.
126 Cf. Lampe, *God As Spirit*, p. 116, p. 50.

and the Son's loving, holy and obedient echo is perhaps what we mean by the communion between the Father and the Son through the Holy Spirit. And it is out of this communion in his spirit with his Father and his obedience from his heart to his Father that Jesus thinks, sees, hears, speaks, teaches, preaches, acts, heals and lives. The spirit in which he does all these is the spirit of holiness, love, compassion, truth, wisdom, and so on, which he shares with his Father. It is out of the spirit of truth and righteousness which he shares with his Father that he preaches to the crowds (e.g., in the Sermon on the Mount, see chapter 3), and it is out of the spirit of compassion which he shares with his Father that he reaches out to the sick and heals them (see, e.g., healing of the leper in chapter 4). This important truth is crystallised succinctly in John 15:9 - 'As the Father has loved me, so have I loved you.' His loving action to the people is founded on his loving communion with his Father. *This is how Jesus Christ on earth reveals his Father in heaven*: knowing his Father's love and his Father's mission for him (cf. Jesus' baptism), trusting in his Father's sovereign rule and providential care (cf. Mt. 6:25-34), in loving response to his Father, in resolute obedience and unity of will with his Father (cf. from the wilderness through Gethsemane to the cross), living and finding rest in the personal presence of his Father (Mt. 11:27-30), breathing in the atmosphere and air of the Spirit, sharing the same spirit of holiness, love and compassion with his Father through the Spirit, in this unity with his Father Jesus thinks, lives, speaks and acts in full consonance and communion with his Father in the power of the same Spirit and thus *reveals* his heavenly Father to the people on earth *in the spirit/Spirit*. This is a *refined* non-linear concept of revelation compared to the non-linear concept of revelation based on the exegesis of Mt. 11:25-30 in 4.0 of chapter 2 - it is refined by virtue of the more comprehensive use of the three senses of 'spirit' and the connection of the inner spirit and outer action by the word 'spirit'.

Barth's scheme of Jesus' revelation of his Father was interpreted to be a linear one in chapters 2 and 4: Jesus on earth, as the Word spoken by the Father, corresponds and conforms to, reflects and reveals his Father in heaven. But how does he do that? It is by a willing *bi-directional communing correspondence* between Jesus and his Father in the Spirit/spirit that he is united with and thereby reveals his Father, i.e., Jesus on earth in *mutual communion* through the Spirit/spirit with his Father in heaven corresponds and conforms to, reflects and reveals his Father in heaven in the Spirit/spirit - a non-linear concept of revelation by virtue of the bi-directional spiritual communion which Barth perhaps did not emphasise. This is how Jesus' *communion* with his Father through the *Spirit* is indispensable to his *revelation* of his Father; this is also how his *obedience* to his Father through the *Spirit* is equally crucial to his *revelation* of his Father, for communion needs to be augmented by and expressed in willing obedience which in turn maintains and completes that communion and unity (see Jesus' unbroken obedience from his baptism to his death in chapter 4).[127] Without the Spirit acting as the communion link between Jesus and his Father (if that was possible), there would have been no communion and there would have been no revelation by Jesus of his Father and no revelation of his relationship with his Father.[128] This is how important the Spirit is in God's revelation in God's economy. If we believe that the economic Trinity, though not exhausting the immanent Trinity, reveals the immanent Trinity, then the personal Spirit, as revealed in the economy, is also the communion link between the Father and the Son in the immanent Trinity, the *vinculum trinitatis*, the personal factor of the personal unity between the Father and the Son. Irving's understanding of the role of the Spirit in the immanent Trinity in this respect is correct and important: 'the Spirit being originated both from the Father and the Son, must in His self-existent being represent the *unity* and harmony of these two self-existent beings.'[129] Any concept of substantial unity of the Trinity must be augmented with this concept of dynamic and spiritual unity through the personal Spirit.

Traditionally the Spirit is understood as the *vinculum caritatis*, the bond of love, between the Father and the Son (Augustine) but there is more to the content of the communion between the Father and the Son through the Spirit as the discussion above shows. There are other qualities in the spirit of God shared by the Trinity which are not expressed by the word 'love' specifically enough or not expressed by

---

127 In the wilderness of temptations, even though Jesus was in communion with his Father through the Spirit, it was still possible for him to disobey his Father. The communion must be augmented with Jesus' will to obey which maintained the communion. Communion can be broken by disobedience. Also, obedience completes Jesus' unity with his Father which is the basis of his revelation of his Father. 'The Son's absolute and unique oneness with the Father is shown precisely in his submitting to the Father's will: "I and the Father are one." (John 10:30) precisely because 'the Father is greater than I' (John 14:28). That is, Jesus exhibits the nature and character of God in the only way in which they can be absolutely and perfectly exhibited in the context of human behaviour, namely, in such a relationship as properly belongs to man over against God, the relationship of glad and willing filial obedience.' C. F. D. Moule, 'The Manhood of Jesus in the New Testament', in *Christ, Faith and History* (Cambridge: Cambridge University Press, 1972), S. W. Sykes and J. P. Clayton (eds.), p. 101.

128 There could only be Jesus' revelation of himself.

129 *The Collected Writings of Edward Irving*, vol. 1, pp. 263-4. See McFarlane, 'The Strange Tongue of a Long Lost Christianity: The Spirit and the Trinity' in *Vox Evangelica*, XXII, p. 69.

this word at all, e.g., wisdom, truth/integrity, faithfulness, authority, freedom, Lordship, humility, purity, holiness. These we can concretely see in Jesus' life, ministry and death and are presumably shared by him with his Father through the Spirit - as the content of their communion - as he lives his life on earth. A more comprehensive understanding of the spirit of God as the content of the communion within the Trinity should therefore be gleaned from what Jesus Christ in his life and death concretely manifests in history, which includes pre-eminently love but also more specifically other qualities such as those mentioned above. The ministry, life and death of Jesus Christ in history therefore become the window into the content of communion within the Trinity, economic or immanent. One application from this concerns the co-authority of Jesus and his Father in his authoritative preaching and mighty works discussed in the last section. It is possible to understand Jesus' exercise of authority in consonance with his Father's authority in the following manner: Jesus in communion with his Father shares the spirit of Lordship and authority with his Father, and knowing the approval and good pleasure of his Father (cf. Phil. 2:9-11) he exercises that sovereign Lordship and divine authority freely as his own, and in so doing reveals his Father's sovereign Lordship and divine authority on earth.

From the above understanding of the refined non-linear concept of revelation, one can see that Jesus the Son resonates through the Spirit with his Father in every aspect of his being, that he remains in oneness with his Father in his will, in his rational, emotional and experiential faculties, in his sense of divine Lordship, freedom and majesty. It is in this comprehensive oneness with his Father that he breathes in the communing presence of his Father, obeys him, fulfils his mission and reveals him.

3.3 Spirit/spirit and Jesus' Revelation of His Relationship with His Father

It has been remarked in chapters 3 and 4 that Jesus' relationship/unity with his Father is both the basis and content (partial) of his revelation. That is, the basis of revelation is also somehow revealed. For example, Jesus' Sonship to the Father, or God's Fatherhood to him, is the basis of his life and revelation. On this basis, he not only teaches and reveals to others the Fatherhood of God but he also expresses and reveals this relationship and basis in his *abba* prayer and his obedience to his Father. Similarly, Jesus' communion with his Father is characterised by knowledge (of his Father's will), love for his Father and trust in his Father. Within this communion, it is in the knowledge of his Father's will, it is in a spirit of love and trust that he works out his obedience in concrete actions. And his obedient actions in some way witness to and reveal his knowledge of his Father's will, his spirit of love for his Father and his trust in his Father.[130] In chapter 3, we have seen how the manner of certainty in which Jesus teaches witnesses to his intimate *knowledge* of his Father's righteous will. In chapter 4, the fearless and courageous manner in which Jesus confronts the religious leaders witnesses to his *trust* in his Father,[131] and his obedience from Jordan to the cross witnesses to his *love* for his Father. What is being brought out here is that what characterise Jesus' relationship with his Father in their spiritual communion - the spirit of Sonship, knowledge, the spirit of trust, rest and love - are not only the basis of revelation but also the content of revelation. The knowledge, the spirit of trust, rest and love in their spiritual communion are inevitably expressed in Jesus' life-act. (Again, the OT connection of the inner and the outer by the concept of 'spirit' is applicable here, where the inner spirit of knowledge, trust, rest and love is expressed in Jesus' outward action.)

The fact of the revelation of the basis of Jesus' revelation of his Father can also be gleaned from the following utterance - 'As the Father has loved me, so have I loved you.' This utterance can be interpreted in two complementary manners. In that communion of love which is the basis of revelation, Jesus' love corresponds to his Father's love which is revealed in his loving actions towards others. Jesus thus reveals his Father - this is the point of the last section. But it is also true that in his loving action towards others, he also reveals his love for his Father (in his obedience). Jesus thus in his action reveals his loving relationship/communion with his Father, which is therefore both the basis and content of his revelation. This is to be expected because if his communion and relationship with his Father in the Spirit/spirit is fundamental to his life and being, this fundamental relationship, this basis of revelation, must inevitably manifest itself in Jesus' life and act. And this manifestation of his spirit of trust, love and knowledge of his Father, which can be seen from Jordan to Jerusalem, reaches its climactic height in the suffering and death of Jesus Christ (see 3.3 of chapter 4). Paradoxically, it is in the Father's abandonment of the Son on the cross that the unity between the Father and the Son, which is the basis of revelation, is climactically revealed.[132]

---

130 See, for example, chapters 3 and 4, see also the comment at the beginning of 2.0 of chapter 4.

131 The rest that Jesus speaks of in Mt. 11:28-30 is manifested in his action.

132 At the level of discipleship, even though a disciple's relationship with the Father cannot be physically visible, his mature life-act, for example, does witness to and reveal his relationship (of knowledge, trust and love) with the Father who is not seen. Jesus' relationship with his Father (and the revelation of this relationship) is then the limiting case of the disciples' relationship with the Father.

CHAPTER 7

The Humanity and Divinity of Jesus Christ

Summary: This chapter explores the relationship between the humanity and divinity of Jesus Christ by developing the concept of 'conformity in spirit' and utilising the refined non-linear concept of revelation. G. Thomasius' kenotic Christology will be examined and critiqued. Crucial to the understanding of Jesus' humanity and divinity are the relationships between authority, mode of existence and person. The mystery of incarnation is affirmed but its location is more clearly identified. The proposed Christology has some claim to be a refined Christology with a paradigmatic shift beyond Chalcedon.

1.0 Introduction

The final issue to be discussed in this book concerns the humanity and divinity of Jesus Christ. Christological discussions after Chalcedon often centre around how the human and divine nature can be united in the person (or *hypostasis*) of Jesus Christ without much reference to the Father and the Spirit. Here, this issue will be explored in a fully trinitarian framework, starting rather surprisingly with Wilhelm Herrmann's comment on Chalcedonian Christology.

Herrmann's objection to the Chalcedon formula was that with its language of natures it does not draw one's attention to one's experience of Jesus in which one apprehends God.[1] For Herrmann, Chalcedon had

---

1   Herrmann, *Systematic Theology*, pp. 139-42.

missed the most crucial basis for the confession of Christ's divinity, i.e., Jesus' capacity to reveal God or his presence.[2] And once that basis is missed, the thought of Jesus' divinity does not connect Jesus with God (the Father). Such divinity of Jesus is confined to and ends in Christ himself, without *connecting* Jesus with the Father. But 'if the confession of the Deity of Christ is to have any meaning at all, it is clear that it must in any case mean that we connect God in our thoughts with the Man Jesus.'[3] Even though this book may not agree with Herrmann totally on his Christology, it does acknowledge his contribution that one must connect Jesus with God via the concept of revelation in thinking about his divinity. It is possible that Barth in this respect, i.e., his emphasis on Jesus' revelation of God in his understanding of Christ's divinity and the Trinity, could have been influenced by his teacher Herrmann. Having explored in greater details the inextricable relationship between communion and revelation in the last chapter above, here the *divinity* of Jesus Christ will be explored in the context of his communion with and revelation of his Father through the Spirit as a genuine *human* being, rather than in the context of how his divinity and his humanity can co-exist together.

2.0 Spirit/spirit, the Humanity and Divinity of Jesus Christ

One can conceive that within the immanent Trinity the Father and the divine Son commune in their ineffable mutual knowledge and presence through the Spirit and in the spirit. The spirit of communion between the Father and the Son is pre-eminently love. But this spirit of love is held in different forms by the Father and the Son. This spirit is held by the Father in the form of his Fatherly love for the Son, and it is held by the Son in the form of his filial love for the Father. Even though the spirit of love is held in different forms by the Father and the Son, one can agree that they share the same essence of love. Spirit is such a dynamic and fluid concept that its form can change but its essence remains intact.[4] Here, the concept of conformity is introduced. The

---

2 For Herrmann it will not do to seek to 'base Christian faith upon the hypothesis that in Christ divine nature is united with human nature.' *Ibid.*, pp. 141-42. The mistake of using the Chalcedon formula as the basis for the acknowledgement of the deity of Christ is 'it had been forgotten ... that Christian faith, if it treats Christ as God, must have before its eyes, without being able to comprehend it, a wonderful fact [i.e., Jesus' inner life which reveals God's presence] which it recognises as the source and the foundation of its own life.' *Ibid.*

3 Herrmann, *The Communion of the Christian with God*, p. 154.

4 A human example of this change of form while retaining the essence is found in the parents' love for their child. The father loves the child as father with his fatherly love

spirit (or mind) of the Son is *conformable* to the spirit (or mind) of the Father, and vice versa, in the sense that they share the same essence despite the difference in form. This concept of conformity will be used to understand how in the economy Jesus' humanity can be related to his divinity.

With the incarnation of the Son, the immanent Trinity is revealed in the economic Trinity. In the economic Trinity, we also see that the Father in heaven and the Son on earth commune with one another in their mutual knowledge and presence through the Spirit and in the spirit. It has been established that revelation depends on Jesus' communion with his Father; it must be stressed that for Jesus' revelation of his Father to take place on earth his communion with his Father has to be of such quality that his spirit (or mind) in his true humanity corresponds or conforms to the spirit (or mind) of his Father in heaven. Otherwise, Jesus does not truly conform or correspond to his Father and revelation fails. Jesus' conformity with his Father in the spirit has the following important implication. Since the human spirit of Jesus on earth (in the economy) and the spirit of the divine Son in eternity are both conformable to the spirit of the Father, they are essentially the same, or conformable to each other. (Note how conformity to and revelation of the *Father* through the *Spirit* is invoked here in relating together the human and divine aspects of Jesus Christ; traditional Christological discussions after Chalcedon often revolve around the human and divine natures of Jesus Christ only, without much reference to the Father and the Spirit.)

How can the human spirit of Jesus Christ in history conform to the divine spirit of the divine Son in eternity? Note the question is not 'How can the human spirit of Jesus Christ in history conform to the divine spirit of the divine Son in history?' The spirit of Jesus in history is deliberately compared to the spirit of the divine Son in eternity. The question is not about the co-existence of two spirits, or two wills, in Jesus as in much traditional Christological discussions but about the conformity between the spirit of Jesus in history and the spirit of the Son in eternity. This conformity is not impossible if we maintain that the spirit of God can be held in its essence in different forms, just as the spirit of the divine Son in eternity is essentially the same as, or conformable to, the spirit of the Father as pointed out above. However, in the case of incarnation, one has to assume that it is possible for the divine spirit of the divine Son in eternity to be held in a conformable

---

while the mother loves the child as mother with her motherly love. Even though the form of love for the child varies between the father and the mother, they share the same spirit or essence of love for their child. Therefore, the spirit or essence of love is retained despite the plurality of form.

human form in history with no loss of essence. How can this assumption be maintained and justified? One cannot maintain this assumption robustly from any vantage point, philosophical or otherwise, other than the fact or actuality of incarnation and the fact of Jesus' true revelation of his Father witnessed by Scripture; that is, from these Scriptural facts and only from these facts, one can conclude that this assumption can be true.[5] For example, as Jesus was moved in compassion to teach the lost and heal the sick (e.g., Mt. 9:36, see 2.1.2 of chapter 4), we have good reasons to believe that this genuinely human compassion of Jesus in history portrayed in the gospel narrative conformed to and revealed his Father's compassion and at the same time conformed to the Son's divine love in eternity. To weaken the sense of the conformity of Jesus' human spirit to the divine spirit of the Father jeopardises his revelation of the Father. To break the sense of the conformity of Jesus' human spirit in history to the divine spirit of the Son in eternity jeopardise the nature of the incarnation.

The conformity between the divine spirit of the Son in eternity and the human spirit of Jesus in history prompts us to think about God's creation of man as the image of God. It is possible that the image of God - humanity - was so designed by his creator that it has the capacity or the potential to conform to the spirit of God through the Spirit of God, even to the degree of without loss of essence in these respects. (Rahner made a very similar point by using the scholastic expression *potentia obedientialis*, obediential or supernatural potency.[6]) This potential could be realised when man in his spirit as a rational, feeling, willing, living personality endowed with insight, wisdom and moral sensitivity is energised and drawn into the personal dialogue, spiritual interaction and integration with the creator God through the creative and life-renewing power of the Spirit, which is nothing less than his personal presence.[7] Jesus Christ through *active and willing obedience* to his Father, then, is the one who as the perfect Image of God on earth has realised this potential and fulfilled this capacity to the fullest; his human spirit in history is then conformable to the spirit of the Father and the

---

5 Here Barth's point about beginning with the fact of incarnation in *CD* I.2, p. 124 is appealed to but this crucial point is now used to understand conformity between divine spirit and human spirit in the incarnation, a move which Barth did not make and perhaps did not wish to make.

6 'What does it mean to say that human nature has the possibility of being assumed by the person of the Word of God? Correctly understood, it means that this *potentia* is not one potentiality along with other possibilities in the constituent elements of human nature; it is objectively identical with the essence of man.' Karl Rahner, 'On the Theology of the Incarnation' in *Theological Investigation*, vol. 4, p. 110.

7 Lampe, *God as Spirit*, pp. 44, 47, 50.

spirit of the divine Son in eternity.[8]

Lampe commented that 'spirit' is one of the bridge words which denotes God's active outreach to humanity.[9] It is possible to postulate that 'spirit' could also be a bridge word between the divine and human in the sense of denoting the conformity of Jesus' humanity in the incarnation to his divinity in eternity, i.e., conformity in spirit through the Spirit. It is interesting that the incarnation of the divine Son in human form was effected by the Holy Spirit. One wonders if an important aspect of the work of the Spirit in the incarnation is in effecting the conformity between the divine spirit of the Son in eternity and the human spirit of Jesus in history. This supposition is reasonable because the Spirit is the most congenial agent to work with and conform the spirit of a person. In any case, it is possible to understand that the Son's divinity in eternity, as the source, has been *expressed* in his perfect humanity in history (though not exhaustively) and his perfect humanity is a witness to his inherent divinity. David Coffey, following Rahner's lead in his understanding of the incarnation, rather boldly writes, '[T]he divinity of Christ is not something different from his humanity; it *is* the humanity, i.e., human nature at the peak of its possibility.'[10] He attributes the wedge 'between the humanity and divinity of Christ' to Greek philosophical thoughts and language.[11] Concerning the *communicatio idiomatum*, Coffey writes, '*whatever* is communicated from God to man in the Incarnation is bestowed in a divine way but received in a human way.'[12] Here, the bestowal and reception between the divine and human is conceived more specifically in terms of conformity in spirit.

It is somewhat surprising that since spirit is the most congenial concept to link the divine and human together, Chalcedonian Christology has no mention of this concept in its attempt to describe the

---

8   For a similar line of thought, see David Coffey, 'The "Incarnation" of the Holy Spirit in Christ', *Theological Studies*, 45 (1984), no. 3, and Rahner, 'On the Theology of the Incarnation', pp. 105-20. Rahner wrote (p. 110), 'The incarnation of God is therefore the unique, *supreme*, case of the total actualisation of human reality, which consists of the fact that man *is* in so far as he gives up himself.'

9   Lampe, *God as Spirit*, p. 35.

10 Coffey, 'The "Incarnation" of the Holy Spirit in Christ', p. 467. But he does point out that Jesus' perfect humanity does not exhaust his divinity. '... to say that the divinity of Christ *is* his humanity is not to say that the divine person of the Son comes to perfect or adequate expression in the human nature of Christ. It is only to say that he comes to the most perfect expression of which humanity is capable, which is different from, and less than, the expression which he has in his divine nature in the eternal Trinity.' *Ibid.*, p. 468.

11 *Ibid.*, p. 468.

12 *Ibid.*, p. 469.

humanity and divinity of Jesus Christ. The more fluid and dynamic notion of spirit is able to accommodate both humanity and divinity together better than the more static notion of substance (or essence). For example, it is not easy to conceive how the divine substance and human substance can be one, or how divine substance can be conformable to human substance, or how the divine substance expresses itself in human substance, while the notion of divine spirit changing its form and conforming itself to the human spirit of Jesus Christ, without compromising its divine content, is more readily acceptable. The notion of the conformity of the divine spirit to the human spirit (through the Holy Spirit) in the incarnation can be sustained by appealing to the conformity of the spirit of the Son to the spirit of the Father through the Holy Spirit in the immanent and economic Trinity. This understanding of conformity in spirit through the Holy Spirit can be summarised as '*spirit remains true to itself while taking different forms*'. This is a valuable *conceptual tool* for conceiving (i) the Trinity and how revelation takes place and (ii) Christology - how Jesus Christ can be human and divine at the same time. This conceptual tool is of course dependent on or derived from the *category* of spirit which has been employed in this book. Although the category of spirit should not replace the category of substance in Christological (and trinitarian) discussions, it should be brought in to augment the category of substance in order to fulfil the roles that are not adequately covered by substance. Had Chalcedon and its ensuing Christological discussions adopted this more dynamic category and its associated conceptual tool, there could have been less difficulties and confusions throughout the centuries in the church's articulation of Jesus Christ. Also, the humanity of Jesus Christ and the role of the Holy Spirit in Christological, Trinitarian and theological discussions would have been much more prominent.

From the discussion above, the following conformities can be collected: the spirit of the divine Son is conformable to the spirit of the Father in eternity; the spirit of Jesus in his true humanity is conformable to the spirit of the divine Son in eternity and to the spirit of the Father. Briefly, the Son has always conformed to his Father in spirit through the Spirit, whether in eternity or history. The Son's conformity to his Father is one of the main keys for understanding the Son's divinity in history (and in eternity). Herrmann's insight is valuable here: the *divinity* of Jesus Christ needs to be spoken of and understood in the context of his connection with and revelation of God in his *humanity*. The approach adopted here concerning Jesus' divinity is the following. Jesus' divinity has already been acknowledged and affirmed in the study of the gospel narratives (chapters 2 to 5). Our attention has now turned to how this divinity of Jesus is *expressed* in his relationship with and revelation of his Father. The divinity of the Son can therefore be understood to be *expressed* in the person of Jesus Christ in the three facts that (i) he has so resolutely willed to obey his Father to maintain the communion and conformity, this dynamic unity with his Father that (ii) he has realised the potential and fulfilled the capacity to commune with and conform to his Father through the Spirit even in his true humanity, and (iii) he freely exercises his inherent authority and Lordship in teaching and in mighty acts which he shares with his Father (which is in no way weakened in his becoming flesh and which cannot be attributed to his humanity, i.e., the authority is proper only to his divinity). Barth's intuitive insight that Jesus Christ has to be God in order to reveal God is a valuable and very important one. However, this precious notion needs to be further unpacked and elaborated in the way outlined above. That is, anyone less than divine cannot obediently commune with God so perfectly/fully in the Holy Spirit and therefore will not be able to correspond and conform to God and reveal him truly on earth. *Revelation (term C) is therefore dependent on Jesus' perfect obedient communion with and correspondence to God (term B) which in turn depends on the divinity of Jesus Christ (term A).* Barth emphasises the aspect of Christ's divinity (term A) and thus his ability to conform to and reveal God (term C). This book has aimed to emphasise equally *the middle term between divinity and revelation* - i.e., perfect obedient communion (term B) which constitutes their dynamic unity. The *divinity* of Jesus implies that he has the capacity to fully *commune* with and conform to his Father through the Spirit in his *humanity*, and he has so realised and fulfilled this capacity through *obedience* that he truly conforms to, is united with and *reveals* his Father on earth.[13] Barth has

---

13 But Barth also has something important to say about (i) the 'giving' and 'receiving' between the Father and the Son (communion) in revelation, and (ii) the capacity of Jesus to fully *commune* with and conform to his Father. '"All things are delivered unto me of my Father." Again in accordance with the sense Schlatter underlines the fact 'that Πάντα [all] does not carry any limitation ... there are no limits for the giver and therefore *no limits* for the recipient.' Therefore, this saying implies the *deity* of Jesus. But it is in complete hiddenness that He is who and what He is. "No man knoweth the Son, but the Father; neither knoweth any man the Father, save the Son, and he to whomsoever the Son will reveal him." But that means that who and what He is as *the human bearer of that unlimited omnipotence*, and who and what is the One who has given it to him, what there is of divine majesty in giving and receiving of it - this and the revelation of it is not something which can be laid down and judged and evaluated from without ... The door to the majesty of Jesus can open only from within. And when it does open it is this door - the poor *humanity of the divine being* and activity, the strange form of the divine majesty, the humility in which God is God and the Son is Son, and to that extent the Father the Father, ...' *CD* IV.1, p. 178; Italics mine. Quoted in 4.0 of chapter 2. '[T]he *revelation* imparted

by no means neglected this middle term (see previous footnote), but with a more weighty introduction of this middle term in his understanding of revelation, the consequent greater emphasis on the Spirit might have made his basically trinitarian understanding of revelation perhaps even truer to his intention.

The idea of conformity which has been used above is not original to this book. Barth uses it in describing Jesus' relation to God in the context of revelation (see 2.1.2 of chapter 4) and in the context of the communion of natures in the person of Jesus.[14] But he tends to see humanity and divinity rather distinctly, without overlap. He gives 'no place for a monistic thinking which confuses or reverses the divine and the human.'[15] However, it is possible that there can be some commonality and conformity between humanity and divinity such that some aspects of the Son's divinity can be expressed in humanity without these divine aspects existing as something materially distinct from and alongside with these conforming human aspects, which have already found their *divine correspondents in his Father*. For example, did Jesus Christ have a materially distinct divine spirit in addition to his human spirit when his human spirit is already conforming and corresponding to his Father's divine spirit?[16] And did Jesus Christ have a materially distinct divine will in addition to his *human will* when his human will already is conforming and corresponding to his *Father's divine will*?[17] Are these divine and human aspects of Jesus necessarily

---

to the νηπίοι (Mt. 11:25 and Luke 10:21) is grounded in a preceding movement in God Himself between the Father and the Son. ... He was the Father who loves the Son and the Son who loves the Father, and as such, *in communion and reciprocity of this love*, as God the Father, Son and Holy Ghost, the God who is self-moved, the living God, *the One who loves eternally and as such moves to love.*' *CD* IV.2, p. 759, in the subsection 'The Basis of Love.' Quoted in 4.0 of chapter 2. Italics mine.

14 'The one will of Jesus Christ is the eternal will of God and it is also - absolutely *conformable* for all its dissimilarity - the motivated human will which determines the way of this human life as such.' *CD* IV.2, p. 116.

15 *Ibid.*

16 Note the discussion above has been deliberately silent on the possibility of the existence of a divine spirit of Jesus materially distinct from his human spirit.

17 In the seventh century, Sergius, patriarch of Constantinople from 610-638, spoke of 'one energy' in Christ and Pope Honorius I, in a correspondence with Sergius, spoke of 'one will' in Christ (monotheletism). But the Third Council of Constantinople in A.D. 680-681 condemned monotheletism and maintained the two wills of Christ. See Gerald O'Collins, SJ, *Christology, A Biblical, historical and systematic study of Jesus Christ* (Oxford: Oxford University Press, 1995), pp. 196-7. For a more detailed discussion of monotheletism, see J. A. Dorner, *History of the Development of the Doctrine of the Person of Christ* (Edinburgh, Scotland: T. & T. Clark, 1880-1897), Division Second, vol. 1, Rev. D. W. Simon (tr.), pp. 199f.

and materially distinct? Following Rahner's lead in his understanding of the incarnation, Coffey proposes that the NT does not see the human and divine aspects of Jesus as necessarily and materially distinct even though humanity does not exhaust divinity.[18] In aiming to see a more prominent role of the Spirit in the incarnation, he seeks to see the actualisation of Jesus' divinity in his humanity, and not unlike Irving, he attributes this possibility *wholly* to the Spirit.[19]

> Modern Christology, like, for example, that of Rahner, takes its cue from biblical Christology and sees Christ's divinity not as something separate or even distinct from his humanity but as its supreme actualisation under grace. I should simply add that the grace in question, the actualizing power, is the bestowal of the Holy Spirit here spoken of. ... The Spirit is the love of the Father for Jesus, poured out on him in a radical and unique way and experienced as such on the part of Jesus. The Spirit, through the answering love it evoked from him, *enabled* him to live his whole life in dedicated obedience to the Father's will.[20]

> [F]undamentally by the word 'love' here we cannot mean either his particular acts of love or the underlying virtue of charity in him, both of which he had in common with all graced men and women (even if to a greater degree), but a reality deeper still and unique to himself, and in his case the source of both his charity and his particular acts. This reality is the Holy Spirit precisely as appropriated by him, 'humanised' in its radical reception by him. This appropriation I have not hesitated to call an

---

18 Coffey, 'The "Incarnation" of the Holy Spirit in Christ', p. 468, '[T]he NT did not conceive the divinity of Christ as something different from his humanity: what it had to say about his divinity was a statement about his humanity, expressed in the language of salvation history, not philosophy.' Mackintosh, *The Doctrine of the Person of Jesus Christ*, p. 470, 'We cannot predicate of Him two consciousnesses or two wills; the New Testament indicates nothing of the kind, nor indeed is it congruous with an intelligible psychology. The unity of His personal life is axiomatic.'

19 But he differs from Irving in that the humanity of Jesus Christ is radically sanctified at the moment of the creation of his humanity by the Spirit. '... the central thesis of our theology of grace, viz. that the Father anointed the man Jesus with the Holy Spirit in an act which at the same time created him, sanctified him and united him in person to the divine Son, is found in seminal form in Scripture.' Coffey, *Grace, the Gift of the Holy Spirit*, p. 130.

20 Coffey, *Deus Trinitas*, p. 37; Italics mine. Coffey's view is also presented in *Grace: The Gift of the Holy Spirit*, e.g., p. 109. Del Colle, *Christ and the Spirit*, p. 124, summarises his view, 'In his own right, Christ is personally holy because he fully possessed the Holy Spirit, and it is this same Spirit sent by him that is the grace of Christians.'

'incarnation' of the Holy Spirit, though the meaning of word here is only analogous to that which it bears in the Incarnation properly so called. The matter might be accurately and succinctly expressed thus: in a way analogous to the Incarnation of divine being in human being in the person of Jesus, there is an incarnation of divine love in human love in the love of Jesus, this latter incarnation being the Holy Spirit.[21]

Although the author agrees with Coffey on the important role of the Spirit in the Son's incarnational life, he does not wish to attribute Jesus' perfect humanity *wholly* to the Spirit. For all the benefits of imparting the communing presence and knowledge of the Father which inclines Jesus towards obedience, the Spirit cannot replace the will of Jesus Christ. Even as he breathes the air of his Father's presence through the Spirit, the possibility and indeed temptation to disobey his Father is still open to him as a genuine human being. He still has to make a conscious decision to choose to keep in step with his Father's will and spirit and so return his filial love and presence to his Father. This is how his perfect humanity is effected - in the communing presence of his Father through the Spirit he deliberately wills to do his Father's will. It should also be noted that his perfect humanity does not exhaust his divinity, as Coffey also points out.[22] *Very importantly, Jesus' inherent and insuperable authority to teach and to exercise the power of the Spirit is not something the Spirit can functionally impart to him nor something intrinsic to humanity. He himself has to be the Lord, even in his true humanity, in order to freely exercise his Lordship in authoritative words and in mighty acts so that he on earth can truly reveal his Father in heaven.* The author sympathises with Coffey's aim to see Jesus' divinity as actualisation under the grace of the Spirit but he wishes to point out that the role of the Spirit as conveying the Father's communing presence to Jesus must be augmented by Jesus' willing obedience to his Father.[23] Any present or future exploration of such actualisation has to take this crucial aspect into consideration, or else a functioning Spirit

---

21 Coffey, *Deus Trinitas*, p. 39. See also his 'The "Incarnation" of the Holy Spirit in Christ'.

22 Coffey, 'The "Incarnation" of the Holy Spirit in Christ', p. 468.

23 Instead of seeing Jesus' divinity as *actualisation* under the grace of the Spirit, the author prefers to speak of the *expression* of Jesus' divinity in his humanity through obedience to the Father who grants his presence to him by the Holy Spirit. Actualisation may give the wrong connotation that Jesus' divinity is dependent on some actions or events empowered by the Spirit (cf. Dunn, 'As the Spirit was the "divinity" of Jesus, so Jesus became the personality of the Spirit.' *Jesus and the Spirit*, p. 325). But 'expression of Jesus' divinity in his humanity' presupposes his inherent divinity which is not the result of some actions or events.

Christology will unnecessarily eclipse a non-functioning Logos Christology. Note also Coffey does not explain how this 'incarnation of divine love in human love in the love of Jesus' is possible except by invoking the Spirit. The preceding discussion provides a possible solution through the notion of conformity in spirit through the Spirit.

3.0 The Kenotic Christology of G. Thomasius

The ideas presented above seek to understand Jesus Christ in his indivisible unity, which are often violated by the notion of dual consciousness or the two wills of Christ. This emphasis on the unity of Christ echoes the concern of Lutheran (and Alexandrian) Christology. With the concept of *communicatio idiomatum* (communication of attributes), Lutheran Christology understands that the human nature of Jesus Christ was capable of receiving or being permeated by the divine nature.[24] Luther himself 'taught the real interpenetration of the two natures and loved the figure of the glowing iron.'[25] But the problem of how divine attributes (or nature) can be communicated to humanity, without violation or annulment of the latter, was not resolved by him. However, he did attempt to address the problem by noting the difference between 'form of God' and 'divine essence', the former corresponding to the state of exaltation with unrestrained manifestation of God's divine glory, the latter being a hidden internal reality which may or may not be expressed; Jesus Christ in his earthly life possessed this divine essence which remained active but was veiled in the form of a servant.[26] The question of the extent to which the divine attributes were manifested in Jesus' earthly life was debated amongst Lutheran theologians in the seventeenth and eighteenth centuries, namely

---

24 'The communion of nature is that most intimate participation and combination of the divine nature of the λόγος and of the assumed human nature, by which the λόγος, through a most intimate and profound perichoresis, so permeates, perfects, inhabits, and appropriates to Himself the human nature that is personally united to Him, that from both, mutually inter-communicating, there arises the one incommunicable subject, viz., one person.' Heinrich Schmid, *The Doctrinal Theology of the Evangelical Lutheran Church* (Minneapolis: Augsburg Publishing House, 1961), H.A. Charles and J.E. Henry (tr.), p. 310. The communion is understood as an active movement from the divine nature to the human nature and the relationship between the two is compared to that between fire and a red-hot iron.

25 W. Pannenberg, *Jesus - God and Man* (London: SCM Press, 2002), p. 338. See also Martin Luther, *Werke: Kritische Gesamtausgabe* (Weimar: Herman Böhlau & Nachfolger, 1883 ff.), vol. 7, p. 53; vol. 6, p. 510.

26 Donald Dawe, *The Form of a Servant* (Philadephia: The Westminster Press, 1963), p. 69-70. See also Luther, *Werke*, vol. 17, pp. 238-9.

between the Tübingen and Giessen schools.[27] While these theologians believed that the God-man Jesus Christ possessed divine attributes (whether he used them or not is a separate question), a nineteenth century Lutheran theologian, Gottfried Thomasius (1802-1875), proposed that Jesus Christ actually divested himself of some of the divine attributes.[28]

Following the idea of Martin Chemnitz (1522-1586) who separated divine attributes into the quiescent and operative attributes of God,[29] Thomasius identified the so-called *immanent* and *relative* attributes of God. The *relative* attributes are omnipotence, omniscience and omnipresence. The relative attributes concern God's relations to the world he has created. Thomasius argued that because God had no need to involve himself in relating to the world before it was created, these relative attributes are not essential to God himself. What are essential to God are his *immanent* attributes - his absolute power (understood as absolute power to determine one's will without failure), truth, holiness and love.[30] The meanings of these attributes become even more apparent in a trinitarian understanding of God.[31] According to Thomasius, in the incarnation the Son of God divested himself of the relative attributes but retained the immanent attributes. Because the relative attributes are not essential to God, he argued that the Son had not lost his divine essence in the incarnation. In contrast with the theologians of Tübingen and Giessen, he stressed that Jesus Christ did not possess, let alone use, the divine attributes of omnipotence,

---

27 For summaries of their debates, see Pannenberg, Jesus - God and Man, pp. 349-52; Dawe, *The Form of a Servant*, pp. 73-8; Barth, *CD* IV.1, pp. 180-183. For a more detailed summary, see Schmid, *The Doctrinal Theology of the Evangelical Lutheran Church*, pp. 388-93.

28 The Tübingen and Giessen theologians both believed that the human nature of Christ possessed the divine attributes (because the human nature was so permeated or 'heated' by the divine nature). While the former believed that Jesus Christ according to his *human* nature actually made use of the divine attributes though under concealment, the latter believed that they were not used, only possessed. However, the latter also believed that according to Christ's *divine* nature, the divine attributes were used - there is a disjunction in Christ's person, that between his divine and human nature. Thomasius resolved this disjunction by the notion of the Logos' self-emptying (kenosis) of some of the divine attributes in truly becoming man, see below.

29 Dawe, *The Form of a Servant*, p. 76.

30 Thomasius' work on kenotic Christology was translated and can be found in *God and Incarnation in Mid-Nineteenth Century German Theology* (New York: Oxford University Press, 1965), Claude Welch (ed., tr.), pp. 25-101. For his treatment on attributes, see pp. 67-9.

31 *Ibid.*, p. 69.

omniscience and omnipresence.

> We say thus that in his life in the flesh the mediator neither used nor possessed the divine omnipotence that is the form of appearance and activation of absolute power in the world; he did not actively rule the world at the same time he walked on earth as man, suffered and died; he exercised no other lordship at all than the ethical one of truth and love, just as he also resorted to no other means than the word of the gospel for the establishment of his kingdom, his whole exercise of power was absorbed in his world-redeeming activity. And it was not as if he were perhaps in a hidden way actively ruling over and through the universe besides; he used the absolute power which dwelt in him only for his meditorial vocation.[32]

> Accordingly, the humiliation is for us not a mere disguise, but an actual kenosis of the designated divine attributes, and surely not merely of their use but of their possession - a distinction which is after all not even applicable here.[33]

In keeping with Lutheran Christology, Thomasius held that human nature is capable of expressing the divine. He appealed to God's creation of humanity in his image for this capability.[34] Of course, this capability only extends as far as God's immanent attributes of power, truth, holiness and love. These immanent attributes were expressed in a truly human consciousness. 'His divine consciousness *became* a human one, in order to develop as human consciousness of his divine essence and his divine glory.'[35] Thomasius denied the co-existence of a divine consciousness and a human consciousness in Jesus Christ because this destroys the unity of the person.[36] The divine consciousness and divine will had become the truly human consciousness and will.

> [T]he human nature is wholly taken up in the divine and completely

---

32 *Ibid.*, p. 70. For the divesting of omniscience and omnipresence, see pp. 70-1.

33 *Ibid.*, p. 71.

34 'The general possibility of such an intimate union of God with humanity in the person of Christ rests on the relation of the two that was established by the creation. ... Thus when the Son enters into humanity he does not betake himself into a sphere inadequate for him but transposes himself into (or appropriates to himself) a nature which he created in his image for the purpose of his self-revelation, and from which he had never wholly withdrawn, even in its deepest corruption.' *Ibid.*, p. 40. See also pp. 41-4.

35 *Ibid.*, p. 48. Italics mine.

36 *Ibid.*, p. 46-7.

penetrated by it. It has neither a distinct human consciousness by itself, nor a distinct human movement of the will by itself in distinction from that of the Logos, just as the latter has nothing that was not directly proper to the assumed humanity; what belongs to the Logos is carried forward in the human thought, will and ability. ... This is one unitary movement, experience and development of life because it is one ego, one divine-human personality (*unio, communio, communication naturarum* [union, participation, impartation of natures]).[37]

Both the Tübingen and Giessen theologians believed the side by side co-existence of Christ's divine and human nature, with the latter permeated by the former as iron is heated by fire (though the Giessen theologians believed that Christ in his *human* nature did not exercise the divine attributes). But Thomasius contended that such side by side co-existence did not exist, the Logos entered into humanity and became the God-man Jesus Christ by way of self-emptying - kenosis - of the relative attributes. If Luther's metaphor for the penetration of the divine into the human is a red-hot iron heated by fire, then an appropriate imagery for Thomasius' kenotic Christology is that of fire actually entering the iron, with certain attributes of the fire being 'extinguished'. Some may say the iron with fire within is not as hot as it should be because of the partial extinguishment. Does not the relinquishment of the relative attributes of omnipotence, omniscience and omnipresence amount to a de-deification and a change in the divine Logos? Criticisms were mounted against Thomasius' kenotic Christology, especially by D.A. Dorner.[38] It seems that Thomasius conceded too much with regard to the Logos' divine attributes as he sought to find a genuine human life in Jesus Christ.

Thomasius' effort to find a satisfactory union of the divine and human in Jesus Christ was based on the concern for the efficaciousness of our justification and reconciliation with God through Jesus Christ - what is not assumed (humanity) is not healed and only the holy God is in a position to reconcile sinful humanity (cf. 3.2 of chapter 2).[39] The reality of Jesus Christ as a genuine human being in communion with God also confirms and fully establishes the possibility of our communion with God through Jesus Christ.[40] The aim of Thomasius is laudable even though the weakness in his attempted solution is exposed

---

37 *Ibid.*, p. 58-9.

38 See Pannenberg, *Jesus - God and Man*, pp. 353-5.

39 Welch, *God and Incarnation in Mid-Nineteenth Century German Theology*, pp. 35-6.

40 Thomasius' attempt was also in line with the concern in the nineteenth century to see Jesus Christ as a truly historical human figure.

to criticisms.

His treatment of God's immanent attributes of absolute power (to determine one's will), truth, holiness and love is very much related to the discussion on conformity in spirit through the Spirit in section 2.0 above. He proposed that these attributes can be received and expressed in a genuine human life, as 2.0 concurs. He also identified the possibility of this reception and expression in the creation of man in God's image. These ideas are useful but they need further development. The discussion in 2.0 in effect develops these ideas although it arose from a different theological basis and focus - the Trinity. Section 2.0 uses the category of spirit and the conceptual tool of 'conformity in spirit' to give greater precision to our understanding of the reception and expression of divinity, and this category and tool originated from a fully trinitarian discussion on the concept of Jesus' conformity to and revelation of his Father through the Spirit, which was not the basis of Thomasius' Christology. Thomasius did mention the role of the spirit in the incarnation but only as an analogy. Welch paraphrases Thomasius' suggestion concerning the analogy between the spirit in humans and the Logos in Jesus Christ,

> [A]s in every man the divine *pneuma* [spirit] forms the basis of Adamic personality ..., in Christ it is the Logos himself, albeit by a self-limitation, who constitutes this basis and is the kernel of the whole divine-human development.[41]

Thomasius was charged with Apollinarianism because of a lack of clarity concerning the existence of a genuine human spirit in Jesus Christ - the place of the human spirit in Jesus seemed to be taken over by the Logos. He later tried to avoid this criticism by stating that the Logos assumed an explicitly human substrate, a human soul.[42] But how was the distance between the divine Logos and human soul to be bridged in the assumption or becoming? Thomasius gave no further answer to this question apart from the possibility availed by creation. The category of spirit is most congenial for linking the divine and the human because of its dynamic and fluid nature (spirit can remain true to itself while taking different forms, divine or human). Had he given more consideration to the use of the category of spirit as a factor of continuity between the divine and human in his Christology, his idea of the Logos assuming a human soul could have been developed into a more satisfactory form and the charge of Apollinarianism would have been avoided or defended more successfully.

---

41 *Ibid.*, p. 45.
42 *Ibid.*

The other defect in his Christology is his misconstrual of Jesus' relationship with the Spirit, which cost him a clearer vision of the divinity of Jesus Christ. In his own way he could see how Jesus related to the Spirit in his humanity. Apart from some inaccuracy in his understanding, the author is sympathetic to his view.[43] When it comes to Jesus' relationship to the Spirit in his true divinity, his misunderstanding is more apparent when he wrote,

> [The miracles] belong to the work of vocation, for which his humanity is anointed with the Holy Spirit.[44]

> He [the Spirit] is now not yet the Spirit of Jesus Christ in the same sense as he is from the resurrection onward, i.e. the incarnate one is now not yet proportioned to this Spirit as the principle determining his activity ...[45]

Chapters 5 and 6 argue at length that Jesus' free exercise of his authority to heal and exorcise in the power of the Spirit relates to his divinity, not his humanity, and even in his earthly life he was already Lord of the Spirit. In seeking to affirm the humanity of Jesus Christ, Thomasius, as other Spirit Christologists (such as Irving and Dunn), neglected this crucial divine aspect of Jesus' relationship with the Spirit. Had Thomasius correctly construed Jesus' relationship with the Spirit, he would not have unnecessarily asserted that the Logos divested himself of his divine relative attributes, which is the chief weakness of his kenotic Christology. The following section aims to establish the fact that the Son of God in truly becoming man needs not divest himself of the divine relative attributes and so retains his genuine divinity while living a truly human life.[46]

---

43 '[T]he Holy Spirit first governs formatively in the depth of his natural and personal life and then imparts himself to him in peculiar fullness for his vocation; the Spirit shows him the temporal moments of the divine will of salvation and mediates to his human nature the ability to carry out that will.' *Ibid.*, p. 66. The author concurs that the Spirit conveys the will of the Father (and the Father's communing presence) to Jesus (see 5.0 of chapter 3) but insists that, for all the benefits the Spirit brings to the humanity of Jesus, these in themselves do not constitute obedience. Jesus Christ in his own will has to choose and determine himself to do his Father's will. This self-determination and decision the Spirit cannot do for him. It is not quite accurate to say that the Spirit mediates to his human nature the *ability* to carry out his Father's will. Jesus' obedience is more intricate than this simplistic picture (see 2.1.3.2 of chapter 6 and the end of 2.0 in this chapter).

44 *Ibid.*, p. 70.

45 *Ibid.*, p. 66.

46 For a well written presentation of kenotic Christology, see Mackintosh, *The Doctrine of the Person of Jesus Christ*, pp. 463-86.

4.0 How Can the Genuinely Human Jesus Exercise Divine Sovereign Power?

The divine relative attributes concern God's sovereign rule of his creation. In his sovereign rule of the world, God exercises his omnipotence, omniscience and omnipresence. In faith, one can readily accept that God exercises his sovereign power to rule the world from his throne in heaven. But when the divine Logos has *become* flesh (John 1:14), how does he exercise this sovereign power while he lives on earth as a genuine human being? The question regarding the Logos' retaining his immanent attributes of absolute power (to determine his will), truth, holiness and love in a truly human life has been addressed in sections 2.0 and 3.0. But the question of the Logos retaining the divine relative attributes in that life presents a formidable challenge. How can a genuinely human Jesus exercise divine sovereign power?

The notion that the genuinely human Jesus exercises divine sovereign power can be found in numerous passages in the gospel narratives, e.g., passages on his healings including healings from a distance (e.g., Mt. 8:5-13, see 1.2 of chapter 4), exorcisms, his miracles in nature (e.g., rebuking and thereby calming storm and waves at Galilee), raising people from the dead (e.g. Lazarus) and supernatural knowledge (e.g., Jesus speaking to the Samaritan woman in John 4:16-18). These miraculous acts manifest Jesus' *capacity* to act sovereignly, with supernatural knowledge and from a distance if necessary. The question one is raising regarding Jesus' exercising sovereign power is not a question of possibility - for Scripture teaches that it is possible - but a question of 'how'.[47] The answer to the question of how, readily given by the gospel narratives, is that Jesus performs these mighty acts by the power of the Holy Spirit. But one may object that the fact that Jesus performs these mighty acts in the power of the Spirit does not necessarily mean that he is sovereign and divine in these acts. After all, Jesus' disciples also perform miraculous acts by the power of the Holy Spirit (see the Book of Acts and the disciples' mini missions in Mt. 10 and Lk. 10). Certainly, Jesus' disciples are not sovereign nor divine. But it has been established in chapter 5 that the gospels, especially Luke, distinguish sharply Jesus' relationship with the Spirit from his disciples' relationship with the Spirit. Jesus is already Lord of the Spirit in his earthly ministry. Schweizer wrote,

> Luke, then, avoids the idea that the Spirit stands over Jesus. The OT view
> of the power of God coming upon men does not satisfy him. Jesus

---

47 The question regarding 'how often' Jesus exercises sovereign power will be
addressed later.

becomes the *subject* of an action in the Holy Spirit. He is not a pneumatic, but the *Lord of the πνεῦμα.*[48]

Because Jesus is Lord of the Spirit, he has the capacity to exercise freely the power of the Spirit as the sovereign Lord. He can act sovereignly in that power in his immediate locality or even from a distance. But does he exercise his sovereign power to rule in every place and corner of the world during his earthly life?[49] Scripture teaches that the Son of God does take on this sovereign rule of the world after he has ascended to the right hand of the Father (see, e.g., Eph. 1:20-22; Phil. 2:9-11) but it gives no hint of this continuous all-governing function of Jesus Christ while he was on earth. In the gospel narratives, Jesus Christ is not presented as having another consciousness, apart from his human one, in which he rules the world.[50] They only witness to the intermittent use of his sovereign power, e.g., in healings and exorcisms. One has to conclude that even though Jesus Christ, the Son of God and Lord of the Spirit, could have chosen to exercise his sovereign power through the Spirit much more than he did, in fact he did not choose to do so because that was not his Father's will for him while he was on earth. The Father's own good pleasure was that he would rule the world as the universal Lord only after his resurrection and exaltation (Phil. 2:9-11).[51]

In view of the above discussion, one is justified in saying that Jesus Christ had divine authority to exercise sovereign power and he exercised this power only when it was his Father's will for him to do so. This reminds us of Luther's notion of 'divine essence' which the Son of God, in the form of a servant, possessed as a hidden internal reality which may or may not be expressed. In terms of possession of divine relative attributes, one can say that Jesus Christ did possess the *capacity*

---

48 *Theological Dictionary of the New Testament*, vol. VI, pp. 404-5. Italics mine.

49 See Barth's discussion on this, the issue of *Extra Calvinisticum* in *CD* IV.1, pp. 180-2. Calvin affirmed this universal rule by the Son of God while he was on earth, see *Institutes of the Christian Religion*, Book II, Chapter XIII, 4.

50 Thomasius also denied this. See, Welch, *God and Incarnation in Mid-Nineteenth Century German Theology*, pp. 46f.

51 The first part of the Christ hymn, Phil. 2:6-8, which concerns the Son's earthly life, gives no indication of his universal reign, while the second part of the hymn, Phil. 2:9-11, explicitly affirms this reign. Because of this sharp contrast, it is reasonable to suggest that the self-humbling, or self-emptying (kenosis), in the first part refers to the relinquishment of universal reign which was enjoyed by the Son before the self-emptying and fully recovered after his resurrection and exaltation. But this does not mean that during the Son's earthly life he completely abstained from any use of his sovereign authority as Lord. He used it whenever it pleased the Father, albeit intermittently.

and *authority* to exercise these attributes through the power of the Holy Spirit even though this capacity was exercised only as far as it was appropriate for the purpose of his Father's kingdom. It is in this sense that he possessed the relative attributes and ascribing this sense of possession to him is entirely Scriptural. We must not allow any preconceived ideas of possession and exercise of relative attributes (such as those belonging to the Tübingen theologians) to be imposed on Jesus Christ.[52] To do so will only bring insoluble difficulties to one's mind.

Even if one accepts the above sense of Jesus' possession of relative attributes, the question still remains: how could a man (Jesus Christ) possess and invoke this divine authority/capacity to freely exercise sovereign power through the Spirit whenever he saw fit, i.e., whenever it pleased the Father? Other men, such as his disciples, certainly could not and did not possess, nor invoke, this divine authority. Is it not true that 'a person who possesses and invokes divine authority must be in a divine mode of existence, i.e., in a glorified and exalted state'? The answer from the gospels is that this statement is *not* true because Jesus Christ was not in a glorified mode of existence and he possessed and invoked his divine authority. That brings us to the interesting and very important relationship between possession of authority, mode of existence and the person involved. This relationship will illuminate the question of how the *person* of Jesus is at once human in terms of his *mode of existence* and divine in terms of his *authority*.

4.1 Authority, Mode of Existence and Person

It can be clearly seen from reason that individuals of the same mode of existence can have differing authorities, or, differing authorities can correspond to the same mode of existence. Three examples will be used to illustrate this. Firstly, within the same mode of human existence, one person can be a Professor and has authority appropriate to the professorship while others may have less authority or other kinds of authority. Secondly, when a person is newly elected as the Prime Minister of the United Kingdom and freshly receives the authority appropriate to the Prime Minister, he does not need to change his mode of human existence to another kind of existence (e.g., more exalted state such as that of an angel) in order to hold that authority; the same mode of human existence can support differing levels of authority. Thirdly,

---

52 The Tübingen theologians believed that the Son of God maintained omnipotence, omniscience and omnipresence throughout his earthly life but this was done under concealment. Scripture gives no support to this view which greatly undermines the humanity of Jesus Christ.

when Jesus' disciples received authority from him to heal and exorcise in his name, there was no need for them to change their mode of human existence. Scripture teaches that *how much authority a human person has is ultimately decided by God* (see, e.g., John 19:11[53]) and potentially the limit can be very high. And if the Son of God should decide, in harmony with the will of the Father, that when he exists in human form he is to retain his sovereign authority over the Spirit as his Father has sovereign authority over the Spirit (*filioque*), his decision will be effective. And when he with that authority exercises the power of the Spirit in healings and exorcisms, he is not exercising the power of the human mode of existence that he is in but the divine power of the Spirit who is the agent or executive power of his action. Likewise, when the Prime Minister exercises his authority to send military personnel to war, he does not exercise his bodily power in combat but his action will be realised by the power of his agents, the military personnel over whom he has authority (but this analogy has its own limitation for Jesus' experience of the power of the Spirit is much more intimate than the Prime Minister's experience of the combating action of his military personnel, see 5.0 below).

From the above discussion, we see that authority is not tied to mode of existence - (i) authority can vary within the same mode of human existence and (ii) the Son of God with his undiminished authority can be in different modes of existence, including the human mode. It is in God's own good pleasure that (i) and (ii) are true. Instead of tying authority to mode of existence, one should tie authority to *person*. That is because God is pleased to give a certain authority to a person. This is true in human society and this is true in the case of the person of the Son of God. The *divine* authority of the Son of God over the Spirit is tied to the *divine* personal subject of the Son of God, not to his mode of existence. And when this personal subject is in the human mode of existence, the personal subject retains this authority which is tied to him. He has not lost his authority over the Spirit; he has remained true to himself with regard to this divine authority despite his change into the human form.[54] His human mode of existence is compatible with the divine authority he holds - *his possession of authority needs not and does not violate his human mode of existence*, it is not necessary to modify his human mode of existence into some 'higher' mode in order for his authority to be preserved. He continues to enjoy authority over

---

53 Jesus said to Pilate, 'You would have no power [ἐξουσίαν/authority] over me if it were not given to you from above.'

54 This treatment of the relative attributes reflects our treatment of the immanent attributes of the Son of God - the Son remains true to himself with regard to his spirit despite the change in form.

the Spirit on earth as his Father does in heaven (*filioque*). The question raised above - how the *person* of Jesus is at once *human* in terms of his *mode of existence* and *divine* in terms of his *authority* - is answered. We can therefore affirm with Scripture that Jesus is at once truly human and genuinely divine.

The argument for Jesus' enjoying personal divine authority with respect to the Spirit can be repeated for his personal divine authority in uttering forgiveness of sins and in teaching the new law in the Sermon on the Mount (which required divine authority because he changed part of the Old Testament, e.g., abrogating provisions for oath and divorce, see 3.3 of chapter 3). He exercises his own *personal* divine authority in these utterances and speeches, without even invoking the name of the Father or the name of the Spirit, when he exists in a truly human form. Again, these authorities of his are tied to his *person*, not to a mode of his existence. And such authorities manifested in his utterances and speeches have an interesting relationship with his authority over the Spirit. The former cannot be verified by the listeners and that is why some people question the validity and appropriateness of Jesus' utterance of forgiveness of sins to the paralytic (Mark 2:6-7). However, the latter is verifiable as, for example, his commands in healings and exorcisms are indeed followed by visible changes to those who are suffering. And Jesus sometimes uses the latter authority with respect to the Spirit to confirm that he indeed has the former less 'visible' authorities. He therefore heals the paralytic (implicitly by the power of the Spirit, Mark 2:9-12) to confirm the former utterance concerning his authority to forgive his sins.

With the above clarification and affirmation of Jesus' possession of his divine authority, we can revisit his intermittent use of his authority without the risk of diluting his divinity. Jesus' divine freedom and authority to exercise the power of the Spirit is not used in a wanton manner; he uses it in the strictest consonance with and obedience to his Father. If it pleases the Father that he should not exercise the authority of the Spirit to sustain and rule the world in his earthly life and he should entrust this responsibility to his Father who does so in the power of the Holy Spirit from heaven, he will obediently comply with his Father's will and his divinity is not diminished. But if in consonance with his Father he has compassion for the sick and demonised and chooses to freely exercise his divine authority to heal or exorcise a demon from a tormented person in the power of the Spirit, his divinity is revealed in this divine action. If it is his Father's will that he should abstain from exercising the power of the Spirit for his own sake, e.g., not turning stone into bread in the wilderness or not retaliating against those who insult and hurt him in his trials by the authorities, he will obediently comply and his divinity is not diminished. We can understand Jesus' intermittent exercise of his divine authority from the perspective of his obedience to and consonance with his Father. Whether he exercises it or not, he does it to his Father's will for he is the truly obedient Son.

5.0 The Mystery of Incarnation

One would be very presumptuous if one considers one has solved the mystery of the incarnation by treating God's relative and immanent attributes in the ways that have been proposed above. The incarnation is still a mystery. But we have to locate where the mystery is and compare this mystery with the mystery supposed by traditional or Chalcedonian Christology. This requires a closer consideration of the process of incarnation, including Jesus' conception by the Holy Spirit.

The mystery supposed by traditional or Chalcedonian Christology is how divine nature and human nature co-exist together in the one person of Jesus Christ, which is the mystery of the hypostatic union. According to Pannenberg, there are insurmountable problems arising from this supposed mystery. He writes,

> The impasse reached by every attempt to construct Christology by beginning with the incarnational concept demonstrates that all such attempts are doomed to failure. We found repeatedly that either the unity of Jesus Christ as person or else his real humanity or true divinity were lost in view.[55]

Pannenberg's pessimistic view is not unjustified but progress is possible as proposed in the discussion above. If we do not begin with the traditional concept of incarnation which majors on the language of substance/essence and only focuses on the second person of the Trinity, if we begin with a fresh concept employing Scriptural terms and ideas, taking the biblical narratives seriously and looking intently at the three persons of the Trinity as presented in the gospel narratives, we may make more positive ground, or break new ground, in our understanding of the God-man Jesus Christ. We will not solve the mystery of the incarnation but we will locate the mystery in a more appropriate form. The is the aim of this section.

The proposal presented above does not begin with the question of the co-existence of divine and human nature in the person of Jesus Christ (and the often attendant intractable problem of reconciling the dual consciousness, two wills or two minds of Christ); it begins with the

---

55 Pannenberg, *Jesus - God and Man*, p. 367.

more fundamental question of how the divine attributes of the Son of God can be retained as the divine personal subject of the Son of God passes from one mode of existence to another, i.e., from a glorified/exalted mode in eternity/heaven to a human mode of existence on earth in time. The question of the simultaneous existence of two natures in one person in time (or in a certain period of time) is answered only after the more fundamental question of *becoming* is addressed, viz, *the passage of the person of the Son of God from eternity/heaven into time/creation such that his divine attributes are preserved.* The proposed solution is crucially based on the notion of *person*, in particular, (i) the spirit of the *person* and (ii) the *personal* authority of the *person*.

With regard to (i), we maintain that the spirit of the *person* of the Son of God (pertaining to the immanent attributes of power for self-determination, love, holiness and truth) can be retained without loss as he moves from the glorified mode of existence into an earthly mode of existence as true man. We substantiate this by using the concept of 'conformity in spirit' through the Spirit and appeal to Jesus' faithful correspondence to the spirit of his Father as he efficaciously reveals his Father on earth concerning these attributes. As the Son of God moves from the glorified mode to the earthly mode, his conformity to the Father in spirit has been maintained and therefore his immanent attributes have been retained despite a change in form.

With regard to (ii), the personal authority of the person of the Son of God, we have shown that authority is tied to the person, not to a mode of existence. Therefore, as the personal subject of the Son of God moves from the glorified mode to the earthly mode, there is no loss of *personal* authority and his relative attributes have been retained, even though the manifestation of his authority and divine relative attributes is in the strictest consonance with the Father's will because the Son loves the Father and obeys him in all he does. By treating the immanent and relative attributes as *personal* attributes which are both tied to the personal subject - the personal subject being the ultimate factor of continuity in the passage from one form to another, we have addressed the question of the passage of the *person* of the Son of God from eternity/heaven into time/creation such that his divine attributes (both immanent and relative) are preserved. But where is the mystery?

The mystery lies both in (i) and (ii) and will be treated in that order. In the transition from the glorified mode to the earthly mode of existence, we do not know how the divine spirit of the Son of God is preserved in the incarnation, especially at Jesus' conception and in his very early childhood. The Spirit provides some answer which nevertheless cannot be complete. Scripture teaches that it is the Spirit who effected Jesus' conception and we have reason to suggest that part of the process of conception involved conforming the divine spirit of the Son of God into the spirit of Jesus Christ by the power of the Holy Spirit, i.e., the divine spirit of the Son of God becomes the human spirit of Jesus Christ through the conforming power of the Holy Spirit without loss in essentiality. It is the Spirit who conforms the divine spirit such that there is no loss in essence in the form of the human spirit. This suggestion concerning the role of the Spirit in the incarnation is a reasonable one because the Spirit is the most congenial agent to work with and conform the spirit of a person. But the mystery is that we do not know how the Spirit conforms spirit without loss. Evidently, the fact that humanity is designed and created as the image of God has much to do with this mystery. It is proper to propose that God has so *designed* the image of God in humanity that his Son at a suitable point in time can conform himself through the Spirit into that image. But all in all, how the Spirit conforms the divine Son of God into the human Jesus in the spirit (including the will as an important element of spirit in a person) is a mystery to us, especially at the point of Jesus' conception and immediately afterward.[56] But we can maintain that the conformity is a success because just as the divine Son of God in eternity has always conformed his spirit to his Father's spirit through obedience, the human spirit of Jesus on earth has also conformed to the spirit of his Father in heaven through obedience (which comes from his genuinely human will). And so, the spirit of the Father (A), the spirit of the divine Son of God in eternity (B) and the spirit of Jesus Christ on earth (C) are all conformable to one another. The mystery is: how is the conformity between the latter two (B and C) effected by the Spirit? But the magnitude of this mystery is somewhat reduced as we look to the 'visible' example of the human Jesus conforming himself to his Father in spirit (A and B) through their communion in the Holy Spirit.

Another aspect of the mystery of incarnation lies in Jesus' experience of the power of the Spirit. We have maintained that Jesus Christ the Son of God retained his authority to exercise the power of the Spirit but how he experienced the Spirit as Lord is something we cannot experience or fathom. In 4.1, an analogy was used to aid our understanding between Jesus' authority and the Spirit's power, viz, the Prime Minister exercises his *authority* to send military personnel who exert their military *power* in the war that the Prime Minister commands them to engage in. But this analogy has a severe shortcoming, i.e., for all the concerns that the Prime Minister may have for the military personnel, he does not actually have a *personal* taste of what that exertion of power and all the attendant struggles and casualties involve. The

---

56 There is an interesting parallel with the Big Bang theory for the origin of the universe.

exertion of power in combat is somewhat remote from the person of the Prime Minister; he certainly does not experience that power as his own power. This is the crucial difference between this analogy and Jesus' exercise of the power of the Spirit. Because Jesus Christ has such an intimate personal relationship with the Spirit which began from the earliest point of his earthly existence and continues throughout his life, he experiences the power of the Spirit not as something extrinsic to him, but intrinsic in him. He breathes and lives in the lasting air of the Spirit. His every movement is a movement in the Spirit; the power of the Spirit is not something alien to him; he personally experiences the power of the Spirit virtually as his own (and the power of the Father in him). This is the mystery of the Trinity and the mystery of the incarnation.

The mystery of the incarnation is a thoroughly *spiritual* one in that this mystery lies in the concept of conformity in *spirit* through the *Spirit* and in Jesus' unique relationship with and experience of the *Spirit*.

6.0 Beyond Chalcedon: Refined Christology with a Paradigmatic Shift

We have based our thoughts on Christology by (i) shifting its focus away from (though not abandoning) the traditional language and concepts of substance and hypostatic union of two substances, (ii) looking more intently at Jesus' relationships with his Father and the Spirit and (iii) employing gospel/biblical narratives to *ground* our understanding of Jesus Christ. We have found the notion of *spirit* as being more dynamic, fluid and 'living' than the notion of substance so that it is more congenial for linking divinity (immanent attributes) and humanity in the passage from one to the other without loss, i.e., the two are conformable in spirit to one another. We have also found the notion of person as being crucial in understanding how *spirit* and *authority* are tied to the *person* of the Son of God as he undergoes change in form but without loss in his *spirit* and *authority*. The notions of spirit, authority and person help us to conceive the incarnation as a transition from eternity into time, from one mode of existence into another such that the divinity of Jesus Christ is upheld and his humanity is genuinely acknowledged. By seeing the incarnation as a transition or passage, one no longer has to contend with the age old, rather intractable and unreasonable problem of reconciling the two wills (two spirits, two minds or dual consciousness corresponding to the two natures) of Christ which exist side by side simultaneously in time, and the irreconcilable problem of being at once limited in space/time and transcending it.[57]

---

57 Mackintosh, *The Doctrine of the Person of Jesus Christ*, p. 470, 'We cannot predicate of Him two consciousnesses or two wills; the New Testament indicates

And by looking more concretely at Jesus' obedience to his *Father*, we can understand that Jesus' genuine human will is orientated to his Father's divine will, rather than the divine and separate will of the Logos.[58] And by paying due attention to the roles played by the *Holy Spirit* in (i) Jesus' conception, (ii) Jesus' communion with his Father and the consequent conforming of Jesus' human will to his Father's will through obedience, (iii) Jesus' relationship with the Spirit and his manifestation of his relative attributes in mighty acts, the Holy Spirit is emphasised and this emphasis is a helpful and necessary remedy to much of Western theological tradition. All in all, a truly trinitarian approach to Christology, incorporating all three persons of the Trinity, is the most promising venue for progress and it is unfortunate that in the history of the study of Christology this approach has been far from prominent.[59]

We have found unsatisfactory the kenotic approach of Thomasius, and the approaches of the Tübingen and Giessen theologians. One of the gravest mistakes in Thomasius' approach was his neglecting the role of the Spirit in Jesus' life and work so that he could not see how Jesus can manifest his divine relative attributes as a genuine human person. A trinitarian approach to Christology would have prevented him from his error of diluting the divinity of Jesus Christ. Also, he did not use the category of 'spirit' for conceiving the communication of divine immanent attributes to the humanity of Jesus Christ. This is also true of modern theologians such as David Coffey (or Rahner). We have proposed that the concept of 'conformity in spirit' through the Spirit, despite ultimately being a mystery in itself, provides some kind of handle in conceiving this communication and locates more accurately where the mystery of incarnation lies.

With regard to the approaches of the Tübingen and Giessen theologians, their belief that the divine attributes, including omnipotence, omniscience and omnipresence, are communicated to Jesus' human nature is a problematic one.[60] The whole idea of the communication of omnipotence, omniscience and omnipresence (later called relative attributes by Thomasius) to Jesus' human nature is a

---

nothing of the kind; nor indeed is it congruous with an intelligible psychology. The unity of His personal life is axiomatic.'

58 See Pannenberg, *Jesus - God and Man*, p. 335, for the complaint of neglecting the will of the Father.

59 Often in non-trinitarian approaches to Christology, the divinity of the Logos is unnecessarily called for to do the work of the Father and the Spirit, which raises many difficult problems.

60 Whether Jesus Christ in his human nature exercises these attributes is a separate question for contention between the two schools.

wrong turn into a blind alley, even though the communication of immanent attributes to the humanity of Jesus is a valid one. Human nature is not capable of receiving these supra-human relative attributes; it is beyond the image of God to exercise divine relative attributes. The only way one can conceive Jesus Christ exercising these attributes is via the crucial notion of divine authority which he can *personally* possess without violating his human mode of existence.

In stressing the role of the Spirit in Christology and trinitarian theology, we have not fallen into the pitfalls where some Spirit Christologists have landed. Some of them, in seeking to find a greater role for the Spirit and to affirm the true humanity of Jesus, has raised the profile of the Spirit at the expense of the divinity, or the active divinity, of Jesus Christ. For example, J.D.G. Dunn could write, 'As the Spirit was the "divinity" of Jesus, so Jesus became the personality of the Spirit.'[61] There is a clear tendency towards adoptionism in Dunn's Spirit Christology. The nineteenth century Scottish theologian, Edward Irving, opted for a divinity of Jesus which is passive or dormant so that space could be made for the activity of the Spirit. G. Lampe, in his *God as Spirit*, denied the divinity of Jesus Christ altogether. In these attempts to promote the profile of the Holy Spirit, they see the divinity of Jesus Christ as a competing source with the divine action of the Spirit so that it must be lowered in order to see the Spirit prominently. In other words, active divine Logos Christology has to give way to Spirit Christology and the humanity of Jesus Christ. However, they all failed to see that Logos Christology and Spirit Christology are complementary to one another: it is precisely in the free and sovereign exercise of the power of the Holy Spirit by the personal subject of the Logos (the 'I' of Jesus Christ), who possesses this divine authority over the Holy Spirit, that the divinity of Jesus Christ is strongly manifested. This kind of Spirit Christology requires and affirms Logos Christology. And Logos Christology requires and implies this kind of Spirit Christology because the personal subject of the Logos (or Son of God) has this divine authority over the Spirit tied to his person. Separating Logos Christology and Spirit Christology amounts to doing violence to the unity of the person of the Son of God whereby one of the key personal attributes tied to his person is truncated from him. Here, we are saying no more than what the important term *filioque* is expressing: the personal subject of the Son of God, even in the genuinely human mode of existence, relates to the Spirit in the same way as the Father does.[62]

---

61 Dunn, *Jesus and the Spirit*, p. 325.

62 In saying that the Father and the Son have authority over the Spirit, one is not denying the divinity of the Spirit. We find the divinity of the Spirit strongly manifested in his divine sovereign executive power which is expressed in his relation

Finally, we need to measure our Christology with the yardstick of Scripture, and compare this measure with other approaches to Christology using the criterion of *faithfulness to Scripture*. It is beyond doubt that Chalcedonian Christology, and some other Christologies derived from Chalcedon, including kenotic Christology (see Pannenberg's survey in *Jesus - God and Man*, pp. 319-68), were intended to be consonant with Scripture, so is the Christology proposed here. A detailed comparison between them is beyond the scope of this book. But in terms of preserving the unity of the person of Jesus Christ and excluding a dual consciousness (which Scripture does not teach), in terms of affirming both the genuine humanity and true divinity of Jesus Christ, in terms of paying due respect and attention to all three persons of the Trinity, in terms of locating the mystery of the incarnation, we have good reasons, as presented above, to claim that the Christology proposed here is as close to Scripture as the author can make it, and in this respect compares favourably with other Christologies in terms of faithfulness to Scripture. This is not surprising because the approach adopted here is firmly based on a careful and detailed study of Scripture, from which some conceptualisations are derived and developed with minimal speculation in order to interpret or make sense of the data given by Scripture. Other Christologies, even though they claim to be derived from or consonant with Scripture, take *too much* liberty in utilising concepts and categories from philosophy extrinsic to Scripture and in so doing create unnecessary and insoluble problems for the generations to come. This brings us to the second and last criterion for comparison with other Christologies.

Apart from the criterion of faithfulness to Scripture, another criterion is the *conceptual elegance* of the proposal and the associated magnitude of the difficulties generated. It is reasonable to expect that a more elegant proposal will incur less number of difficulty. It is prudent to prefer the Christology which is conceptually most elegant and generates the least number of difficulty. It may be said that the above understanding of the incarnation as (i) a *passage* from divinity into humanity without loss of conformity in spirit and (ii) the personal subject of the Son of God retaining his personal authority of the Spirit (*filioque*) in that passage from eternity into time, is conceptually more elegant than attempting to hold two substances (often seen as *disjunctive* and *inflexible*) together in time whereby double centres of consciousness or two distinctive wills have to be reconciled. Moreover, the notion of *authority* being tied to a *personal subject* rather than a certain mode of existence is highly reasonable and allows transcendent attributes (i.e., divine authorities in speeches and in mighty acts) to be

---

to the world including human persons.

predicated to a person, even if the person exists in a human form. This notion is therefore crucial in acknowledging the divinity of Jesus who is also at once held to be truly human. One can say that this notion of *personal authority* is one of the two keys for holding the divinity and humanity of Jesus Christ together in our proposal. Its conceptual elegance and its effectiveness in solving one of the chief difficulties in Christology make it a prime candidate for the most satisfying and elegant concept found in this Christology. However, the concept of 'conformity in spirit through the Holy Spirit' such that the *personal spirit* is retained, which is the other key for holding the divinity and humanity of Jesus Christ together, may have some reasons to challenge for that position of honour. It is interesting to note that both keys hinge on the concept of person: the person is the ultimate factor of continuity in the change in form, and because authority and spirit are tied to the person he can retain his attributes (or essentialities) as he exists in different forms. With regard to the question of the overall comparison with other Christologies using this second criterion of elegance (and the number of difficulty generated), the preferable choice is open for the reader.

Is the Christology proposed here a refined Christology with a paradigmatic shift beyond Chalcedon as the title of this section suggests? It is a move beyond Chalcedon in the following two senses, i.e., it seeks refinement via a shift in *methodology* and *conceptualisation*. Its use of gospel/biblical narratives to *ground* our understanding of Jesus Christ and its attempt to widen its horizon to look intently at all three persons of the Trinity constitute a significant shift in *methodology*. This shift is made all the more evident given the impasse and chasm between biblical studies and doctrinal theology as practised in academic theology. In terms of conceptualisation, its use of the category of spirit and the concept of conformity in spirit (rather than majoring on the category of substance), its employment of personal authority and the application of the idea of passage from divinity to humanity without loss in divine authority and divine spirit - these are the keys for understanding the hypostatic union of divine and human natures - constitute a groundbreaking shift in *conceptualisation* in Christology. Given the comparisons with other Christologies as presented above, the claim of the proposed Christology to refinement and paradigmatic shift can therefore be firmly justified with good reasons. The significant implications of this refined and innovative Christology, and its possible further refinement, await to be explored.

CHAPTER 8

Conclusions

This book, under the influence by Barth who links Trinity and revelation closely together, has aimed to study the Trinity via the theme of revelation. This study began by asking the conceptual question: How does Jesus reveal his Father? In Barth's answer to this question, the divinity of Jesus Christ is paramount. In chapter 2, it was argued/shown that the gospel narratives, Matthew in particular, do present Jesus as the divine Lord not only by title (Mt. 3:3) but also by the literary structure and the presentation of Jesus' words and actions (see chapters 3 and 4). A corollary of this is that a mere confession of Jesus Lordship/divinity is not enough; it needs to be complemented with a 'face to face encounter' with him through the narratives of his life and action. Herrmann, in this respect, unrelentingly attacked doctrinal legalism which treats doctrines, such as Jesus' divinity, as mere information to be confessed.[1] Barth, likewise, does not consider revelation as mere information, even as information contained in the Bible, but as a

---

1 'Information concerning God, therefore, although it may claim to be of divine revelation, can only bring that troubled piety which lives by no delivering act of God, but by men's own exertions. ... For in such doctrines, however true they may be in themselves, we are not brought face to face with that reality which gives faith its certainty; they simply tell us something, and we are then expected by our own efforts to hold that information to be true.' Herrmann, *The Communion of the Christian with God*, p. 58. The face to face encounter with that reality in Herrmann's understanding was the encounter with Jesus Christ, though he stressed more of the aspect of Jesus' inner life in this encounter. This book concentrates more on Jesus' words and actions and derives from these some reasonable inferences of his communion with his Father.

genuine encounter with Jesus Christ in the event of revelation.[2] Such encounter inevitably involves meeting Jesus in his words and actions and this may be one of the reasons why Barth goes to such lengths in *CD* IV.1,2 to expound the gospel narratives. For Barth, this encounter with Jesus Christ is nothing less than the encounter with God because Christ in himself is God and equal with God the Father. Any compromise of Christ's divinity and his sovereign majesty dilutes his correspondence to his Father and the decisive finality of Jesus' revelation of his Father. Jesus' revelation of God is of a different order to the prophets' revelation of God. In the OT, God revealed his will and thoughts through prophets but we cannot say that through these prophets God revealed himself *in person*. For God's revelation *in person* to take place, there has to be a *personal correspondence and likeness* between the person revealing God and God himself. It was this *personal correspondence and likeness* that OT prophets, including Moses and Elijah, lacked but Christ possessed.[3] And being in correspondence to God and likeness of God in person, being in full consonance with God in the spirit of authority, freedom, majesty, compassion, humility, gentleness, wisdom, truth ... through the Holy Spirit, Jesus was able to act as God personally would act and thus faithfully revealed his Father *in person* on earth. In meeting him, we really have to do with meeting the personal God in person.[4] In encountering him by the grace of the Holy Spirit, we are truly seeing God face to face. And the face we see in this direct revelation in person is the same face as the Father, same in terms of spirit, because the Father and the Son are always one in spirit through the unity of the divine Spirit. In this sense, Jesus' revelation of God is of a different and higher order to the prophets' revelation of God.

A detailed exegesis of Mt. 11:25-30 in chapter 2 yielded a so-called 'non-linear concept of revelation' (in contrast to Barth's linear concept

---

2 For Barth's differentiation between information and revelation, see Trevor Hart, 'Revelation' in *The Cambridge Companion to Karl Barth*, pp. 52-3. Barth's criticism of those mentality which equates revelation with information, and his emphasis on encountering with the living Word through the written word in the event of revelation might have been significantly influenced by his teacher Herrmann. For what Barth means by the event of revelation, see *CD* I.1, pp. 111f; see also pp. 230, 244 on how the living Word is present to those who experience him in faith.

3 Lacking direct correspondence to God in terms of possessing divine authority, Elijah *prayed* to God for fire from heaven in the event on Mount Carmel (1 Kings 17). But Jesus, who corresponded to God in person in terms of possessing divine authority, *commanded* or *rebuked* the winds and the waves to stop in Galilee (Mt. 8:26 and parallels). God's revelation through Elijah and God's revelation through Jesus are different kinds of revelation, two kinds of revelation of different order.

4 'Anyone who has seen me has seen the Father.' John 14:9.

of revelation) which incorporates the important notion of Jesus' communion with the Father as the basis of his revelation of his Father. This concept of revelation was used as the interpretative clue/framework, along with the Lordship of Jesus, to study Jesus' words and actions in chapters 3 and 4 (cf. McGrath's comment on the relationship between interpretative framework and narrative in 3.0 of chapter 1). The non-linear concept of revelation was subsequently informed by narrative studies of Jesus' words and actions, and refined in chapter 6 by canvassing the three possible meanings of 'spirit' - the Holy Spirit, the human spirit and the content of communion. The Father reaches out to his Son, communing his loving and holy presence to him through the Holy Spirit in a manner which cannot be adequately captured by human description, sharing with his Son through the same Spirit his spirit of righteousness, compassion, wisdom, truth, freedom, authority, humility and gentleness. The Son with a gentle and humble heart/spirit (Mt. 11:29) receives the presence and spirit of his Father through the Holy Spirit, trusting and finding rest in him (Mt. 11:28-30), and responds to his Father's loving presence with resolute obedience to the very end. Jesus shares the same spirit as his Father so that he can rightly say, 'All that belongs to the Father is mine' (John 16:15). And it is in his loving and holy communion with his Father that he moves to love - 'As the Father has loved me, so have I loved you' (John 15:9). In this perfect obedient communion with his Father, in this fellowship of life to the full, in this rest and freedom in his Father's presence, Jesus corresponds and conforms to his Father, whose love and life thereby flow through the person of his Son and who thus reveals himself through him in the power of the Holy Spirit.

In chapter 7, the inextricable relationship between the divinity of Jesus Christ and his perfect obedient communion with his Father in his true humanity was highlighted; it was not possible to have one without the other. Therefore, this perfect communion in his perfect humanity should not be seen as an extra factor, distinct from and additional to divinity, which is required in Jesus' revelation of his Father. It should be seen as the consequence or expression of Jesus' divinity, or as inherent in his divinity. Thus the exegesis of Mt. 11:25-30 in effect unpacks the meaning of the divine Lordship of Jesus by demonstrating Jesus' capacity to commune with his Father and reveal his Father. Barth's insight (perhaps an intuitive one) - 'But who can reveal God except God Himself?' (*CD* I.1, p. 406) - is a correct one but one which can be further and profitably elaborated/unpacked in terms of communion. However, it has been shown near the end of 4.0 in chapter 2 that Barth did connect the notion of communion with revelation even though perhaps he did not emphasise this important relationship. Barth in principle by no means neglected the communion between the Father and the Son through the Spirit, as his subscription to the doctrine of perichoresis of the Trinity shows.[5] However, he was relatively reticent on this theme and Jesus' spiritual experience of his Father when speaking of Jesus' earthly life. A reason was suggested regarding Barth's relative reticence in these respects - his painful relationship with Liberal Protestantism which had so stressed Jesus' inner life and man's spiritual experience (or consciousness) of God.[6] However, if one takes Jesus' divinity seriously, one has to do the same with his communion with his Father, for the two are inextricably linked together (or the latter is subsumed in the former). That means one has to consider, in addition to Jesus' audible words and visible actions, Jesus' experience of his Father in the Spirit/spirit as his beloved Son. Chapter 6 attempted to elaborate this notion of spiritual communion/experience dynamically and more concretely by exploiting the meanings of 'spirit' and some insights by Lampe. The Father's communing presence to the Son through the Spirit/spirit was the basis of Jesus' life-act, while the Son in obedience to his Father maintained that communion with and correspondence to his Father, and thus revealed his Father in words and actions. There was an integrity between Jesus' visible life-act and his invisible spiritual communion with his Father, which can also be substantiated by a careful consideration of the biblical notion of spirit which connects the outer with the inner. (The author's understanding of this biblical notion of spirit might have been prompted by the Chinese understanding of spirit, 精神, which also connects the outer with the inner.) Barth stressed the outer in interpreting Jesus Christ but perhaps the inner should also be maintained because the two are integrated in the one person of Jesus.[7] In this respect, Barth himself in *CD* III.2 emphasised the indissoluble unity between the inner and outer aspects of man, Jesus Christ in particular.[8] Had he consistently paid due respect to this indissoluble unity and allowed himself to speak more of Jesus' experience of his Father through the Holy Spirit as the basis of his outer words and actions, his pneumatology would have been considerably

---

5 *CD* I.1, pp. 370-1.

6 But there are some signs of the receding of this reticence in *The Christian Life*, where Barth near the end of his life concentrated his attention on the Fatherhood of God. One can only imagine how this heightened sense of God's Fatherhood and a clear focus on the Spirit in the doctrine of redemption might have afforded him a more comprehensive understanding of Jesus' relationship with and experience of his Father.

7 Foe the biblical understanding of spirit, see 3.1 of chapter 6. In the Hebrew language, the word spirit/*rûah* can stand for both thought and action, thus linking them directly together.

8 *CD* III.2 (*The Doctrine of Creation*), pp. 325-436.

strengthened and his theology would have been even more trinitarian.

A corollary of the discussion concerning divinity, communion and revelation is that divinity should not be understood in an individualistic manner. Integral to and constitutive of divinity is the capacity and will to commune and correspond. Divinity and communion should not be seen as two separate distinct concepts. The latter should be subsumed under the former. In that case, 'the divine (and human) Jesus communes with his Father' is an analytic statement, not a synthetic one. The significance of this is: had Chalcedon adopted this understanding of divinity, the divinity of Jesus Christ and Christology would not have been thought of in an individualistic manner - how divinity and humanity co-exist in the one person - but would have rather been understood in a more trinitarian context; the Spirit and possibly the humanity of Jesus would have been more prominent in the centuries of theological thoughts after Chalcedon.

Apart from the conceptual question of how Jesus revealed his Father, this book has also raised the question regarding the content of revelation - what did Jesus reveal of his Father through his concrete words and actions as witnessed by the gospel narratives? The following answer is a very brief summary. The gospels present a Jesus who in his radical spirit of unconditional love reaches out and touches the lives of of the marginalised, the oppressed, the poor, the 'unclean', the sinners, even the gentiles, and in so doing bursts through and transcends the legalistic barriers and ethnic boundaries treasured/insisted by religious leaders. His uncompromising confrontations with the religious leaders on this revolutionary love escalates after his entry into Jerusalem and costs him his life as they crucify him on the cross. This story of a life of radicalism, a ministry of unconditional love which ends in suffering, rejection and death is the story of Jesus' revelation of his Father – the God of radical unconditional love. Another way to summarise his revelation is this: he revealed through his teachings and actions the Fatherhood of God, the righteousness of God (or his kingdom) and the Lordship of his Father. But in each of these he revealed not only his Father but also his relationship with his Father. It is true that Jesus' relationship with his Father is the basis of revelation, but it is also true that this basis of revelation itself is revealed in Jesus' life-act. His relationship with his Father, as manifested in his life-act, is one of unity characterised by knowledge, trust, love, and obedience. And it is in the Father's abandonment of the Son on the cross that this unity, this basis of revelation, is climactically and paradoxically revealed (see 3.3 of chapter 4).

Apart from revealing the Father, Jesus also revealed his own sovereign Lordship in his words and actions. He revealed his Lordship in the sovereign authority that he exercised in his radical teachings, in his revolutionary acts of love transcending all barriers and in his mighty acts of healings and exorcisms which he freely performed in the Spirit. Jesus speaking and acting in his sovereign majesty and divine authority, rather than in the manner of a self-effacing prophet, properly revealed his Lordship. But his own Lordship raises the question of the dual Lordships of Jesus and his Father and the question of his relationship with the Spirit especially in exorcism. These two questions will be considered in the reversed order.

The Spirit Christologies of Dunn and Irving readily attributed the power of exorcism to the Spirit only. But such Spirit Christologies, in their simplistic forms, do not do justice to the inherent sovereign authority and Lordship of Jesus witnessed by the gospel narratives - Jesus was the true subject, Lord and possessor of the Spirit, rather than the object of possession by the Spirit. Chapter 5 argued at length for this point, demonstrating the evangelists' (especially Luke's) considerable effort to distinguish Jesus from the disciples in their relationships with the Spirit. The question of the compatibility of Logos and Spirit Christology was resolved in chapter 6 - according to the gospel narratives Jesus' authority to freely exercise the power of the Spirit as his very own and his movement in his native atmosphere of the Spirit from birth (chapters 4 and 5) witnessed to his divinity, rather than detracted from his divinity. There is a profound unity between Jesus and the Spirit even though they are mysteriously distinct. A corollary from the discussions in chapter 5, especially on Luke's treatment of Jesus' relationship with the Spirit in the context of addressing his spiritually sensitised audience, is that a heightened profile of the Spirit (in relation to figures in the narratives) needs to be balanced by a heightened profile of Jesus Christ, so that the situation of a highly spiritually enthusiastic community neglecting the centrality of the more 'objective' revelation of Jesus Christ can be avoided. But the heightened profiles of the Spirit and Jesus Christ immediately demand an equally heightened profile of the Father in order to avoid the situation of the forgotten Father. In short, the profiles of the Father, Son and Spirit should remain simultaneously high in the consciousness, spirituality and practice of the church, e.g., in preaching, worship, prayer, fellowship and mission.

Jesus' unity with the Spirit has been affirmed but the question of his unity with the Father (i.e., the question of dual Lordships) also requires a solution. This question turned out to be closely related to the controversial question of *filioque* and it was proposed in chapter 6 that both *filioque* and *per filium* are both required by the gospel narratives, the former being a consequence of the divinity of the Son and the latter as a result of the communion between the Father and the Son, rather than a result of the Father begetting the Son, as suggested by

Augustine.[9] (This may have implication for the conception of the immanent Trinity and the East-West dialogue on *filioque*.) By employing the notions of co-authority, communion and sharing the same spirit of authority, the dual Lordships of Jesus and his Father were resolved. Thus, with the profound unity between Jesus and the Spirit having been affirmed, and the unity between Jesus and his Father having been acknowledged, the unity of the Father, Son and Holy Spirit is maintained.

In Dunn's Spirit Christology, the divinity of the Son is not in view and only the unity between the Father and the Spirit can be affirmed. In Irving's Spirit Christology, the divine Son is effectively passive so that there can be no active unity between the three in history. The author sympathises with their (and those of other contemporary theologians such as David Coffey) effort to find a clearer role for the Spirit in Jesus (particularly in Jesus' communion with his Father) and to affirm the true humanity of Jesus,[10] but it must be pointed out that Dunn's approach compromises the divinity of Jesus and Irving's approach compromises his active divinity. On the one hand, against Dunn and Irving the author maintains the insight of Barth - the paramount importance of Jesus' divinity and the active exercise of that divinity in his revelation of his Father (Logos Christology). On the other hand, the author aims also to take the work of the Spirit in Jesus and his humanity seriously in his relationship with and revelation of his Father, as Dunn, Irving and Coffey intended (Spirit Christology). The role of the Spirit in Jesus (i) has indeed been given a prominent place in this book through locating his crucial role in Jesus' communion with his Father in the Spirit/spirit (section 3 of chapter 6), and (ii) has been emphatically

---

9 In the discussion on the issues of *filioque* and *per filium* in 2.2 of chapter 6, it was found that communion is a better context for thinking about these issues than begetting. This raises the thought that eternal begetting, which is quite static and difficult to visualise and understand, might perhaps be understood more dynamically as the Father *communing* to his Son as the Father, and begotten might be understood more dynamically as the Son *communing* to his Father as the Son. Barth remarks, 'How is the Son begotten? ... We do not know, either when we are speaking of the eternal reality or when we are speaking of the temporal reality which can be denoted by these metaphors ...' (*CD* I.1, p. 475). The more dynamic concept of communion gained from history, which involves the action of the Father communicating his spiritual presence to his Son and the action of the Son communicating his obedience to his Father, might give some substance to and thus reveal the meanings of begetting and begotten.

10 Vladimir Lossky criticised the West for their inadequate treatment of the Holy Spirit, see, e.g., *The Mystical Theology of the Eastern Church* (Cambridge: James Clarke, 1957). Criticisms such as this needs to be considered seriously. See also *The Forgotten Trinity*; Colle, *Christ and the Spirit*, chapter 1.

affirmed in Jesus' profound unity with the Spirit from the moment of his conception (see 2.1.4 of chapter 6). How Jesus' humanity has been treated in this book will be taken up later. Here it needs to be pointed out that the answer given in chapters 3 and 4 to the question - what did Jesus reveal of his Father through his concrete words and actions as witnessed by the gospel narratives? - has led to further reflections in chapters 5 and 6 and a more detailed conceptual understanding of the unity between Jesus and the Spirit, Jesus and his Father and the unity of the Trinity, which prompted the formulation of the *refined* non-linear concept of revelation. Thus the narrative *content* of Jesus' revelation has shed light on the *concept* of revelation and the understanding of the Trinity (cf. McGrath's comments on the dynamic relationship between narratives and conceptualisation in 3.0 of chapter 1). A corollary of this is that the input to conceptual or systematic formulations of doctrinal truths are significantly impoverished if biblical stories/narratives are not given their due and careful attention. Conceptualisations and systematic formulations which are over-dependent on preconceived ideas, such as those of Dunn and Irving, run the risk of presenting over-simplistic and distorted pictures which are at variance with the biblical narratives.

It might appear that by emphasising the divine Lordship of Jesus in his revelation of his Father (as Barth did), this book might not have given sufficient attention to the true humanity of Jesus and may put in jeopardy his relevance to his followers. However, the following points can be made to dispel this misconception. *Firstly*, in 2.2 of chapter 2 it was shown that Matthew clearly intended to present Jesus as the true Israel who in his baptism and temptations in the wilderness identified himself with Israel. While Israel - the son of God - sinned in the wilderness, Jesus - the Son of God - remained resolutely obedient to his Father throughout the temptations. All three synoptic gospels present the real temptations to which Jesus as a true human being was subjected. Such temptations reached the high point in the Garden of Gethsemane. *Secondly*, in 4.0 of chapter 2 and 2.0 of chapter 3 it was shown that Jesus in his humanity trusted in the sovereign rule and providential care of his Father who worked out everything, including his suffering and death, according to his purpose. His teachings on prayer, for example, asking the Father to provide for daily needs and that his will be done, may well reflect his own trusting dependence on his Father. It was in this trusting dependence of his Father, in this spirit of gentleness and humility that he in his true humanity experienced rest in his Father's presence through the Holy Spirit (Mt. 11:28-30). *Thirdly*, in 5.0 of chapter 3 it was argued that during the temptations in the wilderness Jesus, as a true human being, was *reliant on the Holy Spirit* working through Scripture to convey to him his Father's specific will for him as the Son of God. And his teaching on the Sermon on the

Mount was probably a result of his meditation on Scripture and his close communion with his Father through the Spirit.[11] In this respect, Jesus did not bypass his humanity in knowing his Father's will for himself and for his disciples. *Fourthly*, in 3.0 of chapter 4, the sufferings, insults and agony that Jesus experienced on the cross were affirmed as true human sufferings, to a degree that surpassed our own human sufferings. Jesus, as the true Israel, identified himself with Israel utterly to the end and so gave his life as a ransom and saved the people from their sins (Mt. 1:21). By acknowledging the real and severe temptations that Jesus faced, the trust that he exercised in his Father and the rest he found in his Father's presence, his reliance upon Scripture and the Holy Spirit in discerning his Father's will, and his real human suffering on the cross, this book has strongly affirmed the true humanity of Jesus Christ. He is truly the obedient and trusting Son of God who can rightly serve as the perfect example for our sonship to the Father, and his experience of rest in his Father's presence is an encouragement for us to seek the same. The gospel narratives find no difficulty in portraying this true humanity of Jesus and his divine Lordship together in his one person. More could be said about how Jesus' genuine human experience of his Father through the Spirit can be relevant to the Christian experience of the communing presence of God through the Spirit, but that will be the subject of another book.

There is, however, one distinctive difference between the humanity of Jesus and humanity in general - Jesus in his humanity did not sin while other human beings do. This crucial difference, i.e., the uniqueness of Jesus' sinless life, needs to be accounted for. Irving explained Jesus' sinless life by the work of the Holy Spirit who freed the human will of Jesus under bondage and sustained him from falling into sin. However, there is no evidence in the whole of the NT that Jesus' will was under bondage (even though he was subjected to severe temptations). While this book emphasises the importance of Jesus' communion with his Father through the Spirit and the beneficial personal presence of his Father which inclined him to obedience, it does not wish to attribute Jesus' obedience *wholly* to this presence granted through the Spirit. It maintains that Jesus as the free agent had to purposefully decide and intentionally choose to align his will to his Father's will. If anything, the gospel narratives present Jesus as the subject who willed to obey his Father more emphatically as the narratives proceed towards the ending in the cross. As already pointed out in the critique of Irving in 2.1.3 of chapter 6, the Spirit was present

---

11 Note, in Mt. 11:27, how 'all things' concerning revelation had been committed to the Son by the Father, and this committing to the Son was realised in the context of communion or mutual knowledge.

in Jesus' baptism and the temptations in the wilderness, but *the Spirit is mentioned neither in Jesus' transfiguration nor in the Garden of Gethsemane! The evangelists, by lowering the profile of the Spirit in Gethsemane, are making a clear space to present quite unambiguously and unequivocally the Son's own active obedience to his Father* (active Logos Christology), notwithstanding whatever benefits the Spirit might have brought (active Spirit Christology). Irving's simplistic notion which attributes Jesus' obedience *wholly* to the Spirit does not correspond to the gospel narratives and gives rise to a non-functioning Logos Christology where the majestic freedom and Lordship of Jesus is hard to find, but the author suggests that by attributing obedience to Jesus in the presence of his Father through the Spirit both Logos Christology and Spirit Christology can be maintained together. Also, to teach Irving's notion in the church, i.e., obedience wholly by the work of the Spirit, would be pastorally irresponsible because it takes away the real responsibility of Christians to actively exercise their will to obey God. Furthermore, attributing Jesus' obedience wholly to the Spirit does not explain the uniqueness of Jesus' sinless life, for it raises the question of why his followers, who have been liberated from bondage to sin by his death, resurrection and the gift of the Spirit (Rom. 8:1-4), fail to achieve the same kind of sinless life. There has to be an important distinction between Jesus and his followers to account for the uniqueness of his sinless life.

By studying what can be gathered from the gospel narratives in Jesus' journey from Galilee to Jerusalem, 3.0 of chapter 4 identifies consistently Jesus' own deliberate decisions to complete his mission from Jordan, through Galilee, to entry into Jerusalem and finally death in Calvary. For his Father's mission to be accomplished, there had to be a series of conscious and deliberate decisions made on Jesus' part, which can only be made by himself. According to the evangelists, Jesus' prayers in the Garden of Gethsemane makes this abundantly clear - not even the Spirit can take his place of obedience. It has to be admitted that according to the narratives Jesus in his human will did not fall into retreat and disobedience. And it also has to be admitted that this obedience in his human will cannot be reduced simply to the work of the Spirit. And it has to be concluded that Jesus' perfect obedient human will is distinct from other human wills in this respect of obedience. If this distinction is evaded, as Irving probably did, the uniqueness of his sinless life cannot be accounted for (unless everything is attributed to the Spirit, which the evangelists denied and is problematic). The distinct human will of Jesus and the uniqueness of his sinless life have to be held together; one cannot have one without the other. One has to maintain Jesus' distinct human will unless one is prepared to forgo his unique sinless life. But does Jesus' distinct human will make him irrelevant to his followers? It does not lead to irrelevance if one maintains that his human will was subjected to the same temptations as we face and at a magnitude beyond what we have experienced or can imagine. The real battle he had to fight in Gethsemane starkly reminds us that he was truly one of us and we, rather than protesting against and being cynical of his unique, human, humble and obedient will, should only be thankful that his human will had not been bent into disobedience, which would have shipwrecked his mission to save the people from their sins.

It is tempting to attribute Jesus' distinct human will to the determination by his divine will, as Barth did (see 2.1.4 of chapter 6). But instead of conceiving of two materially distinct wills operating closely together in Jesus, it is possible, in the light of the discussion in chapter 7 on the conformity in spirit between the divine and human, to think in terms of the incarnation of the divine will into the human will in spirit and through the Spirit.

Jesus' own obedience to his Father has been emphasised as integral to his revelation to his Father and this obedience has finally and unavoidably been traced to the distinct human will of Jesus in the incarnation which can be attributed to his divinity. (Jesus' divinity is seen as crucial to his revelation of his Father, cf. Barth.[12]) Moreover, Jesus' obedience affords us a glimpse into the dynamic unity between the Father, Son and Holy Spirit. The gospel narratives seem to present the picture that it was as Jesus committed his will to obey his Father that he moved in the power of the Spirit; the fullness of Jesus' life in the Spirit was constantly underlaid and maintained by his consistent commitment to obey his Father. According to Luke, Jesus full of the Holy Spirit was led by the Spirit in the wilderness of temptations (4:1). But after the temptations against which he willed to *obey* his Father's will, Luke presents Jesus as returning to Galilee in the *power* of the Spirit, speaking and ministering in the power of the Spirit (4:14). It seems that the Spirit conveyed his Father's will to him in the wilderness, and as he kept in step with the Spirit and in step with his Father's will, he moved in the communing presence of his Father and in the power of the Holy Spirit. *This power of the Spirit in which he moved, he experienced as his own power and at the same time as the power of his Father who was present in him.*[13] *This is the mystery of the Trinity that Jesus himself experienced*, the mystery of the community

---

12 The Son's divinity is expressed in Jesus' obedient communion with his Father, in which he corresponds and conforms to his Father, thus revealing his Father in his words and actions.

13 See Mark 5:30, 2.2 of chapter 5 and 2.1.4 of chapter 6 for Jesus' experiencing of the power of the Spirit as his own.

(comm-unity) and unity of the Trinity expressed in the life-act and experience of Jesus Christ. He could say, 'I and the Father are one, ... The words I say to you are *not just my own*. Rather, it is the Father, living in me, who is doing his work. Believe me, when I say that I am in the Father and the Father is in me.'[14] The Son's oneness in words and actions with the Father was inextricably linked with his communion with his Father through the Spirit. It was the same when he exorcised demons from the possessed. *He* cast out demons by the *Spirit* of *God* (Mt. 12:28). The power he exercises as the subject in exorcism was experienced as *his own inherent power*, which was at the same time experienced as the power of the *Spirit* of his *Father* who was *present* with him through the same Spirit. We cannot fully fathom this mystery of the unity of the Trinity but we are aware that Jesus' unity with the Father through the Spirit was experienced by him and was inextricably linked with their communion in the Spirit. To summarise, the Father wills, the Father conveys his will and communing presence to his Son through the Spirit, the Son in his truly incarnated humanity wills to obey his Father, the Spirit empowers the obedient act of the Son, the Spirit's power is experienced by the Son as his own power and the power of his Father present in him through the Spirit. This is the mystery of the Trinity.

The unity of the humanity and divinity of Jesus Christ is another mystery, which has been addressed in chapter 7. Again, the concept of conformity in spirit has been instrumental in understanding the unity of the person of Jesus Christ as it has been found useful in understanding the unity of the Trinity. An additional conceptual understanding of the relationship between authority, mode of existence and person was found illuminating while Thomasius' kenotic Christology was critiqued. The proposed Christology, based on the idea of the *person* of the Son of God retaining his *personal* spirit and *personal* authority despite a change in the mode of existence, has some claim to innovation and refinement beyond Chalcedon with a paradigmatic shift. The implications from this proposed Christology, and its further refinements, are yet to be explored.

Finally, to end this conclusion three points about the work of the Spirit will be made. The first point concerns the historicity of the gospel narratives. Crucial to the following argument is the ability of the spirit of Christ to take different forms within limits. One cannot expect a verbatim report of Jesus' words and actions in the gospel narratives for it would have required much longer and tedious narratives. What can be preserved in these records are the essence of Jesus' actions and his words, although it is probable that many of his sayings in the gospels

---

14 John 10:30; 14:10-11.

follow closely his original words which were designed to be committed to memory by his disciples, e.g., the sayings beginning with 'I say to you'. The purpose of the gospels is therefore to present to the readers an essential picture of Jesus (see the concept of 'middle distance' mentioned in 3.0 of chapter 1 and David Ford's *Barth and God's Story*). It seems that this essential picture of Jesus has been able to accommodate the spirit of Jesus in such a way that the essence of the spirit of Jesus in his life, ministry, death and resurrection has been faithfully kept in these *forms* in the gospels.[15] Thus, we see in the gospels the spirit of compassion in Jesus, his radical spirit of unconditional love, his spirit of uncompromising Lordship and at the same time his spirit of meekness and humility, his spirit of obedient love for his Father, his spirit of integrity and truth, his spirit of wisdom and courage, and in the end his spirit of self-giving sacrificial love on the cross. This spirit of Jesus is consistently presented throughout the four gospels, albeit in varying forms. And it is possible that the Holy Spirit, the *Spirit of Christ*, leads us in our reading or preaching of the gospel narratives and reveals the *spirit of Christ* to us (1 Cor. 2:10-16), thus granting us his personal presence through the Spirit/spirit.[16] And in knowing this spirit of Christ, one comes to know the spirit of the Father and the Spirit for the three are united in Spirit/spirit. This understanding of revelation may have implications for the preaching of Jesus Christ and the Trinity in the church, and for preaching as a means of God's imparting his personal presence to the church. These are possible fields for further research.

The second point concerns obedience to Christ in the life-acts of his disciples. Since the spirit of Christ can be accommodated and retained in different forms in the lives of the disciples, the Holy Spirit might take the spirit of Christ as witnessed in the gospels and apply it prophetically to the disciples' situations and contexts. In this way, the spirit of Jesus' love, compassion, integrity, radicalism, courage and humility can be preserved and enacted in the obedient lives of the disciples who seek to keep in step with their master in the Spirit/spirit in ever changing contexts.[17]

---

15 Again, the same spirit can be retained in different forms - the form in the actual life and ministry of Jesus, the three forms in the synoptic gospels and the form in the fourth gospel.

16 One wonders how this view of encountering the Word through the word in the Spirit/spirit might be related to Barth's notion of the event of revelation.

17 Lampe's idea that God has been working according to the same Christ Spirit in the OT, NT and beyond has similarities with the idea presented here but this book has maintained the distinct hypostasis of the Spirit and the Son while acknowledging that the Spirit works in the disciples according to the spirit of Christ manifested in the

The third point concerns the life and unity of the church in the Spirit/spirit. The church indeed is a network of relationships maintained by the Spirit and thus the church is constituted by the Spirit.[18] But the discussion in chapter 5 shows that any emphasis on the Holy Spirit needs to be balanced by an emphasis on Jesus Christ; or else, with a Christological vacuum a form of mysticism or some uncontrolled spiritual enthusiasm may result in the church. Furthermore, emphases on Jesus and the Spirit in the church must also come under the emphasis on the Fatherhood of God (cf. Tom Smail's *The Forgotten Father*).[19] Therefore at a more detailed level, the unity of the church is in practice maintained by the Spirit through his granting members of the church the same spirit of Christ (maybe in different forms in different believers), the same spirit of sonship to the Father, the same spirit of love and humility of Jesus. And it may be as members of the church obediently keep in step with Christ in the Spirit/spirit of Christ, praying and calling out to God as 'Abba' and Jesus as 'Lord' in the Spirit, receiving the love of the Father and the Son, trusting in their sovereign rule, serving one another and the world in sincerity and humility, in love and compassion that the personal loving and holy communing presence of the Father is poured into the hearts of the believers through the Son in the power of the Holy Spirit, to the praise of his glory (Rom. 5:5; Eph. 4:16, 3:14-21).

For this reason I kneel before the *Father*, from whom his whole family in heaven and on earth derives its name. I pray that out of his riches he may strengthen you with *power through his Spirit in your inner being*, so that *Christ* may dwell in your hearts through faith. And I pray that you, being rooted and established in *love*, may have power, together with *all the saints*, to grasp how wide and long and deep is *the love of Christ*, and to know this love that surpasses knowledge - that you may be *filled to the measure of all the fullness of God*. Now to him who is able to do

---

incarnation of the divine Son.

18 See *Being as Communion* by John Zizioulas, and *The Forgotten Trinity*.

19 '... we need trinitarian controls on the ecclesiology imagery we use, if it is not to produce one-sided distortions. But it must be *trinitarian* theology as a whole that we use, not unconsidered appeals to persons of the Trinity. Suggestions we considered were that 'Father-only' images are associated with power-lust and domination; 'Jesus-only' images with moralistic activism or individualistic pietism; 'Spirit-only' images with introspective escapism or charismatic excess. We would not necessarily agree with the precise form in which such points are made, particularly in view of the fact that matters of causality in these matters are notoriously difficult to discern. But we do in general agree that conceptions of the Church derived from attention to one person of the Trinity only do tend to give rise to a variety of spiritual ills.' *The Forgotten Trinity*, 1, pp. 28-9.

immeasurably more than all we ask or imagine, according to his power that is at work within us, to him be the glory in the *church* and in Christ Jesus throughout all generations, for ever and ever! Amen. (Ephesians 3:14-21)

Bibliography

Adam, A. K. M., *What is Postmodern Biblical Criticism?* (Minneapolis: Fortress Press, 1995).

Auerbach, Erich, *Mimesis: The Representation of Reality in Western Literature* (Princeton: Princeton University Press, 1953), Willard R. Trask (tr.).

Balchin, John Paul, 'Wisdom and Christ', in *Christ the Lord* (Leicester: Inter-Varsity, 1982), H.H. Rowdon (ed.), pp. 204-19.

Banks, Robert J., *Jesus and The law in the Synoptic Tradition* (Cambridge: Cambridge University Press, 1975).

Barrett, C. K., *The Holy Spirit and the Gospel tradition* (London: SPCK, 1947).

Barth, Karl, *Theology and Church: Shorter Writings, 1920-1928* (London: SCM Press, 1962).

– *Church Dogmatics* (Edinburgh: T. & T. Clark, 1936-1977), G.W. Bromiley, T.F. Torrance (eds.).

– *The Christian Life: Church Dogmatics IV, 4 Lecture Fragments* (Edinburgh: T. & T. Clark, 1981), Geoffrey W. Bromiley (tr.).

Bauckham, R.,'The Worship of Jesus in Apocalyptic Christianity', *New Testament Studies* 27 (1980-1), pp. 322-41.

Beare, Francis Wright, *The Gospel According to Matthew: A commentary* (Oxford: Blackwell, 1981).

Betz, Hans Dieter, *Essays on the Sermon on the mount* (Philadelphia: Fortress Press, 1985), Laurence Welborn (tr.).

Blair, Edward Payson, *Jesus in the Gospel of Matthew* (New York: Abingdon Press, 1960).

Blomberg, Craig, *Jesus and the Gospels: An Introduction and Survey* (Leicester: Apollos, 1997).

Bobrinsky, Borris, 'The Indwelling of the Spirit in Christ: "Pneumatic Christology" in the Cappadocian Fathers', *St. Vladimir's Theological Quarterly*, 28 (1984), no. 1, pp. 49-65.

Bornkamm, Günther, Gerhard Barth and Heinz Joachim Held, *Tradition and Interpretation in Matthew* (London: SCM Press, 1963), Percy Scott (tr.).

Bousset, Wilhelm, *Kyrios Christos: A History of the Belief in Christ from the Beginnings of Christianity to Irenaeus* (Nashville: Abingdon Press, 1970), John E. Steely (tr.).

Bultmann, Rudolf Karl, *Theology of the New Testament* (London: SCM Press, 1952-1955), Kendrick Grobel (tr.).

– *Jesus* (Berlin: Deutsche Bibliothek, 1929).

– *The History of the Synoptic Tradition* (Oxford: Blackwell, 1963), John Marsh (tr.).

Calvin, John, *Joannis Calvini Opera Selecta* (Monachii: C. Kaiser,

1926-1962).

Campenhausen, H. F. von, *Ecclesiastical Authority and Spiritual Power in the Church of the First Three Centuries* (London: Adam and Charles Black, 1969), J.A. Baker (tr.).

Carson, D., 'Christological Ambiguities in Matthew', in *Christ the Lord: Studies in Christology Presented to Donald Guthrie* (Leicester: Inter-Varsity, 1982), Harold H. Rowdon (ed.), pp. 97-114.

Case, Shirley J., *Studies in Early Christianity* (New York & London: Century Co., 1928).

Casey, M., 'Chronology and the Development of Pauline Christology', in *Paul and Paulinism: Essays in Honour of C. K. Barrett* (London: SPCK, 1982), M. D. Hooker and S. G. Wilson (eds.), pp. 124-34.

Catchpole, David R., *The Trial of Jesus: A Study in the Gospels and Jewish Historiography from 1770 to the Present Day* (Leiden: Brill, 1971).

Coffey, David, *Deus Trinitas: The Doctrine of the Triune God* (New York; Oxford: Oxford University Press, 1999).

– *Grace: The Gift of the Holy Spirit* (Manly: Catholic Institute of Sydney, 1979).

– 'The "Incarnation" of the Holy Spirit in Christ', *Theological Studies*, 45 (1984), no. 3, pp. 466-80.

Conzelmann, Hans, *The Theology of St. Luke* (London: Faber, 1960), Geoffrey Buswell (tr.).

Coogan, Michael D. and Bruce M. Metzger, *The Oxford Companion to the Bible* (New York ; Oxford: Oxford University Press, 1993).

Crites, Stephen, 'The Narrative Quality of Experience', *Journal of the American Academy of Religion* 39 (Sept., 1971), pp. 291-311.

Cullmann, Oscar, *Baptism in the New Testament* (London: SCM Press, 1950), J.K.S. Reid (tr.).

Dallimore, Arnold A., *The Life of Edward Irving: Fore-runner of the Charismatic Movement* (Edinburgh; Carlisle: Banner of Truth Trust, 1983).

Davies, W. D. and Dale C. Allison, *A Critical and Exegetical Commentary on the Gospel According to Saint Matthew* (Edinburgh: T. & T. Clark, 1988-1997).

– *The Setting of the Sermon on the Mount* (Atlanta: Scholars Press, 1989).

Dawe, Donald, *The Form of a Servant* (Philadephia: The Westminster Press, 1963).

Del Colle, Ralph, *Christ and the Spirit: Spirit-Christology in Trinitarian Perspective* (New York; Oxford: Oxford University

Press, 1994).

DeVries, Dawn, *Jesus Christ in the Preaching of Calvin and Schleiermacher* (Louisville : Westminster John Knox Press, 1996)

Dodd, C. H., *The Founder of Christianity* (London: Collins, 1971).

Dorner, J. A., *History of the Development of the Doctrine of the Person of Christ* (Edinburgh: T. & T. Clark, 1880-1897).

Dorrien, Gary J., *The Barthian Revolt in Modern Theology: Theology Without Weapons* (Louisville: Westminster John Knox Press, 2000).

Dunn, James D. G., *Jesus and the Spirit: A Study of the Religious and Charismatic Experience of Jesus and the First Christians as Reflected in the New Testament* (London: SCM Press, 1975).

– *Baptism in the Holy Spirit: A Reexamination of the New Testament Teaching on the Gift of the Spirit in Relation to Pentecostalism Today* (London: SCM Press, 1970).

– *Christology in the Making: A New Testament Inquiry into the Origins of the Doctrine of the Incarnation* (London: SCM Press, 1989²).

– 'The Messianic Secret in Mark', in *The Messianic Secret* (London: SPCK, 1983), C. Tuckett (ed.), pp. 116-31.

– 'Baptism in the Spirit: A Response to Pentecostal Scholarship on Luke-Acts', *Journal of Pentecostal Theology*, 3 (1993), pp. 3-27.

– 'Rediscovering the Spirit', *Expository Times* 84 (1972-73), pp. 7-12, 40-44.

– 'Rediscovering the Spirit - 2', *Expository Times* 94 (1982), pp. 9-18.

Dupré, Louis K, *Passage to Modernity: An Essay in the Hermeneutics of Nature and Culture* (New Haven; London: Yale University Press, 1993).

England, Edward (ed.), *Living in the light of Pentecost* (Crowborough: Highland, 1990).

Fee, Gordon, 'Paul and the Trinity', in *The Trinity: An Interdisciplinary Symposium on the Trinity* (Oxford: Oxford University Press, 1999), Stephen T. Davis, Daniel Kendall, Gerald O'Collins (eds.), pp. 49-72.

Flew, R. Newton, *Jesus and His Church: A Study of the Idea of the Ecclesia in the New Testament* (London: Epworth, 1938).

Ford, David, 'System, Story, Performance: A Proposal about the Role of Narrative in Christian Systematic Theology', in *Why Narrative? Readings in Narrative Theology* (Grand Rapids: Eerdmans, 1989), S. Hauerwas and G. Jones (eds.), pp.191-215.

– *Barth and God's Story: Biblical Narrative and the Theological Method of Karl Barth in the "Church dogmatics"* (Frankfurt: Lang,

328 *Bibliography*

1981).

France, R. T., *The Gospel According to Matthew: An Introduction and Commentary* (Leicester: Inter-Varsity, 1985/7).

– *Matthew: evangelist and teacher* (Exeter: Paternoster, 1989).

– *Jesus and the Old Testament* (London: Tyndale Press, 1971).

– 'The Worship of Jesus: A Neglected Factor in Christological Debate?', in *Christ the Lord: Studies in Christology Presented to Donald Guthrie* (Leicester: Inter-Varsity, 1982), Harold H. Rowdon (ed.), pp. 17-36.

– 'Development in New Testament Christology', in *Themelios*, 18 (1993), no 1, pp. 4-8.

Freedman, D. and David F. Graf (eds.), *The Anchor Bible Dictionary* (New York; London: Doubleday, 1992).

Frei, Hans W., *Theology and Narrative: Selected Essays* (New York; Oxford: Oxford University Press, 1993), George Hunsinger and William C. Placher (eds.).

– *Types of Christian Theology* (New Haven ; London: Yale University Press, 1992), George Hunsinger and William C. Placher (eds.).

– *The Eclipse of Biblical Narrative: A Study in Eighteenth and Nineteenth Century Hermeneutics* (New Haven; London: Yale University Press, 1974).

– *The Identity of Jesus Christ: The Hermeneutical Bases of Dogmatic Theology* (Philadelphia: Fortress Press, 1975).

Gärtner, Bertil, *The Temple and the Community in Qumran and the New Testament: A Comparative Study in the Temple Symbolism of the Qumran Texts and the New Testament* (Cambridge: Cambridge University Press, 1965).

Green, Joel B., Scot McKnight and Howard Marshall (eds.), *Dictionary of Jesus and the Gospels* (Downers Grove; Leicester: InterVarsity Press, 1992).

Guelich, Robert A, *The Sermon on the Mount: A Foundation for Understanding* (Waco: Word Books, 1982).

Gundry, Robert H., *Matthew: A Commentary on His literary and Theological Art* (Grand Rapids: Eerdmans, c1982).

Gunton, Colin E., *The promise of Trinitarian Theology* (Edinburgh: T. & T. Clark, 1991).

– *The One, the Three and the Many: God, Creation and the Culture of Modernity* (Cambridge: Cambridge University Press, 1993).

– *The Triune Creator: A Historical and Systematic Study* (Edinburgh: Edinburgh University Press, 1998).

– 'Two Dogmas Revisited: Edward Irving's Christology', *Scottish Journal of Theology*, 41 (1988), pp. 359-76.

Hagner, Donald A., *Matthew 1-13*; *Word Biblical Commentary; vol.33A* (Dallas: Word Books, 1993).
- *Matthew 14-28*; *Word Biblical Commentary* ; *vol.33B* (Dallas: Word Books, 1995).
Hammerton-Kelly, R. G., 'A Note on Matthew 12:28 par. Luke 11:20', *New Testament Studies,* 11 (1964-65), no. 2, pp. 167-8.
Hanson, Anthony T., *The Image of the Invisible God* (London: SCM Press, 1982).
Hart, Trevor, 'Revelation', in *The Cambridge Companion to Karl Barth* (Cambridge: Cambridge University Press, 2000), J. Webster (ed.), pp. 37-56.
Hawthorne, Gerald F, *Philippians*; *Word Biblical Commentar* (Waco: Word Books, 1983).
Heinrich Schmid, *The Doctrinal Theology of the Evangelical Lutheran Church* (Minneapolis: Augsburg Publishing House, 1961), H.A. Charles and J.E. Henry (trs.).
Hendry, George Stuart, *The Gospel of the Incarnation* (London: SCM Press, 1959).
Heron, A., '"Who Proceedeth from the Father and theh Son", The Problem of the Filioque', *Scottish Journal of Theology*, 24 (1971), pp. 149-66.
Herrmann, Wilhelm, *Systematic Theology* (London: G. Allen & Unwin, 1927), Nathaniel Micklem and Kenneth A. Saunders (trs.).
- *The Communion of the Christian with God: Described on the Basis of Luther's Statements* (London: SCM Press, 1972), R.T. Voelkel (ed), J.S. Stanyon (tr.).
Hill, D., *The Gospel of Matthew (New Century Bible)* (London: Marshall, Morgan and Scott, 1972)
Houston, James, 'Spirituality and the Doctrine of the Trinity', in *Christ in Our Place: The Humanity of God in Christ for the Reconciliation of the World: Essays Presented to Professor James Torrance* (Exeter: Paternoster, 1989), Trevor A. Hart and Daniel P. Thimell (eds.), pp. 48-69.
Hughes, J., 'John the Baptist: The Forerunner of God Himself', *Novum Testamentum* 14 (1972), pp. 191-218.
Hunsinger, George, 'Karl Barth's Christology', in *The Cambridge Companion to Karl Barth* (Cambridge: Cambridge University Press, 2000), John Webster (ed.), pp. 127-42.
- 'The Mediator of Communion: Karl Barth's Doctrine of the Holy Spirit', in *The Cambridge Companion to Karl Barth* (Cambridge: Cambridge University Press, 2000), John Webster (ed.), pp. 177-94.
Hunter, A.M., 'Crux Criticorum - Matt. XI. 25-30 – A Re-appraisal'

New Testament Studies, 8 (1961/62), pp. 244-5.

Hurtado, Larry W., *One God, One Lord: Early Christian Devotion and Ancient Jewish Monotheism* (London: SCM Press, 1988).

– 'New Testament Christology: A Critique of Bousset's Influence', *Theological Studies,* 40 (1979), pp. 306-17.

Irving, Edward, *The collected writings of Edward Irving, in Five Volumes* (London, Alexander Strahan, 1864/65), G. Carlyle (ed.).

– *Christ's Holiness in Flesh, the Form, Fountain Head, and Assurance to us of Holiness in Flesh* (Edinburgh: John Lindsay & Co., 1831).

Jeremias, Joachim, *The Prayers of Jesus* (London: SCM Press, 1967).

– *New Testament Theology* (London: SCM Press, 1971), John Bowden (tr.).

Johnson, Luke T., *The Gospel of Luke; Sacra Pagina Series* (Collegeville: Liturgical Press, 1991), Daniel J. Harrington (ed.).

Jüngel, Eberhard, *The Doctrine of the Trinity: God's Being is in Becoming* (Edinburgh: Scottish Academic Press, 1976), Horton Harris (ed.).

Käsemann, Ernst, *Essays on New Testament Themes* (London: SCM Press, 1964).

Kelly, J. N. D., *Early Christian Creeds;* (London: Longman, 1972[3]).

Kelsey, David H., *The Uses of Scripture in Recent Theology* (London: SCM Press, 1975).

Kim, Seyoon, *The Origin of Paul's Gospel* (Tübingen: J.C.B. Mohr, 1984[2]).

Kingsbury, J., 'The Title "Kyrios" in Matthew's Gospel', *Journal of Biblical Literature,* 94 (1975), pp. 246-55.

– 'The Composition and Christology of Matt 28:16-20', *Journal of Biblical Literature,* 93 (1974), pp. 537-84.

– 'The Place, Structure, and Meaning of the Sermon on the Mount Within Matthew', *Interpretation,* 41 (1987), pp. 131-43.

– *Matthew: Structure, Christology,* Kingdom (Philadelphia: Fortress, 1975).

– 'The Figure of Jesus in Matthew's Story: A Literary-Critical Probe', *Journal for the Study of the New Testament,* 21 (1984), pp. 3-36.

– *Matthew as Story* (Philadephia: Fortress, 1988[2]).

LaCugna, Catherine M., *God for Us: The Trinity and Christian Life* (Harper; SanFrancisco, 1991).

Lampe, G. W. H., *God as Spirit* (Oxford: Clarendon Press, 1977).

Leisegang, H, 'Pneuma Hagion' in, *Studies in Early Christianity* (New York & London: Century Co., 1928), Shirley J. Case (ed.). Presented to Frank Chamberlin Porter and Benjamin Wisner

Bacon.

Liefeld, W., *The Expositor's Bible Commentary*: *Vol. 8; Matthew, Mark, Luke* (Grand Rapids: Regency Reference, 1984) Frank E. Gaebelein (ed.).

Lindbeck, George A., *The Nature of Doctrine: Religion and Theology in a Postliberal Age* (London: SPCK, 1984).

Longman, Tremper III., *Literary Approaches to Biblical Interpretation* (Leicester: Apollos, 1987/9)

Lossky, Vladimir, *The Mystical Theology of the Eastern Church* (Cambridge: James Clarke, 1957).

Loughlin, Gerard, *Telling God's Story: Bible, Church and Narrative Theology* (Cambridge: Cambridge University Press, 1996).

Louw, Johannes P. and Eugene A. Nida, *Greek-English Lexicon of the New Testament: Based on Semantic domains* (New York: United Bible Societies, 1988).

Luther, Martin, *Werke: Kritische Gesamtausgabe* (Weimar: Herman Böhlau & Nachfolger, 1883 ff).

Luz, Ulrich, *Matthew 1-7: A Commentary* (Edinburgh: T. & T. Clark, 1990), Wilhelm C. Linss (tr.).

– *The Theology of the Gospel of Matthew* (Cambridge: Cambridge University Press, 1995), J. Bradford Robinson (tr.).

– *Matthew 8-20* (Minneapolis: Fortress, 2001), Helmut Koester (ed.), James E. Crouch (tr.). .

MacDonald, A.N., *The Interpreter Spirit and Human Life* (London: SPCK, 1944).

Mackintosh, H. R., *The Doctrine of the Person of Jesus Christ* (Edinburgh: T. & T. Clark, 1948²).

Manson, Thomas W., *The Teaching of Jesus: Studies of its Form and Content* (London: Cambridge University Press, 1931).

Marshall, I. Howard, 'Incarnational Christology in the New Testament', in *Christ the Lord* (Leicester: Inter-Varsity, 1982), H. H. Rowdon (ed.), pp. 1-16.

McClendon, James, *Biography as Theology* (Nashville: Abingdon Press, 1974)

McCormack, Bruce, *Karl Barth's Critically Realistic Dialectical Theology: Its Genesis and Development 1909-1936* (Oxford: Clarendon Press, 1995).

McFarlane, Graham, *Christ and the Spirit: the Doctrine of the Incarnation According to Edward Irving* (Carlisle: Paternoster, 1996).

– *Edward Irving: the Trinitarian Face of God* (Edinburgh: Saint Andrew Press, 1996).

– 'The Strange Tongue of a Long Lost Christianity: The Spirit and the Trinity' in *Vox Evangelica*, XXII (London: London Bible College, 1992), pp. 63-70.

McGrath, Alister E., *The Genesis of Doctrine: A Study in the Foundations of Doctrinal Criticism* (Oxford: Basil Blackwell, 1990).

– *Understanding Doctrine: Its Relevance and Purpose for Today* (London: Hodder & Stoughton, 1990).

Menzies, Robert Paul, *The Development of Early Christian Pneumatology with Special Reference to Luke - Acts* (Sheffield: JSOT Press, 1991).

Moltmann, Jürgen, *The Crucified God: The Cross of Christ as the Foundation and Criticism of Christian Theology* (London: SCM Press, 1974), R.A. Wilson and John Bowden (trs.).

– *The Trinity and the Kingdom of God: the Doctrine of God* (London: SCM Press, 1981), Margaret Kohl (tr.).

Montague, George T., *The Holy Spirit: Growth of a Biblical Tradition* (New York: Paulist Press, 1976).

Moule, C. F. D., *The origin of Christology* (Cambridge: Cambridge University Press, 1977).

– 'Fulfilment-Words in the New Testament', *New Testament Studies,* 14 (1967-68), pp. 293-320.

– 'The Manhood of Jesus in the New Testament' in *Christ, Faith and History* (Cambridge University Press: 1972), S. W. Sykes and J. P. Clayton (eds.), pp. 95-110.

Murphy-O'Connor, J., 'Christological Anthropology in Phil 2:6-11', *Revue Biblique* 83 (1976), pp. 25-50.

Newbigin, Lesslie, *Trinitarian Doctrine for Today's Mission* (Carlisle: Paternoster, 1998; first published: Edinburgh House press, 1963).

Niebuhr, Reinhold, *The Nature and Destiny of Man: a Christian Interpretation* (London: Nisbet, 1943).

Nolland, John, *Luke; Word Biblical Commentary, Vol. 35A, B and C* (Dallas: Word Books, 1989-1993).

O'Collins, Gerald, SJ, *Christology, A Biblical, Historical and Systematic Study of Jesus Christ,* (Oxford: Oxford University Press, 1995).

Pannenberg, Wolfhart, *Systematic Theology* (Edinburgh: T. & T. Clark, 1991-3), Geoffrey W. Bromiley (tr.).

– *Jesus - God and Man* (London: SCM Press, 2002)

Parker, T. H. L., *Essays in Christology for Karl Barth* (London: Lutterworth Press, 1956).

– *Calvin's Preaching* (Edinburgh : T. & T. Clark, 1992).

Petersen. Norman R, *Literary Criticism for New Testament Critics* (Philadelphia: Fortress, 1978).

Powell, Mark Allan, *The Bible and Modern Literary Criticism: A Critical Assessment and Annotated Bibliography* (New York; London: Greenwood Press, 1992).
– *What is Narrative Criticism?: A New Approach to the Bible* (London: SPCK, 1993).
Rahner, Karl, *The Trinity* (London: Burns and Oates, 1970), Joseph Donceel (tr.).
– 'On the Theology of the Incarnation' in *Theological Investigation, vol. 4,* (London: Darton, Longman and Todd, 1966), Kevin Smyth (tr.), pp. 105-120.
– *Foundations of Christian Faith: An Introduction to the Idea of Christianity* (London: Darton, Longman and Todd, 1978), William V. Dych (tr.).
Rosato, Philip J., *The Spirit as Lord: the Pneumatology of Karl Barth* (Edinburgh: T. & T. Clark, 1981).
Ryle, Gilbert, *The Concept of Mind,* (London, Hutchinson, 1949).
Schleiermacher, F., *The Christian Faith* (Edinburgh: T. & T. Clark, 1956).
Schweizer, Eduard, *The Good News According to Matthew* (London: SPCK, 1976/75), David E. Green (tr.).
– *Jesus* (London: SCM Press, 1971), David E. Green (tr.).
– 'Christus und Geist im Kolosserbrief', in *Christ and the Spirit in the New Testament, in Honour of Charles Francis Digby Moule* (Cambridge: Cambridge University Press, 1973), B. Lindars and S. Smalley (eds.), pp. 297-213.
Schwöbel, Christoph (ed.), *Trinitarian Theology Today: Essays on Divine Being and Act* (Edinburgh: T. & T. Clark, 1995).
Scott, Ernest Findlay, *The Spirit in the New Testament* (London: Hodder & Stoughton, 1923).
Smail, Thomas A., *The Forgotten Father* (London: Hodder and Stoughton, 1980).
– *The Giving Gift: the Holy Spirit in Person* (London: Hodder and Stoughton, 1988).
Stanton, G., 'The Origin and Purpose of Matthew's Gospel: Matthean Scholarship from 1945 to 1980', in *Aufstieg und Niedergang der römischen Welt* (Berlin: Walter de Gruyter, 1982).
– 'Matthew 11:28-30: Comfortable Words?', *Expository Times ,* 94 (1982) pp. 3-9.
– *A Gospel for a New People: Studies in Matthew* (Edinburgh: T. & T. Clark, 1992).
Stern, J. P., *On Realism* (London: Routledge & Kegan Paul, 1973).
Strachan, Gordon, *The Pentecostal Theology of Edward Irving* (London: Darton, Longman and Todd, 1973).

Strecker, Georg, *The Sermon on the Mount: An Exegetical Commentary* (Edinburgh: T. & T. Clark, 1988), O. C. Dean, Jr. (tr.).

Stroup, George W., *The Promise of Narrative Theology* (London: SCM Press, 1981/84).

Taylor, Vincent, *The Formation of the Gospel Tradition* (London: Macmillan, 1960²).

– *The Gospel According to St. Mark: The Greek Text* (London: Macmillan, 1952).

The British Council of Churches, *The Forgotten Trinity* (London: The British Council of Churches, 1989-91).

Theissen, Gerd, *The Shadow of the Galilean: The Quest of the Historical Jesus in Narrative Form* (London: SCM Press, 2001).

Thompson, John, *Modern Trinitarian Perspectives* (New York; Oxford: Oxford University Press, 1994).

– *The Holy Spirit in the Theology of Karl Barth* (Allison Park: Pickwick Publications, 1991).

– *Christ in Perspective: Christological Perspectives in the Theology of Karl Barth* (Edinburgh: Saint Andrew, 1978).

Tillich, Paul, *Systematic theology* (Welwyn: James Nisbet, 1968).

Tödt, Heinz Eduard, *The Son of Man in the Synoptic Tradition* (London: SCM Press, 1965), Dorothea M. Barton (tr.).

Torrance, Alan J., *Persons in Communion: An Essay on Trinitarian Description and Human Participation, with Special Reference to Volume One of Karl Barth's Church Dogmatics* (Edinburgh: T. & T. Clark, 1996).

Torrance, James, *Worship, Community, and the Triune God of Grace* (Carlisle: Paternoster Press, 1996).

Torrance, Thomas F., *The Trinitarian Faith: The Evangelical Theology of the Ancient Catholic Church* (Edinburgh: T. & T. Clark, 1988).

– *The Christian Doctrine of God: One Being, Three Persons* (Edinburgh: T. & T. Clark, 1996).

– *Trinitarian Perspectives: Toward Doctrinal Agreement* (Edinburgh: T. & T. Clark, 1994).

Tuckett, Christopher, (ed.), *The Messianic Secret* (Philadelphia; London: Fortress Press ; SPCK, 1983).

Turner, Max, *The Holy Spirit and Spiritual Gifts: Then and Now* (Carlisle: Paternoster, 1996).

– 'Prayers in Gospels and Acts', in *Teach Us to Pray: Prayer in the Bible and the World* (Exeter: The Paternoster Press and Baker Book House, 1990), D. A. Carson (ed.), pp. 58-83.

– 'Luke and the Spirit: Studies in the Significance of Receiving the

Spirit in Luke-Acts', Ph.D thesis (Cambridge University, 1980)
- 'The Spirit of Christ and Christology', in *Christ the Lord* (Leicester: Inter-Varsity, 1982), H. H. Rowdon (ed.), pp. 168-90.
- 'The Spirit of Christ and "Divine" Christology', in *Jesus of Nazareth* (Grand Rapids; Carlisle: Eerdmans; Paternoster Press, 1994), Joel B. Green and Max Turner (eds.), pp. 413-36.
Wallace, Mark, 'The New Yale Theology', in *The Best in Theology, Vol 3* (Carol Stream: Christianity Today Inc, 1989), J. I. Packer (ed.), pp. 169-186.
Webster, John, *Barth* (London: Continuum, 2000).
- *The Cambridge Companion to Karl Barth* (Cambridge: Cambridge University Press, 2000), J. Webster (ed.).
Welch, Claude (ed., tr.), *God and Incarnation in Mid-Nineteenth Century German Theology* (New York: Oxford University Press, 1965).
Wenham, David, *The Rediscovery of Jesus' Eschatological Discourse* (Sheffield: JSOT Press, 1984).
Wiles, Maurice F, *Working Papers in Doctrine* (London: SCM Press, 1976).
Williams, Rowan, 'Barth on the Triune God', in *Karl Barth: Studies of His Theological Method* (Oxford: Clarendon Press, 1979), S. W. Sykes (ed.), pp. 147-93.
Windisch, H, 'Jesus und der Geist nach synoptischer Ueberlieferung', in *Studies in Early Christianity* (New York & London: Century Co.: 1928), Shirley J. Case.
Wright, N. T., *Jesus and the Victory of God* (London: SPCK, 1996).
- *New Testament and the People of God* (London: SPCK, 1992).
- 'ἁρπαγμός and the Meaning of Phil 2:5-11', *Journal of Theological Studies*, 37 (1986), pp. 321-52.
Zizioulas, John D, *Being as Communion: Studies in Personhood and the Church* (London: Darton, Longman and Todd, 1985).
- 'The Doctrine of the Holy Trinity: the Significance of the Cappadocian Contribution', in *Trinitarian Theology Today* (Edinburgh: T&T Clark, 1995), Christoph Schwöbel (ed.), pp. 44-60.

Scripture Index

Author Index

Subject Index

Paternoster Biblical Monographs

(All titles uniform with this volume)
Dates in bold are of projected publication

Joseph Abraham
Eve: Accused or Acquitted?
A Reconsideration of Feminist Readings of the Creation Narrative Texts in Genesis 1–3
Two contrary views dominate contemporary feminist biblical scholarship. One finds in the Bible an unequivocal equality between the sexes from the very creation of humanity, whilst the other sees the biblical text as irredeemably patriarchal and androcentric. Dr Abraham enters into dialogue with both camps as well as introducing his own method of approach. An invaluable tool for any one who is interested in this contemporary debate.
2002 / 0-85364-971-5 / xxiv + 272pp

Octavian D. Baban
Mimesis and Luke's on the Road Encounters in Luke-Acts
Luke's Theology of the Way and its Literary Representation
The book argues on theological and literary (mimetic) grounds that Luke's on-the-road encounters, especially those belonging to the post-Easter period, are part of his complex theology of the Way. Jesus' teaching and that of the apostles is presented by Luke as a challenging answer to the Hellenistic reader's thirst for adventure, good literature, and existential paradigms.
2005 / 1-84227-253-5 / approx. 374pp

Paul Barker
The Triumph of Grace in Deuteronomy
This book is a textual and theological analysis of the interaction between the sin and faithlessness of Israel and the grace of Yahweh in response, looking especially at Deuteronomy chapters 1–3, 8–10 and 29–30. The author argues that the grace of Yahweh is determinative for the ongoing relationship between Yahweh and Israel and that Deuteronomy anticipates and fully expects Israel to be faithless.
2004 / 1-84227-226-8 / xxii + 270pp

Jonathan F. Bayes
The Weakness of the Law
God's Law and the Christian in New Testament Perspective
A study of the four New Testament books which refer to the law as weak (Acts, Romans, Galatians, Hebrews) leads to a defence of the third use in the Reformed debate about the law in the life of the believer.
2000 / 0-85364-957-X / xii + 244pp

Mark Bonnington
The Antioch Episode of Galatians 2:11-14 in Historical and Cultural Context

The Galatians 2 'incident' in Antioch over table-fellowship suggests significant disagreement between the leading apostles. This book analyses the background to the disagreement by locating the incident within the dynamics of social interaction between Jews and Gentiles. It proposes a new way of understanding the relationship between the individuals and issues involved.

2005 / 1-84227-050-8 / approx. 350pp

David Bostock
A Portrayal of Trust
The Theme of Faith in the Hezekiah Narratives

This study provides detailed and sensitive readings of the Hezekiah narratives (2 Kings 18–20 and Isaiah 36–39) from a theological perspective. It concentrates on the theme of faith, using narrative criticism as its methodology. Attention is paid especially to setting, plot, point of view and characterization within the narratives. A largely positive portrayal of Hezekiah emerges that underlines the importance and relevance of scripture.

2005 / 1-84227-314-0 / approx. 300pp

Mark Bredin
Jesus, Revolutionary of Peace
A Non-violent Christology in the Book of Revelation

This book aims to demonstrate that the figure of Jesus in the Book of Revelation can best be understood as an active non-violent revolutionary.

2003 / 1-84227-153-9 / xviii + 262pp

Robinson Butarbutar
Paul and Conflict Resolution
An Exegetical Study of Paul's Apostolic Paradigm in 1 Corinthians 9

The author sees the apostolic paradigm in 1 Corinthians 9 as part of Paul's unified arguments in 1 Corinthians 8–10 in which he seeks to mediate in the dispute over the issue of food offered to idols. The book also sees its relevance for dispute-resolution today, taking the conflict within the author's church as an example.

2006 / 1-84227-315-9 / approx. 280pp

Daniel J-S Chae
Paul as Apostle to the Gentiles
His Apostolic Self-awareness and its Influence on the Soteriological Argument in Romans
Opposing 'the post-Holocaust interpretation of Romans', Daniel Chae competently demonstrates that Paul argues for the equality of Jew and Gentile in Romans. Chae's fresh exegetical interpretation is academically outstanding and spiritually encouraging.
1997 / 0-85364-829-8 / xiv + 378pp

Luke L. Cheung
The Genre, Composition and Hermeneutics of the Epistle of James
The present work examines the employment of the wisdom genre with a certain compositional structure and the interpretation of the law through the Jesus tradition of the double love command by the author of the Epistle of James to serve his purpose in promoting perfection and warning against doubleness among the eschatologically renewed people of God in the Diaspora.
2003 / 1-84227-062-1 / xvi + 372pp

Youngmo Cho
Spirit and Kingdom in the Writings of Luke and Paul
The relationship between Spirit and Kingdom is a relatively unexplored area in Lukan and Pauline studies. This book offers a fresh perspective of two biblical writers on the subject. It explores the difference between Luke's and Paul's understanding of the Spirit by examining the specific question of the relationship of the concept of the Spirit to the concept of the Kingdom of God in each writer.
2005 / 1-84227-316-7 / approx. 270pp

Andrew C. Clark
Parallel Lives
The Relation of Paul to the Apostles in the Lucan Perspective
This study of the Peter-Paul parallels in Acts argues that their purpose was to emphasize the themes of continuity in salvation history and the unity of the Jewish and Gentile missions. New light is shed on Luke's literary techniques, partly through a comparison with Plutarch.
2001 / 1-84227-035-4 / xviii + 386pp

Andrew D. Clarke
Secular and Christian Leadership in Corinth
A Socio-Historical and Exegetical Study of 1 Corinthians 1–6
This volume is an investigation into the leadership structures and dynamics of first-century Roman Corinth. These are compared with the practice of leadership in the Corinthian Christian community which are reflected in 1 Corinthians 1–6, and contrasted with Paul's own principles of Christian leadership.
2005 / 1-84227-229-2 / 200pp

Stephen Finamore
God, Order and Chaos
René Girard and the Apocalypse
Readers are often disturbed by the images of destruction in the book of Revelation and unsure why they are unleashed after the exaltation of Jesus. This book examines past approaches to these texts and uses René Girard's theories to revive some old ideas and propose some new ones.
2005 / 1-84227-197-0 / approx. 344pp

David G. Firth
Surrendering Retribution in the Psalms
Responses to Violence in the Individual Complaints
In *Surrendering Retribution in the Psalms*, David Firth examines the ways in which the book of Psalms inculcates a model response to violence through the repetition of standard patterns of prayer. Rather than seeking justification for retributive violence, Psalms encourages not only a surrender of the right of retribution to Yahweh, but also sets limits on the retribution that can be sought in imprecations. Arising initially from the author's experience in South Africa, the possibilities of this model to a particular context of violence is then briefly explored.
2005 / 1-84227-337-X / xviii + 154pp

Scott J. Hafemann
Suffering and Ministry in the Spirit
Paul's Defence of His Ministry in II Corinthians 2:14–3:3
Shedding new light on the way Paul defended his apostleship, the author offers a careful, detailed study of 2 Corinthians 2:14–3:3 linked with other key passages throughout 1 and 2 Corinthians. Demonstrating the unity and coherence of Paul's argument in this passage, the author shows that Paul's suffering served as the vehicle for revealing God's power and glory through the Spirit.
2000 / 0-85364-967-7 / xiv + 262pp

Scott J. Hafemann
Paul, Moses and the History of Israel
The Letter/Spirit Contrast and the Argument from Scripture in 2 Corinthians 3
An exegetical study of the call of Moses, the second giving of the Law (Exodus 32–34), the new covenant, and the prophetic understanding of the history of Israel in 2 Corinthians 3. Hafemann's work demonstrates Paul's contextual use of the Old Testament and the essential unity between the Law and the Gospel within the context of the distinctive ministries of Moses and Paul.
2005 / 1-84227-317-5 / xii + 498pp

Douglas S. McComiskey
Lukan Theology in the Light of the Gospel's Literary Structure
Luke's Gospel was purposefully written with theology embedded in its patterned literary structure. A critical analysis of this cyclical structure provides new windows into Luke's interpretation of the individual pericopes comprising the Gospel and illuminates several of his theological interests.
2004 / 1-84227-148-2 / xviii + 388pp

Stephen Motyer
Your Father the Devil?
A New Approach to John and 'The Jews'
Who are 'the Jews' in John's Gospel? Defending John against the charge of antisemitism, Motyer argues that, far from demonising the Jews, the Gospel seeks to present Jesus as 'Good News for Jews' in a late first century setting.
1997 / 0-85364-832-8 / xiv + 260pp

Esther Ng
Reconstructing Christian Origins?
The Feminist Theology of Elizabeth Schüssler Fiorenza: An Evaluation
In a detailed evaluation, the author challenges Elizabeth Schüssler Fiorenza's reconstruction of early Christian origins and her underlying presuppositions. The author also presents her own views on women's roles both then and now.
2002 / 1-84227-055-9 / xxiv + 468pp

Robin Parry
Old Testament Story and Christian Ethics
The Rape of Dinah as a Case Study

What is the role of story in ethics and, more particularly, what is the role of Old Testament story in Christian ethics? This book, drawing on the work of contemporary philosophers, argues that narrative is crucial in the ethical shaping of people and, drawing on the work of contemporary Old Testament scholars, that story plays a key role in Old Testament ethics. Parry then argues that when situated in canonical context Old Testament stories can be reappropriated by Christian readers in their own ethical formation. The shocking story of the rape of Dinah and the massacre of the Shechemites provides a fascinating case study for exploring the parameters within which Christian ethical appropriations of Old Testament stories can live.

2004 / 1-84227-210-1 / xx + 350pp

Ian Paul
Power to See the World Anew
The Value of Paul Ricoeur's Hermeneutic of Metaphor in Interpreting the Symbolism of Revelation 12 and 13

This book is a study of the hermeneutics of metaphor of Paul Ricoeur, one of the most important writers on hermeneutics and metaphor of the last century. It sets out the key points of his theory, important criticisms of his work, and how his approach, modified in the light of these criticisms, offers a methodological framework for reading apocalyptic texts.

2006 / 1-84227-056-7 / approx. 350pp

Robert L. Plummer
Paul's Understanding of the Church's Mission
Did the Apostle Paul Expect the Early Christian Communities to Evangelize?

This book engages in a careful study of Paul's letters to determine if the apostle expected the communities to which he wrote to engage in missionary activity. It helpfully summarizes the discussion on this debated issue, judiciously handling contested texts, and provides a way forward in addressing this critical question. While admitting that Paul rarely explicitly commands the communities he founded to evangelize, Plummer amasses significant incidental data to provide a convincing case that Paul did indeed expect his churches to engage in mission activity. Throughout the study, Plummer progressively builds a theological basis for the church's mission that is both distinctively Pauline and compelling.

2006 / 1-84227-333-7 / approx. 324pp

David Powys
'Hell': A Hard Look at a Hard Question
The Fate of the Unrighteous in New Testament Thought
This comprehensive treatment seeks to unlock the original meaning of terms and phrases long thought to support the traditional doctrine of hell. It concludes that there is an alternative—one which is more biblical, and which can positively revive the rationale for Christian mission.

1997 / 0-85364-831-X / xxii + 478pp

Sorin Sabou
Between Horror and Hope
Paul's Metaphorical Language of Death in Romans 6.1-11
This book argues that Paul's metaphorical language of death in Romans 6.1-11 conveys two aspects: horror and hope. The 'horror' aspect is conveyed by the 'crucifixion' language, and the 'hope' aspect by 'burial' language. The life of the Christian believer is understood, as relationship with sin is concerned ('death to sin'), between these two realities: horror and hope.

2005 / 1-84227-322-1 / approx. 224pp

Rosalind Selby
The Comical Doctrine
The Epistemology of New Testament Hermeneutics
This book argues that the gospel breaks through postmodernity's critique of truth and the referential possibilities of textuality with its gift of grace. With a rigorous, philosophical challenge to modernist and postmodernist assumptions, Selby offers an alternative epistemology to all who would still read with faith *and* with academic credibility.

2005 / 1-84227-212-8 / approx. 350pp

Kiwoong Son
Zion Symbolism in Hebrews
Hebrews 12.18-24 as a Hermeneutical Key to the Epistle
This book challenges the general tendency of understanding the Epistle to the Hebrews against a Hellenistic background and suggests that the Epistle should be understood in the light of the Jewish apocalyptic tradition. The author especially argues for the importance of the theological symbolism of Sinai and Zion (Heb. 12:18-24) as it provides the Epistle's theological background as well as the rhetorical basis of the superiority motif of Jesus throughout the Epistle.

2005 / 1-84227-368-X / approx. 280pp

Kevin Walton
Thou Traveller Unknown
The Presence and Absence of God in the Jacob Narrative
The author offers a fresh reading of the story of Jacob in the book of Genesis through the paradox of divine presence and absence. The work also seeks to make a contribution to Pentateuchal studies by bringing together a close reading of the final text with historical critical insights, doing justice to the text's historical depth, final form and canonical status.
2003 / 1-84227-059-1 / xvi + 238pp

George M. Wieland
The Significance of Salvation
A Study of Salvation Language in the Pastoral Epistles
The language and ideas of salvation pervade the three Pastoral Epistles. This study offers a close examination of their soteriological statements. In all three letters the idea of salvation is found to play a vital paraenetic role, but each also exhibits distinctive soteriological emphases. The results challenge common assumptions about the Pastoral Epistles as a corpus.
2005 / 1-84227-257-8 / approx. 324pp

Alistair Wilson
When Will These Things Happen?
A Study of Jesus as Judge in Matthew 21–25
This study seeks to allow Matthew's carefully constructed presentation of Jesus to be given full weight in the modern evaluation of Jesus' eschatology. Careful analysis of the text of Matthew 21–25 reveals Jesus to be standing firmly in the Jewish prophetic and wisdom traditions as he proclaims and enacts imminent judgement on the Jewish authorities then boldly claims the central role in the final and universal judgement.
2004 / 1-84227-146-6 / xxii + 272pp

Lindsay Wilson
Joseph Wise and Otherwise
The Intersection of Covenant and Wisdom in Genesis 37–50
This book offers a careful literary reading of Genesis 37–50 that argues that the Joseph story contains both strong covenant themes and many wisdom-like elements. The connections between the two helps to explore how covenant and wisdom might intersect in an integrated biblical theology.
2004 / 1-84227-140-7 / xvi + 340pp

Stephen I. Wright
The Voice of Jesus
Studies in the Interpretation of Six Gospel Parables
This literary study considers how the 'voice' of Jesus has been heard in different periods of parable interpretation, and how the categories of figure and trope may help us towards a sensitive reading of the parables today.
2000 / 0-85364-975-8 / xiv + 280pp

Paternoster
9 Holdom Avenue,
Bletchley,
Milton Keynes MK1 1QR,
United Kingdom
Web: www.authenticmedia.co.uk/paternoster

July 2005

Paternoster Theological Monographs
(All titles uniform with this volume)
Dates in bold are of projected publication

Emil Bartos
Deification in Eastern Orthodox Theology
An Evaluation and Critique of the Theology of Dumitru Staniloae
Bartos studies a fundamental yet neglected aspect of Orthodox theology: deification. By examining the doctrines of anthropology, christology, soteriology and ecclesiology as they relate to deification, he provides an important contribution to contemporary dialogue between Eastern and Western theologians.

1999 / 0-85364-956-1 / xii + 370pp

Graham Buxton
The Trinity, Creation and Pastoral Ministry
Imaging the Perichoretic God
In this book the author proposes a three-way conversation between theology, science and pastoral ministry. His approach draws on a Trinitarian understanding of God as a relational being of love, whose life 'spills over' into all created reality, human and non-human. By locating human meaning and purpose within God's 'creation-community' this book offers the possibility of a transforming engagement between those in pastoral ministry and the scientific community.

2005 */ 1-84227-369-8 / approx. 380 pp*

Iain D. Campbell
Fixing the Indemnity
The Life and Work of George Adam Smith
When Old Testament scholar George Adam Smith (1856–1942) delivered the Lyman Beecher lectures at Yale University in 1899, he confidently declared that 'modern criticism has won its war against traditional theories. It only remains to fix the amount of the indemnity.' In this biography, Iain D. Campbell assesses Smith's critical approach to the Old Testament and evaluates its consequences, showing that Smith's life and work still raises questions about the relationship between biblical scholarship and evangelical faith.

2004 / 1-84227-228-4 / xx + 256pp

Tim Chester
Mission and the Coming of God
Eschatology, the Trinity and Mission in the Theology of Jürgen Moltmann
This book explores the theology and missiology of the influential contemporary theologian, Jürgen Moltmann. It highlights the important contribution Moltmann has made while offering a critique of his thought from an evangelical perspective. In so doing, it touches on pertinent issues for evangelical missiology. The conclusion takes Calvin as a starting point, proposing 'an eschatology of the cross' which offers a critique of the over-realised eschatologies in liberation theology and certain forms of evangelicalism.
2006 / 1-84227-320-5 / approx. 224pp

Sylvia Wilkey Collinson
Making Disciples
The Significance of Jesus' Educational Strategy for Today's Church
This study examines the biblical practice of discipling, formulates a definition, and makes comparisons with modern models of education. A recommendation is made for greater attention to its practice today.
2004 / 1-84227-116-4 / xiv + 278pp

Darrell Cosden
A Theology of Work
Work and the New Creation
Through dialogue with Moltmann, Pope John Paul II and others, this book develops a genitive 'theology of work', presenting a theological definition of work and a model for a theological ethics of work that shows work's nature, value and meaning now and eschatologically. Work is shown to be a transformative activity consisting of three dynamically inter-related dimensions: the instrumental, relational and ontological.
2005 / 1-84227-332-9 / xvi + 208pp

Stephen M. Dunning
The Crisis and the Quest
A Kierkegaardian Reading of Charles Williams
Employing Kierkegaardian categories and analysis, this study investigates both the central crisis in Charles Williams's authorship between hermetism and Christianity (Kierkegaard's Religions A and B), and the quest to resolve this crisis, a quest that ultimately presses the bounds of orthodoxy.
2000 / 0-85364-985-5 / xxiv + 254pp

Keith Ferdinando
The Triumph of Christ in African Perspective
A Study of Demonology and Redemption in the African Context
The book explores the implications of the gospel for traditional African fears of occult aggression. It analyses such traditional approaches to suffering and biblical responses to fears of demonic evil, concluding with an evaluation of African beliefs from the perspective of the gospel.

1999 / 0-85364-830-1 / xviii + 450pp

Andrew Goddard
Living the Word, Resisting the World
The Life and Thought of Jacques Ellul
This work offers a definitive study of both the life and thought of the French Reformed thinker Jacques Ellul (1912-1994). It will prove an indispensable resource for those interested in this influential theologian and sociologist and for Christian ethics and political thought generally.

2002 / 1-84227-053-2 / xxiv + 378pp

David Hilborn
The Words of our Lips
Language-Use in Free Church Worship
Studies of liturgical language have tended to focus on the written canons of Roman Catholic and Anglican communities. By contrast, David Hilborn analyses the more extemporary approach of English Nonconformity. Drawing on recent developments in linguistic pragmatics, he explores similarities and differences between 'fixed' and 'free' worship, and argues for the interdependence of each.

2006 */ 0-85364-977-4 / approx. 350pp*

Roger Hitching
The Church and Deaf People
A Study of Identity, Communication and Relationships with Special Reference to the Ecclesiology of Jürgen Moltmann
In *The Church and Deaf People* Roger Hitching sensitively examines the history and present experience of deaf people and finds similarities between aspects of sign language and Moltmann's theological method that 'open up' new ways of understanding theological concepts.

2003 / 1-84227-222-5 / xxii + 236pp

John G. Kelly
One God, One People
*The Differentiated Unity of the People of God in the Theology of
Jürgen Moltmann*
The author expounds and critiques Moltmann's doctrine of God and highlights
the systematic connections between it and Moltmann's influential discussion of
Israel. He then proposes a fresh approach to Jewish–Christian relations building
on Moltmann's work using insights from Habermas and Rawls.
2005 / 0-85346-969-3 / approx. 350pp

Mark F.W. Lovatt
Confronting the Will-to-Power
A Reconsideration of the Theology of Reinhold Niebuhr
Confronting the Will-to-Power is an analysis of the theology of Reinhold
Niebuhr, arguing that his work is an attempt to identify, and provide a practical
theological answer to, the existence and nature of human evil.
2001 / 1-84227-054-0 / xviii + 216pp

Neil B. MacDonald
Karl Barth and the Strange New World within the Bible
Barth, Wittgenstein, and the Metadilemmas of the Enlightenment
Barth's discovery of the strange new world within the Bible is examined in the
context of Kant, Hume, Overbeck, and, most importantly, Wittgenstein.
MacDonald covers some fundamental issues in theology today: epistemology,
the final form of the text and biblical truth-claims.
2000 / 0-85364-970-7 / xxvi + 374pp

Keith A. Mascord
Alvin Plantinga and Christian Apologetics
This book draws together the contributions of the philosopher Alvin Plantinga to
the major contemporary challenges to Christian belief, highlighting in particular
his ground-breaking work in epistemology and the problem of evil. Plantinga's
theory that both theistic and Christian belief is warrantedly basic is explored and
critiqued, and an assessment offered as to the significance of his work for
apologetic theory and practice.
2005 / 1-84227-256-X / approx. 304pp

Gillian McCulloch
The Deconstruction of Dualism in Theology
With Reference to Ecofeminist Theology and New Age Spirituality
This book challenges eco-theological anti-dualism in Christian theology, arguing that dualism has a twofold function in Christian religious discourse. Firstly, it enables us to express the discontinuities and divisions that are part of the process of reality. Secondly, dualistic language allows us to express the mysteries of divine transcendence/immanence and the survival of the soul without collapsing into monism and materialism, both of which are problematic for Christian epistemology.

2002 / 1-84227-044-3 / xii + 282pp

Leslie McCurdy
Attributes and Atonement
The Holy Love of God in the Theology of P.T. Forsyth
Attributes and Atonement is an intriguing full-length study of P.T. Forsyth's doctrine of the cross as it relates particularly to God's holy love. It includes an unparalleled bibliography of both primary and secondary material relating to Forsyth.

1999 / 0-85364-833-6 / xiv + 328pp

Nozomu Miyahira
Towards a Theology of the Concord of God
A Japanese Perspective on the Trinity
This book introduces a new Japanese theology and a unique Trinitarian formula based on the Japanese intellectual climate: three betweennesses and one concord. It also presents a new interpretation of the Trinity, a co-subordinationism, which is in line with orthodox Trinitarianism; each single person of the Trinity is eternally and equally subordinate (or serviceable) to the other persons, so that they retain the mutual dynamic equality.

2000 / 0-85364-863-8 / xiv + 256pp

Eddy José Muskus
The Origins and Early Development of Liberation Theology in Latin America
With Particular Reference to Gustavo Gutiérrez
This work challenges the fundamental premise of Liberation Theology, 'opting for the poor', and its claim that Christ is found in them. It also argues that Liberation Theology emerged as a direct result of the failure of the Roman Catholic Church in Latin America.

2002 / 0-85364-974-X / xiv + 296pp

Jim Purves
The Triune God and the Charismatic Movement
A Critical Appraisal from a Scottish Perspective
All emotion and no theology? Or a fundamental challenge to reappraise and realign our trinitarian theology in the light of Christian experience? This study of charismatic renewal as it found expression within Scotland at the end of the twentieth century evaluates the use of Patristic, Reformed and contemporary models of the Trinity in explaining the workings of the Holy Spirit.
2004 / 1-84227-321-3 / xxiv + 246pp

Anna Robbins
Methods in the Madness
Diversity in Twentieth-Century Christian Social Ethics
The author compares the ethical methods of Walter Rauschenbusch, Reinhold Niebuhr and others. She argues that unless Christians are clear about the ways that theology and philosophy are expressed practically they may lose the ability to discuss social ethics across contexts, let alone reach effective agreements.
2004 / 1-84227-211-X / xx + 294pp

Ed Rybarczyk
Beyond Salvation
Eastern Orthodoxy and Classical Pentecostalism on Becoming Like Christ
At first glance eastern Orthodoxy and classical Pentecostalism seem quite distinct. This ground-breaking study shows they share much in common, especially as it concerns the experiential elements of following Christ. Both traditions assert that authentic Christianity transcends the wooden categories of modernism.
2004 / 1-84227-144-X / xii + 356pp

Signe Sandsmark
Is World View Neutral Education Possible and Desirable?
A Christian Response to Liberal Arguments
(Published jointly with The Stapleford Centre)
This book discusses reasons for belief in world view neutrality, and argues that 'neutral' education will have a hidden, but strong world view influence. It discusses the place for Christian education in the common school.
2000 / 0-85364-973-1 / xiv + 182pp

Hazel Sherman
Reading Zechariah
The Allegorical Tradition of Biblical Interpretation through the Commentary of
Didymus the Blind and Theodore of Mopsuestia
A close reading of the commentary on Zechariah by Didymus the Blind
alongside that of Theodore of Mopsuestia suggests that popular categorising of
Antiochene and Alexandrian biblical exegesis as 'historical' or 'allegorical' is
inadequate and misleading.
2005 / 1-84227-213-6 / approx. 280pp

Andrew Sloane
On Being a Christian in the Academy
Nicholas Wolterstorff and the Practice of Christian Scholarship
An exposition and critical appraisal of Nicholas Wolterstorff's epistemology in
the light of the philosophy of science, and an application of his thought to the
practice of Christian scholarship.
2003 / 1-84227-058-3 / xvi + 274pp

Damon W.K. So
Jesus' Revelation of His Father
A Narrative-Conceptual Study of the Trinity with Special Reference to
Karl Barth
This book explores the trinitarian dynamics in the context of Jesus' revelation of
his Father in his earthly ministry with references to key passages in Matthew's
Gospel. It develops from the exegeses of these passages a non-linear concept of
revelation which links Jesus' communion with his Father to his revelatory words
and actions through a nuanced understanding of the Holy Spirit, with references
to K. Barth, G.W.H. Lampe, J.D.G. Dunn and E. Irving.
2005 / 1-84227-323-X / approx. 380pp

Daniel Strange
The Possibility of Salvation Among the Unevangelised
An Analysis of Inclusivism in Recent Evangelical Theology
For evangelical theologians the 'fate of the unevangelised' impinges upon
fundamental tenets of evangelical identity. The position known as 'inclusivism',
defined by the belief that the unevangelised can be ontologically saved by Christ
whilst being epistemologically unaware of him, has been defended most
vigorously by the Canadian evangelical Clark H. Pinnock. Through a detailed
analysis and critique of Pinnock's work, this book examines a cluster of issues
surrounding the unevangelised and its implications for christology, soteriology
and the doctrine of revelation.
2002 / 1-84227-047-8 / xviii + 362pp

Scott Swain
God According to the Gospel
Biblical Narrative and the Identity of God in the Theology of Robert W. Jenson
Robert W. Jenson is one of the leading voices in contemporary Trinitarian theology. His boldest contribution in this area concerns his use of biblical narrative both to ground and explicate the Christian doctrine of God. *God According to the Gospel* critically examines Jenson's proposal and suggests an alternative way of reading the biblical portrayal of the triune God.
2006 / 1-84227-258-6 / approx. 180pp

Justyn Terry
The Justifying Judgement of God
A Reassessment of the Place of Judgement in the Saving Work of Christ
The argument of this book is that judgement, understood as the whole process of bringing justice, is the primary metaphor of atonement, with others, such as victory, redemption and sacrifice, subordinate to it. Judgement also provides the proper context for understanding penal substitution and the call to repentance, baptism, eucharist and holiness.
2005 / 1-84227-370-1 / approx. 274 pp

Graham Tomlin
The Power of the Cross
Theology and the Death of Christ in Paul, Luther and Pascal
This book explores the theology of the cross in St Paul, Luther and Pascal. It offers new perspectives on the theology of each, and some implications for the nature of power, apologetics, theology and church life in a postmodern context.
1999 / 0-85364-984-7 / xiv + 344pp

Adonis Vidu
Postliberal Theological Method
A Critical Study
The postliberal theology of Hans Frei, George Lindbeck, Ronald Thiemann, John Milbank and others is one of the more influential contemporary options. This book focuses on several aspects pertaining to its theological method, specifically its understanding of background, hermeneutics, epistemic justification, ontology, the nature of doctrine and, finally, Christological method.
2005 / 1-84227-395-7 / approx. 324pp

Graham J. Watts
Revelation and the Spirit
*A Comparative Study of the Relationship between the Doctrine of Revelation
and Pneumatology in the Theology of Eberhard Jüngel and of
Wolfhart Pannenberg*
The relationship between revelation and pneumatology is relatively unexplored.
This approach offers a fresh angle on two important twentieth century
theologians and raises pneumatological questions which are theologically crucial
and relevant to mission in a postmodern culture.
2005 / 1-84227-104-0 / xxii + 232pp

Nigel G. Wright
Disavowing Constantine
*Mission, Church and the Social Order in the Theologies of John Howard Yoder
and Jürgen Moltmann*
This book is a timely restatement of a radical theology of church and state in the
Anabaptist and Baptist tradition. Dr Wright constructs his argument in dialogue
and debate with Yoder and Moltmann, major contributors to a free church
perspective.
2000 / 0-85364-978-2 / xvi + 252pp

Paternoster
9 Holdom Avenue,
Bletchley,
Milton Keynes MK1 1QR,
United Kingdom
Web: www.authenticmedia.co.uk/paternoster

St John's College, Nottingham

70404

July 2005